CHOICES

Interviewing and Counselling Skills for Canadians

Second Edition

Bob Shebib

Douglas College

Prentice
Hall

Toronto

To Joyce

National Library of Canada Cataloguing in Publication Data

Shebib, Bob
       Choices: interviewing and counseling skills for Canadians

2nd ed.
Includes bibliographical references and index.
ISBN 0-13-066585-1

     1. Counseling.   2. Interviewing.   I. Title.

BF637.C6S52 2002   158'.3   C2001-904288-4

0-13-066585-1

Vice President, Editorial Director: Michael J. Young
Acquisitions Editors: Heather McWhinney/ Jessica Mosher
Marketing Manager: Judith Allen
Developmental Editor: John Polanszky
Production Editor: Tammy Scherer
Copy Editor: Alex Moore
Senior Production Coordinator: Peggy Brown
Page Layout: Jansom
Art Director: Mary Opper
Cover Design: Lisa Lapointe
Front Cover Image: Photodisc

6   06 05

Printed and bound in Canada.

CONTENTS

TO THE INSTRUCTOR

It is not for him to pride himself who loveth his own country, but rather for him who loveth the whole world. The earth is but one country, and mankind its citizens.
—Bahá'u'lláh

Purpose

This text is a snapshot of my lifetime work in the fascinating and complex field of counselling. My intention is to provide a practical guide that assists professionals in the helping disciplines to develop knowledge, skills, and attitudes for effective interviewing and counselling. Although the book is intended primarily as a textbook for Canadian introductory counselling and interviewing courses, it is also designed as a reference text for more advanced practitioners. The book is targeted to students of counselling and professionals in disciplines such as social work and youth counselling. It may also be of interest to practitioners in allied disciplines such as psychology, criminology, teaching, and nursing who wish to develop their interviewing and counselling skills.

This book aims to contribute to the development of professional competence in four ways:

1. It introduces basic concepts and models to help learners understand the theory and reasoning behind the use of skills.

2. It provides a range of realistic examples that illustrate concepts in action.

3. It contains challenging exercises that promote skill development, conceptual understanding, and self-awareness.

4. It emphasizes the notion of a range of skill choices for interviewing, rather than rules and recipes.

The first edition of this textbook was published under the title *Choices: Practical Interviewing and Counselling Skills*. This revised edition was written to respond to a long unmet need for a counselling textbook with a Canadian perspective. Throughout the book, case examples and ethical references were updated to reflect Canadian realities. Chapter 2 is now linked to the Canadian Counselling Association and the Canadian Association of Social Workers codes of ethics. Chapter 10, dealing with multicultural counselling in Canada, is a major addition to this edition. New material has also been added on spirituality and working from a strengths perspective. The inclusion of spirituality reflects growing interest and acceptance of the importance of spiritual issues in counselling. Drawing on feedback from reviewers, readers, and students, selected portions of the text have been reworded for clarity, or expanded to include current research.

I believe in the importance of intelligent choice in the use of skills and strategies. This requires counsellors to develop a wide range of practice skills that are based on the unique needs of clients and situations as well as supported theory (science) and proven practice. This book emphasizes cultural competence by encouraging counsellors to consider culture as a major component of rational choice. Clearly, this is true when working with clients who are culturally different, but since everyone is unique, with their own mix of values and beliefs, culture is a variable for work with all clients. When working with clients from visible minorities and those who are marginalized by poverty or discrimination, examination of the socio-political realities that frame their circumstances becomes crucial. Counsellors need to develop sufficient self-awareness to escape or manage any tendency to be culture-bound—assuming that all clients share their values, perspectives, and ambitions, or, worse still, that their clients' differences represent deficiencies. By sustaining a multicultural perspective that recognizes and prizes diversity, counsellors can avoid the pitfalls of ethnocentrism (the belief that one's one views and culture are superior). There is substantial research that documents the fact that traditional counselling approaches and techniques are ineffective or limited when used with racial and ethnic minority populations (Sue, 1992). Commitment to a multicultural perspective will engage counsellors in cooperative effort with clients to mobilize strategies that more closely meet their clients' needs and worldviews. It reminds counsellors that their clients' communication styles, comfort with eye contact, or emotional disclosure, for example, are influenced by their culture. Clients do not always respond in the manner preferred by their counsellors, nor do they necessarily need to do so. In fact, culturally competent counsellors will view cultural differences as opportunities to widen their horizons and deepen their versatility. They remember to be humble enough to learn from their clients.

Central Values and Assumptions

Choices and Respect for Diversity.   Diversity includes differences in such major variables as race, religion, age, sex, sexual orientation, physical and mental ability, economic capacity, language, culture, values, beliefs, preferences, and ways of thinking and behaving. This diversity of today's counselling caseloads requires that counsellors develop a range of interviewing and counselling skills. Competent counsellors are able to vary their style depending on the unique needs of different clients and situations. In simplest terms, the more choices counsellors have, the greater they are able to match their work to the needs and wants of their clients and the less they need to repeatedly use the same skill. Effective counsellors can use particular skills, but they are wise enough to know when not to use them. Similarly, the goal of counselling is to help clients achieve versatility in their capacity to solve problems and achieve goals. Effective clients are also able to vary their responses based on the differing needs of situations.

Counsellors need to be aware of their own personal and cultural values and how they might affect their dealings with clients from different cultures, members of minority groups, and disempowered groups. Counsellors must be sensitive to ensure that they do not abuse their power when relating to marginalized groups who may have suffered economic, social, and political disadvantage.

Self-Awareness.   Knowledge of self, including consciousness of one's values and beliefs and the impact of one's behaviour on others, is a prerequisite for effective counselling. When counsellors lack self-awareness they may confuse their clients' feelings with their own, or they may assume that clients will feel as they do. When counsellors are unaware of their own needs, including those that are unmet, they risk unconsciously using their counselling relationships to meet personal goals instead of client goals. Without self-awareness, counsellors will be ignorant of those areas of practice in which they are competent and those in which it will be difficult for them to work with objectivity.

Everyone, including professional counsellors, has personal values and beliefs. Competent professionals know themselves, and they ensure that their values do not become a burden to their clients. They accept that exploring and reflecting on one's competence and the limits of one's role and expertise are fundamental to professional practice. For counsellors, this process of self-examination continues throughout their careers.

Self-Determination.

Whenever possible, counselling should draw on the expertise of clients to participate in decisions related to the goals and process of counselling. To facilitate this involvement, counsellors will need to develop comfort and ability to openly discuss their work and methodology with clients. By so doing, the work of counselling is demystified. Moreover, commitment to client self-determination restrains counsellors from unhelpful behaviours, such as advice giving and abuse of power or control.

By promoting client self-determination counsellors use a strengths approach that empowers clients by assuming their capacity to cope and change. In practice this means

> ... believing that people are capable of making their own choices and decisions. It means not only that human beings possess the strengths and potential to resolve their own difficult life situations, but also that they increase their strength and contribute to society by doing so. The role of the social worker in clinical practice is to nourish, encourage, assist, enable, support, stimulate, and unleash the strengths within people; to illuminate the strengths available to people in their own environments; and to promote equity and justice at all levels of society. To do that, the social worker helps clients articulate the nature of their situations, identify what they want, explore alternatives for achieving those wants, and achieve them. (Cowger, 1994:264)

Although it is a topic beyond the scope of this book, counsellors should consider their responsibility to extend beyond their role as counsellors to social and political action. As advocates for social justice, they strive to reduce gender, cultural, and other forms of discrimination. They promote changes in social policy as well as modification in the functioning of formal organizations and institutions to better meet the needs of clients.

The Nature of Counselling and Interviewing.

Interviewing is an information-gathering process that is free from any conscious attempt to influence the subject. Interviewing is the foundation of counselling, a process that goes beyond interviewing to enable clients to cope with the problems of daily living. Counsellors negotiate a working relationship with clients to accomplish some agreed-on purpose, such as assisting clients to make decisions, deal with painful feelings, solve problems, or learn new skills.

Counselling is a complex blend of skill, attitude, and art. Although core skills can be learned and practised, they are not recipes. The ideas in this book are presented as a starting point with the hope that they will be customized and adapted to fit individual counsellor–client interactions. Skill and technique can be impressive, sometimes even appearing to be magical, but alone they are insufficient. Counsellors need to be genuine, they need to have warm and caring regard for their clients, and they need to recognize the inherent worth of people. To some extent professional training can shape these beliefs and values, but to a greater extent they must come from the hearts and souls of counsellors. Kadushin discusses the important mix of skill and feeling:

Many might say that if they had to choose between feeling and technique they would choose feeling as the more important prerequisite. Perhaps so, but if one has to make a choice between these qualifications, an injustice has already been done to the client. It should be possible to offer the client an interviewer who is both attitudinally correct and technically proficient. (1990:xii)

The counselling model featured in this book rests on the assumption that counselling and interviewing are most effective when:

- Interviews and counselling relationships have a clear contract and purpose.
- Working relationships with a clear understanding of roles are established.
- A climate of trust and safety in taking risks is established.
- Counsellors' responses are genuine, or based on real feelings and attitudes.
- Counsellors respect their clients' independence and their right to self-determination.

The Four Phases of Counselling

In this book, counselling relationships and interviews are described as evolving through four phases: preliminary, beginning, action, and ending. Each phase involves common as well as unique tasks and skills. For example, the beginning phase usually focuses on relationship development and problem exploration. Predictably, skills in developing relationships such as active listening will be favoured, whereas skills such as confrontation are not recommended. In contrast, the action phase focuses on helping clients develop new perspectives, set goals, and implement change strategies; thus, skills such as reframing and confronting may be used more extensively in this phase. In Chapter 1 the model will be described in more detail and elements of the preliminary and ending phases will be discussed.

The four phases are developmental, with success at one phase dependent in part on success at previous phases. Thus, clients are more willing to accept confrontation if a solid relationship or trust is present. In general, reference to the four phase model allows counsellors to make some predictions about the climate of the interview and what skills and tasks will be in the foreground at different points. However, practitioners must be cautious in applying the model to individual counselling interviews, in which the sequence of events may differ sharply from the model.

Structure of the Book

The book is divided into ten chapters.

Chapter 1 explores the basic nature of counselling skills and strategies. In this chapter four major skill clusters are introduced: relationship building, exploring/probing, empowering, and challenging. A four-phase model of counselling (preliminary, beginning, action, and ending) is proposed as a model for understanding the evolution of the counselling relationship.

Chapter 2 introduces readers to the basic concepts of ethics, values, and self-awareness.

Chapter 3 examines the helping relationship and considers the core conditions necessary for counselling to be effective.

Chapters 4, **5**, and **6** explore the active listening skills of attending, silence, paraphrasing, and summarizing (Chapter 4), questioning (Chapter 5), and empathy (Chapter 6).

Chapter 7 is concerned with action phase skills that motivate clients to think differently and to make changes in their lives.

Chapter 8 presents information for working in difficult situations, such as when clients are resistant or potentially violent.

Chapter 9 looks at concepts for working with various populations, including those who are seeking work, dealing with mental disorders, contemplating suicide, or coping with an HIV-positive diagnosis or AIDS.

Chapter 10 explores important concepts and issues related to counselling clients from different cultures.

Appendix A reproduces the Canadian Counselling Association's Code of Ethics.

Appendix B reproduces the Canadian Association of Social Worker's Code of Ethics. These are followed by a **Glossary** of key terms and concepts, and a list of **References**.

Features

People learn in different ways, so this book includes a range of features designed to assist learners to understand at cognitive, emotional, and behavioural levels. Each chapter contains the following elements:

- **Chapter preview:** key concepts that will be addressed in the chapter.

- **Summary:** a short review at the end of each chapter that reviews important ideas.

- **Conversations:** a unique addition, offering debate or opinions on frequently asked questions.

- **Sample interviews:** annotated interview excerpts that illustrate and explain chapter concepts.

- **Exercises:** end-of-chapter reflective questions that are designed to give readers practice in the development of skills or questions framed to promote self-awareness and creative thinking.

- **Weblinks:** links to Web sites related to the chapter's material.

TO THE STUDENT

If you are studying this book as part of a course on counselling skills, you will probably have the opportunity to develop skill competence in a number of different ways, including:

- Watching instructor demonstrations.
- Conducting practice interviews using role-played or (preferably) real-life scenarios.
- Completing the chapter exercises.
- Receiving feedback and evaluation from instructors and student colleagues who observe your work.
- Using audio and video recordings to understand and assess your verbal and non-verbal responses.
- Working with clients.

In most counselling skills courses, learning groups are used to practise skills. Usually, these learning groups use classroom simulations and practice interviews, in which you assume the roles of client, counsellor, and observer. Each of these roles offers unique challenges and opportunities for learning.

Being a Client. The client's role offers a powerful opportunity for you to understand the feelings and expectations that clients may bring to the session. You may find that your reactions are similar to those that clients experience, including:

- Ambivalence about sharing feelings or details about personal issues.
- Feelings of vulnerability, including fear of being judged, embarrassed, or ridiculed.

As a client, it will be up to you to control how much you wish to disclose; however, by taking reasonable risks, your learning opportunities and insights are enhanced.

Being a Counsellor. When you are asked to practise your newly learned skills as a counsellor, you may feel clumsy and insecure. As a counsellor you will be encouraged to change established communication patterns or to experiment with new skills and strategies, and this can be unsettling. As a student with limited training, you may be reluctant to ask questions that seem to invade the privacy of your colleagues. When dealing with sensitive issues, you may fear that your lack of experience may damage your clients. You may fear that your colleagues will judge you as inept. When you are observed by others, the intense focus on your work can be unsettling and anxiety-provoking. These reactions are common, and you will probably find that your colleagues feel the same way. For most professional counsellors it takes many years of practice and study to become competent and comfortable using a full range of skills. What is important is that you persist and avoid the natural temptation to stick with familiar patterns of communicating. Skills that seem awkward at first may, with practice, become part of your natural and preferred style.

Minuchin & Fishman (1981) offer this interesting conclusion, "Only a person who has mastered technique and then contrived to forget it can become an expert ..." (1). Elsewhere, they observe that:

> Unfortunately, the teaching of new skills often disorganizes the beginning student. As in any learning or relearning process, the student finds himself concentrating so much on the trees that he misses the forest... As in the training of the samurai, the student needs a number of years to achieve expertise and many more to achieve spontaneity. (Minuchin & Fishman, 1981:10)

Being an Observer. Student observers are responsible for watching the interview and for providing feedback to other student colleagues who are practising their counselling skills. You may be reluctant to offer feedback, perhaps worrying that your remarks will generate anger or hurt feelings. The observer's role gives you an excellent opportunity to develop and practise giving feedback.

Helpful feedback is energizing and does not detract from another person's self-esteem. As people learn and practice interviewing and counselling skills, they may feel vulnerable and awkward. Hence, the importance of remaining sensitive to their emotional and psychological needs while balancing their needs for information and correction. Feedback may be of two types: supportive or corrective.

Supportive feedback reinforces or acknowledges achievements—"catch them doing something right." However obvious this idea seems, many people are problem-oriented and fail to recognize strengths. Consider how you respond differently when your strengths are acknowledged rather than when your weaknesses are targeted. Supportive feedback, to be effective, must be genuine (true), and delivered without rescuing or patronizing. If you lie to others in order to avoid hurting them, your credibility as a source of feedback will diminish.

Corrective feedback challenges others to examine or change behaviour. Before giving corrective feedback, consider your relationship with the other person. If your relationship is based on trust and caring, corrective feedback has the potential to be effective. However, if your relationship is stressed, for example, in situations where there is unresolved conflict, corrective feedback is more likely to be perceived as an attack. If people think your feedback is harsh, demanding or controlling, there is a higher probability of them resisting.

Don't use corrective feedback as a means to control, impress, or to punish. Pay attention to your tone of voice and other nonverbal behaviour. Make sure that you avoid lecturing and pointing fingers. Timing and pacing are important. Supportive feedback is more useful when self-esteem is low. It's best to give feedback as soon as possible, but ensure that personal privacy is protected. Avoid overwhelming others by remembering that you do not have to accomplish everything at once. As a general rule, ask people to self-evaluate before offering your opinions. You may be surprised to find that they already have insight into the problem areas. Then, the number of areas where you have to provide direct feedback is reduced.

Feedback has the most potential for success if it is invited and/or targeted to perceived areas of need. Contract with others to receive feedback. Ask questions such as: "Would you like me to offer my ideas on what happened?" or, "Are there specific issues that you are concerned about?" When you work with others (clients or colleagues), don't forget individual differences. Some people prefer feedback to be direct and to the point. Others may prefer it "sandwiched" between positives. Some need time to reflect before responding or they may profit from visual and written illustrations.

People may have an immediate reaction to your feedback that differs from their reaction once they have time to ponder what you have said. Thus, a person who responds defensively or even with anger may on reflection come to accept your input. The opposite can also be true—people who react favourably may develop other feelings such as resentment or confusion. Checking back during future encounters is one strategy for keeping abreast of others' reactions.

Finally, remember that giving helpful and caring feedback is one way of developing and strengthening relationships. If you are honest and supportive with others, you greatly increase the probability they will be honest and supportive with you when you ask for their helpful feedback.

Developing an Effective Learning Group.
When you work with student colleagues in each of the three roles, it is helpful to candidly discuss your fears as well as your expectations of one another. You will need to work to develop a contract or agreement on how you will work together.

Practice interviews will be more powerful learning opportunities if they are based on real rather than role-played feelings and issues. Consequently, it will be important to establish a climate of safety, where confidentiality will be respected. Some important principles to remember:

- Colleagues who are in the client's role are disclosing personal issues and feelings, so it is essential that their dignity and right to privacy are respected.

- Everyone has different capacities for intimacy. Don't expect that all members of a learning group will disclose at the same level. Accept individual differences.

- Learning the skills of counselling requires a certain willingness to give up familiar patterns of communication and to attempt new approaches. Expand your limits by taking appropriate risks to try new skills and be tolerant of colleagues who are engaged in similar risk taking.

- Expect that the process of learning and experimenting with new skills will result in a period of awkwardness and self-consciousness. For a time it may seem as though your capacity to counsel others is regressing.

- Feedback for others is an important part of learning. Therefore, try to make it easy for others to give you feedback and respond in a nondefensive manner. Help others give specific feedback by asking targeted questions.

Keeping a Personal Journal.
A personal "for your eyes only" journal can be a significant adjunct to your learning. The journal is a tool for introspection that provides a private means for documenting and exploring your thoughts and feelings related to the development of your counselling skills. There are no rules for journal writing other than the need to make entries on a regular basis and to try to avoid self-censorship.

Using This Book.   If you are using this book as part of a course on counselling, your teacher will propose a suggested reading schedule that structures your reading over the semester and he or she will assign or adapt the chapter exercises to fit your learning needs. Another way to use the book is on an "as you need it" basis and to use the index or chapter headings to research content that fits your needs. As well, you are encouraged to use other books, journals, and tools, such as Internet research, to supplement your learning. However, you should read this book (or any book) critically and seek to understand and explore the ideas and try them out, but don't forget that there is room for other perspectives.

Counselling Skills as a Way of Life.   You may be surprised to discover that the skills of counselling are also the skills of effective everyday communication and that the process of developing your counselling competence begins to influence your personal relationships. As counselling skills become part of your style, you may find yourself becoming a little more inquisitive and more sensitive to the feelings of others. However, you may find that others in your life do not welcome the changes in your manner and style. When you change, others around you have to accommodate your changes. If you become more probing in your questions, they must be forthcoming with their answers. When you become more empathic, their feelings become more transparent. These changes move the relationship to a deeper level of intimacy, which may be frightening for some, particularly if the pace is too fast for their comfort level.

ACKNOWLEDGMENTS

The editorial staff at Pearson Education Canada has been instrumental in helping me to bring the manuscript to publication. In particular, I wish to thank Heather McWhinney, Jessica Mosher, John Polanszky, Tammy Scherer, and Alex Moore, who provided outstanding assistance in the writing of the second edition.

My colleagues Bob Martel, John Fox, and Sharon Smith assisted me by reviewing selected sections. I want to express special appreciation for their many helpful comments and suggestions. I also appreciate the support and suggestions of my colleagues at Douglas College, Doug Estergaard, Nancy Newman, Lawrence Becker, Julie Roper, and especially Dave Burgess, who contributes ongoing thoughtful criticism. I wish to thank the faculty at Vancouver Community College—Joanne Rykers, Lee McLeod, Susan Runytu, and Sara Menzel—who have given me many helpful suggestions that have been incorporated in this book. Thanks also to Jackie Yurick at Surrey Community Services and Ellen Edwards at NETWERRC for their continued support and helpful suggestions.

The students of the Community Social Service Worker program at Douglas College offered candid and helpful recommendations to me when I field tested the ideas in this book. Similarly, Sandy Cook, Jim Edwards and the great team at Covenant House in Vancouver offered insightful comments and suggestions.

I have been aided by many reviewers who critically evaluated pre-publication drafts, including Jeff Arbus at Sault College, Marilyn Jeske at Grant MacEwan College, and Lourdes A.D. de la Cruz at Sheridan College. I want them to know that their input was extremely useful and much appreciated.

This book is dedicated to Joyce Shebib, to whom I owe an enormous debt of gratitude. Her constant support, encouragement, and painstaking review of every chapter through many rewrites made the final product much better than it would have been otherwise.

Bob Shebib
Douglas College

AN INTRODUCTION TO THE SKILLS AND PROCESS OF COUNSELLING

PREVIEW

After reading this chapter you should be able to:

- Define the range of counselling activities.
- List the people who provide counselling services.
- Explain why it is important for counsellors to be versatile.
- Describe the necessary range of skill versatility.
- Classify the four skill clusters of counselling.
- Describe why counselling fails.
- List the four phases of counselling.
- Summarize the developmental objectives of the four phases of counselling.

AN OVERVIEW OF COUNSELLING

Training as a Counsellor

A large number of people at various levels of training are counsellors, including social workers, psychologists, psychiatrists, and psychiatric nurses. Many counsellors are members of professional associations such as the Canadian Association of Social Workers (CASW), the Canadian Counselling Association, and the US-based National Association of Social Workers (NASW). As members, they are subject to codes of ethics governing acceptable professional behaviour. Membership in these associations usually requires a university degree and, in some cases, a master's degree or a Ph.D.

Social workers generally have university training with a bachelor's degree in social work (B.S.W.) or a master's degree in social work (M.S.W.) In addition, they may have specialized training in specialty areas such as family therapy or group work. Social workers might work in private practice or be employed in hospitals, prisons, schools, or community social service agencies, for example, working with people who have drug addictions. Many social workers work for government agencies investigating incidents of child abuse and neglect.

Counselling psychologists are usually qualified at the Ph.D. level, but some jurisdictions allow registration for those with a master's degree. Psychologists may work as counsellors, or they may specialize in other areas such as in administering and interpreting psychological tests. Psychologists are often employed in private practice, but they also may work in settings such as prisons, hospitals, schools, and private industry.

Psychiatrists are medical doctors with advanced training in psychiatry. They are specialists in the treatment of people with mental disorders. Psychiatrists are the only counselling professionals who are licensed to prescribe medication. Psychiatric nurses generally have two to four years of training. Historically, they worked in psychiatric hospitals and wards, but increasingly, they are working in community-based mental health settings.

Volunteers and paraprofessional counsellors who have one to two years of university or college training also may provide counselling services. In addition, the professional counselling community is often supported or replaced by an array self-help support groups. Frequently, counsellors work with clients who are attending a self-help group such as Alcoholics Anonymous (AA) or Narcotics Anonymous (NA).

The Scope of Counselling

Counselling involves a time-limited relationship in which the counsellor helps clients increase their ability to deal with the demands of life. Typically, people seek or are referred to counsellors because of some unmanageable crisis, such as the loss of a job, relationship problems, or feelings of distress. The immediate goal of counselling is to provide assistance so that people seeking help (clients) can gain some control over their problems. The long-term goal of counselling is to work with clients to restore or develop their ability to cope with the changing demands of their lives.

The focus of counselling depends on three variables: the needs and wants of the client, the mandate of the counselling setting, and the expertise or competence of the counsellor. Professional counsellors know when their competence limits are exceeded and when they need to make an appropriate referral. They are also aware of their own needs and unresolved issues, and they refer clients to other professionals when they cannot work with reasonable **objectivity**. They accept that no one is qualified to work with all clients. Table 1.1 summarizes how counselling knowledge and skill evolves from beginning to advanced levels.

The work of counselling may entail a broad range of activities, including the following:

- helping clients cope with painful feelings
- teaching clients new skills
- helping clients develop problem-solving skills
- mediating relationship communication difficulties
- aiding clients in identifying and accessing resources
- helping clients make decisions and implement action plans
- supporting or motivating clients

Social Work and Counselling

One special feature that distinguishes social work counselling from that performed by other professionals is its dual focus on working with the individual as well as the environment. Social workers assume that an individual can only be understood in the context of their environment and they pay particular attention to the interaction of the person and

Table 1.1 Beginning to Advanced Level Counsellors

Beginning Level Counsellors	Advanced Level Counsellors
Basic use of core listening and responding skills.	Exemplary use of broad range of listening and counselling skills and strategies. Capacity to be creative to meet unique needs of individual clients.
Sensitivity to overt nonverbal cues.	Responsive to subtle nonverbal cues and themes.
Basic content knowledge of field of practice.	In-depth knowledge of current science and practice in the field. Ability to analyze and adapt published material.
Rudimentary understanding of self.	Sophisticated knowledge of self, one's impact on others and the ability to selectively use aspects of self to influence others.
Struggle to manage biases, personal reactions.	"Second nature" capacity to stay appropriately detached and in-control of self.
Tendency to "mimic" mentors and textbook responses.	Capacity to customize approach, development of individual styles.
Self-consciousness.	Focus on clients.
Tendency to want to fix, rescue or solve client problems.	Recognition of the need to empower clients to problem solve.

their environment. Like other professionals in the helping field, social workers may counsel clients to help them develop insight, problem solve, deal with emotional pain, or to enhance relationships. They may support clients by providing information, social skills training or resources. Unique to social work is the important responsibility that the profession gives social workers to promote change or adaptation in social and political systems so that they can respond more effectively to the needs of clients. Specht (1990) underscores that one defining feature of social work must be its continuing mission to build better systems and communities that are structured to provide social support and helping networks to its clientele.

> It is a mission to deal with the enormous social problems under which our society staggers: the social isolation of our aged, the anomie experienced by our youth, the neglect and abuse of children, homelessness, drug addiction, and AIDS. (354)

Counselling, while an important component of helping individuals cope, is insufficient in dealing with these great challenges. Thus, while the intent of this book is to explore the counselling component of social work practice, practitioners are cautioned to approach this task with the broader mission of social work in mind. Chapter 10 of The Code of Ethics of the Canadian Association of Social Workers (1994) outlines the obligations of social workers to advocate for social change.

10. A social worker shall advocate change
　　(a) in the best interest of the client, and
　　(b) for the overall benefit of society, the environment and the global community.

10.1. A social worker shall identify, document and advocate for the elimination of discrimination.

10.2 A social worker shall advocate for the equal distribution of resources to all persons.

10.3 A social worker shall advocate for the equal access of all persons to resources, services, and opportunities.

10.4 A social worker shall advocate for a clean and healthy environment and shall advocate the development of environmental strategies consistent with social work principles.

10.5 A social worker shall provide reasonable professional services in a state of emergency.

10.6 A social worker shall promote social justice.

CONVERSATION 1.1

COUNSELLING AND PSYCHOTHERAPY

STUDENT: What's the difference between counselling and psychotherapy?

TEACHER: The terms **psychotherapy** and counselling are often used interchangeably to describe the application of specific skills to assist clients in a process of change. Both counselling and psychotherapy strive to help clients to learn skills, deal with feelings, and manage problems. In counselling and psychotherapy, appropriate relationships with clients are the medium for promoting change. In both psychotherapy and counselling, these relationships with clients are crucial to success. They provide an important foundation of safety and security for clients to undertake the change process.

Although there is no clear dividing line between the two terms, the major difference between counselling and psychotherapy is that psychotherapy tends to be more long term than counselling, with an emphasis on severe emotional and behavioural difficulties or disorders. On the other hand, counselling is targeted toward assisting clients in managing situational problems.

Interviewing skills are indispensable to effective counselling. The goal of **interviewing** is to acquire and organize relevant information through timely listening and responding skills. When the interview is used as an information-gathering process, interviewers do not try to promote change. However, clients may feel relief from sharing, and organizing their thoughts in response to a systematic interview may allow them to grow.

Good interviewers are comfortable with silence and know when to listen without interrupting. Counsellors who listen to clients give them a chance to air their feelings, and this step can be therapeutic in itself. Patient listening shows clients that counsellors are willing to accept them without judgment and without burdening them with quick-fix solutions to complex problems and feelings.

At the beginning of counselling sessions or interviews, silent listening may give counsellors valuable clues about the potential focus of the interview. Listening helps counsellors understand something about their clients' priorities. It reveals which methods clients may have used and not used to try to solve their problems.

Good listeners also know when and how to respond. A range of skills, including paraphrasing, summarizing, questioning, and showing empathy, completes the foundation of effective listening. These skills enable counsellors to focus and deepen the interview. Questions may be used to clarify meaning and to seek detail and example, whereas paraphrasing and summarizing responses are useful for confirming understanding and for sorting out important from less important information. A good interview involves methodical questioning and exploration of issues, a process that can help clients to clarify and organize their thoughts. Counsellors use empathy skills to confirm their understanding of the client's feelings.

THE NEED FOR VERSATILITY

The typical counselling caseload is characterized by **diversity**. Culture, gender, age, religion, sexual orientation, language, education, economic ability, and intellectual capacity, as well as beliefs, values, preferences and personal style, make every client different. Therefore, a "one size fits all" model of counselling is precluded. Respect for client diversity requires counsellors to be versatile in adapting their methods to fit the needs of each client or context. Counsellors who persist in using the same strategy for all clients, without regard to individual differences, will be ineffective. As Haley observes, skilled counsellors expect that they "will approach each new person with the idea that a unique procedure might be necessary for this particular person and social situation" (1987:7).

Expert counsellors draw on research theory and experience as guides in determining which skills and procedures will best meet their clients' needs. They work from a model or process for exploring problems and helping clients build solutions, but they adapt that model to each client situation. Every client and problem circumstance will favour different skills, and each situation requires counsellors to know how to use skills, as well as when to use them. Many counsellors consider themselves eclectic, and they use concepts and skills from 400 or more varieties of psychotherapy (Lazarus and Beutler, 1993). In the process, they may use an assortment of counselling tools, including drama, role play, toys, music, art, films, visual charts such as genealogical diagrams, personality tests, and audio or visual recordings. Lazarus and Beutler remind us that no one theoretical orientation has all the answers, but they caution against selecting skills and procedures haphazardly, arguing that counsellors must act based on "a logical decisional process that takes into account the client, setting, problem, and the nature of the counselor's skills" (1993:384).

At the same time, this need for **versatility** does not mean that counsellors have to deny their basic personality. It does not require counsellors to compromise their professional ethics, nor to ignore the core conditions or values of clients. Successful counsellors model a high level of congruence between who they are and how they act. They are sincere and real in the way they relate to clients.

Competence Using a Wide Range of Skills

The element of versatility requires that counsellors understand and perfect new skills. Only then will they have choices. With choices, counsellors have freedom to relate to each client differently. When one strategy fails, counsellors can use others. They have the ability to use a skill, but they also have the ability to refrain from applying it compulsively.

Skill versatility enables counsellors to customize their approach. For example, although most clients respond favourably to empathy, some clients may see empathy as intrusive and respond with defensiveness, preferring to keep their feelings private, at least for a while. Effective counsellors are alert to such reactions and have the ability to use skills other than empathy with such clients.

Knowing how to use a skill is not the same as knowing when it is wise to use it. Being able to predict an outcome is an important part of timing. Although counsellors can make some generalizations about when a particular skill is appropriate, they need to apply these generalizations with caution and consideration for individual differences. For example, at the start of a counselling relationship, the counsellor usually wants to use skills that promote the development of the working alliance and, thus, avoids more demanding strategies, such as confrontation. Conversely, once they have established a firm working relationship, counsellors will want to use skills that help clients gain new perspectives, so confrontation may be warranted. As another example, empathy often encourages clients to share deeper feelings. Therefore, counsellors who use empathy should be willing to invest the time that this sharing requires. If the interview is near an end, the counsellor might decide to avoid empathic responses that stimulate emotions that cannot be dealt with in the time available.

Matching the Language of Clients

Careful listening tells counsellors about the language and metaphors that characterize their clients' communication styles. In turn, this knowledge helps guide counsellors to modify their language to fit that of their clients. Skillful counsellors are alert to their clients' use of humour and metaphor. Counsellors also need to pay attention to such variables as voice tone, volume, and tempo, and to then respond appropriately. To a depressed client, a high-energy, fast-talking counsellor might be annoying. Similarly, the counsellor who responds in a monotone to a client who is ecstatic about finding a job might come across as cold and indifferent.

Grinder and Bandler (1976) suggest that everyone has a different way of using language to represent their experiences. According to their theory, people process ideas in one of three major modalities: in the visual mode through pictures and images; in the auditory mode with sounds; and in the kinesthetic or feeling mode. A person who thinks visually will be more likely to say, "I see what you mean," whereas a person who processes in the auditory mode might say, "I hear you." Someone else might say, "I have a handle on my problem" or "I feel in touch with..."; these responses suggest that they process in the kinesthetic mode. Counsellors may find it easier to establish rapport and build trust when they match their clients' words with similar language (see Table 1.2).

Other Versatility Variables

Counsellor adaptability also includes the need to be flexible regarding such variables as where the interview takes place, how long the interview lasts, the pace of the interview, the fees, and the people who are involved. Although some counsellors still work in office settings with scheduled 45-minute or hour-long interviews, many work in settings where counselling interviews are less structured. Process versatility gives counsellors choices regarding the sequence and pace of counselling activities. With most clients, the beginning phase is concerned with exploring problems and feelings, but with other clients, counsellors may move immediately to action and problem solving. With some clients, counsellors spend a great deal of time helping them explore their feelings, but with others, counsellors spend little or no time in this activity.

The need for versatility also extends to other factors, such as the amount of eye contact that is expected or desired, seating arrangements, and physical distance. Some clients are comfortable in an office setting, but others prefer to work in their own home or to meet in a neutral setting. Adolescent boys, for example, might prove more approachable if counselling interventions are combined with some activity. Some clients favour an open seating arrangement with no desk or obstacle between them and their counsellors. Others prefer to work over the corner of a desk (Kadushin, 1990).

Table 1.2 Matching Clients' Language Styles		
Style	**Client Statement**	**Sample Counsellor Response**
Visual	My view of the problem is...	If I get the picture correctly, the way you see it is...
Auditory	When I listen to myself I know what I have to do.	Tell me more about what you are saying to yourself.
Kinesthetic	I can't seem to get a handle on my problem.	What prevents you from grasping the solution?

VALUES AND ETHICS

Ethics are principles of acceptable conduct. Professional associations such as the Canadian Association of Social Workers and the Canadian Counselling Association have formal statements that define ethics and standards of practice. These documents define the responsibilities of its members. **Values** are what individuals and groups consider important or worthwhile. The behaviour of counsellors in their interviews is influenced to a great extent by their values, including their philosophical view of people and of how they are motivated. Counsellors who see people as basically good and goal-directed will behave very differently than those who believe people are evil and must be monitored or controlled. In counselling, two values are of particular importance:

1. belief in the dignity and worth of people
2. respect for the client's right to self-determination, i.e., for freedom of choice and the right to control their own lives

These professional values are at the root of the counselling model described in this book. By respecting the dignity of people, counsellors try to be nonjudgmental in their work and to treat all clients with respect and caring. The self-determination principle values the right of clients to be involved in decision making and to control decisions that affect their lives. Chapter 2 considers these concepts in greater depth.

SKILL CLUSTERS

Today, there is no standardized method for classifying counselling skills. Nevertheless, it is useful to think about skills in terms of their function or intended purpose. In this book four major **skill clusters**, based on their intended purpose, are used: (1) relationship building; (2) exploring or probing; (3) empowering; and (4) challenging. Each major skill is further categorized into subclusters of related skills (see Table 1.3).

Significantly, some skills achieve multiple purposes. Sensitive active listening, for example, contributes to the development of the relationship because it communicates acceptance and the sincere desire to understand. At the same time, active listening is essential for getting information, so these skills are also classified as exploring/probing. Building on the need for versatility, practitioners need to be versatile in seeking to build competence based on knowledge of (1) what particular skills involve, including their intended purpose; (2) when and how to use individual skills; and (3) their own skill strengths and limitations.

Relationship-Building Skills

Relationship-building skills are the basic tools for engaging clients, developing trust, and defining the purpose of the counselling. They are of central importance during the beginning phase of helping, but effective counselling requires that the relationship be sustained and deepened through all phases of helping. Listening is at the heart of this cluster of skills. When clients feel heard, they respond with further disclosure. Unless counsellors listen, there is no way for them to understand the complexities and uniqueness of their clients' situations. Other relationship-building skills involve conveying interest, warmth, and willingness to become involved.

Table 1.3   Skill Clusters

Relationship Building	Exploring or Probing	Empowering	Challenging
Active listening • Attending • Using silence • Paraphrasing • Summarizing • Questioning • Showing empathy	Active listening • Attending • Using silence • Paraphrasing • Summarizing • Questioning • Showing empathy	Searching for strengths • Defining client capacities and rights • Defining problems as opportunities • Identifying resources	Confronting • Providing critical feedback • Promoting strengths • Encouraging • Correcting distortions • Reframing • Asking clients to take responsibility
Promoting core conditions • Showing congruence or genuineness • Showing empathy • Revealing positive regard	Other interviewing skills • Using directives • Providing simple encouragers • Using counsellor self-disclosure • Using humour	Teaching • Providing skills training • Modeling • Role playing	Action planning • Defining clear and measurable targets for change • Helping clients identify and evaluate alternatives for reaching goals • Helping clients choose, develop, and carry out change strategies
Defining the relationship • Contracting • Using immediacy • Using counsellor self-disclosure		Information giving • Offering advice and information • Referring	
		Supporting • Reassuring • Fostering optimism • Reinforcing • Advocating • Providing direct aid • Praising	Use of Power and Authority • limit setting • enforcement

Active Listening. **Active listening** involves six separate skills: attending, using silence, paraphrasing, summarizing, questioning, and showing empathy. **Attending** is the manner in which counsellors communicate that they are physically and psychologically interested in what their clients are saying or doing. Appropriate **silence** gives clients time to think and respond. Effective counsellors understand the multiple meanings of silence. Is the client confused? Have we reached the end of the topic? Is the client thinking? Skilled counsellors know when to interrupt a silence and when to allow it to continue. **Paraphrasing** involves restating (usually in shortened form) the client's thoughts to clarify the essence of what he or she has said. **Summarizing** is an interviewing tool used to condense the essential content and to identify essential themes and ideas. **Questioning** involves probing for information to confirm understanding and seek clarification, such as by saying, "Do you mean that...?" **Empathy** is "the process of accurately understanding the emotional perspective of another person and the communication of this understanding" (Shebib, 1997:177).

Active listening skills provide psychological incentive for clients to open up. When clients experience a deep sense of having been heard, they are motivated to open up. They learn to trust the listener when their ideas are not judged or rejected and when their feelings are validated. This trust results in a climate of safety, and clients begin to reveal more. Furthermore, active listening skills provide a structure for exploring thoughts and feelings. Paraphrasing and summarizing, for example, help clients to organize ideas, identify key points, and recognize priorities. Questions provide a systematic way of exploring ideas for detail, definition, and example. Empathy opens opportunities for understanding and accepting feelings.

Active listening says to the client, "I have heard you," "I am willing to understand your problems and feelings without judgment," and "I accept you." Consequently, active listening is a powerful tool for establishing rapport and understanding, the basis for a strong working relationship. The skills of active listening will be discussed in depth in Chapters 4, 5, and 6.

Promoting Core Conditions.

The values of this model are inspired by the views of Carl Rogers (1961; 1980) and his belief that people are essentially good, self-deterministic (able to make their own decisions), and goal directed. Rogers identified three factors that are essential for helpers: congruence, empathy, and positive regard. In Chapter 3, these core conditions will be explored further.

Congruence, or **genuineness**, is the capacity to be real and consistent with clients. Congruent counsellors are open with their reactions and feelings and demonstrate consistency in what they believe, say, and do. Congruency requires counsellors to be "transparent," or without hidden agendas or false demeanours. Rogers believed that the more counsellors are aware of their feelings and the more they genuinely express these feelings in the counselling relationship, the more effective the counselling will be.

Empathy as a core condition means being able to see the world through the eyes of the clients. Essential to empathic understanding is the ability to understand feelings without imposing one's own feelings or reactions. "Empathy becomes judgmental when the counselor not only reflects the client's feeling state but also applies his or her own emotional yardstick in measuring its appropriateness for the client" (Gilliland and James, 1998:117–18).

Positive regard, or respect for clients, is the ability of counsellors to recognize the inherent worth of people, regardless of their behaviour. As Gilliland and James conclude, "At any given time, the counselor needs to be willing to accept the confusion, fear, anger, resentment, courage, sorrow, and multiplicity of other feelings the client may have. Such caring is total and nonpossessive and lacks prior conditions of rightness or appropriateness of the client's feelings" (1998:117).

Defining the Relationship.

Rogers emphasized the importance of avoiding moral judgment of clients in order to develop an effective helping relationship. He vividly captured the significance of nonjudgmental exploration to the development of the relationship: "It is only as I understand the feelings and thoughts which seem so horrible to you, or so weak, or so sentimental, or so bizarre—it is only as I see them as you see them, and accept them and you, that you feel really free to explore all the hidden nooks and frightening crannies of your inner and often buried experience" (1961:34).

Three major skills are associated with defining the relationship: contracting, immediacy, and self-disclosure. Contracting involves negotiating the intended purpose of the counselling relationship, including agreeing on the expected roles of both counsellor and client. The counselling contract is an agenda of the activities and tasks that counselling will address, but the contract may change, sometimes frequently, as the work proceeds. Contracting defines a plan for the work that is individualized to meet the needs of each client. Consider, for example, three women who seek counselling with an identical problem, a relationship breakdown. As a result of contracting, client one may identify her need as help in managing her stress and pain. Client two may want to focus on developing her assertive communication skills for dealing with an abusive spouse. Client three, on the other hand, might want help with decision making in choosing between leaving the relationship or remaining in hopes of solving the relationship problems.

Immediacy (Egan, 1998) is a tool for examining and deepening the counselling relationship. It involves a process of evaluation that addresses the quality of the relationship in terms of its contracted objectives. Thus, the skill of immediacy means prompting candid discussion regarding how the relationship might be changed in order to better serve its objectives. Counsellor self-disclosure can be an important component of immediacy, or it can be used as a skill that reduces a client's sense that "I'm the only one who thinks and feels this way."

Exploring/Probing Skills

Exploring/probing skills are the basic tools of interviewing that counsellors use to gather information, clarify definitions, seek examples, and obtain necessary detail. These skills enable counsellors to avoid making **assumptions**. Questions are central to probing, but other skills also have the effect of encouraging clients to tell their stories.

Other Interviewing Skills. **Directives** such as "Tell me more" or "Please expand on your feelings" are statements that are used to control the direction and pace of the interview. As well, directives can be used to focus the client on relevant priorities. Directives are the "road signs" of the interview.

Simple encouragers are short verbal and nonverbal cues that motivate clients to continue. Verbal statements such as "Uh huh" or "Yes" and short directives such as "Please continue," along with nonverbal signals such as head nods and an attentive posture, are the essence of this skill set.

Counsellor self-disclosure, used sparingly, can be a useful tool that models appropriate sharing of feelings. As discussed above, counsellor self-disclosure may reduce the clients' sense that their experiences or feelings are strange or abnormal. Subsequently, when experiences are "normalized" clients are more apt to open up and share. In this way, counsellor self-disclosure acts as an exploring/probing skill.

Humour, if it is timely, can be used as a way to reduce tension or to encourage clients to take a lighter view of their situation. Humour must be used cautiously so that it does not offend clients or trivialize their problems.

Empowering Skills

Empowering skills are used to help clients develop confidence, self-esteem, and control over their lives. Five skill subclusters are the essence of empowering: searching for strengths, teaching, supporting, giving information, and managing anxiety.

Searching for strengths moves counselling from a process of identifying deficits and problems to one in which clients' strengths, capacities, and resources are recognized. Strengths are the resources that enable clients to overcome problems, so they cannot be ignored. Helping clients realize their strengths empowers them with the belief that they are capable of change. Sometimes reframing how clients think about problems can help them to see their problems as opportunities.

Teaching may be used in counselling as a way to assist clients in developing strengths. Skills training, role playing, and other tools can be used as ways to help clients develop their capacities.

Information giving empowers clients with knowledge of alternative courses of action, including resources that might assist them in dealing with their problems. Counsellors may also offer suggestions and advice regarding problem management.

Supporting is used to help bolster clients' energy and optimism. To some extent, all counselling skills are supportive. Supporting reduces clients' feelings of isolation and provides the incentive for clients to address their problems, express their feelings, and begin a process of change. Supporting can be used to tell clients that they are on the right track and to inform clients that their feelings and reactions are normal. Supporting helps clients manage anxiety and stress, thus increasing their energy, self-confidence, and capacity for problem solving.

Cowger (1994) offers this important reminder that the role of social workers is not to change, treat, or empower people:

> To assume a social worker can empower someone else is naive and condescending and has little basis in reality. Power is not something that social workers possess for distribution at will. Clients, not social workers, own the power that brings significant change in clinical practice. A clinical social worker is merely a resource person with professional training on the use of resources who is committed to people empowerment and willing to share his or her knowledge in a manner that helps people realize their own power, take control of their own lives, and solve their own problems. (264)

By using a **strengths approach** social workers identify and reinforce client competence. In this sense, client assessment moves beyond identifying obstacles and problems to discussion of personal and environmental resources. Such an approach reduces some of the power differential that comes when client vulnerabilities and deficits are given priority.

Challenging Skills

Challenging skills are used to encourage clients to critically evaluate their behaviour and ideas. They push clients toward change and growth and in this way fulfill the fundamental reason for the counselling relationship. Excessive or premature reliance on challenging skills may strain the counselling relationship. As Young puts it, "when challenging skills are used, the aura of safety and support, so carefully constructed by the helper, is at risk. There is a fundamental shift from relationship building to a focus on the goals set by the client and helper, conveying to the client that the helping relationship is not a friendship but a business partnership" (1998:100).

Two subclusters are contained within this skill set: confronting and action planning. **Confrontation** prods clients to critically examine their actions and/or consider other viewpoints. This process may involve counsellors in providing critical or corrective feedback, identifying overlooked strengths, correcting distortions, suggesting other viewpoints (reframing), and requesting that clients assume responsibility. Confrontation skills are most effective when there is a strong relationship of trust and when clients understand and accept the value of their use. Brill offers this perspective on the challenging skill of confrontation:

> Misuse of confrontation can be devastating, destroying all previous efforts. Workers must assess the amount and quality of confrontation the client is willing or able to use, and they must be able to give support if the reality is overwhelming. Workers must not use confrontation to express their own anger and frustration, although these are certainly a part of the reality with which both workers and clients must deal. (1998:166)

Ideally, confrontation skills will increase clients' motivation for change. Counsellors develop the credibility necessary for successful confronting when they have listened to clients and have persuaded them that they are accepted and understood. With this base, clients may be appropriately confronted when they

- are working from false assumptions or incomplete information
- misread the actions of others
- lack **self-awareness** regarding the impact of their actions, for example, when they blame others for their problems rather than examine their own responsibility
- demonstrate contradictions in their behaviour, thoughts, and feelings
- deny or do not recognize their personal strengths, capacities, or resources

Action planning is a way of helping clients bring about changes in their lives. These changes may include finding new ways of managing feelings, forming strategies for modifying ways of thinking, or developing new skills or behaviours. Action planning helps clients to define clear and measurable targets for change (goals), to identify and evaluate alternative strategies, and to select and develop plans for reaching these goals.

Use of Power and Authority

Social workers derive or are given power by virtue of their position. Such power comes from many sources: competence, knowledge, education, control of resources, position in the agency/status in the community, or simply the fact that the client is the one who is in the position of needing or seeking help. Social workers are representatives of agencies that wield power. They have the right and responsibility to make decisions and judgments that impact clients' lives. Notwithstanding the personal style of the social worker, however gentle and caring, from the perspective of clients, social workers are perceived as persons with power and influence, and often as people to be feared. As such, social workers should heed Compton and Galaway's (1999) caution to accept and use power wisely.

> Questions of power and authority are particularly relevant when we are required to enter a situation by court order or agency decision. Prior experiences of the misuse of professional

authority may underlie the family's negative expectations, lack of trust and fear of commitment. When we intervene in people's lives at the request of others, we must be prepared to explain very clearly—many times, if necessary—what authority and power we carry, what the limits of our authority and power are, and how we will use it. This is often difficult because of our own feelings about authority. (1999:181.)

FAILURE IN COUNSELLING

It is inevitable that counselling will sometimes fail, so counsellors need to develop their capacity to systematically investigate and review failure. They need to be able to distinguish between failures that are beyond their control and those that originate from their own mistakes. Failure may originate with the client; it may arise from personal issues associated with the counsellor, such as faulty technique or lack of skill; or it may come from factors that are out the client's and counsellor's control.

Client Variables

Client variables that could lead to failure include unrealistic expectations, poor motivation, unconscious self-sabotage, destructive personality, organic factors, and poor capacity for insight (Kottler, 1993:18). For example, substance abuse or mental disorders may make it difficult or impossible for clients to engage with the work of counselling. Clients may resist or undermine counselling because of secondary gain, where the payoffs from maintaining the problem outweigh the benefits of change. Or clients may resist change because of unconscious fear of success, because they expect to fail, or because the risks of change are too frightening to face.

Kottler suggests using caution to ensure that counsellors are not too quick to blame failure on clients. "Many of us avoid dealing with our failures by blaming clients for not cooperating. If only they were more motivated and less ambivalent, if only they were willing to work harder and take greater risks, if only they did what we asked of them, if only they would act more like we would prefer, then counseling could work out quite nicely" (1993:17).

Counsellor Variables

Intellectually and emotionally secure counsellors are willing to examine their methods and attitudes, and they are willing to take their share of responsibility for poor counselling outcomes. Counsellor variables include such factors as mental attitudes, moods, and behaviours, which can dramatically affect how counsellors relate to and assess their clients. Counsellor variables that can affect counselling outcomes may arise from burnout, personal problems, or loss of objectivity.

Burnout. A career working with people in crisis may be intensely satisfying, but it can also be emotionally stressful and draining. Counsellors may experience unrelenting pressure in workplace demands, including high caseloads, limited resources, and crushing paperwork. Counsellors can become depleted from trying to respond to the needs of their clients and the organization. In addition, counsellors are subject to their own family and economic stress and trauma. Counsellors may be resilient, but even the most sturdy person can become debilitated by stress.

Burnout is a state of emotional, mental, and physical exhaustion that hinders or prevents people from performing their jobs. Burnout may affect people in different ways, but certain symptoms are typical. The stress of burnout may show itself as a general state of physical exhaustion, including signs of diminished health such as headaches, sleep disruptions, and digestive upset. Emotional and mental burnout may be revealed as increased anxiety, inability to cope with the normal demands of work, depression, excessive worry, discouragement, pessimism toward clients, loss of a sense of purpose, general irritability, and inability to find joy in one's career or life.

Counsellors who suspect that they suffer from burnout should first consult a physician to rule out any medical condition that might be factor. The best way to deal with burnout is to prevent it from happening. For counsellors, this means balancing the demands of their work life by taking care of themselves. Counsellors need to develop personal wellness plans that address their own emotional, physical, and spiritual needs. An essential part of this plan is time away from the job. Counsellors need to avoid becoming over-involved such as by working unreasonably long hours and weekends or by skipping vacations. Counsellors need to make intelligent decisions about the limits of what they can do.

Counsellors can also prevent burnout by setting up and using a support system of family, friends, supervisors, and colleagues. By doing so, they ensure that they have people to whom they can turn for assistance and emotional support. Work colleagues and supervisors are essential for helping counsellors manage their emotional reactions toward clients, such as fear and anger. Counsellors need to recognize that being able to accept help from others is a sign of strength and that they should model this belief in their own behaviour. Talking to others reduces isolation and allows for team participation and support with difficult decisions or situations. It is particularly important for counsellors to have someone to debrief with after stressful interviews, such as those with angry or assaultive clients.

Continued professional development is another important strategy for preventing burnout. Attending seminars, courses, and conferences exposes counsellors to new ideas and the latest research and can help them renew their enthusiasm and creativity.

Personal Problems. Counsellors are subject to the same stresses in life as other people. They can become depressed, their children can become ill, their marriages can fail, or they can become responsible for caring for ailing and elderly parents. Responsible counsellors accept that there may be times when they need help too. They recognize the importance of having people in their lives to whom they can turn for assistance. When counsellors have healthy reciprocal relationships with others, they are less likely to subconsciously use their clients to meet these needs.

During acute periods of stress, counsellors recognize their vulnerability and take steps to protect their clients. These steps might include taking a temporary reduction in workload, shifting to a less demanding caseload, taking a "mental health" break, and seeking increased supervision or consultation to monitor their work. In extreme circumstances, they may choose to take extended leave or switch careers.

Loss of Objectivity. **Objectivity** is a measure of counsellors' capacity to relate to clients without allowing their own feelings and biases to distort their judgment (see Chapter 2 for a detailed discussion). A number of factors can lead to a loss of objectivity, including unresolved personal problems, difficulty dealing with particular emotions or topics, attraction or revulsion to clients, overidentification with clients, and excessive or unrealistic fear of particular clients.

Counsellors who are not self-aware of their values, their beliefs, and the impact of their behaviour on others are limited in their ability to monitor their level of objectivity. Counsellors who seek to increase their objectivity make themselves available for feedback or supervision. Moreover, they recognize their personal limitations and the fact that they may be unable to work with objectivity with every client. They know when to refer clients to other professionals.

Process or Technique Variables

Process variables that can lead to failure include pseudo-counselling, inappropriate advice giving, rescuing, and miscellaneous problems with technique or procedure.

Pseudo-Counselling. The goal of every counselling relationship is to improve the quality of life for the client. Achieving this goal may involve problem resolution, assistance with decision making, or management of painful feelings. Counsellors need to screen their responses and activities to ensure that their work supports the objectives of counselling.

Pseudo-counselling involves what Shulman (1992) describes as the **illusion of work**— counselling sessions are animated and active, but they are essentially empty and without real meaning. The illusion of work can be created through:

* interesting but irrelevant exploration of issues that do not contribute to problem solving, including an excessive focus on finding the root causes of problems
* use of clichés and patronizing platitudes
* overly intellectual exploration of issues
* avoidance of subjects or feelings that involve pain in favour of safe topics (of course, it is sometimes appropriate to shift the focus to safe areas of discussion, for example, if the interview is almost over or if clients are clearly unable to handle additional stress)

Inappropriate Advice Giving. Society conditions us to seek advice from experts, so it's not surprising that many clients come to counsellors expecting "expert advice" on how to manage their lives and solve their problems. Students and beginning counsellors often believe that counselling requires them to listen patiently to their clients' problems, then offer advice on what they should do. However, they need to learn that this approach is rarely helpful and is sometimes harmful for clients, particularly when such advice is based on values that are inconsistent with the client's lifestyle or culture.

Clients often seek advice even when they know what to do to manage their problems. Seeking advice can be a way of expressing dependency or transferring responsibility for decisions and outcomes to someone else. This dependency inhibits the right of clients to make choices, and it may leave clients feeling resentful or frustrated, particularly if the advice was unsolicited.

Advice giving may increase counsellors' self-esteem by underscoring their ability to be resourceful and helpful, but it may undermine clients' self-esteem, leaving them feeling inadequate because they have been unable to figure out their problems for themselves or because they lack the will or resources to act on the "good advice." Counsellors who tend to give advice can become overly concerned about whether clients follow their advice, and if so, whether the advice is successful. They can become disappointed when clients do not follow advice.

As Compton and Galaway conclude, the wisdom of counsellors "lies less in the substantive areas of knowing what is best for the client and more in the process area of assisting clients to develop alternatives for themselves, make decisions among the alternatives, and implement decisions" (1984:73). This is the essence of empowering and **self-determination:** instead of giving advice, counsellors can encourage clients to generate their own ideas. Some leads counsellors may use to accomplish this goal are:

- What are your thoughts about what to do?
- What ideas have you considered but rejected?
- What advice could you give yourself?
- What alternatives have you considered?
- What would your friends or family encourage you to do?
- What advice do you think I will give you?
- What do you see as your choices? (Shebib, 1997:31)

The injunction against advice giving does not mean that counsellors should withhold information or ideas that might benefit their clients. Examples of information or advice that counsellors might provide are listed below.

- tentative suggestions regarding alternative courses of action that the client has overlooked. However, "when counsellors are unwilling or unable to present and explore all viable alternatives neutrally, they have an ethical responsibility to refer the client to another counsellor, or at the very least, to make their biases or limitations explicit" (Shebib, 1997:33).
- expert information based on research or knowledge (e.g., job search techniques, child-rearing principles)
- ideas for improving communication or problem solving
- suggestions regarding the process of problem resolution
- opinions and information that will help clients avoid unforeseen consequences (dangers) to themselves or impulsive or poorly considered action

Where there is a range of individual choices such as decisions related to marriage or career, advice giving is inappropriate. In such circumstances the role of counsellors is to assist clients in identifying alternative courses of action, then to help them weigh the advantages and disadvantages of each alternative. Counsellors may suggest alternatives, but they should do this in such a way that clients feel free to reject their suggestions.

Rescuing. **Rescuing**, or band-aiding, involves actions that prevent or protect clients from dealing with issues or feelings. Rescuing arises from the counsellor's need to avoid tension and keep the session cheerful, but it is misguided because rescuing diverts clients from addressing important though difficult issues in their lives. Rescuing is a misuse of the support function of helping. Counsellors may become so preoccupied with avoiding or reducing tension that they interfere with their clients' ability to cope or problem solve. If problem situations are to be worked through successfully, clients must be allowed to experience and express painful emotions and, when necessary, confront reality (Shebib, 1997).

There are three major types of rescue behaviour:

1. **responses that minimize tension, such as avoiding tough but otherwise timely and important topics and feelings by changing the subject, using humour to cut off discussion, or suggesting a coffee break**

   Rodney was finally willing to address his sadness over the death of his father. As he began to talk, he cried softly. As he did so, his counsellor reached out and put her hands on his shoulders, reassuring him that his grief would pass.

   Par hesitated for a moment as he struggled to collect his thoughts. Sensing that this might be a painful moment for him, his counsellor suggested that he might prefer to talk about something else.

   Counsellor responses such as these impede the work of counselling by preventing or discouraging clients from dealing with their feelings. For clients to learn how to manage emotions, they must be allowed to experience their pain. If counsellors communicate discomfort or disapproval with expressed emotions, important opportunities for work may be lost.

2. **placating by withholding potentially helpful but critical confrontation or by offering false feedback and empty reassurance**

   Tara expressed fear about contacting her father, with whom she had not had contact for five years. Her counsellor offered support: "Everything is going to work out well. I'm sure your father will be ecstatic to see you."

   Shirley decided not to confront her client over an obvious hygiene problem. She concluded that it would be best not to upset her client and jeopardize a strong relationship.

3. **behaviours that impede independence, such as speaking for clients and doing for clients what they are able to do for themselves**

   Jessie's counsellor wanted to be seen as helpful and resourceful. She offered to rewrite her client's résumé and pick up application forms from local employers.

Jose was having trouble understanding a school assignment. His child-care counsellor phoned his teacher to ask for clarification, even though Jose was capable of talking to the teacher himself.

For clients to become independent, they need to develop the skills and strength to deal with their lives. This may be a difficult process for clients, requiring counsellors to be supportive without stifling their clients' growth. Counsellors must avoid unduly protecting their clients by interfering with their opportunities and capacity to face their difficulties. This requires counsellors to be fully aware of their own need for power and control and to accept that successful counselling requires clients to be their own problem solvers. Furthermore, counsellors must rid themselves of any fantasy that their clients can be saved only by them.

CONVERSATION 1.2

RESCUING AND SUPPORTING

STUDENT: What is the difference between supporting clients and rescuing them?

TEACHER: Rescuing robs clients of legitimate opportunities for growth. Supporting promotes self-determination by providing encouragement or resources to motivate clients toward growth and change. Timing is also a factor. Rescuing occurs when clients have the strength to deal with difficult areas or feelings, but their counsellors avoid the work or pain that this would entail. On the other hand, if clients are overwhelmed, some direct assistance by counsellors to lessen their burden is supportive. It may be wise to avoid excessive intimacy in the beginning of a relationship, and it may be hazardous to explore highly emotional topics near the end of an interview. An important question for counsellors to consider is "Whose needs are being met, mine or the client's?" Rescuing behaviour meets counsellors' needs under the guise of helping clients, but supportive behaviour helps clients to realize their objectives. In the long run, there are times when it is more supportive to allow clients to face their struggles and experience their pain. Effective counsellors are courageous enough to allow clients to express their pain and accept the reality that they cannot provide solutions to all problems.

Faulty Technique. Some of the problems that arise in counselling can be attributed to counsellors' inept use of skills. Poor technique can lead to missed opportunities and, in extreme cases, can be harmful to clients. For example, counsellors might fail to respond to individual differences (e.g., gender and culture), or they may cling to a rigid "one style fits all" approach to counselling. They may be poor listeners, or they may lack empathy. They might push clients too quickly, or they might allow them to stagnate by neglecting to motivate them to make changes.

Uncontrollable Variables. Large caseloads may preclude counsellors from spending sufficient time with their clients. Resources may not be available to support clients in the change process, such as detox facilities for a client who wants treatment for heroin addiction.

Unexpected events and crises, such as illness, death, or job loss, may frustrate progress. In some cases, client changes may be subverted by family and friends who are unprepared to support change.

THE PHASES OF COUNSELLING

This book is based on a model of four **phases of counselling**: (1) preliminary; (2) beginning; (3) action; and (4) ending (Shebib, 1997). This organization builds on similar models presented by others such as Egan (1998), Shulman (1992), and Young (1998). Each phase of counselling is characterized by common as well as unique objectives and skills.

One common objective of each phase is forming and sustaining a working relationship. This counselling relationship is the vehicle for change and provides a base of safety and security for clients to explore and understand their emotions and difficulties. The counselling contract, an agreement on the goals and roles of the participants, is the reference point for the relationship. It is continually reviewed and revised as the work progresses.

A second common objective of all phases is to establish open, honest, and productive communication. Effective communication enables counsellors to learn about their clients' needs and feelings. As well, it empowers clients to learn new ways of handling old problems.

The third common objective of all phases is evaluation. Ongoing evaluation can be targeted to the essential elements of the counselling plan, the working relationship, its goals and methods, and the overall satisfaction of all participants with the pace of the work and its results. By using a problem-solving approach, counsellors and clients can explore ways to ensure that the work is relevant and efficient.

Each phase is distinguished by its focus on different activities. The preliminary phase is essentially for planning. Proper planning increases the likelihood that clients will perceive that their needs can be met through counselling. The beginning phase is a time of engagement, when both the client and the counsellor make decisions about whether they will work together and, if so, under what structure. The beginning phase is also a time for exploring problems and feelings. Although clients may begin to change their behaviour or manage their feelings more effectively during the beginning phase, the action phase is more concerned with initiating change. During the ending phase, the working relationship is brought to a close, perhaps with a referral to another resource or counsellor.

Skill clusters were introduced as a way to organize skills based on function. Since each phase of counselling supports different activities, it seems logical that each phase would also favour different skills. For example, during the beginning phase of counselling, relationship-building skills are the priority, whereas challenging skills are usually avoided, at least until a foundation of trust and safety is established. Exploration/probing skills are also vital during the beginning phase. They enable counsellors to acquire information for understanding and to avoid any tendency to make assumptions. Challenging and directing/teaching skills tend to be more effective in the action phase, when a strong relationship and a solid base of understanding have been established. Table 1.4 summarizes the principal activities and priority skills of each phase.

Counselling tends to move through the phases sequentially, with success at each phase depending, in part, on the success of preceding phases. For example, the preliminary phase is designed to support the work of the beginning phase. It allows the counsellor to complete the preparations that will help welcome clients to the agency. As well, it works

Table 1.4 Counselling Activities and Skills		
Phase	**Principal Activities**	**Priority Skills**
Preliminary	• Interview preplanning • Preparing the interview setting	• Planning • Establishing self-awareness
Beginning	• Establishing a working relationship • Interviewing for understanding • Evaluation	• Active listening • Promoting core conditions • Defining the relationship • Searching for strengths
Action	• Goal setting • Action planning • Helping clients change behaviour, manage feelings, change perceptions • Revising the contract, deepening the relationship, managing communication difficulties • Evaluation	• Teaching • Information giving • Supporting • Confronting • Action planning
Ending	• Ending the helping relationship • Referring to other resources • Evaluation	• Information giving • Supporting

as a kind of warm-up, so counsellors can be ready and sensitive to the needs of their clients. Weak planning results in weak beginnings. Similarly, effective work in the action phase is easier when the beginning phase has been successful. A solid base of understanding will permit counsellors and clients to set more pertinent goals, and a foundation of trust allows counsellors to be more challenging in their approach. In contrast, counsellors who attempt to challenge clients from a thin base of trust are likely to meet with resistance or rejection. In the action phase, it is important to try to sequence the steps. If clients try to develop action plans before they have set clear goals, their action plans are more likely to be vague and directionless.

Although counselling work tends to evolve sequentially through the four phases, flexibility in applying the model is necessary, since counselling does not always advance in a linear fashion. Counsellors cannot insist that clients move through the phases in a neat and orderly manner.

> The phases of counselling provide a systematic and useful way of organizing our thoughts and actions. Acting as a kind of checklist, the phases remind counsellors of the essential activities and logical steps that are part of any process of change or problem solving. The model can act as a reference point to plan our actions, to predict what might come next, and to understand the reactions of our clients. Practical experience shows, however, that each counselling encounter is different, each relationship is uniquely complex, and the work may evolve in unpredictable ways. (Shebib, 1997:71)

By referring to the phases of counselling, counsellors and clients can remain clear on where they are in the counselling process, what has been done, what remains to be accomplished, and what options remain open. Sometimes clear divisions between the phases of counselling are apparent. More frequently, there will be overlap between the phases and shifts forward and back between one phase or another, and in some cases phases may be skipped. Some typical counselling scenarios are provided below.

> *Jessica, a very private person, was distraught over the breakup of her marriage. Aware of her inability to cope and not knowing what to do, she attended several sessions with a counsellor. Her counsellor proceeded slowly, gently encouraging Jessica to talk about her feelings. Jessica was surprised that during the second counselling session she began to weep. Afterward, she remarked that she felt as if a great weight had been lifted from her shoulders. She never felt the need to return for a third session.*

> *Clint was not interested in exploring his problem beyond a superficial level. Anxious to effect change in his life, he wanted to brainstorm ideas for dealing with his problems. Counselling work focused on helping him set goals. As this work progressed, Clint became more trusting, and the sessions began to focus on exploring his feelings.*

> *As Fernando talked about his problem, he suddenly realized that his situation was not as hopeless as he thought. Discovering another way to look at his problem, he identified several new ways to solve it.*

> *After a single session, Bob remarked to his counsellor, "My problem is the same as when I came in here, but somehow it doesn't seem to bother me as much."*

CONVERSATION 1.3

WHY COUNSELLING WORKS

STUDENT: What is the difference between a conversation with a helpful friend and a counselling interview?

TEACHER: The goal of a friendship is to meet the needs of both people. Friends (and family) are important. If they are understanding, caring, and supportive, they can be an effective source of help. Much like a counselling relationship, just talking to a friend can be cathartic to the individual, but there may be limits in what friends can offer. Sometimes friends and families don't have specialized knowledge, or they may not know what resources or services are available to deal with specific problems. Friends and family may be so emotionally involved with you that it is hard for them to be objective. They may have a great deal of difficulty separating their feelings from the situation, and when this happens they may resort to giving well-intentioned but not very helpful advice.

Effective counsellors are comfortable discussing feelings, and they don't tell clients how they should feel. Good counsellors are excellent listeners, and they invest time to make sure they accurately understand clients' feelings and concerns. Counsellors know how to systematically explore problems, set goals, and develop plans for action. They assist clients in identifying and evaluating alternatives, while recognizing that the clients must choose for themselves. Therefore, counsellors do not impose advice or try to rescue clients by taking on their problems. Unlike friendships, counselling relationships are directed to meet the needs of one person only—the client.

The Preliminary Phase

The preliminary phase is essentially a time of planning. The planning targets two important areas: First, the agency setting is made attractive for clients so they are motivated to engage and remain with the agency. Second, counsellors prepare themselves for the interview.

The Agency Setting. Ideally, the agency is set up to appeal to the client groups that it serves. A drop-in counselling centre for teens would be very different from a day program for seniors. Dim lighting and beanbag chairs meet the needs of teens but present a safety hazard for seniors. Tea is appropriate for seniors, but soda pop makes more sense when the clients are teens. Ideally, the agency should:

- have uncrowded waiting rooms
- allow for reception and interview space that is private and confidential
- have procedures so that clients are greeted in a warm and friendly manner
- provide for the needs of children (by supplying a play area, appropriate toys)
- allow for wheelchair access
- have posters and other art that do not violate the values, religion, or culture of the agency's clients (generally, they should be politically neutral)
- have up-to-date reading material for clients who are waiting

Counsellors should take precautions to ensure that the interview time is protected from phone calls and other interruptions that will impede the flow of conversation. When counsellors allow their interviews to be interrupted, the message to clients may be "I have other concerns that are more important than you. Hurry up and finish."

The office should be structured to favour flexibility. Some clients and many counsellors prefer an unobstructed arrangement without a desk between the participants, but others favour working over the desk. The office needs to be arranged with careful consideration to the messages that the design communicates. Chairs and desks should be arranged so that no psychological advantage or power is given to the counsellor. Seating arrangements should allow for adequate personal space between counsellors and clients. A comfort zone of about 1 to 2 m (4 to 7 feet) is adequate for most clients, but other factors might result in a need for more or less distance. Counsellors need to be careful in choosing personal items to display. Pictures and memorabilia that punctuate differences between counsellors and their clients ought to be avoided. Of course, clients may have different reactions. For example, some clients expect and appreciate seeing their counsellor's degrees or diplomas hung on the wall. For these clients, knowing something about the training and credentials of their counsellors helps to establish confidence and credibility. Other clients, however, may react negatively to such a display. For them, the display sets up social and intellectual barriers. Generally, counsellors should structure their offices with the needs and background of their clients in mind. In this respect, clients can be an invaluable source of consultation. Their opinions on office decor and layout should be solicited.

Client Files. Some clients will have a history with the agency, and counsellors may have access to considerable information about these clients before their first contact. Depending on the agency, various kinds of useful information can be obtained from client files, including age, place of birth, address, marital status, work history, educational background, prior experiences with counselling, and assessments of personality, values, past problems, ability to handle stress, communication patterns, and so on. Client files can also alert counsellors to any past incidents of violence and point out any need to take special precautions in dealing with a particular client.

Ideally, counsellors should give clients reasonable access to the records concerning them. In many jurisdictions, legislation gives clients the right to access information held by organizations. Usually, the onus is on the agency or government department to provide a reason for withholding information. Counsellors need to be familiar with the regulations in their area.

A review of client files can greatly speed the intake process, but it is important to maintain an open mind and avoid prejudgment, particularly with respect to the assessments other counsellors have made regarding such variables as manner and personality. Client reactions are influenced in part (and occasionally to a great extent) by the personality and behaviour of their counsellors, as shown in the following example:

> Russ waited for his counsellor, who was half an hour late for the scheduled interview. Russ was stressed because of personal problems and was anxious to get home to care for his sick children. Estelle, his counsellor, was also stressed owing to a difficult week of work. She was also aware that her next appointment was already waiting for her to finish with Russ. Determined to catch up, she moved quickly with questions to complete her assessment of Russ's situation. Russ, taken aback by Estelle's abrupt style, proceeded cautiously, hesitating to share personal information too quickly. Later, when completing her file notes on the interview, Estelle wrote: "Client was defensive and guarded. He appeared unusually resistant to exploring his feelings."

CONVERSATION 1.4

SHOULD I READ THE FILE?

STUDENT: If there's already a file on the client, should I read it before seeing the client for the first time?

TEACHER: There are reasons for reading and not reading files. It's important to be aware of the risks of either route. Some counsellors prefer to conduct their first interviews without reading their clients' files. They argue that by not reading the files they are prevented from being unduly influenced (biased) by prior information. After a first interview, they feel more able to objectively evaluate the validity of previous records. In addition, they argue that clients can change, and approaching the interview with a fresh perspective makes it easier to relate to the client's present condition. Remember that you may be biased against some workers, even to the point of rejecting what would otherwise be valid assessments.

STUDENT: But suppose the client has a history of violence that is reported in the file. How would I be able to get that information in order to protect myself, but still keep an open mind? Is there a way of getting only the pertinent information from the file that would allow me to identify those problems?

TEACHER: That's one of the drawbacks of not reading the file. I like your idea of setting up some kind of process for identifying clients who might be dangerous. Clients who present safety concerns could be "red flagged" in some way.

STUDENT: I think another drawback is that if you don't look at the file, you will miss out on knowing what's been done, what worked, what issues are key, and so forth. Is there a way of reading a file without being influenced by other writers?

TEACHER: Being aware of the potential for influence is crucial. It is important to remind ourselves that opinions in files are not those of the clients, but of the person writing the record. Ideally, records should be shared with clients and the conclusions jointly supported. Of course, this is not always possible.

STUDENT: Could I share the file with the client to get his or her reactions?

TEACHER: Probably not, at least not without the permission of the person who wrote the record. Depending on where you live, freedom of access to information legislation may give clients the right to petition for access to the file.

Interview Preparation. Counsellors can anticipate in the preliminary phase how the interview time will be utilized and consider decisions related to the time, place, and structure of the interview. As well, counsellors might begin thinking about specific questions and responses for working with particular clients and then map out a tentative structure for the interview; however, they should avoid using this structure as a script or rigid agenda. This is also a time when counsellors can seek any facts that will help them understand their client's problem. For example, a counsellor may have advance knowledge that the client has a child who has been diagnosed with Tourette's syndrome. The counsellor's credibility will be greatly increased in the client's eyes if the counsellor grasps the essential nature and implications of this condition. Knowing something about Tourette's syndrome provides an important starting point for exploration.

Shulman (1992) suggests that for a variety of reasons clients often do not share feelings and concerns directly. They may be ambivalent about sharing, or they may hold back because of societal and cultural taboos about talking about sex, authority, and money. As a result, clients may raise these concerns indirectly, and counsellors must be alert to recognize clues about their clients' concerns. For example, a single parent who asks her welfare worker if he has ever been on welfare may be indirectly expressing her fear that the worker will be insensitive to the stress she faces in trying to cope with a limited budget. Sometimes, questions regarding personal background or circumstances may be indirect ways clients have of exploring concerns about trust.

Shulman introduces the preliminary phase skill of tuning in as a tool for anticipating the feelings and concerns that clients might bring to the interview. By tuning in, counsellors can think about what clients might express and how they will do so. The preliminary phase is also a time when counsellors examine their own readiness. For example, counsellors can take a few moments prior to each interview to self-examine through questions such as the following:

- Am I dealing with personal stress or problems that might make me less effective or more vulnerable?
- Am I sufficiently disengaged from my last client to be open and objective?
- What personal biases do I need to manage in order to work effectively with this client?
- What reservations do I have about meeting this client?
- Do I have unfinished business with this client that I have not addressed?
- What feelings do I have toward this client that might impede my objectivity?

The Beginning Phase

When it is successful, the preliminary phase establishes a base for developing a helping relationship. Counselling relationships are formed to provide a safe and trusting vehicle for clients to work toward their goals. The relationship between counsellors and their clients influences whether clients will be willing to risk disclosure and is a significant variable that determines whether clients will continue with counselling. The objective at this stage is to negotiate a working relationship that is goal directed and based on trust and mutual understanding of expectations. This relationship is time limited and based on a contract that outlines the objectives and terms of the relationship.

Some clients come willingly to counselling, perhaps as a result of an unresolved crisis or because they have been persuaded by others to seek help. Other clients are involuntary. They may also be coming as a result of a current crisis, or pressure from others. An employer, for example, may insist that a staff member seek counselling to address attitudinal or addiction problems.

Many clients are under considerable stress, and this stress is intensified if the clients perceive counsellors negatively. To some extent, this view is under the control of the counsellor. However, clients' past experiences with other agencies and counsellors also shape their perceptions and expectations. Clients who have had bad experiences with counsellors will understandably be guarded against further disappointment. Because counsellors are often in a position of authority, or clients see them in such a position, clients' past experiences with others in authority will come into play. Most clients, however strongly they may be motivated, will have some degree of resistance or ambivalence to change. Involuntary clients, in particular, may be especially resistant and in some cases hostile. They may perceive any initiative by their counsellors, however well meaning, as a hostile act.

The relationship between counsellors and clients is fundamental to counselling success. Even in short, one-session encounters, when a high level of intimacy is not crucial, clients will be more apt to engage and share when the counsellor gives some attention to developing the relationship. Chapter 3 more fully explores the importance of the helping relationship and specific skills for developing and maintaining it.

A second major task of the beginning phase is to acquire and deepen understanding of the client's situation or problem. Simply put, clients are asked to tell their stories, describe their feelings, and explore their problems and dilemmas. For their part, counsellors must be prepared to listen, and this means being prepared to learn. Preliminary phase work may help counsellors predict possible themes, and experience may teach counsellors a great deal about common needs and issues. However, in the beginning phase, counsellors need to put aside any assumptions as they attempt to appreciate the unique nature of each client. Active listening skills of attending, using silence, summarizing, paraphrasing, questioning, and showing empathy are the basic tools for this exploration. These skills tend to motivate clients to gradually open up, organize their thoughts, and identify their feelings. They move the relationship beyond superficiality and help both the counsellor and the client achieve shared understanding. Active listening enables counsellors to probe for details, definitions, and examples—information that is essential for preventing assumptions. Active listening skills will be explored in depth in Chapters 4 to 6.

The Therapeutic Value of the Beginning Phase. Even though the beginning phase focuses on developing the counselling relationship and on exploration, clients often deepen their understanding and become empowered by the process. The therapeutic value of counsellors listening without judgment can be enormous. Since intense listening is rare in everyday encounters, clients may be visibly moved when they feel heard. When counsellors accept clients without judgment, clients become better able to accept themselves.

Effective counsellors probe for detail by asking questions systematically. They identify feelings and mirror them with empathic statements. This work enables clients to better organize their thinking and to explore and accept their feelings. When clients are confused or indecisive, orderly questioning helps them to categorize information and to pinpoint details or issues that they may have overlooked.

Effective counsellors encourage clients to explore the emotional components of their lives. When clients share emotions, counsellors need to be careful not to sabotage this sharing by rescuing, telling clients not to feel as they do, changing the subject, or conveying discomfort or judgment. As clients talk, they may release a flood of emotions. A client might remark, "I've told you things that no one else knows." As clients open up, they may begin to feel unburdened, a process that is known as **catharsis**, which Barker defines as a "verbalization and other expression of ideas, fears, past significant events, and associations, the expected result of which is a release of anxiety or tension, resulting in improved functioning; also called **ventilation**" (1995:49).

A Caution. Some clients don't return for the next scheduled interview. Sometimes they decide not to return because they feel they don't need to. A single session may be sufficient to meet their needs. The cathartic release of emotions in a single session empowers them enough to deal with their problems.

Other clients may quickly respond to the power of the counselling relationship and disclose at a level they would not have predicted. Later, they may feel embarrassed, fearing that they have gone too far, or they may resent their counsellors for probing into areas they would have preferred to keep private. In response, clients may cut off the counselling relationship prematurely, or they may come to the next session but remain distant and guarded in order to protect themselves from overdisclosing.

One way to prevent problems is to be sensitive to individual pacing needs. Clients may give clues that the session is moving too quickly. The counsellor should watch for indicators such as hesitation, questioning why the counsellor wants to know something, or statements that the client would rather not discuss particular issues.

Another strategy is to candidly discuss with clients how they feel about the session. The following excerpt illustrates this technique:

COUNSELLOR: *Later tonight, when you think about our time together, how do you think you will feel?*

CLIENT: *I think I'll have mixed feelings. It was really good to talk, but I wonder if I told you too much. I hope you won't think less of me.*

COUNSELLOR: *You took a real risk with me in sharing your private thoughts and feelings. I think it's reasonable to worry about how I reacted. Would you like to know?*

CLIENT: *Yes, very much.*

COUNSELLOR: *Do you trust me enough to believe that I won't lie to you or tell you something just to make you feel better?*

If client says yes, the counsellor might candidly share his/her reaction to the client disclosure:

I admire your courage to face such painful issues. As a result, I feel closer to you and better able to understand your struggle. No, I don't think less of you.

If client says no, counsellor initiates discussion of what work needs to be done to establish trust:

Perhaps we could talk a bit about what needs to happen between you and me in order for you to trust me.

In the above example, the counsellor helps the client anticipate feelings that might arise after the session. By doing so, the counsellor can help prevent the client from reaching false conclusions or making erroneous assumptions about what happened. In order for counsellors to have such discussions with clients, a high level of counsellor self-awareness is crucial. Counsellors need to be willing to examine how they are relating to their clients. They should be adept at identifying any personal biases (positive and negative) that they need to manage in order to work effectively with their client.

The Action Phase

The action phase is a time of change, a time when clients set goals, explore alternatives, and develop strategies for reaching their objectives. In the beginning phase, counsellors work to understand their clients' perspectives. Now, in the action phase, counsellors look for opportunities to assist clients in identifying other ways of looking at or dealing with their situation. This can happen or be facilitated in two ways.

First, clients may make discoveries or reach insight spontaneously from exploring issues, feelings, and problems. Skilled interviewers ask questions systematically, probing for detail as appropriate. This process alone helps clients organize their thoughts on complex issues. As well, summary, paraphrase, and empathy responses provide an important mirror for reflecting clients' feelings and ideas. As a result, clients may see their problems in a different light, or they may discover choices for action that they had overlooked.

Second, counsellors may play a key role by providing new information, ideas, or perspectives. This role could involve challenging distortions in the way clients think about problems or encouraging them to consider overlooked aspects. As well, counsellors need to encourage the work of change by ensuring that clients set clear and specific goals, which form the basis for the development of realistic action plans. Subsequently, counsellors may assist clients in implementing their plans. This assistance includes helping them to anticipate and address potential problems, as well as supporting them through the struggles of the change process. Counsellors also help clients develop new strategies for coping through a variety of skill acquisition strategies, such as role playing, or by teaching techniques for managing self-defeating thought patterns.

When clients experience **core conditions** of congruence, empathy, and positive regard, they become better able to accept themselves, less defensive, and more open to experiencing and accepting their feelings. Client attitudes and feelings change as counselling progresses successfully. Some of the important signals that clients are changing and growing include the following:

- cues that they feel less apprehensive about counselling and the counselling relationship
- increased acceptance of feelings and more honest expression of previously denied feelings
- diminished negativism, self-doubt, and blaming of others and increased optimism and self-acceptance
- increased acceptance of responsibility for behaviours or choices
- reduced sense of responsibility for the actions and choices of others
- increased empathy for others (Gilliland and James, 1998:115)

Frequently, beginning and action phase activities happen simultaneously. Shifts between beginning and action phase work are also common. Clients may explore a problem in depth, begin a change program, then revert to beginning phase work to tackle another problem area. Some common scenarios are the following:

Angelo's counsellor encouraged him to describe his situation. As he talked, he discovered aspects of his problem that he had overlooked and that suggested new possibilities for immediate action.

Pari tended to keep her feelings so well hidden that she was unaware of their effect or intensity. With gentle encouragement from her counsellor, she began to open up. Talking about her feelings represented a dramatic shift in her behaviour. The therapeutic value of this change was enormous, as she unburdened herself from a lifetime of pent-up emotions.

Chapter 7 will explore how to assist clients through the work of the action phase.

The Ending Phase

Successful termination starts in the beginning phase, when the nature and limits of the counselling contract are defined. When counsellors and clients agree on the activities and goals of counselling, the point of termination is defined. This point of termination becomes a target of all counselling work, and though it may change as client needs and progress are reevaluated, counsellors should reinforce termination as one reality of the counselling relationship.

Although evaluation is a component of all phases of counselling, the ending phase is a major opportunity to assess what was accomplished and what remains to be done. It is a time to help clients make the step to independence, and it is a time for clients to consider new directions and goals. It may be a point of transition as counsellors refer clients to other services. The ending phase is also a time to evaluate the counselling relationship. This evaluation may involve addressing any unresolved feelings or concerns and expressing feelings about the ending of the relationship.

Counsellors need to be able to make intelligent decisions about when to terminate the relationship. Termination of counselling relationships may be warranted for a number of reasons. First, the relationship may be ended when the goals of counselling have been reached. Counselling relationships are time limited, and when clients have developed a sufficient capacity to work on their own, it is time to end the relationship. Second, counsellors may end the relationship if they do not have the time or competence to fulfill their clients' needs. In such cases, the ending will include referral other counsellors or agencies. Third, counsellors may determine that they are unable to work with sufficient objectivity. Here, again, referral is the preferred alternative. Finally, if evidence shows that counselling has not worked and that there is little potential that it will become successful, it is time to terminate or refer.

Counselling relationships can be exceptionally intimate, and the termination of the relationship may evoke painful feelings of loss for both counsellors and clients. This sense of loss may be especially pronounced in long-term relationships, but even short-term relationships that have dealt with crises or intimate matters may rouse feelings of sadness as the relationship ends. Clients who have difficulty with transitions and who have become dependent on their counsellors may experience the ending as a crisis.

Young suggests that "a helper's feelings of loss at termination may also be due to a reliance on helping relationships to meet needs for intimacy (friendship) as well as a conscious or unconscious sexual attraction" (1998:286). The termination may also remind counsellors of other losses in their lives. When these losses remain unresolved, there is a risk that counsellors may be unable to appropriately handle termination with the client. They may feel guilty for leaving the client, and they might delay or avoid termination in order to elude their own feelings of pain.

The ending phase can be a time of continuing growth for clients. As Hess and McCartt Hess conclude,

> Clients should be empowered through the termination process to embark upon a self-directed course of action based upon realistic assessment of their problem-solving strengths. Mastery of termination issues supports client self-esteem and reinforces the client's hopes that ongoing progress can be achieved. The work of the ending also frees the client to reinvest energy in appropriate life tasks and ongoing relationships which support problem solving. (1984:562)

Termination of the counselling relationship will be considered in more detail in Chapter 2.

Summary

Counselling involves a time-limited relationship designed to help clients increase their capacity to deal with the demands of life. Counselling work may include many activities, such as helping clients deal with feelings, learn new skills, make decisions, and access resources.

Counselling is conducted by a wide range of people at various levels of education. Interviewing skills are imperative for effective counselling. Interviewing is essentially an information-gathering process; however, clients may experience some therapeutic relief from sharing their stories.

Counselling caseloads are characterized by diversity in culture, gender, age, religion, sexual orientation, language, education, economic ability, and so on. Working with diversity requires counsellors to be adaptive. Expert counsellors use research theory and experience as guides to determine which skills and procedures best meet the needs of their clients. Competent counsellors use a wide range of skills; they know when to use skills; they match the language of their clients; and they adapt other variables, such as the time and place of the interview.

Four major skill clusters define the range of necessary skills: (1) relationship-building; (2) exploring/probing; (3) empowering; and (4) challenging skills. Counsellors use relationship-building skills for engaging clients and developing trust. Counsellors use exploring/probing skills in order to gather information, clarify definitions, seek examples, and obtain necessary detail. They use empowering skills to help clients develop confidence, self-esteem, and control over their lives. As well, counsellors help clients manage anxiety and stress and use challenging skills to encourage clients to critically evaluate their behaviour and ideas.

Many variables can lead to poor outcomes in counselling. Client variables include unrealistic expectations and poor motivation. Counsellor factors such as burnout, personal problems, and loss of objectivity can also lead to failure. Process or faulty techniques, including pseudo-counselling, advice giving, and rescuing, can contribute to failure. Finally, failure may arise from factors outside the control of counsellors and clients.

The four counselling phases are: (1) preliminary; (2) beginning; (3) action; and (4) ending. Each phase is characterized by unique tasks and skills. The preliminary phase focuses on preparing for the interview and setting up the right environment for counselling. The beginning phase is concerned with establishing the counselling relationship and with exploring for understanding. In the action phase, the focus shifts to goal setting and implementing change. In the ending phase, the relationship is concluded. During different phases of the relationship different skill clusters assume priority.

Exercises

1. Assess the following statements as "true" or "false." Be prepared to defend your answers.

   a. It is important for counsellors to develop a personal style so that all clients are treated in the same way.

   b. The counselling process has a lot in common with the process used by other professionals, such as doctors and lawyers; thus, competent counsellors gather information, diagnose the problem, and offer solutions or advice to their clients on the best resolution.

  c. Usually clients who seek help are in crisis, and their ability to make decisions is significantly impaired. Therefore, it is important that counsellors are comfortable with making important decisions on behalf of their clients.

  d. Application of skills or techniques detracts from spontaneity.

  e. Professional counsellors are free from biases.

  f. Personal experience with the same problem or issues as clients is necessary for counsellors.

  g. The counselling process evolves sequentially through a number of phases, with each phase having defined skills and tasks.

  h. Effective counsellors are consistent, and they use the same skills in the same way throughout the counselling process.

  i. If the principles of counselling are applied effectively, all clients will be helped.

  j. Everything that happens in the counselling interview must be treated as confidential and must be shared with no one.

  k. Effective counselling involves blending the client's needs with those of the counsellor so that everyone involved is satisfied.

  l. The skills of counselling are also the skills of effective everyday communication.

2. Write a short essay supporting the following argument: The capacity to accept help from another person is a sign of strength.

3. Imagine that you are responding to the following client questions: What is counselling? How does it work?

4. Explore the extent to which you tend to give advice or rescue. Seek feedback from others who know you to see if their perceptions agree with your self-evaluation.

5. In what ways might advice giving disempower clients?

6. Think of a recent or current problem that you are facing. Describe the ways that counselling might be used to assist you in addressing this problem. Using concepts from this chapter, identify what might be the major activities for each phase of counselling.

7. Review the tasks of each of the phases of helping. With which phase do you feel most comfortable? Least comfortable?

8. What do you think are the advantages and disadvantages of working from a four-phase model of counselling?

9. Reflect on your competence across the broad range of counselling skills listed in this chapter. Rate yourself on a scale of 1 to 5 for each of the following counselling skills.
    5 = very strong
    4 = strong
    3 = satisfactory
    2 = needs development
    1 = needs considerable development

a. Active listening

___ attending

___ allowing appropriate silence

___ paraphrasing

___ summarizing

___ questioning

___ showing empathy

b. Promoting core conditions

___ communicating with genuineness

___ showing positive regard

c. Defining the relationship

___ contracting (defining roles and the purpose of counselling)

___ promoting immediacy (open discussion and evaluation of the relationship)

___ allowing self-disclosure and admitting feelings

d. Other interviewing skills

___ using directives

___ using small encouragers ("Yes," "Tell me more," head nods)

___ using humour

e. Searching for strengths

___ defining client capacities, skills, and abilities

___ redefining problems as challenges and opportunities for learning

___ identifying resources

f. Teaching

___ training in skills

___ modelling behaviours, skills, or attitudes

___ role playing/rehearsing behaviours

g. Information giving

___ offering opinions or advice

___ making referrals

h. Supporting

___ reassuring

___ expressing optimism

___ reinforcing (rewarding, praising)

___ acting as an advocate for the client

i. Confrontation

___ providing feedback to help clients recognize inappropriate reactions

___ confronting strengths (pointing out client capacities and strengths)

___ encouraging or urging

___ correcting distortions/testing reality

___ asking the client to take responsibility

j.   Action planning

___ assisting and motivating clients in defining clear and measurable targets for change

___ helping clients identify and evaluate alternatives

___ helping clients choose, develop, and carry out change strategies

k.   Use of Power and Authority

___ limit setting

___ enforcement

10. Based on your ratings identify:

   a.   three main skill strengths

   b.   the skills you are more likely to use

   c.   the skills that you typically have difficulty using

   d.   three priority areas for development/goal setting

11. Identify and explore clients' legal rights to access file information in your jurisdiction.

Weblinks

The Counseling Web: Counseling and Psychology Resources provides access to a variety of counselling, psychology and mental health resources on the Web.
seamonkey.ed.asu.edu/~gail/resource.htm#research

About Counseling provides information about a wide variety of counselling issues and links to professional organizations.
www.allaboutcounseling.com/aboutc.cfm

Counselling Link offers books with an emphasis on self-help.
www.counsellinglink.com.au

ETHICS, VALUES, AND SELF-AWARENESS

PREVIEW

After reading this chapter you should be able to:

- Explain the importance of ethics.
- List core standards of ethical behaviour, including principles governing confidentiality.
- Identify principles for resolving ethical dilemmas.
- Explain the principle of self-determination.
- Describe how counsellors can understand and work with diversity.
- Understand the importance of counsellor objectivity and self-awareness.
- Know how to increase self-awareness.
- Understand and manage personal needs and values in counselling.

PROFESSIONAL BEHAVIOUR

Ethics

Ethics are the principles and rules of acceptable or proper conduct. All professions have ethical guidelines that define the limits of permissible behaviour and the sanctions or remedies that might be applied if members violate ethical standards. Codes of ethics protect both counsellors and clients.

Professionals can use their codes to assist them with decision making and as reference for their practice. Clients are offered some shelter from incompetent practice. Ethical codes also provide guidance on how counsellors can deal fairly with colleagues. The codes detail expectations and procedures for protecting clients from unethical conduct by other members of the profession. Unethical behaviour typically arises from issues related to the following: breaking confidentiality, misrepresenting or working beyond one's level of expertise, conducting improper relationships, including sexual activity with clients, and causing conflicts of interest, such as entering into business or other **dual relationships** with clients.

Professional associations are responsible for monitoring their own policies and for investigating and resolving violations of ethical conduct. The Canadian Association of Social Workers (CASW) and The Canadian Counselling Association (CCA) are examples of professional bodies that may formally discipline members who violate their codes of ethics. Alternatively, counsellors who are not members of professional associations may work with agencies that provide guidelines for ethical behaviour and decision making.

Legislation may define and restrict the use of certain titles, such as social worker, psychologist, and psychiatrist, to those who have completed the appropriate degree or training. The clients of these professionals can report misconduct or concerns to the appropriate professional association. However, there may be no legislation preventing people from offering counselling services under a wide range of other titles, such as counsellor, personal therapist, family and marital counsellor, and personal growth consultant. These practitioners may not have had formal preparation or training, and clients should be cautious when they seek their services.

The Canadian Counselling Association Code of Ethics and Standards of Practice (CCA, 1999) is included in this book as Appendix A and the Canadian Association of Social Workers Code of Ethics (CASW, 1994) is included as Appendix B. Ethical guidelines such as the CCA and CASW codes are designed to protect and respect clients' needs and interests. Ethical codes recognize that clients may be vulnerable and subject to manipulation and abuse of power by professionals, so they constrain professionals from taking advantage of clients. As well, codes of ethics contain standards of behaviour for dealing with colleagues, other professionals, and society in general. Codes outline the responsibility of its members to address the unethical conduct of colleagues. Although the codes are the primary source for professional decision making, counsellors should also consider relevant theory, research, laws, regulations, and agency policy. When faced with **ethical dilemmas** they should consider consultation with colleagues, supervisors, professional associations and legal counsel. In addition, the Canadian Counselling Association has published an ethics casebook (Shulz, 2000) designed to assist counsellors to clarify ethics and standards of practice.

Philosophical Base

The CASW code outlines the foundational philosophy of social work in its preamble:

> The profession of social work is founded on humanitarian and egalitarian ideals. Social workers believe in the intrinsic worth and dignity of every human being and are committed to the values of acceptance, self-determination and respect of individuality. They believe in the obligation of all people, individually and collectively, to provide resources, services and opportunities for the overall benefit of humanity. The culture of individuals, families, groups, communities and nations has to be respected without prejudice.

> Social workers are dedicated to the welfare and self-realization of human beings; to the development and disciplined use of scientific knowledge regarding human and societal behaviour; to the development of resources to meet individual, group, national and international needs and aspirations; and to the achievement of social justice for all. (CASW, 1994:7)

These ideals are echoed by the Canadian Association of Counselling which articulates the following fundamental principles as the basis for ethical conduct:

a. respect for the dignity of persons
b. not wilfully harming others
c. integrity in relationships
d. responsible caring
e. responsibility to society
f. respect for self-determination (CCA, 1999:1)

Core Standards of Ethical Behaviour

Ethics are derived from values. Values are principles or qualities that individuals and groups consider important or worthwhile. Values represent beliefs about what is desirable and good. Personal values describe what individuals consider desirable and what they believe is right and wrong. Professional values describe fundamental beliefs that the profession holds about people and how the work of the profession ought to be conducted. Clearly, professional values (as reflected in ethical codes of conduct) and personal values have a major impact in shaping the practice of counselling professionals. The key values of counselling are discussed below.

The Belief in the Dignity and Worth of People. Belief in the dignity and worth of people is the core value of counselling. This value has a number of implications for practice. Central to this value is the commitment to ensuring that clients are treated with regard for their rights. It obligates counsellors to demonstrate acceptance of the individual and to uphold confidentiality. Counsellors who value the dignity of their clients appreciate diversity and reject stereotyping, labelling, and other dehumanizing practices. This means that counsellors must treat clients fairly, regardless of their personal feelings toward them. For example, they must resist the natural temptation to spend more time with clients they favour and less time with those whom they find difficult. Discriminatory practices are strictly prohibited by both major codes, and these directives may exceed those specified in most human rights legislation.

Counsellors actively work to understand the diverse cultural background of the clients with whom they work, and do not condone or engage in discrimination based on age, colour, culture, ethnicity, disability, gender, religion, sexual orientation, marital, or socioeconomic status. (CCA, 1999:B9)

A social worker in the practice of social work shall not discriminate against any person on the basis of race, ethnic background, language, religion, marital status, sex, sexual orientation, age, abilities, socio-economic status, political affiliation or national ancestry. (CASW, 1994:1.2)

These ethical guidelines underscore the need for professionals to actively engage in learning about other cultures. They need to increase their sensitivity regarding how their values and beliefs have affected their behaviour worldview and their way of relating to others. This topic will be explored in more depth in Chapter 10.

Counsellors are expected to apply their skills and knowledge at an optimum level for each client, regardless of their personal reaction toward any client. Clients may have behaved in ways that counsellors perceive to be offensive, but this belief does not give counsellors licence to be disrespectful or to withhold service.

Compton and Galaway (1984:70) suggest five guidelines for putting this value into practice:

1. Be sensitive and aware of what we are communicating regarding client dignity by the way we organize and administer our services.

2. Avoid stereotyping clients.

3. Help clients to discover and use their strengths.

4. Expect client participation in problem solving.

5. Focus on clients' wants rather than on clients' needs.

Counsellors who work with high-risk clients, such as those with chronic addiction problems, need to careful that their view of and attitudes toward clients do not become jaded. Jaded counsellors have abandoned any optimistic view of human nature, including the belief that people are generally goal directed and capable of change. In place of this view they have developed, sometimes gradually over a period of years, a more cynical and pessimistic perspective of the willingness and capacity of their clients to change and grow. Counsellors who believe that clients are incapable of growth are likely to invest less energy in supporting change. Moreover, they may be more prone to use controlling responses because of their expectation that the "clients cannot do it on their own." What would you predict to be the likely outcome of a counselling session when the counsellor labels the client as "a hopeless alcoholic"?

The Importance of Avoiding Dual Relationships. The essential purpose of the counselling relationship is to meet the needs of clients while respecting their individuality and rights. This goal has a number of implications for ethical practice. Counsellors must not misuse professional relationships for personal gain. A dual or multiple relationship is one that involves both a counselling relationship and another type of relationship (e.g., friendship, sexual, business, supervisory). Dual relationships "are problematic because they reduce the counselor's objectivity, confuse the issue, and often put the client in a position of diminished consent" (Cormier and Cormier, 1985:19). In dual relationships, the counsellor has a personal interest that may conflict with the client's interest. This may lead to intended or unintended exploitation, harm, manipulation, or coercion of clients. To prevent these problems and any conflict of interest, dual relationships should be avoided, particularly when they could potentially harm the client. Counsellors who are emotionally stable will not want or need to involve themselves in dual relationships to meet their own needs.

Not surprisingly, the codes of ethics for the various counselling professions strictly prohibit certain types of dual relationships, especially sexual involvement. The CCA position on sexual intimacy outlines this obligation and makes the significant point that termination of the worker/client relationship does not release counsellors to enter into other ties with clients.

> Counsellors avoid any type of sexual intimacies with clients and they do not counsel persons with whom they have had a sexual relationship. Counsellors do not engage in sexual intimacies with former clients within a minimum of three years after terminating the counselling relationship. This prohibition is not limited to the three year period but extends indefinitely if the client is clearly vulnerable, by reason of emotional or cognitive disorder, to exploitative influence by the counsellor. Counsellors, in all such circumstances, clearly bear the burden to ensure that no such exploitative influence has occurred, and to seek consultative assistance. (CCA, 1999:B12)

Notwithstanding these injunctions, abuses continue to occur. Reviewing the available research, Thoreson et al. (1993) found that the incidence of sexual contact between counsellors and clients ranges from 3.6 to 12.1 percent, with as many as 80 percent of counsellors who had sexual contact with clients engaging in it with more than one client. Conducting their own study, the researchers found after surveying 1000 randomly selected male members of the American Counselling Association (ACA) that 1.7 percent of the respondents reported engaging in sexual contact with a client during a professional relationship, and 7 percent reported engaging in sexual contact after a professional relationship (Thoreson et al., 1993).

The CCA and CASW codes are silent on the issue of physical contact such as hugging, but the United States-based National Association of Social Worker's (NASW) suggestion that physical contact may be reasonable as long as workers set "clear, appropriate, and culturally sensitive boundaries" (NASW, 1996: 1.10) can be considered as a starting reference point. Although the NASW code does not give examples of when physical contact might be acceptable, one of the authors of the code suggests elsewhere that, "comforting a distraught child who has been removed from his home because of parental neglect or holding the hand of a nursing home resident who spouse has died" (Reamer, 1998:18) may be permissible.

The Need to Promote Client Self-Determination.

The principle of client self-determination promotes the rights of clients to have autonomy and freedom of choice. Adherence to the principle does not prevent counsellors from helping clients understand how their actions might violate the rights of others, nor does it prevent counsellors from helping clients appreciate the potential consequences of their actions. Some clients, such as people with mental disabilities and young children, may be unable to make competent choices. If so, counsellors may prevent them from acting in ways that are potentially harmful to themselves or others, but as Cottone and Tarvydas (1998) warn, expert knowledge does not give counsellors the moral authority to act on behalf of their clients with the assumption that only they know what is best for them.

Choice is an integral part of client self-determination. When clients have no choices or believe that they have none, self-determination is not possible. Counsellors can assist clients in self-determination through a number of strategies. First, they can help clients identify their choices. Sometimes clients have overlooked alternatives or need concrete information regarding their options. Counsellors can also provide information to help clients make informed choices. Second, counsellors can use advocacy skills to help clients access resources or remove barriers to existing options.

The principle of self-determination obligates counsellors to avoid behaviours that control and manipulate clients and to instead employ strategies that empower clients. Empowerment is the process of assisting clients to discover personal strengths and capacities. Empowerment seeks to help clients take control of their lives and realize that they can improve their situation through their actions. As much as possible, clients should be encouraged to make independent decisions.

Sometimes, beginning counsellors are misinformed about the nature of counselling. They believe that their role is to listen to their clients' problems, then offer helpful advice or solutions. This gives rise to what Dumont describes as the rescue fantasy, a belief that the counsellor's role is save people and put happiness back into their lives. He concludes that when this notion is communicated to clients, "they have no choice other than to rebel and leave or become even more helpless, dependent and sick" (1968:6).

When counsellors understand the principle of self-determination, they avoid advice giving by helping clients identify and explore options, then encouraging them to make their own decisions. This puts clients clearly in the position of being the major decision makers and problem solvers. For their part, counsellors play a major role in orchestrating the process.

Effective counsellors accept that clients have a right to be involved in counselling decision making. They have the right to be treated as active partners in the counselling process and to participate in decisions affecting their lives. This right is underscored in the CCA code of ethics:

> **Clients' Rights and Informed Consent.** When counselling is initiated, and throughout the counselling process as necessary, counsellors inform clients of the purposes, goals, techniques, procedures, limitations, potential risks and benefits of services to be performed, and other such pertinent information. Counsellors make sure that clients understand the implications of diagnosis, fees and fee collection arrangements, record keeping, and limits to confidentiality. Clients have the right to participate in the ongoing counselling plans, to refuse any recommended services, and to be advised of the consequences of such refusal. (1999:B4)

Thus, counsellors should promote client awareness of the issues affecting counselling. They should encourage clients to ask questions about their counselling techniques and strategies. They should welcome client involvement in evaluating the progress of counselling and the counselling relationship itself. When dealing with clients who are receiving services involuntarily, such as those under court order, counsellors should provide information to them regarding the limits of their right to decline service, as well as the possible consequences of such denial.

The Need for Professional Development. Professional counsellors need a core knowledge base, which typically requires two or more years of academic training,

including supervised clinical experience in a recognized counselling or social service setting. Moreover, throughout their careers, counsellors should expect to spend time reading books and journals to increase their knowledge. As well, regular attendance of courses, seminars, and conferences should be a part of everyone's professional career.

By keeping their knowledge base current, counsellors are better able to be empathic because they are more aware of the issues and feelings that their clients face. Moreover, keeping up-to-date will help counsellors avoid any judgmental responses that might occur if they reacted from only their own frames of reference. The range of knowledge that counsellors need to pursue includes the following:

- Specific issues, problems, and challenges that their clients are facing. For example, counsellors working in corrections need to know something about finding a job if one has a criminal record and coping with the stigma of a criminal record. Many clients are dealing with poverty, and counsellors need to be aware its social and psychological effects.

- Relevant medical and psychiatric conditions (e.g., attention deficit disorder, multiple sclerosis, **schizophrenia**, bipolar disorder). Counsellor credibility and competence is greatly enhanced if their knowledge of these conditions is current.

- Lifestyle variation (e.g., same-sex relationships, single parents, extended families, and blended families).

- Cultural awareness about the values, beliefs, and customs of others.

- Lifespan development (i.e., developmental changes and milestones from birth to death). Life experience can greatly increase a counsellor's capacity for empathy and understanding. Of course, life experience may also cloud judgment and objectivity, so it is important that counsellors seek training and consultation to increase their understanding of others' experiences.

Confidentiality

The rules regarding confidentiality are integral to every code of ethics (See Table 2.1 on page 44 for guidelines.). Ethical guidelines stress that the confidentiality of clients must be protected. Indeed, most clients enter counselling with an expectation that what they say will be kept private. For the most part, counsellors can assure clients that they will keep their disclosures confidential. However, it is often not so simple. **Absolute confidentiality** means that client disclosures are not shared with anyone. **Relative confidentiality** means that information is shared within the agency with supervisors or colleagues, outside the agency with the client's permission, or in courts of law owing to legal requirements, such as child abuse legislation. Usually, clients can be assured only of relative confidentiality.

In order to provide optimum service to clients, information about them must be shared within the agency. To monitor the quality of work and help counsellors improve their skills, supervisors need to review client files, or they may consult with counsellors by reviewing audio and video recordings of their interviews. Other counsellors within the agency also have access to files.

Many people believe that counsellors and other professionals enjoy "privileged communication," i.e., that they are legally protected from having to share information that they have obtained while exercising their professional duties. However, the courts may subpoena counsellors' records. A recent U.S. Supreme Court decision (*Jafee v. Redmond*, cited in Remley, Herlihy, and Herlihy, 1997) held that communication between licensed psychotherapists (those with master's degrees) and their clients does not have to be disclosed in federal court. However, protection for unlicensed psychotherapists has not been established. Canada has no legislative protection for licensed or unlicensed psychotherapists.

There are valid reasons, including some legal requirements, for sharing information. For example, all jurisdictions in North America have legislation that requires counsellors to report suspicions of child abuse and neglect to the appropriate authorities. Similarly, counsellors might have to break confidentiality when they believe that clients might harm themselves or others. Counsellors need to become familiar with the precise wording of relevant statutes in their area since laws may vary significantly between jurisdictions.

One often quoted legal precedent is the *Tarasoff* case, in which the client had told his counsellor of his intent to kill his girlfriend. The counsellor told the campus police of the threat, but he did not warn his client's girlfriend or her family. The client, a student at the school, subsequently carried out his threat and killed the young woman. The young woman's parents brought a successful lawsuit against the counsellor and the university. This litigation established that when counsellors believe that a client represents "a serious danger of violence to another" they have a **duty to warn** potential victims (*Tarasoff v. Regents of the University of California* [1976], cited in Woodside and McClam, 1990:267). Since the *Tarasoff* decision, there have been numerous state laws and legal precedents that address the duty-to-warn issue. Reamer (1998) concluded that although some court rulings have been contradictory, trends suggest that four conditions warrant disclosure of confidential information without a client's permission:

1. There must be evidence that the client is a threat to another person.

2. Based on a client's behavior, there should be evidence that the violent act is likely to occur.

3. There should be evidence suggesting that the violent act is imminent.

4. Social workers and other professionals should be able to identify the potential victim.

The ACA code permits counsellors to notify persons who are at risk of contracting a communicable and fatal disease from a client, providing that the counsellors are certain that the client has not informed the person and does not intend to: "A counselor who receives information confirming that a client has a disease commonly known to be both communicable and fatal is justified in disclosing information to an identifiable third party, who by his or her relationship with the client is at a high risk of contracting the disease" (1995:B.1.d).

Zastrow (1990:64) notes that breaking confidentiality may be warranted or required when:

• a client formally authorizes the release

• a professional is called to testify in a criminal case

• a client files a lawsuit against a professional

• a client threatens suicide

- a client threatens to harm his or her therapist
- a professional becomes aware that a minor has committed a crime, that a minor is being used by adults as an accessory in a crime, or that a minor is a victim of criminal actions
- there is evidence of child abuse or neglect
- a client's emotional or physical condition makes his or her employment a clear danger, such as when an airline pilot has a serious drinking problem

Clients have a right to be fully informed regarding the limits of confidentiality, including any legal and ethical responsibilities that require counsellors to share information. Through discussions regarding confidentiality, counsellors can reassure clients that computer and file records are not shared indiscriminately.

There are a number of steps that counsellors can take to protect client confidentiality. They should discipline themselves not to discuss clients in public places and at parties or other social events. Counselling work is demanding, and an important part of dealing with the stress of the job is to unwind by talking about difficult cases and personal reactions with colleagues and supervisors. This is a healthy and necessary component of professional wellness. Unfortunately, time pressures and large caseloads may leave little or no time for this process during the working day, so it is easy to fall into the trap of discussing clients over lunch or in other settings where confidentiality cannot be ensured. The obvious risk is that the conversation will be overheard. Even when names are not used, accidental listeners may think that they know the person being discussed. In addition, they may decide that they would never go for counselling because what they say will soon be all over town.

Although it is tempting for counsellors to discuss clients with family and friends because they are available as supportive listeners, they should avoid doing so. Family and friends are not bound by the same ethics as counselling professionals and could accidentally disclose what they have heard, perhaps with a seemingly innocent observation or comment.

Sometimes counsellors breach confidentiality by failing to take simple precautions. For example, taking phone calls during a counselling session can lead to careless breaches of confidentiality and suggests to clients that the counsellor treats their private matters casually. In addition, counsellors should remove all case records, phone messages, and notes from their desk. This prevents clients from seeing the names of other clients and reinforces the fact that the counsellor will not leave private records in public places.

When counsellors leave phone messages for clients, they should leave only their first name and say nothing about their title or the nature of their call. Clients may not have informed roommates or family members that they are seeing a counsellor.

The interview itself should be conducted in private, not in the waiting room or where other staff or clients may overhear. When greeting a client in the waiting room, counsellors should refrain from using surnames. However, they need to be sensitive to the fact that many seniors and people from some cultures are insulted by the casual use of their first names.

Sometimes counsellors meet clients by chance in public places. When this happens, counsellors should ensure that they maintain confidentiality, even when the client appears unconcerned. They should gently shift the conversation to a neutral topic or suggest a private time and place to continue the discussion. At that time, counsellors can explain why they avoided public discussion.

Table 2.1 Confidentiality Guidelines

- Involve clients. Keep them informed and seek their permission to release information. Remember that freedom of information statutes may give clients the right to access your files.

- Become familiar with relevant legal statutes (e.g., child abuse or mental health legislation) that define and limit confidentiality. Disclose only that information that is required.

- Review professional guidelines such as the CASW Code of Ethics and CCA Code of Ethics.

- Protect client records with secure filing systems. Do not leave files, notes, or phone messages about clients where they may be read by others. Insure that electronically stored data is protected.

- Insure that consultations concerning clients with others are legitimate and conducted in private and professional manner. This precludes conversations about clients at social gatherings or in a public place such as a restaurant.

- Insure that interviews are private and free from interruptions.

- Counsellors may discuss clients with supervisors and they may use support staff for processing necessary paperwork and documentation.

CONVERSATION 2.1

BLACK HUMOUR

STUDENT: I've just started my field placement and I'm disturbed by what's happening. When we go for coffee, everyone jokes and makes fun of the clients. If they knew the way their counsellors talked about them, they would never come back. I didn't know that professionals could be so cold hearted. Isn't their behaviour unethical?

TEACHER: Many professionals deal with the enormous stress of their jobs through "black humour" (also known as "gallows humour") by making jokes about tragic events or clients' misfortunes. It's one way that counsellors sustain their emotional well-being. It doesn't mean that they've become hardened or uncaring toward their clients; rather, it's a way of unwinding and relieving constant pressure. As you've discovered, one of the dangers of black humour is that others will overhear it and draw conclusions about the person's attitudes. Is it unethical? What do you think?

Ethical Dilemmas

Ethical codes attempt to define acceptable behaviour, and although they cannot provide precise guidelines for resolving all dilemmas, they provide an important reference for decision making. Ethics have their origin in the values of the profession, but "because people interpret abstract imperatives differently, they often disagree about what constitutes ethical behavior or 'appropriate actions'" (DuBois and Miley, 1996:123).

Codes of ethics provide guidelines for making ethical decisions, but they usually do not offer answers to specific situations that arise for counselling professionals. An ethical dilemma exists when a choice must be made between competing values. A common example is the potential conflict between a client's right to confidentiality and the rights of society, for example, when a client discloses an intention to harm someone else. Such a dilemma might be resolved with the conclusion that the rights of an intended victim supersede the rights of the client. Other examples of ethical dilemmas include:

- A 15-year-old girl discloses that her father has been abusive, but in recent weeks he seems to have changed. She asks that you do not make a report to the authorities. She says she knows her father will retaliate if he finds out that she told anyone.

- A 17-year-old girl asks for your help to obtain an abortion without involving her parents.

- Your client informs you that he has tested positive for HIV, but he hasn't informed his partner.

- A 16-year-old boy tells you that he is working as a prostitute.

- Your client casually mentions that he robbed a bank several months ago but was not caught.

Cottone and Tarvydas (1998:135) identify five ethical rules or principles that can be used to help resolve ethical dilemmas: autonomy, beneficence, nonmaleficence, justice, and fidelity. They describe the obligations of each principle as follows:

1. *autonomy*: to honour the right to individual decisions

2. *beneficence*: to do good to others

3. *nonmaleficence*: to do no harm to others

4. *justice*: to be fair, give equally to others

5. *fidelity*: to be loyal, honest, and keep promises

Under ideal conditions, counsellors can honour all five principles, but ethical dilemmas by nature represent competing principles, and different choices involve unique consequences. Ethical decision making involves identifying and weighing which of the five principles ought to have priority in any given situation. As well, professional judgment for resolving ethical dilemmas can be enhanced by consulting legislation and codes of ethics and by consulting with supervisors or colleagues.

EXAMPLE:

A 50-year-old man confides that he often thinks of killing himself, but he pleads with you not to tell his spouse or anyone else. Here the principle of autonomy, which respects the client's right to self-determination, appears to be in conflict with the beneficence principle. The counsellor must decide whether to sacrifice the client's right to make his own decision or to interfere with his autonomy because of a belief that intervention will be better for him in the long term. In addition, if the counsellor keeps his client's secret (fidelity principle) and the client subsequently commits suicide, the counsellor might be held responsible for not acting to prevent his actions (nonmaleficence).

The Canadian Counselling Association in its Code of Ethics attempted to integrate various models of ethical decision making. They suggest a six-step sequence for ethical decision making and for resolving ethical dilemmas.

Step One - What are the key ethical issues in this situation?

Step Two - What ethical guidelines are relevant to this situation? The second important step consists of referring to the CCA Code of Ethics to see if the situation is dealt with under one or more of the articles in the Code.

Step Three - What ethical principles are of major importance in this situation?
a.   respect for the dignity of persons
b.   not wilfully harming others
c.   integrity in relationships
d.   responsible caring
e.   responsibility to society
f.   respect for self-determination

Step Four - What are the most important principles, and what are the risks and benefits if these principles are acted upon? The fourth step consists of choosing the most important principles and relevant ethical articles and beginning to implement some possible action by:
(a) generating alternatives and examining the risks and benefits of each,
(b) securing additional information, including possible discussion with the client
(c) consulting with knowledgeable colleagues, with provincial or CCA ethics committees, or with other appropriate sources, and
(d) examining the probable outcomes of various courses of action.

Step Five - Will I feel the same about this situation if I think about it a little longer? Until this point, this decision-making process has concentrated on fairly cognitive, rational steps, so at the fifth step counsellors should acknowledge and include in their decision making process the feelings and intuitions evoked by the ethical challenge. In so doing, they could use such techniques as:
(a) Quest - a solitary walk in the woods or park where your emotions evoked by the ethical challenge are brought into full awareness,
(b) Incubation - "sleep on it,"
(c) Time projection - projecting the ethical situation into the future and thinking about the various probable scenarios.

Step Six - What plan of action will be most helpful in this situation? The sixth step consists of taking some action. Counsellors should follow a concrete action plan, evaluate the plan, and be prepared to correct any negative consequences that might occur from the action taken. (CCA, 1999:iv - 2).[1]

Shultz (2000) presents an example demonstrating the six steps in action. A high school counsellor developed a strong relationship with John, a Grade 11 student, who confided that he was making extra money by stealing from his employer. The counsellor struggled with what to do since he had assured John that their conversations would be confidential. Key ethical issues in this situation (step one) play off the promise of confidentiality with the illegal nature of the student's actions. As well, the potential that the student might be caught with serious consequences must be considered. The key ethical articles (step two) include those related to confidentiality with an exception for circumstances where there is a danger to others. Ethics also require counsellors to maintain first responsibility to help the client. As well, counsellors must inform clients regarding potential exceptions to

---

1. See Shultz (2000:12-13) for a detailed example using the six-step model.

confidentiality at the onset of counselling. Step three involves identification of the most important ethical principles. Of the six principles listed in the CCA code (see Step Three in the CCA text) Shultz suggests five are significant in this case: integrity in relationships, responsible caring, not willfully harming others, responsibility to society, and respect for self determination. Step Four considers the risks and benefits of various courses of action such as reporting the theft and not reporting the theft and continuing to work with the client. In this particular situation the counsellor concluded (after consultation with a colleague) that "responsible caring" and "responsibility to society" should be the priorities. After "sleeping on it" (Step Five) the counsellor took action (Step Six) by informing his client that he had concluded that he would not be acting responsibly by allowing the stealing to continue and that confidentiality must be broken. However, he worked with his client to identify several options including the client reporting the theft himself, or the counsellor going with the client to inform the employer of his illegal actions. Shultz proposes that decision making can be organized using charts such as Table 2.2.

Application of the CCA model for ethical decision making (or any other model) does not mean that resolution of ethical dilemmas will be easy. When values and ethics compete, the decision as to which one should have priority can be painfully difficult. Hepworth, Rooney and Larsen (1997) propose the following four principles as guidelines:

1. The right to life, health, well-being, and necessities of life take precedence over rights to confidentiality and opportunities for additive 'goods' such as wealth, education, and recreation.
2. An individual's basic right to well-being takes precedence over another person's right to privacy, freedom, or self-determination.

Table 2.2 Decision-Making Chart

Action Choices	Benefits	Risks	Potential Outcomes
Choice 1 Avoid confronting the issue in counselling.	May be the easiest.	The problem behaviour continues. Avoidance may implicitly condone the clients behaviour	Counsellor could lose his job. Unchecked, the client's illegal activity might escalate with potential serious consequences.
Choice 2 Keep counselling the client. Encourage him to change his behaviour and make restitution	Maintains counselling relationship.	Client may continue to come for counselling but not alter his behaviour	If stealing continues, client's employer is further victimized. Client's behaviour may escalate.
Choice 3 After telling client, report the activities to the appropriate authorities	In the long run this may help the client to act more responsibility. Respects rights of employer.	Lose client. Possibly other clients.	Initially, client may be angry, But this action would clearly communicate to him that the stealing had to stop.

Source: Adapted from Shulz W.E. *Counselling Ethics Casebook 2000.* Ottawa, ON: Canadian Counselling Association, 2000:13.

3. People's right to self-determination takes precedence over their rights to basic well-being.
4. Person's rights to well-being may override laws, policies, and arrangements of organizations. (85-86)

Intimate knowledge of ethical principles and legal guidelines can make the decision-making process clearer, albeit no less difficult. For example, a client's right to confidentiality and self-determination must be given up when they disclose child abuse and the "duty to warn" principle means that professionals must warn potential victims. However, it is not always clear the extent that a client's behaviour constitutes danger to the safety of others. Another example: Hepworth, Rooney and Larsen (1997) assert that people have a right "to carry out actions that appear contrary to their best interests, providing they are competent to make an informed and relevant decision" (85). This would protect the rights of people to make errors and carry out actions that others might consider wrong. However, counsellors must consider when application of this principle must be abandoned because the individual's behaviour might result in death such as in a case where clients threaten suicide. While counsellors have a clear legal and ethical responsibility to intervene to prevent suicide, other challenges are not so easy to resolve. For example, homeless persons' lifestyles may reach the point where their hygiene, living, and eating habits become dangerous for them. The point at which their right to self-determination should yield to their right to health and well-being is not easy to establish.

Objectivity

Effective counsellors may become intimately familiar with the lives of their clients. Objectivity is defined as the capacity to understand situations and people without bias or distortion. When counsellors are objective, they understand their clients' feelings, thoughts, and behaviours without allowing their personal values, beliefs, and biases to contaminate their understanding. When counsellors are objective, they do not directly or subtly try to impose their preferred solutions on clients.

There are a number of ways that counsellors can fail to be objective. The first is to make assumptions. Assumptions are distortions or false conclusions based on simplistic reasoning, incomplete information, or bias. Counsellors who have had similar experiences to their clients' may assume that their clients' problems and feelings are the same. Consequently, they do not take the time to investigate the distinctive viewpoints of their clients. Counsellors also may make assumptions about the meaning of words. This danger can be avoided if counsellors remain alert to the need to probe for individual client definition and meaning, as in the following example:

CLIENT (SPEAKING TO A FIRST NATIONS COUNSELLOR): *I moved here about five years ago. I guess you know how tough it is for an Indian in this city.*

COUNSELLOR (CHOICE 1): *I sure do. Prejudice is everywhere.*

COUNSELLOR (CHOICE 2): *Like you say, it's not easy. But it's different for everyone. I need your help to understand better what it's been like for you.*

In this example, Choice 1 may cut off discussion and the counsellor will lose a valuable opportunity to appreciate his client's experience. Choice 2, on the other hand, offers gentle empathy then probes for more detail. This response reduces the risk that the counsellor will make errors of assumption.

A second way that counsellors can lose objectivity is by overidentifying with clients. When overidentification occurs, counsellors lose their capacity to keep sufficient emotional distance from their clients. Their own feelings and reactions become mixed up with those of their clients, clouding their judgment. Counsellors who find themselves in this position may find that personal counselling or consultation with a supervisor is sufficient to help them regain objectivity, or they may conclude that referral to another counsellor is necessary.

A third way that counsellors can lose objectivity is by becoming overly involved with clients. This overinvolvement includes dual relationships prohibited by ethical codes, as well as relationships in which counsellors rely on clients to meet their social and psychological needs. To prevent this from happening, counsellors need to make sure that they are meeting their personal needs in other ways. As well, counsellors should be alert to signs that they may be overinvolved with particular clients.

Table 2.3 on page 50 summarizes protective strategies counsellors can use to avoid loss of objectivity.

CONVERSATION 2.2

PERSONAL INVOLVEMENT WITH CLIENTS

STUDENT: Is it ever okay to be sexually intimate with clients?

TEACHER: No! Universally, ethical codes of behaviour prohibit sexual intimacies with clients. For example, the CASW code succinctly states that "the social worker shall not have a sexual relationship with a client." (1994:4.3) An expectation explicitly stated in the CCA code is that counsellors "do not counsel persons with whom they have had a sexual relationship" (1999:B12).

STUDENT: That seems straightforward. What about becoming involved with former clients?

TEACHER: That's a more difficult question. My opinion is that you never should, but you should consult individual codes of ethics for specific guidelines. For example, the CCA code requires a minimum of three years between the end of the counselling relationship and the beginning of a sexual relationship. The period is extended indefinitely if the client is clearly vulnerable. In any case counsellors "clearly bear the burden to ensure that no such exploitative influence has occurred" (1999:B.12). A recent review of the literature concluded that harm to clients does occur when professionals have sexual contact with clients including "denial, guilt, shame, isolation, anger, depression, impaired ability to trust, loss of self-esteem, difficulty expressing anger, emotional liability, psychosomatic disorders, sexual confusion, and increased risk of suicide" (Beckman, Turner, Cooper, Polnerow, & Swartz, 2000:2).

STUDENT: What about other types of involvement? If you are a counsellor in a small town, it's impossible to avoid social contact with clients. Your client might be the owner of the only grocery store in town.

TEACHER: Codes of ethics for the various counselling professions (e.g., psychology or social work) frown upon dual relationships when there is a possibility of counsellors losing objectivity or when there is potential for client exploitation. In large cities, it's usually easy to refer clients in order to avoid the conflict of interest of dual relationships. As you point out, it's much more difficult in a small town, and some dual relationship arrangements may be inevitable, but these relationships should never include sexual intimacy with current clients.

Table 2.3 Maintaining Objectivity	
Loss of Objectivity	**Protective Strategies for Counsellors**
Making assumptions	Attempt to understand your prejudices and preferences.
	Listen to but don't be controlled by the opinions of others.
	Develop self-awareness regarding personal needs and values.
	Be inquisitive, and explore each client's situation to discover his or her unique perspective.
	Brainstorm other points of view or seek other opinions.
	Check your conclusions with clients to see if they match theirs—seek definition, detail, and example.
	Monitor cultural and gender bias.
Overidentification	Monitor reactions and discover areas of vulnerability; be alert to strong negative or positive reactions to clients.
	Refer clients when you cannot be impartial.
	Know why you want to be a counsellor—understand your needs.
	Use colleagues to critique your reactions and to give you feedback.
	Use tools such as video recordings to review interviews for inappropriate attempts to influence or control.
Overinvolvement	Avoid promoting client dependency.
	Develop a wellness program to ensure that you are not relying on your clients to meet your needs for social and psychological involvement and acceptance.
	Recognize warning signs (e.g., interviews that consistently run overtime, relief when a client does not show up for an interview, excessive worry about clients, reluctance to end a counselling relationship that has reached a point of termination).

WORKING WITH COMPETENCE

High self-awareness enables counsellors to make important decisions regarding areas in which they are competent and those in which referral to other professionals is warranted. Counsellors must practise only within the range of their competence, and they should not misrepresent their training or experience. This helps to ensure that they do no harm to clients. As Mehr succinctly put it, "Do your best, do what you know how to do, do not get in—or stay in—over your head, and do not take advantage of a client for your own needs" (1998:190). The CASW and CCA codes provide references on practising within the boundaries of competence. The following list provides general guidelines for working with competence:

1. Counsellors should offer counselling services that are within the limits of their professional competence as measured by education and professional standards. Competent counsellors know that the support and assistance of other professionals is necessary for issues that exceed their expertise.

2. Counsellors should monitor their work and seek supervision, training, or consultation in order to evaluate their effectiveness. Continued professional development should be pursued in order to increase their competence and to keep their knowledge current.

3. Until counsellors have received the necessary training, they should not work in specialized areas of practice, such as interviewing children in abuse situations or administering or interpreting psychological tests. Untrained counsellors should not attempt to make psychiatric diagnoses.

4. Counsellors should endeavour to base their work on accepted theory and empirical knowledge. Counsellors need to keep abreast of the latest research in order to increase the probability that their efforts are successful. People would not want to see a doctor whose last training was in medical school. Similarly, clients should not be expected to work with counsellors who are not current in their field.

5. When access to other professionals is limited or unavailable, such as in rural settings or urban areas where there are long waiting lists, counsellors must not conclude that "the provision of well-intentioned but unskilled service [is] ... better than no service at all" (Daniluk and Haverkamp, 1993:18).

6. Counsellors need to know when particular topics or problems are sensitive for clients. They need to be aware of when their clients' problems parallel unresolved issues in their own lives. This knowledge is important to help them to know when to seek consultation or supervision, when to refer clients to other workers, and when to enter counselling to address their own needs. Clients have a right to expect that their counsellors are able to be objective about the issues being discussed and that their judgment is not impaired by bias, unresolved personal problems, or physical illness. The CASW code states:

> Where a social worker has a physical or mental health problem, disability or illness that affects the ability of the social worker to provide competent service or that would threaten the health or well-being of the client, the social worker shall discontinue the provision of social work service to a client
> (a) advising the client of the reason and,
> (b) ensuring that the client is referred to another professional person if the client agrees to the referral. (CASW:1994:12)

Interviewing is a process of gathering information without any expectation of influencing or changing clients. Competent interviewing requires an ability to explore and understand clients' attitudes, feelings, and perspectives. The basis for this competence is a nonjudgmental attitude and intelligent application of the active listening skills of attending, using silence, paraphrasing, summarizing, and asking questions (see Chapters 4 to 6). Although the principal goal of interviewing is information gathering, the process of interviewing may lead clients to unexpectedly release painful or forgotten feelings. Thus, adept interviewers are capable of dealing with unpredictable reactions that the interview may promote or of referring clients to appropriate alternative resources. Moreover, they know when and how to probe effectively.

Counselling requires skilled interviewing but includes the additional goal of helping clients with such activities as problem solving, dealing with painful feelings, and developing new skills. Psychotherapy involves intensive counselling with emphasis on personality change or the treatment of more severe mental disorders. Working within the limits of one's ability requires counsellors to use only those techniques and strategies that they have been adequately trained to apply. For example, attendance at a short seminar on hypnosis would not qualify counsellors to use hypnosis in their work. As well, it is expected that counsellors will use methods that have a reasonable chance of success, supported by experience and research evidence.

Large caseloads and the emotional demands of counselling work may result in emotional and physical fatigue, thereby weakening their competence. "Counsellors must be cognizant of their own limits and must act to protect themselves and their clients from the consequences of burnout" (Daniluk and Haverkamp, 1993:18). Competent counsellors know how to set limits on the amount of work they are able to provide. They know when to seek consultation and when to seek support or personal counselling.

CONVERSATION 2.3

I'm Just a Beginner

STUDENT: I'm just a beginner, so if I'm supposed to work within the limits of my competence, I shouldn't do anything.

TEACHER: Like a lot of counsellors who are just starting, you may feel a bit overwhelmed.

STUDENT: I don't want to say or do the wrong thing. What if I don't know the right answers or if I don't say the right thing to clients?

TEACHER: First, there's rarely a single right way to respond. Most often, there is a range of choices of things to say or do in any situation. Second, no one knows all the right answers. Be honest with clients about the fact that you are still a student, and don't be afraid to admit your limitations, as this provides great modelling for clients. One goal of training is for you to expand your range of choices so that you can respond based on the needs of your clients and their situations. Remember, learning to be an effective counsellor is a lifelong process. At this stage, your professional responsibility is to make effective use of supervisors to monitor your work. Use them to develop your skills. Make it easy for them to give you feedback. Seek it out, and then try to be nondefensive. Look for opportunities to apply your developing knowledge base by taking some risks to learn new skills.

SELF-AWARENESS

We live in a house of mirrors and think we're looking out.
—Fritz Perls

The Importance of Self-Awareness

Competent counsellors need to acquire a high level of awareness of who they are. Until counsellors develop self-awareness of their own needs, feelings, thoughts, and behaviours, including their personal problems and their areas of vulnerability, they will be unable to respond to their clients with objectivity.

Table 2.4 contrasts the characteristics of counsellors who have high levels of self-awareness with those who have low levels of self-awareness.

Counsellors who lack self-awareness and those who are not motivated to pursue it are destined to remain unaware of the ways they influence clients. They may, for example, be unaware of how their nonverbal reactions to controversial topics betray their biases and discomfort. They may avoid particular topics, or they may behave in certain ways to mask their insecurities or to unconsciously meet their personal needs. For example, counsellors who have personal needs for control may meet this need through excessive and inappropriate advice giving.

Increasing Self-Awareness

Counsellors who are serious about developing their self-awareness are secure enough to risk exploring their strengths and limitations. Self-awareness involves counsellors

Table 2.4   Self-Awareness

Counsellors with Self-Awareness	Counsellors without Self-Awareness
Identify and label their personal feelings	Avoid or are unaware of their feelings
Know where their feelings end and those of their clients begin	Project personal feelings onto clients
Recognize and accept areas of vulnerability and unresolved issues	Respond inappropriately because unresolved problems interfere with their capacity to be objective
Understand personal values and their influence on the counselling relationship	React emotionally to their clients but don't understand why or how
Recognize and manage internal dialogue (discussed later in this chapter)	Unconsciously use clients to work out their own personal difficulties
Understand and control personal defence mechanisms	Remain blind to defensive reactions
Know when and how clients are reacting to their style	Behave nonassertively (using excessive caution, placating behaviour, etc.) because they are unaware of the limiting effects of self-defeating thought
Realize how they influence outcomes	Remain unaware how their behaviour influences others
Modify behaviour based on reactions of clients	Behave based on personal needs and style rather than in response to the needs and reactions of clients
Set professional goals based on knowledge of personal and skill strengths and limitations	Avoid or limit goal setting because they are unaware of personal and professional needs

becoming alert and knowledgeable about their ways of thinking, acting, and feeling. This means that they are strong enough to be open to discovering aspects of themselves that they might prefer to keep hidden. For counsellors, this is a continuing process throughout their careers. It requires counsellors to honestly look at themselves and how they relate to others, but as Harris and Maloney (1996) suggest, some behaviours, including racism, sexism, ageism, and heterosexism, operate unconsciously. Consequently, counsellors must overcome any natural tendency to be defensive. They can do this by asking others for feedback.

Colleagues, supervisors, and clients can be extremely helpful sources of information, but their feedback needs to be cultivated. Generally, people are reluctant to deliver critical feedback, however helpful it may be. Thus, the onus is on counsellors to create the conditions to encourage feedback. They can invite input from others through a number of strategies.

The first strategy is to create a safe climate. People balk at giving feedback to others because they fear how it will be received. One concern is the risk of retaliation. "If I say something, will I be attacked or made to feel guilty?" Another common worry is that feedback will damage the relationship. The major concern also might be that feedback will cripple the other person's self-esteem.

Therefore, it is important for counsellors to demonstrate that they are ready, willing, and able to respond nondefensively to feedback. Counsellors have a responsibility to consider feedback and when appropriate, to act on it. This means that they do not have to unconditionally agree with what has been said to them. It does mean that they listen with responses that are nonaggressive, in other words, without blaming or making excuses. Sometimes, such control can be difficult to sustain, particularly if feedback is delivered in an uncaring and hostile manner. A general rule when dealing with clients is no matter what clients say or do, counsellors must maintain a professional role. Of course, this does not preclude setting appropriate limits, nor does it mean that counsellors have to tolerate personal or physical abuse. It means staying calm, being nondefensive, and refraining from retaliatory responses such as name calling or punishing statements.

The second strategy is to use active listening skills to ensure that feedback is concrete or specific. Counsellors can ask questions for details, definitions, examples, and clarification. Summarizing and paraphrasing can be used to confirm understanding.

Who Am I?

The essence of self-awareness is the answer to the question "Who am I?" This question needs to be explored on a number of different dimensions, including understanding personal feelings, thoughts, and behaviour; personal needs; counsellors' impact on clients; the limits of competence; personal and cultural values; and areas of vulnerability.

Feelings, Thoughts, and Behaviour. Counsellors need to know and understand their feelings, thoughts, and behaviours, including the defence mechanisms that they use to protect themselves from stress. Effective counsellors are comfortable discussing a wide range of emotions. They don't avoid feelings; in fact, they recognize that for many clients understanding and managing painful emotions is the greatest outcome from counselling. To understand clients' emotions, counsellors must be in tune with their own emotional reactions. Empathy, the basic tool for understanding the feelings of others, will be contaminated unless counsellors are fully in touch with their own feelings. This includes knowing where their feelings end and those of their clients begin.

Self-Defeating Thought. Counsellors need to be aware of their own internal dialogue—the inner voices that evaluate their actions. Counsellors with low self-worth typically find that the inner voice is critical, issuing messages such as "I'm no good." Negative self-talk can lead to emotional distress and interfere with counselling performance in a number of ways:

- Counsellors may be reluctant to be assertive with clients and may be excessively gentle or nonconfrontational.

- General feelings of incompetence may lead to structuring "the counseling process to meet our own self-image problems or to confirm our negative self-pictures" (Cormier and Cormier, 1985:13).

- Counsellors may be unable to objectively assess counselling relationship outcomes, since they tend to interpret problems as personal failures and to discount positive feedback or outcomes.

Significant research has been conducted regarding the ways that personal beliefs can influence performance and lead to maladaptive emotions and behaviour (Cormier and Cormier, 1985; Ellis, 1984). Counsellors need to become watchful of negative self-talk as a crucial first step in developing a program to combat its effects. Subsequently, systematic techniques such as thought-stopping techniques can be used to replace depreciating self-talk with affirmations or positive statements. Negative thoughts can be interrupted by mentally saying, "Stop," or by snapping an elastic band on the wrist as a reminder to divert the self-talk (Young, 1998; Martin and Pear, 1992).

Defence Mechanisms. Sigmund Freud first described defence mechanisms in 1894, and over a period of 40 years he identified most of the ones we still use today (Vaillant, 1988). A **defence mechanism** is a mental process or reaction that shields a person from undesirable or unacceptable thoughts, feelings, or conclusions that, if accepted, would create anxiety or damage one's self-esteem. Significantly, defence mechanisms usually involve some distortion of reality and are unconscious (Corsini, 1984). All people, including counsellors, use defence mechanisms to protect themselves. Simply put, defence mechanisms help us guard our feelings and self-esteem. Most people use one or more methods to defend themselves from perceived threats. Simple defences include blaming others or making excuses for their own failures. Counsellors might take credit for counselling successes but blame failure on their clients. Common defence mechanisms used by counsellors include the following:

- *Denial*: People refuse to acknowledge the existence of feelings or problems. When counsellors use denial, they fail to consider that their actions might be the reason for their clients' inappropriate behaviour.

- *Displacement*: People relate with the feelings that they should express toward others; for example, counsellors deal with their own work stress by behaving aggressively with clients.

- *Rationalization*: People develop excuses or explanations to protect their self-image; for example, counsellors justify their inability to confront clients by concluding that it is best to offer only positive feedback.

- *Suppression*: People avert stressful thoughts by not thinking about them; for example, counsellors refuse to consider that personal biases might be affecting their decisions.

- *Regression*: People deal with conflict or stress by returning to behaviour from an earlier stage of their lives; for example, counsellors deal with aggressive clients by becoming overly compliant or by trying to please.

Counsellors should be alert to circumstances when they use defence mechanisms rather than confront reality. Facing reality requires courage and taking risks, for to give up one's defences means sacrificing safety. Feedback from others can be threatening because it challenges people to let down their defences by addressing aspects of their situations that they might prefer to avoid.

When counsellors understand themselves, they recognize when their defences are up and can take steps to change their reactions and behaviour. They know when and where they are vulnerable, then they use this knowledge to cue or trigger nondefensive alternatives. For example, when clients are angry or hostile, counsellors can discipline themselves to take time to empathize and encourage clients to ventilate, rather than respond more naturally by fighting back.

Personal Needs. Counsellors have the same basic needs as everyone else, including the need to be loved, respected, and valued by others. This is natural, but counsellors must understand how their personal needs can adversely affect counselling outcomes. Lack of self-awareness regarding personal needs can lead to unconscious structuring of the session to meet counsellors' needs instead of the clients' (Kell and Mueller, 1966; Brammer, 1985; D'Augelli, D'Augelli, and Danish, 1981). "Sometimes helpers want to help themselves with their own problems through assisting others, or satisfaction is acquired through the power and influence over others afforded by the helping relationship" (Brammer, 1985:25).

Corey and Corey warn that lack of self-awareness can impede counsellors from keeping their clients' remarks in proper perspective: "As a beginning helper you are especially vulnerable to believing everything positive that your clients tell you about yourself. Thus, if clients tell you how sexually attractive you are, how understanding you are, and how different from anyone else they have met, it may be very difficult for you to resist believing what they tell you" (1989:192).

Therefore, even positive feedback from clients must be interpreted cautiously. Clients may try to placate counsellors or use ingratiating tactics to manipulate, or it may be their way of relating to authority.

A range of counsellor needs may interfere with counselling, including the need to be liked; achieve status or prestige, control, and perfection; and cultivate social relationships. Table 2.5 summarizes the major warning signs and risks of these needs.

Need To Be Liked. In the next chapter we will explore the importance of a warm and trusting counselling relationship. To a great extent, counselling depends on establishing and maintaining a safe environment, one in which clients feel safe enough to take risks. Obviously, this is easier if clients like their counsellors, but counsellors need to remember that having clients like them is not the primary goal of counselling. The aim of counselling is to support client change or problem management. This means that counsellors have to be assertive enough to risk making reasonable demands on their clients, which, in turn, may generate tension and anxiety. Otherwise, clients can easily stay locked into established but unhealthy patterns. The need to be liked becomes problematic when it becomes more important than achieving the goals of counselling.

Table 2.5 Managing Personal Needs in Counselling	
Personal Need	**Warning Signs and Risks**
Need to be liked and to be helpful	• Withholding potentially helpful but critical feedback • Inappropriately avoiding controversy or conflict • Trying to ingratiate (e.g., excessively praising, telling clients what they want to hear) • Acting with rescuing behaviour • Expecting or reaching for compliments from clients
Need for status, prestige	• Trying to impress with "exotic" techniques or brilliant interpretations • Taking credit for client success • Name dropping • Bragging about successes
Need for control	• Advice giving • Interfering with client self-determination (e.g., unnecessarily using authority, manipulating, dominating) • Imposing personal values • Stereotyping clients as needy and inadequate (which creates a role for someone to be "helpful")
Perfectionism	• Focussing on mistakes • Pushing clients toward unrealistic goals • Responding with self-depreciation to mistakes (e.g., "I'm a failure")
Need for social relationships	• Becoming overinvolved with clients (e.g., meeting clients socially, continuing counselling relationships beyond the normal point of closure) • Indiscriminate self-disclosure

One beginning counsellor, a young male, wrote in his journal: "When a client says something negative or behaves in a self-destructive way, I realize I hold back. I don't say anything because I want to be liked. I want the client to like me, not see me as an authority figure. I'd rather be seen as a pal or a friend." This journal entry highlights the dangers and signals an important insight that will help the counsellor question some of his assumptions about counselling. He will need to reevaluate how his behaviour may be sabotaging client progress.

Need for Status or Prestige. Counsellors who have an excessive need to impress others, perhaps because of insecurity, may become technique-centred instead of client-centred. With this switch in priorities, the needs of the client may be overlooked as counsellors act to impress clients or others. The priority of counselling should be to bolster the self-esteem of clients.

Need for Control. Codes of ethics recognize that clients are vulnerable to exploitation. Consequently, substantial attention is given to prohibiting behaviours that will result in undue control of clients. The principle of self-determination (introduced earlier in this chapter) is a basic value that upholds the right of clients to make independent decisions. Counsellors interfere with this right when they attempt to take over clients' problems and orchestrate their solutions.

In some settings, such as government agencies, counsellors may have the legal mandate to impose their services. This situation requires counsellors to be especially vigilant. As Brammer and MacDonald observe, helpers in these settings "must be wary of identifying too closely with the power of the agency under the guise of carrying out the agency's mission. Often the helpee becomes lost in such settings, and the helping services tend to support the power of the organization. The result may be an exaggerated emphasis on adjustment or pacification rather than on actualization and liberation" (1999:40).

Perfectionism. Perfectionism, an unrealistic pursuit of excellence, can negatively affect counselling. Counsellors who are perfectionists may be unable to realistically appraise their work, and they may have an unjustified tendency to blame themselves for client failures. Sometimes, counsellors who are perfectionists push clients toward unrealistic goals or challenge them to move at too fast a pace.

Unmet Social Needs. Counsellors with unmet social needs risk overinvolvement with clients. If counsellors do not have outlets in their own lives for social interaction, they may misuse the counselling relationship for that purpose.

Effect on Clients

Counsellors need to take time to discover how clients are reacting to them. Personal needs and defence mechanisms may lead counsellors to blindly assume that problems in the counselling relationship arise from their clients' inadequacies or failings. Although effective counsellors have confidence in their own abilities, they know and accept that occasionally they may say or do the wrong thing. Counsellors need to be mature and open enough to evaluate their work and to take responsibility for their errors and insensitivities. For example, open-minded counsellors consider the possibility that clients may be angry for good reason, perhaps because of oppressive agency routines.

Counsellors who lack self-awareness may fail to understand or accept the needs of their clients, and they are more likely to take their clients' behaviour too personally. As Wells and Masch remark, "Clients who should be open, confiding, and grateful for assistance often aren't—and often with good reason. The untrained worker, however, remains unaware of the reasons and ultimately feels like a failure, very angry, or even ill-used and burned-out" (1991:19). Ultimately, counsellors need to be self-aware enough to know which client reactions are reactions to their behaviour or personalities and which client reactions are the result of other variables beyond their control.

Self-aware counsellors know their skill strengths and limitations. This self-awareness enables them to consciously avoid overusing particular skills simply because they are strengths, and it helps them to know when it is appropriate to refer clients to other counsellors. It also helps them to set goals for professional skill development. Knowing the limits of one's ability is a measure of competence.

Work and personal stress may negatively affect a counsellor's capacity to relate effectively to clients. Counsellors must be aware of situations that are stressful and understand how they react to them. Self-aware counsellors avoid or reduce stressors, or they develop personal wellness plans for coping with the inevitable demands of the job.

Personal and Cultural Values

Counsellor self-knowledge of personal values and preferences is indispensable for effective counselling. Values constitute a frame of reference for understanding and assessing clients and for making decisions and choices.

Self-awareness of personal values is an important element of competence. All counsellors have personal values, and it is crucial that they understand what these values are in order to avoid imposing them on clients. Self-awareness of personal values is a first step for counsellors to manage the bias that comes from interpreting clients' behaviour from their own perspectives or cultures rather than from the clients'.

Cultural self-awareness refers to knowledge of the customs, traditions, role expectations, and values of one's culture of origin. Language is a particularly important variable. The word authority will have very different meaning for individuals who come from totalitarian countries and for those who come from democracies. Cultural self-awareness prepares counsellors to recognize and value the diversity of other cultures. Such awareness needs to be accompanied by a belief that one's own ethnic group is only one of many and that there are other appropriate beliefs and behaviours.

It is inevitable that the personal values of counsellors will influence how they assess clients, the techniques and procedures they use, and the goals that they deem reasonable, including which topics will get more or less attention. Moreover, certain topics are more value charged (e.g., abortion, assisted suicide, sexual orientation, religion, abuse), and the beliefs of counsellors may bias their work in these areas. For example, counsellors who find that they never discuss sexuality in their counselling work need to find out why. Are they avoiding this topic because of personal inhibitions? Are they unconsciously judging the sexual behaviour of their clients?

One way for counsellors to address this problem is to disclose their values to their clients. However, they should do this in such a way that clients do not feel pressured to adopt similar values. Clients should feel free to maintain their own values without fear that they are in some way disappointing their counsellors.

A counsellor's value system is an important variable that influences the methods and outcomes of counselling. In general, counsellors are most effective when their values reflect an optimistic and nonjudgmental view of people. Intellectually and emotionally, they accept and treasure the widest possible variations in lifestyle. They believe in the inherent strength and capacity of people and in their intrinsic right to freedom of choice. Table 2.6 on page 60 examines some of the values that might impede or enhance counsellors' effectiveness. When counsellors have values that hinder, they are more likely to find themselves behaving contrary to the ethics of the field, such as by acting in ways that inhibit self-determination or by failing to respect the dignity of their clients. Conversely, counsellors who have values that enhance their ability are more naturally inclined to support the ethics of the profession, and they are more likely to behave in ways that empower.

Table 2.6   Values, Beliefs, and Attitudes that Help and Hinder Counsellors' Effectiveness

Values That Hinder	Values That Help
To accept help from others is a sign of weakness.	To accept help is a sign of strength.
Some people are just not deserving of our respect or caring.	Everyone has intrinsic worth and the capacity to be productive.
People are inherently evil. Unless you are careful, they will take advantage of you.	People are essentially good.
I know what is best for my clients.	People are capable of finding their own answers and making decisions.
It is essential that my clients like me.	The purpose of counselling is to help clients exercise choice, not to make clients like me.
I've been there myself, so I know what my clients are feeling.	I can't know what my clients are feeling until I take the time to let them teach me.
People are incapable of changing.	People can and do change.
My religion/culture/viewpoint is the best.	I can accept a wide variety of cultures, religions, and viewpoints.
In this world, it's survival of the fittest.	We depend on one another and we have a responsibility to help others.
Counsellors have a right to impose service when it is in their clients' best interest.	Clients have a right to refuse service.

Summary

Professional codes of ethics define the acceptable limits of behaviour for professionals. These codes recognize the potential vulnerability of clients and seek to protect them from misuse of position and power by professionals. Every counselling profession has its own code of ethics, but certain core principles are common: they put the needs of clients first, and they strictly prohibit sexual and exploitive relationships.

Ethics are the principles and rules of acceptable conduct. Ethical principles are derived from values, or what individuals and groups consider appropriate or worthwhile. The values of the counselling profession are rooted in a few basic principles: belief in the dignity and worth of people, respect for diversity, and respect for the client's right to self-determination. The principle of self-determination values the right of clients to have control and autonomy over matters that affect their lives. The needs of clients are foremost.

Confidentiality is an integral part of ethical practice. Confidentiality can be absolute, meaning that information is not shared with anyone, or it can be relative and shared for legal and operational reasons. Most client communication is subject to relative confidentiality, as legal constraints may require reporting. As well, the internal operation of the agency necessitates some sharing of information.

An ethical dilemma exists when a choice must be made between competing values. Five principles can be considered when resolving ethical dilemmas: autonomy, beneficence, nonmaleficence, justice, and fidelity. Ethical decision making involves weighing the five principles and deciding which ought to have priority in a given situation.

Although it is recognized that counsellors' values will influence their work, counsellors need to be objective and to understand their clients without allowing their personal views, feelings, or preferences to contaminate their counselling role. Objectivity is the capacity of counsellors to understand situations and people without bias or distortion. Counsellors can lose their objectivity by making assumptions, overidentifying with clients, and becoming overly involved with their clients.

Counsellors need to work at an optimum level for each client regardless of their own feelings or reactions. They need to work within the limits of their competence by using techniques and strategies that they are qualified to deliver and that have a reasonable chance of success.

Self-awareness is essential in order for counsellors to work with objectivity. Self-aware counsellors know themselves—their feelings, thoughts, behaviour, personal needs, and areas of vulnerability. They understand how they affect clients, and they know the limits of their competence. They can answer the question "Who am I?"

Exercises

1. Can we promise our clients absolute confidentiality? Why or why not?

2. What are some advantages and disadvantages to allowing clients access to files?

3. Under what conditions would you make exceptions to the principle of self-determination?

4. Consider the following questions of ethical decision making. Imagine that you are the counsellor in each of the following situations. Use chapter concepts including the CCA's six-step approach to guide your thinking.

   a. An elderly, frail woman suffering from inoperable cancer decides to kill herself.

   b. A client decides to give his life's savings to his church.

   c. A client boasts that if his girlfriend tries to leave him, he will kill her.

   d. A client from a counselling relationship that terminated six months ago phones to ask you for a date. (Imagine that you are not in a current relationship.)

   e. Your client leaves your office in anger, determined to "teach my wife a lesson for the way she treated me."

   f. Knowing that you are in the market for a new car, your client, a used-car salesperson, offers to help you buy a car for wholesale price.

   g. A client inquires about your sexual orientation.

   h. Your client asks for your e-mail address so that he can keep in touch.

   i. Your client, a bisexual male, has tested HIV positive but informs you that he does not wish to tell his wife. He says that he will practise safe sex. (Variation:

Imagine that you receive a call from the client's wife. She says she is concerned about her husband and asks whether you think her husband might be gay.)

j. Your colleagues begin to talk about a client. You are with them at a local restaurant.

k. One of your colleagues tells you that she has just returned from a one-day workshop on hypnosis. She says that she can hardly wait to try it on some clients.

l. You encounter one of your colleagues having lunch with a client. You notice that they are drinking a bottle of wine.

m. You have an erotic dream about one of your clients.

n. While you are counselling a student (in your role as school counsellor), he discloses that he is selling marijuana to classmates. (Would your answer be different if you were a counsellor in a community agency unconnected to the school?)

o. You are a counsellor working with a young, gay client. He has been socially isolated and is slow to trust anyone, but over time you have managed to form a strong working relationship. Imagine that he approaches you with a request that you walk with him in the annual gay pride parade. What variables would you consider in making your decision? What are the implications of going with him? What are the implications of not going?

p. Your client is down to her last two dollars. She offers to buy your coffee. Do you accept? What are the implications of your decision?

q. Your car is broken and requires an expensive repair. Your client has been struggling to set up a mobile repair service, but business has been slow. He offers to fix your car for a discounted price. Do you accept? Why or why not?

5. Consider the following case study. A good friend invites you to a small dinner party. When you arrive you are introduced to the other guests, including a woman client. You have been seeing her and her husband for the past year for marital counselling. You note that her companion for the evening is not her husband. From observing their behaviour, there is no doubt that this is a romantic relationship. She has never mentioned this relationship in the past.

a. What would you do for the rest of the evening?

b. Do you have an obligation to disclose this relationship to the woman's husband?

c. If she asks you to keep your knowledge of this relationship from her husband, could you continue to see them for marital counselling?

6. Assess the extent to which you believe that each of the following counsellor behaviours might be acceptable. Use the following rating scale:

5 = always
4 = often
3 = sometimes
2 = seldom
1 = never

Be prepared to defend your answer. How might your answer vary depending on the circumstances?

____ seeing a client after having had one alcoholic drink

____ accepting an invitation for dinner at a client's home

___ hugging a client

___ inviting a former client to a party at your home

___ dating a former client

___ having sex with a client

___ driving your client home

___ discussing your client with a supervisor

___ assisting a client to end his or her life

___ accepting a client's decision to commit suicide

___ allowing your teenager to babysit for your client

___ buying a car from your client

___ lending money to a client

___ reporting your client to the police (after the client tells you that he or she committed a crime)

___ reporting suspected child abuse by your client

___ sharing personal experiences, feelings, problems, and so on, with your client

___ getting angry with your client

___ discussing a client with your family or friends (without mentioning names)

___ giving a present to a client or receiving a present from a client

___ sharing information about clients with other counsellors

___ warning a person that your client has threatened to harm him- or herself

___ telling a client's partner that he or she is HIV positive

___ advising a client to leave an abusive marriage

___ crying in the presence of a client

___ counselling a friend or neighbour at your agency

(adapted from Shebib, 1997)

7. Give examples of appropriate physical contact between social workers and clients. Be prepared to justify your answer.

8. The case recording below is excerpted from a case record completed by a social work student. Use the CCA and CASW codes to evaluate the appropriateness of the language used.

   I visited the Smith home to investigate allegations of child neglect. I was met at the door by Mrs. Smith, a single parent. I was surprised by her size; she was morbidly obese and smelled as if she hadn't showered in weeks. Rolls of fat hung out of Mrs. Smith's shirt, and portions of her legs were covered with dirt. Mrs Smith's slovenly appearance suggests she is unable to care for herself, much less her children (Reamer, 1998:93).

9. Explore the issues involved in discussing clients with friends and relatives. Is it acceptable to discuss clients if you change their names and other identifying data? Defend your answer.

10. Should some clients be forced to attend counselling?

11. Do you think black humour is ethical? Defend your answer.

12. What strong beliefs do members of your cultural/ethnic group hold?

13. Use the questions and situations below to examine your values related to sexual orientation issues.

    a. If your client were gay or lesbian, how might it influence the way you work with him or her?

    b. What would you do if a friend told you an antihomosexual joke or story? What if the person telling the joke were a client or a colleague?

    c. Do you have gay or lesbian friends?

    d. Do you think homosexuality is an illness?

    e. Your daughter discloses that she is lesbian. Predict how you might feel, think, and behave.

    f. Your best friend confides that he feels he is the wrong gender.

    g. What are your views on same-sex marriage?

14. Write an essay answering the question "Who am I?"

15. Explore your views regarding the following value-charged issues:

    a. Are people basically good or bad?

    b. Should people have the right to take their own lives?

    c. What religion(s) are acceptable?

    d. Should immigrants be required to speak the language of their new homeland?

16. The following questions will help you to examine your values and beliefs. Work in a small group to explore and debate your answers. Use this process as a tool to reevaluate your position on matters you deem important.

    a. What are the characteristics of the client you would most want to work with? (Be specific regarding as many variables as possible, such as age, gender, personality, culture, and religion.) Why would you choose these characteristics?

    b. What are the characteristics of the client you would least want to work with (e.g., age, gender, personality, culture, religion)?

    c. What topics or issues are likely to evoke strong personal reactions from you?

    d. What does authority mean to you? How do you behave and feel when you are relating to people in authority?

    e. In your opinion, what is the meaning of life?

    f. Where do you draw your strength?

    g. When you die, what do you most want to be remembered for?

17. Examine your reasons for wanting to become a counsellor. What needs do you expect to meet through your work? In what ways might your personal needs be an impediment?

18. What are your five most important values?

19. Work in a small group to explore your spiritual values through the following questions.

    a. Are religions basically good or bad?

    b. Are some religions better than others?

    c. Should cults be illegal?

    d.   What does spirituality mean to you?

    e.   Should spiritual issues be introduced by counsellors?

    f.   When is it appropriate to discuss religion with clients?

    g.   What are the implications of your religious views when working with someone with a similar perspective and when working with someone with radically different view?

20. Explore your personal strengths and limitations. Use the following topics to structure your assessment:

- capacity to be assertive (as opposed to shyness or aggressiveness)
- degree of self-confidence
- comfort dealing with a wide range of emotions
- need to control or be in charge
- capacity to relate to diverse populations (age, gender, culture, religion, etc.)
- ability to give and receive feedback (positive and critical)
- need to be helpful
- anxieties and fears
- competence in initiating relationships (beginnings)
- ability to deal with conflict
- self-awareness regarding how others see you
- overall awareness of personal strengths and limitations
- values and attitudes that will help or hinder your work as a counsellor
- capacity and willingness to change

Based on your answers, identify what you consider to be your five major strengths and your five major limitations.

21. Evaluate your capacity for handling feedback from others. Are you generally open and nondefensive when others critically evaluate your behaviour or performance? Do you tend to avoid asking for feedback, or do you actively solicit it? Interview friends and colleagues to see if their opinions on how you respond to feedback agree with your self-evaluation.

22. Are you excessively dependent on your clients? Rate each statement below and rate yourself using the following scale:

4 = always
3 = frequently
2 = sometimes
1 = rarely
0 = never

    ____ a.   I often feel responsible for the feelings, thoughts, and behaviour of my clients.

    ____ b.   I get angry when my help is rejected.

    ____ c.   I feel worthless and/or depressed when clients don't change.

    ____ d.   I feel compelled to help people solve problems by offering unwanted advice.

    ____ e.   I want to take care of my clients and protect them from painful feelings.

___ f.   When clients don't like me, I feel rejected or inadequate.

___ g.   I do things to make my clients like me, even if what I do is not helpful.

___ h.   I avoid confronting or challenging clients.

___ i.   I tell clients what they want to hear.

___ j.   I feel most safe when I'm giving to others.

___ k.   When clients fail, I take it personally.

___ l.   I spend an excessive amount of time trying to prove to myself and my clients that I'm good enough.

___ m.   I tend to be very controlling with clients.

___ n.   I tolerate abuse from clients to ensure they keep liking me.

___ o.   I feel responsible for solving my clients' problems.

Interpretation: Carefully review any statements that you scored 4 or 3. See whether there are any patterns in your behaviour and in the beliefs that you hold. Are you able to identify particular ways that you are dependent on your clients? What self-defeating thoughts are associated with each? Use your awareness of problem areas to develop a program of self-change by following this process:

- Think about where you are vulnerable.
- Set some change goals.
- Develop a concrete action plan to achieve your goals.
- Develop a plan to learn about the cultures in your community.
- Develop a plan to increase your understanding of world religions.

23. Imagine that you are a client. What might your counsellor need to know about you (e.g., values, needs, preferences) in order to work effectively with you?

24. How do you deal with the demands of an increasingly diverse society?

25. Take an inventory of your friendship circle. To what extent do your friends come from the same cultural and values base as your own? Predict what might happen if you broadened your circle to include more diversity.

Weblinks

The Canadian Counselling Association site contains links to Canadian counselling and mental health professional associations as well as guidance and professional development information.
www.ccacc.ca/ccacc.htm

The Canadian Association of Social Workers site has links and information for social workers.
www.casw-acts.ca/framepg1.htm

This British site provides resources for those interested in counselling ethics and philosophical issues related to counselling.
members.aol.com/timlebon/counsethics.htm

RELATIONSHIP: THE FOUNDATION FOR CHANGE

PREVIEW

After reading this chapter you should be able to:

- Define the characteristics of a counselling relationship.
- List the essential relationship-building objectives of each of the four phases of counselling.
- Explain the importance of the core conditions of warmth, empathy, and genuineness.
- Describe the core conditions.
- Describe the counselling contract.
- Demonstrate the ability to negotiate a counselling contract.
- Define immediacy.
- Use basic immediacy skills.
- Explain how transference and countertransference influence counselling relationships.
- Describe the importance of empowering clients.
- Explain the importance of relationship endings.

WHAT IS A COUNSELLING RELATIONSHIP?

A **counselling relationship** is a time-limited period of consultation between a counsellor and one or more clients in order to assist the client in achieving a defined goal. Developing and sustaining an effective counselling relationship is widely accepted as critical to success in counselling (Kadushin, 1990; Shilling, 1984; Shulman, 1992; Rogers, 1980; Young, 1998). In fact, the relationship itself is often viewed as having primary importance (Kadushin, 1990). Capuzzi and Gross conclude that "specific procedures and techniques are much less important than the alliance between counselor and client" (1997:65). Almost 40 years ago, Carl Rogers (1961) emphasized that a counsellor's attitudes and feelings are more important than technique and noted that the client's perception of the counsellor's attitudes is what is most crucial.

Young echoes these sentiments: "Without a strong therapeutic alliance, the goals of therapy cannot be reached" (1998:155). Moreover, the quality of the counselling relationship is a major determinant of whether the client will continue with counselling (Brammer and Shostrom, 1982).

Rogers, in his counselling classic, *Client-Centered Therapy* (1951), described the experience of a client who successfully completed counselling. This success followed an unsuccessful experience with another counsellor. The second counsellor asked the client why he had been able to work through his problems on his second attempt. The client responded, "You did about the same things he did, but you seemed really interested in me" (Rogers, 1951:69).

Counselling relationships are not always comfortable. In fact, as Keith-Lucas proposes, "The attempt to keep the relationship on a pleasant level is the greatest source of ineffectual helping known" (1972:18). The helping relationship provides the necessary security for clients to disclose their feelings and ideas. As trust develops in relationships, so does the capacity of clients to become increasingly open to revealing themselves. Drawing from the strength of their relationships with counsellors, clients may risk new ways of thinking and behaving, and in this way the relationship becomes the medium for change. In positive counselling relationships, clients perceive their counsellors as allies. Clients become increasingly willing to disclose because they do not fear that they will be rejected, judged, or coerced to change in ways that they find unacceptable. In its purest form, the counselling relationship becomes a collaborative endeavour.

Counselling relationships have some of the same components of intimacy, caring, and support that characterize deep personal relationships. High-level communication skills are as important to friendships as they are to counselling. In fact, many of the skills of counselling are also the skills of effective everyday communication. Friendships grow out of mutual attraction and common interest, whereas counselling relationships focus on helping clients achieve goals such as resolving crises, making decisions, and learning new skills. Counselling relationships are structured for the primary purpose of reaching these goals, and once the clients have achieved them, the counselling relationships are terminated.

Personal relationships can be terminated for personal reasons. However, counsellors are expected to persist in their efforts on behalf of clients even when they are frustrated by lack of progress or client resistance. Counselling may be ended when there is little likelihood of reaching its goals, but not simply because the counsellor prefers other clients. One measure of professionalism is the capacity of the practitioner to sustain commitment, patience, and caring despite frustrating obstacles.

CREATING A COUNSELLING RELATIONSHIP

Rogers (1961) asserted the importance of seeing others as "becoming." This notion underscores a fundamental belief in the capacity of people to change. Clients are not bound by their past, and counsellors should not use diagnosis and classification as tools for depersonalizing clients and treating them as objects. In counselling, clients need to be seen for their potential, strength, inner power, and capacity to change. Rogers' philosophy continues to have an enormous impact on counselling thought and procedures. His convictions suggest a number of questions for counsellors to ponder regarding their attitudes and behaviour in helping relationships:

- *How can I act so that clients will perceive me as trustworthy?* This means counsellors do what they say they will do and act in a way that is consistent with how they feel. It requires counsellors to communicate without ambiguity and contradiction.

- *Can I permit myself to experience positive attitudes of warmth, caring, liking, interest, and respect toward clients?*

- *Can I be strong enough as a person to be separate from my clients?* This requires a high level of maturity, self-awareness, and courage. Rogers summarizes this challenge:

  Am I strong enough in my own separateness that I will not be downcast by his depression, frightened by his fear, nor engulfed by his dependency? Is my inner self hardy enough to realize that I am not destroyed by his anger, taken over by his need for dependence, nor enslaved by his love, but that I exist separate from him with feelings and rights of my own? (1961:52)

- *Am I secure enough to permit clients their separateness?* Clients are not under counsellors' control, nor are they to be moulded as models of what counsellors feel they should be.

- *Can I let myself fully empathize with my clients' feelings and world perspectives without evaluating or judging?*

The Phases of Counselling

Each of the four phases of counselling—preliminary, beginning, action, and ending—has associated relationship tasks and challenges (Shebib, 1997). In all phases, counsellors need to develop effective skills and attitudes for engaging and retaining clients, including the following: sincerity, perceptiveness, honesty, respect for diversity, capacity to initiate conversations, ability to be a good listener, comfort with discussing feelings, empathy, ability to communicate confidence without conceit, and warmth.

Preliminary Phase. The goal of the preliminary phase is to create the necessary physical and psychological conditions for the relationship to begin. The counselling environment (e.g., agency setting, office layout, reception procedures) can have a dramatic impact on the client's mood and expectations even before the interview begins (Kadushin, 1990; Shebib, 1997). Preliminary phase work attempts to create first impressions that say to clients, "You will be respected here. You are important. This is a place where you will be supported."

Beginning Phase. The relationship goal in the beginning phase is to develop rapport, trust, and a working contract, or agreement regarding the purpose of the work and the roles of the participants. The relationship at this phase must provide enough safety for clients that they will engage and continue with counselling. Counsellors create this environment of safety by communicating that they do not judge the client and that change can occur. The relationship enables clients to feel sufficiently free to take on the first risks of counselling—sharing their feelings and concerns.

Action Phase. In the action phase, the relationship continues to develop and strengthen, and new counselling risks are taken as clients find the courage and strength to change their ways of thinking, feeling, and behaving. During this phase, relationship work may need to focus on addressing communication problems, including, at times, tension, or conflict.

Ending Phase. Termination of the counselling relationship comes when counselling has served its purpose and clients have reached their goals. Termination focuses on reviewing the work accomplished, helping clients consolidate learning, and saying goodbye.

Core Conditions

Truax and Carkhuff (1967) built on the work of Carl Rogers (1951, 1961, 1980) and defined three aspects of attitude as prerequisites to forming and maintaining effective helping relationships: warmth, empathy, and genuineness. Knowledge and skill are critical to success in counselling, but it is important to remember that clients will "not pay attention to how much the worker knows until they know how much he or she cares" (Sheafor, Horejsi, and Horejsi, 1991:83). Although counsellors can use certain behaviours and skills to demonstrate core conditions, the conditions must represent the authentic values and attitudes of counsellors. When counsellors exhibit these core conditions, the potential for positive relationships with clients is increased. However, there is no guarantee that clients will interpret warmth, genuineness, and empathy (or any communication) in the way that they were intended. Prior experiences and expectations, as well as cultural and individual differences, can easily lead to discrepancies in how communication is perceived. Counsellors can expect to be rejected as least some of the time despite their best efforts. A client may perceive empathy as an intrusive attempt to "get into my head" and caring as manipulation. Secure professionals accept this reality, knowing that considerable resistance may be encountered as they work to develop the helping relationship.

Warmth. Rogers (1961) urged counsellors to shun any tendency to keep clients at a distance by treating them as objects with detailed diagnostic labels. Instead, he argued that counsellors need to learn that it is safe to express their **warmth** and to let clients know that they care. Warmth, although a difficult concept to define, is an expression of nonpossessive caring. As Mehr interprets it:

> People who lack warmth are described as cold, uncaring, or uninvolved. Thus, warmth implies involvement. The expression of warmth requires a non-judgmental attitude and an avoidance of blaming. Warmth involves acceptance of the equal worth of others ... Nonpossessive warmth entails a feeling of caring and concern without placing conditions on the relationship. (1998:182)

Warmth is a precursor to trust. It attracts clients to take risks because it indicates the goodwill and motivation of their counsellors. In the beginning, clients often come to counselling reluctantly, perhaps driven by external pressure or by the weight of their problems. The first task of treatment, then, is to find a way of communicating cues to the counsellor's attitude so the client will engage with the work and return for subsequent visits. Warmth seems to say, "I'm approachable, you don't need to be afraid of me. I won't take advantage of your vulnerability. I'm a kind person." As a result, warmth is particularly important during the formative or beginning stage of the relationship. Warmth is also crucial for supporting clients during a crisis, and it is a necessary partner to caring confrontation. Clients will be more receptive to receiving feedback when they are persuaded that it originates from a caring attitude.

Although the nature of warmth can be defined behaviourally to some extent, it must arise from genuine feelings of caring for the client. Otherwise, the counsellor's actions will appear lacking in genuineness. Warmth is demonstrated by smiling appropriately and by showing sincere interest in the comfort of the client. Counsellors show warmth when they communicate nonverbally that they are totally focused on their clients. Simple courtesies, such as eliminating distractions from the interview, asking clients if they are physically comfortable, offering them a beverage, and making eye contact, convey warmth. Well-timed humour can also add a warm touch to the interview.

Brammer and MacDonald suggest flexibility in the amount of expressed warmth and caring depending on the comfort level of clients. From their research, they conclude, "From a multicultural perspective, overt expression of emotion must be used sensitively. Asian American helpees might be quite uncomfortable receiving strongly emotional care, especially early in the relationship. In the Hispanic American culture, overt warmth might be more acceptable between female helpers and helpees, but not so for males" (1999:32).

Being warm doesn't preclude dealing with difficult topics. Nor does it imply that a great deal of the interview needs to be spent making small talk, as one might do during a social visit.

Sometimes in busy social service agencies caseloads become unmanageable and the pace of the work is frantic. Constant crises and unrelenting paperwork can exhaust even the most energetic and caring workers, who may begin to lose the "spark" they had when they first entered the field. Unless controlled, the office routine can begin to feel more like an assembly line than a counselling service, as clients become numbers and the work becomes increasingly task oriented. How does one continue to feel and express warmth under such conditions? The answer must be discovered individually, but we can learn something from the observations of one worker, a senior caseworker with over 25 years' experience.

> What works for me is to remind myself that no matter how overwhelmed I feel, it's worse for my clients. Often, they're broke, in crisis and not sure whether they want to live and die. They don't need me to be part of the problem. What doesn't work for me is to get caught up in coffee room negativism. You know what it's like—the ones who never have anything good to say and always expect things to get worse. It also helps if I take a few moments, sometimes precious seconds, between interviews to meditate. When I meet my client, I try to spend some time just being friendly.

Empathy. Empathy describes the capacity to understand the feelings and views of another person. Empathic attitudes and skills can generate powerful bonds of trust and rapport. With empathic skill, counsellors are able to communicate understanding and acceptance to their clients. An empathic attitude is characterized by one's willingness to learn about the world of another and begins with suspending judgment. To be nonjudgmental requires considerable discipline in controlling personal biases, assumptions, and reactions that might contaminate understanding. "Without judging (or perhaps even liking) a client, the worker tries to understand the person's problem, accepting feelings without necessarily condoning his or her acts" (Schram and Mandell, 1997:123).

Counsellors need to be able to enter the emotional world of their clients without fear of becoming trapped in their pain. Counsellors who are secure with themselves and their feelings have the capacity to enter their clients' worlds without fear of losing their own identity. Brill notes that when a counsellor communicates acceptance, the client has "freedom to be oneself—to express one's fears, angers, joy, rage, to grow, develop, and change—without concern that doing so will jeopardize the relationship" (1998:97).

Chapter 6 explores the skills of communicating empathy, but a preview of the components of this important skill is provided here. Empathic skill has two components. First, counsellors must be able to perceive their clients' feelings and perspectives. This requires counsellors to have abundant self-awareness and emotional maturity so that they do not contaminate their clients' experience with their own. As Garvin and Seabury observe, "The concept of empathy relates to the act of experiencing something in a manner similar to another person while still retaining a sense of who one is and what one's separate responses may be" (1984:110).

The second component of empathy is to make an empathic response. This involves putting in words the feelings that the client has expressed. This task can be particularly difficult, since clients often communicate their feelings in abstract, ambiguous, or nonverbal ways. Empathic responses require a vocabulary of words and phrases that can be used to precisely define feelings. At a basic level, empathic responses acknowledge obvious and clearly expressed feelings. At a more advanced or inferred level, empathic responses are framed from hints and nonverbal cues.

Genuineness. Being genuine means one is authentic and real in a relationship. Counsellors who are genuine show high consistency between what they think and do, and between what they feel and express. Rogers (1961) used the term congruent to describe this quality and emphasized the importance of self-awareness to unambiguous communication. Counsellors need to be aware of how they are feeling and how they are transmitting their feelings in order to avoid giving contradictory messages.

Counsellors who are genuine are highly trustworthy. They don't lie to clients. They are willing to provide feedback that is timely and helpful. They show respect for clients by being open and honest while maintaining warmth and empathy in the relationship. They do not work from hidden agendas, nor do they put on "masks" or play roles to hide their true feelings. As well, genuine counsellors are reliable. They do what they say they are going to do. Mehr offers this perspective on arriving at genuineness or congruence: "Awareness is the first step toward achieving congruence between internal experiences and outward behavior. Genuineness also, however, requires the maturity and skills to be able to express these feelings in the context of a warm and empathic relationship" (1998:183).

Benjamin (1981) emphasizes the importance of being human in the interview and discarding false facades or professional equipment that might create distance and barriers in the relationship. "If the interviewer is remote and cold, can the interviewee be expected to come close and be warm? When the interviewer is cautious and wary, can the interviewee be unguarded? Will the latter be free to express openly his thoughts and feelings to someone barricaded behind a wall of professionalism?... We must be sincere, genuine, congruent—not act so, but be so" (53–54).

CONVERSATION 3.1

GENUINENESS

STUDENT: How far should I go with genuineness? What if I'm angry with my client? Should I say so? Or suppose I find my client disgusting. Should I express that too?

TEACHER: You've identified an important dilemma. On the one hand, the need for genuineness suggests that we should be open and honest with our clients. We shouldn't put on false fronts, lie to clients, or fake our feelings. At the same time, ethical principles clearly prohibit us from doing harm. Being genuine doesn't entitle counsellors to "dump" on their clients. Genuine counsellors are truthful, but they are also timely. They share personal perceptions and feelings in an assertive way in order to meet their clients' needs. They might express their anger, but they do so without intending to punish, ridicule, or trap their clients. As for feeling disgust toward a client, I can't see how sharing that information would serve any purpose. On the other hand, it may be useful to the client if you explored the specific behaviours or attitudes that gave rise to those feelings. With sensitive feedback, your client can have the benefit of learning about his or her impact on others. One final point: Strong reactions toward our clients may hint at our own vulnerabilities. If you find a client disgusting, I'd want to ask you, "Where does that feeling come from? Are you sure it is related only to the client?"

STUDENT: Maybe the client "pushes my buttons" the same way my father did.

TEACHER: Exactly.

THE CONTRACT

A **contract** is a negotiated agreement between the counsellor and the client regarding important variables that will define the work. Since clients and counsellors often have different ideas about the objectives and methods of counselling, it is important for them to reach understanding regarding the nature of the work (Gladding, 1996). Such understanding results in a contract that "helps clarify the counselor-client relationship and give it direction; protect the rights, roles, and obligations of both counselors and clients; and ensure the success of counseling" (Gladding, 1996:117).

The contract is like a route map that provides general directions on how to get from A to B. It confirms that all parties are working toward the same ends. When counsellors and their clients are working toward agreed-upon objectives, it is much more likely that clients will "own" the work, rather than see it as something that has been imposed on them. Contracting reduces suspicions that counsellors may have hidden agendas.

A counselling contract predicts an end point to the relationship. Defining tasks and goals makes it clear when the relationship should be ended. In this way, the counselling relationship is clearly distinguished from a friendship, which may last for a lifetime.

Shulman's (1992) research confirmed the importance of contracting to counselling success. In particular, his findings supported the relevance of helping clients participate in setting the contract. Egan underscores the empowering nature of contracting. He describes the contract as a kind of charter that can "give clients a flavor of the mechanics of the helping process, diminish initial client anxiety and reluctance, provide a sense of direction, and enhance clients' freedom of choice" (1998:56).

Contracts may be formal and signed by both the counsellor and the client, but more frequently they are informal and ratified with verbal agreement or a handshake. The simplest form of contract concerns agreement on the purpose of the interview or counselling relationship.

The essential elements of the contract include:

1. definition of the objective or purpose of the counselling relationship

If there is no agreement on the purpose of counselling, the work is apt to be directionless. Without agreed-upon purpose, counsellors tend to make assumptions about the needs and wants of their clients. The problem with assumptions is that they are so frequently wrong. The multiple purposes of counselling can include helping clients with problem solving, decision making, and managing feelings; providing support; giving information; and fostering skill acquisition.

2. discussion of the roles and expectations of the participants

Counsellors should know something about what clients want from them. Do clients expect them to provide advice on how to manage their problems? Do they want to be challenged with new information and new perspectives? Are they looking for someone who is warm, gentle, and supportive or someone who will just listen? Similarly, counsellors need to tell clients about any expectations they have of them. Role discussion may also address issues such as how the participants might address conflict and how they can provide feedback to each other.

3. discussion of the methods and routines of counselling

Counsellors do not need to work from a secret script with mysterious techniques that they hide from clients. Counsellors should develop their ability to describe their work in simple, nonjargonistic language. In this way, clients can know something about what is happening as well as what remains to be done.

4. practical details

These include issues such as the time and place of meetings and any fees for service. Ethical issues, including the limitations of confidentiality, are also part of the contract.

Home builders usually prewire new homes so that future installation of services such as cable television will be easy. In the same way, relationships can be "prewired" to make resolution of communication difficulties easier. Contracting strategies, such as discussing in advance how conflict will be addressed and working to develop and refine open communication, are the tools for prewiring relationships. If conflicts occur, a mechanism is already in place for resolving them.

Counsellors generally initiate contracting on the purpose of counselling early in the first interview. However, rigid adherence to a negotiated contract is hazardous. Counselling contracts need to be periodically revisited and updated as necessary. Clients may develop new insights that change their priorities. Increased trust may enable clients to address more difficult topics and feelings that they were unwilling to consider at the beginning of the relationship. As well, new problems and issues may emerge as a result of changing circumstances.

Contracting on the Roles and Purpose of Counselling

Every counselling agency has a purpose that defines and limits its service. Specialty agencies such as employment counselling centres may focus on career testing and job search skills, while a transition home may provide crisis counselling and shelter. A community centre might provide a broad range of counselling, education, and group support services.

Counsellors define and limit their role based on their position in the agency and their training. An intake worker, for example, may be restricted to initial screening and assessments, while a community outreach worker might specialize in reaching clients who do not voluntarily seek service.

Clients have specific wants and needs that may or may not mesh with the mandate of the agency or its workers. Abraham Maslow's (1954) famous hierarchy of needs can be a useful way of understanding client priorities. Maslow suggested that people normally seek to fulfill their basic needs before pursuing higher order needs. He arranged his hierarchy in the following order:

1. physiological or basic survival needs (air, water, and food)
2. safety needs (personal security, stability, protection, and freedom from fear)
3. belonging/love needs (relationships)
4. self-esteem needs (sense of worth and importance)
5. self-actualization needs (achieving one's full potential)

Maslow's theory can be useful reference for counsellors. As one counsellor put it, "You can't counsel a client who hasn't eaten." In simplest terms, counsellors need to begin by ascertaining where clients are in terms of unmet needs. As basic and higher order needs are met, the goals of counselling need to be adjusted accordingly.

Contracting explores three variables: agency, counsellor, and client. Contracting is viable when the client's needs match the agency's mandate and the counsellor's competence. When the service the client needs is beyond the mandate of the agency or the competence of the counsellor, referral to another counsellor or agency is appropriate.

The contracting process aspires to establish a relationship of equality between clients and counsellors, while recognizing each person's role. Zastrow's observation about social workers is relevant to understanding role:

> The expertise of the social worker does not lie in knowing or recommending what is best for the client. Rather, the expertise lies in assisting clients to define their problems, to develop and examine the alternatives for resolving the problems, to maximize the client's capacities and opportunities to make decisions for themselves, and to help clients to implement the decisions they make. (1990:62)

Clients may be aware of their pain and recognize and accept the need for change and help, but they may have no idea what form this help might take. In such situations, counsellors need to be able to help them understand the potential assistance that counselling can provide.

Some clients have unrealistic expectations of their counsellors or the process. They may believe that counsellors will tell them what to do and solve all their problems. Or they may have no faith in the process whatsoever. As Wicks and Parsons describe it, when people enter counselling, they often anticipate "either a miracle or complete failure" (1984:175). Contracting is a significant opportunity for demystifying the process and for challenging unreasonable positive or negative expectations. The following example is taken from the mid-point of a second interview. It illustrates how the counsellor gently encourages the client to reexamine some self-imposed restrictions on the relationship.

CLIENT: *Let's keep my feelings out of this. I simply want to look at ways to improve my relationship with my son. If you could teach me some techniques, I'd be most grateful.*

COUNSELLOR: *Of course you're entitled to privacy on issues or feelings that you don't want to share with me. At the same time, I wonder if you might be too hasty in restricting what we can discuss.*

CLIENT: *I don't get it. What do you mean?*

COUNSELLOR: *Well, you've been through a lot. With your son's arrest and his disappearance for over a month, I'd be surprised if you weren't feeling stress.*

CLIENT: *Who wouldn't?*

COUNSELLOR: *That's exactly my point. When I don't talk about feelings that are bothering me, I have to keep them inside or pretend they're not there. I've found that doesn't work. Sooner or later, I have to face my feelings.*

CLIENT: *I'm just afraid that if I start crying, I won't be able to stop.*

COUNSELLOR: *That tells me that the pain must be very deep. (silence as the client tears up)*

COUNSELLOR: *I won't push you, but I hope our relationship can become a safe place for you. It's okay with me if you cry.*

Many clients are slow to develop trust, perhaps for good reason. They may have lifelong experiences of betrayal or abuse by people they trusted. Why should it be any different with a counsellor? As a result, it is understandable that they approach counselling with a degree of mistrust. Wicks and Parsons provide a compelling observation: "Though there may seem to be a great distance between counselors and their clients during the beginning phase of counseling, they should not be discouraged because at that point their clients may be closer to them than anyone else" (1984:168). In fact, counsellors can foster relationship development if they try to match their responses to their clients (Huber and Backlund, 1991). For example:

CLIENT: *I really don't see the point in being here. My situation is hopeless. I've been to other counsellors and nothing worked. I'm only here because my wife insisted. She thought you might be able to help.*

COUNSELLOR (CHOICE 1): *You certainly do sound discouraged. But I think you should give counselling a chance. Maybe by talking about your problems we can discover some solutions you've overlooked.*

COUNSELLOR (CHOICE 2): *Given your past experiences, I can see why you're pessimistic. You're wise to be skeptical until you find out if you can trust me. In the end, the results will be the most important thing.*

In this example, Choice 1 is well meaning but ill timed. Responses such as this may "impede the client's cooperation ... especially if the client has already been discouraged by previous counselors who began treatment on a positive, optimistic note, only to end counseling efforts with no improvement" (Huber and Backlund, 1991:24). Choice 2, however, is not condescending and does not provide false hope.

Shulman (1992) emphasizes the need for workers to provide clear, nonjargonistic statements that describe the range of services available. This is particularly important in settings where the counsellor may be the one who initiates first contact. When the purpose of the meeting is explicit, clients do not have to worry about workers' hidden agendas, and they are in a more informed position to take advantage of assistance. In the example below, a school counsellor is attempting to engage with an 11-year-old boy who has transferred to the school in the middle of the academic year. His teacher, who is concerned that he seems depressed and alone, has referred him.

> **COUNSELLOR:** *My name is Mr. Smith. I'm here because your teacher thought I might be able to help you with some of the problems you're having at school. I know that it can be tough to be the new kid. Sometimes it's just not much fun. Maybe we could meet and see if we can figure out a way to make things better. What do you think?*

Interview 3.1 on page 78 illustrates part of the contracting process. The excerpt is taken from about the 15-minute mark of a first session with a parent of a teen who is abusing drugs. Sometimes, contracting can start very early in the interview. At other times, such as in this example, it is helpful to give clients some space to describe their feelings and problems before proceeding to contracting.

IMMEDIACY

Immediacy is a tool for exploring, evaluating, and deepening counselling relationships. The goal of immediacy is to strengthen the counselling relationship. Egan (1990; 1998) describes two major types of immediacy: relationship immediacy and here-and-now immediacy.

Relationship Immediacy

Relationship immediacy refers to the process of evaluating the general working climate of the counsellor–client relationship. The focus is not on a particular incident but on the way the relationship has developed and how it is helping or standing in the way of progress. "The relationship is evaluated or reviewed, and relationship strengths and weaknesses are examined by exploring the respective feelings, hopes, and frustrations of the parties involved" (Shebib, 1997:114).

Relationship immediacy might be used effectively when feelings such as anger, resentment, or resistance to the work seem to be adversely affecting the relationship. Similarly, positive feelings of liking or attraction might also need to be addressed if these feelings are clouding objectivity or progress. The example below illustrates how a counsellor might initiate relationship immediacy.

> **COUNSELLOR:** *I want to put aside what we've been talking about and take a look at what's happening between us. I think we have great rapport, and we both seem relaxed when we're together. But I believe I've become reluctant to be totally honest. Maybe it's because I don't want the relationship to become unpleasant. If I'm not mistaken, you seem to hold back too.*

INTERVIEW 3.1 CONTRACTING

DIALOGUE	ANALYSIS
Counsellor: This might be a good time to pause and talk about how we might work together. Then we'll both have a shared sense of direction.	A simple, nonjargonistic statement initiates the contracting process. The importance of contracting is identified.
Client: Yes, I was wondering where we go from here.	
Counsellor: Perhaps you have some ideas on what you'd like to achieve. I'd like to hear them, then, if you wish, I can add some of my own.	By seeking input, the counsellor communicates respect for the client's needs and signals that the counsellor is not going to take control and make all the decisions. This helps to empower the client and minimize any tendency for the client to become overly dependent.
Client: As I told you, my big goal is to keep my son alive. I don't want to receive a call from the hospital saying he has overdosed.	
Counsellor: Whether your son uses drugs is not under your control. But we could talk about some of the ways you could deal with his behaviour, like how to handle it when he breaks curfew or what to do when you think he's high.	The counsellor attempts to gently contain the work within areas that the client can control, namely her behaviour.
Client: That would be great! Those are two of my biggest problems.	The client's reaction confirms understanding and provides agreement on one target for work.
Counsellor: Obviously this is a time of stress for you. One of the ways I may be able to work with you is to help you deal with your feelings. Sometimes you might feel overwhelmed by everything that's happening, and I'd be happy just to listen or to help you sort out your feelings.	Counsellors can use statements of purpose to suggest additional ideas to help clients make the best use of the services available. In this statement, the counsellor attempts to introduce feelings as one of the areas on which counselling might focus.
Client: You have no idea how tough this has been for me as a single parent. My father was addicted to alcohol, and my son brings back all those memories.	The client's willingness to begin to share some of her feelings signals to the counsellor that she has accepted the offer to explore feelings.
Counsellor: So, you're no stranger to the pain that is caused by addiction.	Empathy is the preferred response to strong feelings.
(five minutes later)	

(continued)

Counsellor: What do you need and want from our relationship?

Client: I want you to be honest with me.

Counsellor: What do you mean?

Client: Don't try to spare my feelings. If you think I'm wrong, say so. Don't sugarcoat the truth.

Counsellor: So, if I have some ideas about how you might do things differently or another way of looking at things, I'll just tell you.

Client: Exactly.

Counsellor: Can I expect the same from you?

Client (hesitates): I guess so.

Counsellor: You seem unsure. Would it be tough to confront me if you thought I were wrong?

Client: I'm the kind of person who likes to keep those kinds of things inside.

Counsellor: Sometimes it makes sense to hold back. But it's better to have choices. I'd like to convince you to risk telling the truth to me. Then you can decide if that works better, at least in dealing with me.

(a few minutes later)

Client: About a year ago, I went to a family counsellor for help. That was a disaster.

Counsellor: You might be worried that this will turn out the same way.

Client: Yes.

Counsellor: Now I'm worried too. (counsellor and client laugh) Tell me what went wrong; then we can talk about how we can avoid the same problems here. Just tell me what happened, but don't tell me who your counsellor was.

This work sets the stage for feedback. It gives the counsellor a clear picture of the client's preferred style. Knowing this, the counsellor can tailor any feedback to fit the client's expectations. Notice that the counsellor makes no assumptions of meaning and asks the client to define the vague term "honest."

Later, if the counsellor wishes to challenge the client, he or she can use an introductory statement such as the following to remind the client of the contract: "Remember when we agreed that if I had some ideas that were different from yours, I should be honest." Because there has been prior agreement, the client is more likely to support the process and to be open to feedback or challenges.

Some clients have trouble dealing with persons in authority. Others are simply shy and have habitual patterns of taking a passive approach to relationship problems. The counselling relationship can be an opportunity to experiment with new ways of relating. When counsellors create conditions of safety for risk taking, clients can learn skills that they can transfer to other relationships.

The purpose of this process is not to engage the client in a gossip session about the mistakes of colleagues. Candid discussions about what was effective and ineffective provide important information on the client's expectations and fears for the current relationship. This gives the counsellor a chance to customize counselling to meet the needs and wants of the client. Reviewing the client's counselling history may enable both the client and the counsellor to learn and build on the mistakes of the past. Of course, this discus-

(continued)

Client: Well, for one thing, he never gave me any information. If I asked for a brochure or something on heroin, he'd always say sure, then he'd forget.

(a few minutes later)

Counsellor: Do you have any questions?

Client: Who gets to see my file?

sion must be conducted in a professional manner that does not involve maligning colleagues.

A little humour adds warmth to the relationship.

Discussion regarding the limits of confidentiality and any other ethical concerns that the client has can now be addressed.

Remember that the counselling contract should be reviewed on a regular basis. Exploration of problems may promote insight, and this may lead to changed expectations and revised goals. As the counselling relationship matures, the roles of counsellors and their clients must also evolve.

Here-and-Now Immediacy

Here-and-now immediacy focuses on counsellor–client interactions as they occur within the interview. With here-and-now immediacy, counsellors reveal their current feelings and perspectives. Here-and-now immediacy addresses and deals with relationship issues such as tension, lack of trust, and lack of direction in the session (Egan, 1998; Young 1998).

All relationships, including the counselling relationship, are occasionally tested with minor or serious personality conflicts and communication breakdowns. Describing the counselling relationship, Compton and Galaway conclude that "it is not necessarily pleasant or friendly; sometimes the problem is worked out in reaction and anger, in conflict as well as in collaboration or bargaining" (1994:226). Handled wisely, these conflicts have the potential to deepen rather than impair relationships.

Here-and-now immediacy is a tool for preventing communication breakdowns. By addressing relationship difficulties as they arise, more serious problems are prevented from developing from the build-up of unresolved feelings. This does not imply that every relationship issue must be explored. Here-and-now immediacy should address significant feelings and issues that affect the relationship as they occur, but it is important for counsellors to be sensitive to timing and pacing. Generally, here-and-now immediacy should not be introduced at the end of a session, when there is no time for resolution, or before sufficient trust has developed in the relationship. However, immediacy has the potential to build trust.

Counsellors can ensure the appropriateness of using here-and-now immediacy by asking: Would immediacy be useful for the client? Does the client have the capacity (personal strength and resources) to profit from immediacy at this time? Immediacy is a way to get closer to clients.

In the following example, the counsellor uses here-and-now immediacy to identify a sharp change in the mood of the interview.

EXAMPLE 1:

COUNSELLOR: *You seem to have become somewhat quiet. When I ask a question, you give me one- or two-word answers. Usually, you're quite expressive. Is something wrong?*

CLIENT: *Now that you mention it, yes. I'm just not sure how much I'm willing to trust you. At first it was okay, but now you seem intent on pushing me to deal with things I'd rather keep private.*

COUNSELLOR: *Perhaps I'm moving too fast or bringing up issues we haven't agreed to talk about.*

CLIENT: *Mostly, you don't take no for an answer. When I say I don't want to talk about something, I mean it.*

COUNSELLOR: *Like earlier today when I kept coming back to how you felt when you broke up with your wife.*

CLIENT: *That's a perfect example.*

COUNSELLOR: *I guess I was pushy. I knew you would rather avoid the topic. At the same time, I could see that there was so much pain involved that I thought it might be useful to talk about your feelings.*

CLIENT: *You're probably right. I should face it, but I'm afraid.*

When responding with immediacy, it is important to use **I-statements** to underscore responsibility and ownership of feelings. In general, the emphasis should be on statements such as "I'm uncomfortable," not "You make me feel uncomfortable."

EXAMPLE 2:

COUNSELLOR: *Let's stop for a moment. I'm feeling confused, and I'm not sure where we're headed. What's happening for you?*

CLIENT: *We do seem to be headed in circles. I'm lost too.*

COUNSELLOR: *All right, lets talk about how we can get back on track.*

In Interview 3.2 on page 82, the counsellor uses immediacy to address concerns that his client has become dependent. Initially, the client is reluctant to discuss this issue, but the counsellor's persistence sets the stage for the client to emerge with some important feedback. Changes in the relationship can then be negotiated. Moreover, the process models communication and relationship problem-solving skills that are transferable to other situations.

Transference

Transference is a concept first introduced by Freud to describe the tendency of clients to communicate with their counsellors in the same way that they communicated with significant people in the past. Transference can include reactions of both attraction and aversion. When

INTERVIEW 3.2 IMMEDIACY

DIALOGUE	ANALYSIS
Counsellor: I'd like to suggest that we take a few minutes to talk about you and me. I think it might be useful to look at what's working and what's not working.	The counsellor signals an interest in looking at the relationship and provides a brief rationale (relationship immediacy).
Client: I think it's been great. You always seem to know what to say. I don't know if I could cope if it weren't for you.	Many clients are uncomfortable with immediacy discussions, perhaps because of past failures. The client's praise of the counsellor may be justified, or it may be an attempt to avoid the issue.
Counsellor: Thanks. To be honest, I have mixed reactions to what you're saying. It's nice to be appreciated, but I'm also concerned. I wonder if by relying on me so much, it's becoming harder for you to do it on your own.	The counsellor discloses feelings (here-and-now immediacy).
Client: I can't do it on my own.	Without attempting to argue with the client, the counsellor gently persists in encouraging the client to look at the issue. The client is able to identify an important parallel to her relationship with her father (transference).
Counsellor: Okay, so you need help. Being able to seek and accept help is a sign of strength. My concern is that I may be doing things for you that you need to do yourself.	
Client: Now you sound like my father. He's always saying that I should stand on my own two feet more and not rely on him so much. But every time I try to be independent, he interferes.	
Counsellor: Does that happen between you and me?	
Client (hesitates): A little.	
Counsellor: Can you elaborate?	The counsellor uses a simple probe to make sure that he understands. An empathic response recognizes the client's **ambivalence**, or mixed feelings. Asking for an example is important to confirm that both counsellor and client have the same reference point.
Client: Don't get me wrong, I really want your help, but sometimes it seems like you've already decided what I should do. I figure that you probably know what is best, so I just go along with your plan.	
Counsellor: It sounds as though you have mixed feelings. On the one hand, you value my help, but at the same time I also sense some reluctance. I wonder if part of you knows it isn't	

(continued)

good for you if you don't have the freedom to make your own decisions.

Client: That's right.

Counsellor: Can you think of a recent example? I want to make sure I understand.

Client: Earlier today when I mentioned that I wanted to go back to school you were really supportive, and I appreciated that, but it seemed like you were bulldozing me to take art. I like to paint, but it's a hobby, not something I want to pursue as a career.

Counsellor: That's a good point. Thanks for the feedback. Let's talk about how we can change our relationship to avoid similar problems. I'll try to be more sensitive to interfering. I'll need your help. If you think I'm pushing, will you tell me?

Client: I promise to do that.

Immediacy enables the counsellor and the client to negotiate changes in their relationship.

transference is strong, clients have intense feelings and reactions that are unconnected to experiences with their counsellors. Transference is likely present when there are strong feelings of liking or disliking another person on the basis of first impressions (Young, 1998). For example, a client might relate to the authority of a counsellor with the same withdrawal and inner anger that characterized earlier relationships with family. In addition, as Egan notes, "Some of the difficulties clients have in their day-to-day relationships are also reflected in their relationships to helpers. For instance, if they are compliant outside, they are often compliant in the helping process. If they become aggressive and angry with authority figures outside, they often do the same with helpers" (1998:180).

Below are some examples of relationships in which client transference is apparent:

- Kevin desperately wants to be liked. He gives his counsellor unsolicited praise and gifts. Increasingly, he begins to act and talk like his counsellor.

- Claire suffered abuse from her father and both of her brothers. In the first session with a male counsellor, she immediately begins to cry, despite the fact that she felt optimistic and self-confident before she entered his office.

- Amar has a strong need for approval. He withholds information that he thinks might provoke the counsellor's disagreement.

- Jaimie, a six-year-old who has been abused, behaves in a sexually provocative way.

- Toby, age eighteen, has had a very strained relationship with his father. His counsellor notes how easily he becomes angry during the interview at the slightest provocation.

With transference, unresolved issues result in distortions in the way that others are perceived. Consequently, successful examination and resolution of counsellor–client relationship difficulties helps clients develop communication and problem resolution skills that will be useful to them in their daily lives. It is important that counsellors distinguish client reactions and feelings that arise from the current relationship from those that arise from transference. Counsellors should not be too quick to rationalize clients' feelings and behaviours as transference. Their clients' responses may be valid reactions to what has transpired in the counselling session.

Countertransference

Countertransference is the tendency of counsellors to inappropriately transfer feelings and behaviours to clients. Young views countertransference as an ethical issue that should be addressed by supervision so counsellors can get help to "monitor the tendency to be too helpful, and to deal with feelings of sexual attraction as well as anger, fear, and insecurity" (1998:169). Corey and Corey warn of the dangers of countertransference: "The emotionally intense relationships that develop with your clients can be expected to bring your unresolved conflicts to the surface. Because countertransference may be a form of identification with your client, you can easily get lost in the client's world, and thus your value as a helper becomes limited" (1989:94).

Countertransference issues are emotional reactions to clients, whereby counsellors come to see clients as projects, sexual objects, friends, or even extensions of themselves (Young, 1998:169). Below are some signs that countertransference is happening or that a risk for countertransference is present for counsellors:

- having intense feelings (e.g., irritation, anger, boredom, sexual attraction) for clients you hardly know
- feeling attraction or repulsion
- being reluctant to confront or tending to avoid sensitive issues or feelings
- continually running overtime with certain clients and wishing that others would not show up for scheduled appointments
- acting with rescuing behaviour, such as by wanting to lend money, adopt abused children, or protect clients
- being reminded by clients of other people you know
- dealing with clients who have similar problems or personal histories
- employing unnecessary or excessive self-disclosure
- feeling reluctant to end the counselling relationship

CONVERSATION 3.2

SELF-DISCLOSURE

STUDENT: I think that many counsellors misunderstand self-disclosure. Some of my colleagues make a point of telling their clients about their past, whereas others share little or nothing about their private lives.

TEACHER: Counsellor self-disclosure can be an important part of effective counselling. The problem is knowing what to share, how much to share, and when to share it.

STUDENT: I agree. I think some disclosure conveys that the counsellor is warm and human, and it helps clients overcome the common mistaken belief that they are the only ones with problems.

TEACHER: Self-disclosure models appropriate sharing of feelings and give clients the courage to open up. Some clients may feel reassured knowing that their counsellors have faced similar problems, but unless it's handled carefully, clients may see their counsellors as needy.

STUDENT: Back to your earlier statement. What do you share? How much? When?

TEACHER: The answers will vary depending on the client and the situation. In general, a moderate level of self-disclosure is appropriate (Cormier and Cormier, 1985), but some situations may warrant a great deal of self-disclosure, and some none at all. Depending on the situation, too much self-disclosure may be as bad as too little.

STUDENT: As I see it, the most important principle is that self-disclosure should be an option, not a compulsion. Counsellors need to be able to self-disclose, but they also should be able to constrain themselves from always disclosing. If the session is moving smoothly without self-disclosure, then it's probably unnecessary. Self-disclosure must strengthen the relationship or otherwise contribute to the work. The primary goal is to meet the client's needs.

TEACHER: For me, the most important principle is to avoid letting counsellor self-disclosure shift the focus of the interview from clients to counsellors. That leads to role reversal, with clients counselling counsellors. As I said earlier, too much self-disclosure leads clients to see counsellors as incapable and to lose confidence in the process and the capacity of their counsellors to help. The counselling relationship is not mutual, with each person taking turns sharing a problem.

STUDENT: What's often forgotten is the fact that self-disclosure involves more than sharing details of your past or your personal problems. Sharing your feelings with clients about the relationship or the work is also self-disclosure and a key element of the skill of immediacy. Rogers (1961; 1980), a central figure in counselling and the founder of client-centred (person-centred) therapy, emphasized the importance of being transparent and real in the relationship by sharing moment-to-moment feelings that are relevant to the relationship. After all, if we can't be open about our feelings, how can we expect clients to be?

Dependent Relationships

A **dependent relationship** arises when clients become overly reliant on their counsellors for decision making. Common indicators that a dependent relationship exists include excessive permission seeking, frequent phone calls or office visits for information, and an inability to make simple decisions or take action without consulting the counsellor. A dependent relationship undermines the principle of self-determination by shifting power away from clients and preventing them from developing independence.

Reactions to Power and Authority

Transference happens to some degree in all relationships, but it is much more likely to occur in relationships in which authority is present. However, to some extent all counselling relationships involve power and authority. Counsellors may have roles of authority when clients have clear social control issues. Counsellors such as probation and parole officers may have formal power, or they may work with clients as part of a court order. Counsellors may have power because clients perceive them as having superior or expert knowledge. Some counsellors, such as those in welfare settings, have control over services and benefits that clients are seeking. Clients also may react to other variables, such as age, socioeconomic status, position, gender, marital status, appearance, size, intelligence, and social demeanour.

Need for Empowerment

Often, clients come to counselling with low self-esteem and confidence. Seligman's (1975) concept of **learned helplessness** is a useful perspective for understanding. He suggests that individuals can become demoralized through failure to the point that they give up trying to alter their circumstances, even in situations in which change is possible. Persons with learned helplessness can be difficult and frustrating to work with because "to initiate changes, you must envision that your actions are possible and your effort will make a difference. You must believe that you are capable of taking action and garnering resources to augment your own" (DuBois and Miley, 1996:24). Persons who have learned helplessness do not believe that their efforts will make a difference.

If clients are locked into seeing themselves as victims, they are likely to resist change, or they may enter into dependency relationships in which they relinquish power and control to others, including their counsellors. In working with clients who show signs of learned helplessness, it is crucial that counsellors remember that "helplessness is a perception and not an accurate description of an individual" (Arnhold and Razak, 1991:102). The reality is that "many who are afflicted with crippling low self-esteem are in fact quite capable in some respects—the problem is that they think and feel otherwise about themselves" (Arnhold and Razak, 1991:102).

Counsellors need to be self-aware so that they may take steps to manage their own unmet needs that might impede their capacity to be helpful. For example, if they have a high need for control, they can potentially take power from clients, who for their part, may freely give it away. The concept of **empowerment** gives priority to assisting clients to maintain or assume control over their lives. Empowerment is concerned with giving clients access to resources and with enabling clients to achieve a sense of control over matters that affect their lives. As clients become empowered, there is an increase in their self-respect, confidence, knowledge, and skills.

Strategies for Empowering Clients. Counsellors who are committed to empowering their clients must start with a basic belief that their clients are capable of managing their own lives. They must relinquish the mistaken notion that clients depend on them for advice, decision making, and problem solving. Clients are empowered when they participate in decisions about counselling goals and procedures.

An empowerment attitude gives priority to clients' capacities and strengths. Thus, counsellors should search for and recognize their clients' strengths and resources. Questions and statements can be used to shift the focus of the interview in this direction, such as "What's working well for you?" "Let's talk about how you were able to cope with this problem for so long." "When you were able to manage, what were you doing that helped you succeed?"

"Why don't we take an inventory of your strengths?" Sometimes counsellors can offer other perspectives that empower. For example, responding to a woman who has struggled for six months to find work and get off welfare, a counsellor might say, "I'm impressed with your ability to hang in there. Many people would have given up." Ignoring or questioning self-depreciating remarks that reinforce low self-esteem are other choices for focusing on strength.

The principle of self-determination introduced in Chapter 2 promotes empowerment by helping clients recognize choices and by encouraging them to make independent decisions. To avoid promoting unhealthy client dependency, counsellors should not do for clients what clients can and should do for themselves. Furthermore, when clients are successful as a result of their actions, their confidence and self-esteem will increase. Counsellors should acknowledge and give clients credit for their success.

Strengths Approach. Clients are often besieged by debilitating problems and surrounded by chaos in their lives. Counsellors cannot ignore real problems, but in the process they should not focus all their attention on problem situations and what is dysfunctional in their clients' lives. Counsellors should adopt a strengths approach to clients in order to acquire a balanced perspective. The strengths approach assumes the inherent capacity of people. Individuals and communities are seen to have assets and resources that can be mobilized for problem solving. Sheafor, Horejsi and Horejsi (2000), Saleeby (1997), Cowger (1994) and others have discussed techniques and guidelines for maintaining a focus on client strengths. Building on their work, the following suggestions are offered:

1. Trust that clients have the capability to change, and that they can learn to cope with their problems and challenges. Every experienced counsellor can relate amazing stories of people who have recovered from adversity and overwhelming odds.

2. Stay interested in strengths. Acknowledge clients' skills, resourcefulness, motivation, and virtues. When workers value their clients' strengths, clients learn to value themselves. Discovering overlooked abilities, knowledge, and experience can energize counsellors and clients.

3. Ask questions or make statements that uncover strengths such as: Think of a time when you were able to handle problem such as this. What skills and resources enabled you to cope? What are the things in your live that you feel good about? What's working well for you? What would your friends say are your best qualities?

4. Negotiate a partnership with clients where they share responsibility for identifying priorities, goals, and preferred ways of proceeding. Accept that they are the "experts" on their own lives, and with encouragement they can make decisions on what will and will not work. Counsellors need to be flexible and accept that every intervention plan will be individualized to the unique needs and attributes of each client. What works with one client may be counterproductive with another.

5. Avoid diagnostic labels as a way of describing clients. Labels tend to ignore strengths by focusing on pathology and deficits.

6. Focus on problem solving and goal setting rather that on discussions of blame or on finding the root causes of current behavior or problems. There may be cathartic benefit to discussing history, but once this purpose is achieved the focus of the work should shift to present and future events. Setting goals energizes clients to action and it mobilizes their resources and motivation for change.

7. Consider that families, neighbourhoods, and communities have formal and informal resources that are potential sources of help and strength for clients. Challenge clients to identify and discover these resources. Ask questions such as: Who do you trust? Who supports you when you need help? Use community directories to pinpoint agencies, services, and self-help groups that could be supportive.

ENDING THE COUNSELLING RELATIONSHIP

Counselling relationships vary in length from a single interview or a short encounter to many years. Some are superficial, with minimal emotional investment by the participants, while others result in considerable intimacy and emotional involvement, but all relationships, regardless of their length, have the potential to be intimate. The counselling relationship is not designed to be permanent, but, owing to its intimacy, the ending of the relationship may trigger powerful feelings and behaviours in both clients and counsellors. For some clients, intense satisfaction and feelings of accomplishment punctuate their success, but others may feel abandoned and deserted. The ending may remind them of the pain and sadness of other endings, and they may need help dealing with their loss and grief (Shebib, 1997; Shulman, 1992). Hess and McCartt Hess note that the end of the helping relationship brings attention to the fact that "the impending separation is a violation of the wish intrinsic in most meaningful attachments that the relationship would remain permanently active" (1984:561).

The initial reaction of both clients and counsellors to a pending termination of an intimate counselling relationship is often denial (Hess and McCartt Hess, 1984; Shulman, 1992). Counsellors need to be sensitive to signals that clients are having trouble with endings. Some clients who have shown progress might regress to previous ways of coping, or they may present new and complex concerns that seem to say, "I'm not ready for this to end."

Other clients might express their pain about the ending by expressing unfounded anger and resentment (in effect, avoiding the pain of the ending or denying the importance of the relationship). Still others fail to show up for the final meeting as another way to avoid dealing with the pain of the ending.

Counsellors who have invested heavily in the relationship will also have to deal with their own feelings about the ending. This may result in a variety of denial reactions such as:

*   denial of the ending by allowing or encouraging clients to remain in counselling longer than necessary. The counselling relationship is not designed to be lifelong. The counselling contract should include defining an end point to the relationship. As well, individual interviews should be structured within a time frame. With a time frame, "both worker and client tend to mobilize their efforts more effectively to accomplish the tasks of the contract within the time designated" (Kadushin, 1983:239). Then the relationship ends.

*   denial of the ending by making false or unrealistic concessions or promises, for example, by promising to visit or correspond with clients

*   denial of feelings by behaving apathetically or avoiding discussion of feelings about the ending

*   denial of feelings by abruptly ending without warning

Dealing with Endings

One way to assist clients in dealing with endings, including denial responses, is to teach them about "the predictable reactions to loss and to aid them in identifying those reactions when either directly or indirectly expressed" (Hess and McCartt Hess, 1984:561). The ending phase, when handled effectively, offers rich potential for work. Surprisingly, many books on counselling do not examine the therapeutic possibilities of the ending phase. With trust firmly established in the relationship and the urgency of the end approaching, clients may broach significant themes and topics (Shulman, 1992). Shulman describes the phenomenon of **doorknob communication**, whereby clients bring up important issues at the end of the interview/relationship when there is little or no time to address them. Clients are typically ambivalent about dealing with the issues, but their need to address them finally overcomes their need to avoid them.

A second strategy is for counsellors to honestly express their feelings about the termination of the relationship. This models appropriate sharing for clients, and it stimulates them to risk sharing their reactions and feelings. Of course, this discussion requires counsellors to be open to strong feelings, such as sadness and anger. Shulman (1992) underscores the importance of counsellors sharing their own feelings, but he acknowledges that this is a difficult skill to develop. In part, this arises from the fact that workers may be struggling with their own sense of loss as they prepare to end their relationship with a valued client. Continued self-examination can help counsellors develop self-awareness about their own behaviours and feelings regarding endings and separations.

Interview 3.3 illustrates how the ending process can be used to address feelings. The client is a young adolescent about to be discharged from a residential treatment centre. For the last six weeks, he and his counsellor have been actively planning for his return home. The client has been looking forward to more freedom and release from the rules and restrictions of the centre. As part of his prerelease planning, he has spent two weekends with his family.

INTERVIEW 3.3 ENDINGS

DIALOGUE	ANALYSIS
Counsellor: If I'm not mistaken, you look a little glum today.	The counsellor risks empathy by picking up on nonverbal cues from the client. The counsellor suspects that the client's anger may be connected to the ending of the relationship.
Client: Can't you ever let anything pass? Why don't you just get off my back?	
Counsellor: Tomorrow, you will be leaving the centre to return home. Maybe we could talk about that. I'm wondering how you feel about it. I wouldn't be surprised if you had mixed feelings of being happy to be leaving, but also sad to be leaving your friends here.	The client's first reaction is to deny his feelings by discounting the value and importance of the relationship.

(continued)

Client: It's no big deal, but why should you care?

Counsellor: I feel sad knowing you're leaving. We've become very close and I'll miss our time together.

Client: It's been all right. I guess you're okay.

Counsellor: Thanks, and you're okay with me too. (ten seconds of silence) How do you feel about us not seeing each other anymore?

Client: I wish it wasn't happening. I don't know if I'm ready to go.

Counsellor: It's very scary thinking about leaving.

Client: I want to go home, but my mother and I always seem to end up fighting. You and I can talk and not fight. Why can't it be that way with my mother?

Counsellor: Maybe you have more control than you think. What do you do differently with me than with your mother?

By sharing her own feelings, the counsellor communicates her willingness to deal with emotions. This acts as a model for the client. Of course, any feelings the counsellor shares must be genuine.

Although his anger softens, he is still reluctant to acknowledge his feelings. The counsellor persists.

Although the client has trouble labelling his feelings, he begins to open up. The counsellor uses empathy to acknowledge the feelings suggested by the client's remark.

The client risks talking about his feelings about going home. The counsellor tries to get the client to accept credit for success in the counselling relationship. She challenges him to consider how he can transfer some of his behaviour in the client–counsellor relationship to his relationship with his mother.

Summary

The counselling relationship is negotiated in order to assist clients to achieve defined goals. Developing and sustaining an effective counselling relationship is widely accepted as critical to success in counselling. It is characterized by some of the same elements of a deep friendship, but it differs in important ways, such as its time-limited nature and its emphasis on goal achievement.

Over the four phases of counselling—preliminary, beginning, action, and ending—the counselling relationship needs to be developed, sustained, and then ended. Throughout all phases, counsellor warmth, empathy, and genuineness are essential.

The counselling contract is an important tool that enables counsellors and their clients to agree on their respective roles and the purpose of the counselling relationship. The contract is negotiated early in the relationship, but periodic revision is necessary because of changing client needs and priorities. Counselling relationships are formed for one or more broad purposes, such as to offer support, assist with problem solving, help clients learn skills, or help them deal with painful feelings.

Immediacy is a tool for exploring, evaluating, and deepening counselling relationships. Relationship immediacy refers to the process of evaluating the general working climate of the counsellor–client relationship. Here-and-now immediacy focuses on counsellor–client interactions as they occur within the interview.

Counsellor self-disclosure has an important place in counselling, but counsellors must use it intelligently to ensure that it meets the needs of their clients and that it does not move the focus of the interview away from their clients.

Transference is the tendency of clients to communicate with their counsellors in the same way that they communicated with significant people in their past. Countertransference is the tendency of counsellors to inappropriately transfer feelings and behaviours to clients. It is important that counsellors are able to distinguish between client reactions and feelings that arise from the current relationship and those that arise from transference. All counselling relationships involve power and authority; thus, clients are particularly vulnerable to transference reactions.

Persons with learned helplessness believe that change is not possible through their own efforts. Counsellors need to look for ways to empower such individuals so that they can assume control over their lives. The strengths approach assumes the inherent capacity of people, individuals, and communities as having assets and resources that can be mobilized for problem solving.

The inevitable ending of the counselling relationship may trigger powerful feelings in both clients and counsellors. The ending phase, when handled effectively, offers rich potential for work.

Exercises

1. What were (or are) the attributes of your most positive relationship with another person? The most negative? How can you use this information to be a more effective counsellor?

2. Interview friends and colleagues on the topics of warmth, empathy, and genuineness. Ask them to describe how they know when someone exhibits these inner qualities.

3. Talk to people who are happy in their work. Ask them to describe how they sustain their energy and enthusiasm.

4. Pay attention to the people you see and meet over the next week. Who evokes strong emotional reactions? Who seems most similar to your parents or other authority figures? Now examine your feelings and try to identify transference reactions—feelings that you carry over from prior relationships and that are not based on objective reactions to the current relationship.

5. Orchestrate an immediacy encounter. Contract with a colleague with whom you have a working relationship to spend one hour evaluating and strengthening your relationship. Use the following open-ended statements to develop themes for your discussion, but be sure to explore your ideas and responses:

    • The thing I value most in this relationship is…

    • The one thing that is missing in our relationship is...

    • When I first met you, my reaction was...

    • You are most like...

- When I think about sharing feelings with you...
- In order for us to become closer, I would have to...
- What I want most from you is...
- When I think of the future of our relationship, I...

Periodically, share how you are feeling using a statement such as "Right now I am feeling ..." You are free to add other significant themes in your relationship that are not suggested in the above list. When you are finished, discuss what changes you would like to make in your relationship.

6. Imagine that you wished to use immediacy in each of the following situations. Develop an introductory response to begin the encounter.

   a. You are dealing with a client who hints that he or she is sexually attracted to you.

   b. You are counselling a client who has become demanding.

   c. You are feeling confused and you are not sure what to do next in the interview.

   d. Your client continually questions your training.

7. Do you agree with the observation made by Keith-Lucas (1972:18) that "the attempt to keep the relationship on a pleasant level is the greatest source of ineffectual helping known"? Examine your own needs with respect to keeping the counselling relationship warm and pleasant. How far would you go to ensure this as an outcome? Under what conditions might you need to sacrifice pleasantness?

8. Imagine that you are the designated counsellor in each of the following situations and that you are about to see each client for the first time. What barriers might you anticipate in developing a relationship with each client? Develop a relationship-building strategy.

   a. Hospital setting: A man, age 64, has just learned that he has terminal lung cancer. The ward nurses tell you that he is angry with his doctor and that he blames him for not making an earlier diagnosis.

   b. A young woman (age 21) has just been released from prison and is about to see you, her probation officer. Reports from the prison note that she has considerable difficulty dealing with persons in authority.

   c. Employment counselling setting: A middle-aged man with 25 years' experience and four university degrees has been laid off after 15 years with the same company. As you walk to your office, he remarks, "I don't see the point of this. I think this is a big waste of time, but the company is paying for it, so I might as well get all I can."

   d. School counselling office: A teenager is referred by her teacher, who suspects that she might be using drugs.

   e. Crisis line: A man, age 33, is threatening suicide.

   f. Health clinic, working with a physician colleague: A woman is HIV positive. Your task is to tell her about her HIV-positive diagnosis.

   g. Home visit: You are a social worker interviewing parents to investigate anonymous allegations that their children are suffering physical abuse.

   h. Mediation centre: You are working with a couple who have sought mediation assistance to work out custody and visiting rights.

    i.   Community counselling agency: The client, age 35, has a long history at the agency. Other counsellors have noted that the client has a tendency to become dependent and makes daily phone calls for advice.

    j.   Transition home: A woman is returning to the house for the third time after being severely abused by her husband. On previous occasions she has vowed never to go back to her husband, but each time she has reconciled.

    k.   A mental health counselling centre: A man is seeking assistance for depression. He has considerable difficulty relating to women.

9. What are the issues (pros and cons) involved in counselling friends?

10. This exercise is designed to expand your self-awareness regarding issues that might affect your counselling relationships. Complete each sentence quickly, without attempting to edit your thoughts.

   - The one thing I have to have from other people is...
   - What's missing in my personal life is...
   - Something that people do that bothers me is...
   - The one type of person I'd hate to work with is...
   - Relationships would be better if...
   - What I like most about people is...
   - What I dislike most about people is...

11. Most of us tend to repeat established patterns when we begin new relationships. Interview others who have observed you during your "beginnings." Explore questions such as the following:

   - What first impressions are you likely to leave with others?
   - How do their perceptions compare with your intentions or inner feelings?
   - Now consider the following questions:
   - What are your typical beginning feelings, thoughts, and behaviours?
   - How are beginnings the same or different for you when you are relating to different individuals or groups, for example, clients, colleagues, or supervisors?
   - What works for you?
   - What doesn't?

12. Based on your observations and insights from the previous question, begin the process of developing a range of different skills and strategies for beginning relationships. This will help you avoid becoming locked into established patterns. Define personal goals for development, related to how you handle beginnings. As part of this, detail three different beginning styles you wish to add to your skill repertoire. Describe when and how you will experiment with these three approaches. What problems do you anticipate might interfere with achievement of these goals?

13. Think about significant relationships in your life that have ended because of separation, death, or other reasons. How did you respond emotionally and behaviourally to these endings? In retrospect, are there things you wish you had said or not said? What remains unresolved in these relationships? (Suggestion: If this exercise evokes strong emotions, you may find it useful to debrief with a friend or colleague.)

14. In your answer to the previous question, what behavioural patterns are evident? What are the implications of your insights for your work as a counsellor?

15. Rate the extent to which you think it would be appropriate for you to disclose the information listed below. Use the following scale:

5 = always appropriate
4 = usually appropriate
3 = sometimes appropriate
2 = usually not appropriate
1 = never appropriate

Be prepared to defend your answers with examples.

___ a. details of your education and training

___ b. your philosophy of counselling

___ c. information about your age, marital status, and number of children

___ d. your sexual orientation

___ e. particulars about your life, such as personal problems that you have faced

___ f. details about your everyday life, such as your hobbies, reading preferences, and vacation plans

___ g. intimate details about your personal life, such as marital problems and recovery from addictions

___ h. feelings such as anger, boredom, confusion, or sexual attraction that are influencing the interview

To what extent were your answers influenced by your comfort level with each of the categories?

16. Under what conditions do you think it would be wise for a counsellor to avoid self-disclosure?

17. Evaluate your general comfort with self-disclosure. What areas of your life are you reluctant or unwilling to talk about? To what extent would your friends and colleagues describe you as open or closed? Do you tend to be guarded about sharing information, or do you generally disclose a great deal to others? How does your comfort with disclosure vary depending on whom you are talking with (e.g., family, friends, authority figures, clients, colleagues, strangers)?

18. What are the implications of your answers to the previous question for your work as a counsellor?

19. Evaluate the potential appropriateness of each of the following counsellor self-disclosures (the counsellor is speaking to a client).

a. Your situation reminds me of my own problems. Maybe we can pool our energies and find a solution that works for both of us.

b. I'm sorry to say that it's none of your business whether I have children.

c. When my husband abused me for the first time, I knew the marriage was over and I left.

d. (addictions treatment centre, meeting a client for the first time) Hi, I'm John and I'm a recovering alcoholic, so I know what you're going through.

e. I'm feeling confused. I think we need to stop for a minute and decide where we're going.

f. Your problems are really getting to me. They remind me so much of my own struggles. They bring back all my pain.

g. You have the most beautiful eyes.

h. I like what you're wearing today. It's really sexy.

i. Generally, I like to try to establish open communication in my relationships, so I push myself to be open with my feelings even when it's difficult.

j. Your attitude really makes me want to just give up on you.

k. This has been a bad day for me. There have been some cutbacks at the agency and I'm worried about losing my job, so if I seem a little preoccupied today I hope you'll understand.

l. What a weekend! We partied all night. I could hardly make it to work today.

20. Describe how counsellor self-disclosure might be appropriate in response to each of the following client statements or questions. Suggest a response.

a. Have you ever felt so angry that you wanted to kill someone?

b. My mother never gives me the support I need.

c. I began using drugs when I was 11.

d. Are you gay?

e. I'm terrified about going back to school. I don't think I can handle it. It's been so many years since I wrote an essay or read a book.

f. My teenage son is driving me crazy.

g. I think this counselling session is a waste of time.

h. I really like you.

i. I don't think anyone has ever been as depressed as I am.

Weblinks

"The Foundation of Person-Centered Therapy" by Jerold D. Bozarth.
personcentered.com/therapist.html

"An Analysis of Carl Rogers' Theory of Personality" by Dagmar Pescitelli.
www.wynja.com/personality/rogersff.html

This Carl Rogers site covers Rogerian theory and includes a biography of the man.
www.ship.edu/~cgboeree/rogers.html

LISTENING: THE BASIS FOR UNDERSTANDING

PREVIEW

After reading this chapter you should be able to:

- Explain the importance of listening.
- Define the components of effective listening.
- List common obstacles to listening.
- Describe techniques for overcoming listening obstacles.
- Explain the importance of active listening.
- Describe the components of attending.
- Demonstrate attending skills.
- List and explain the multiple meanings of silence in counselling.
- Identify a range of choices for dealing with silence.
- Define and describe what is meant by paraphrasing.
- Demonstrate paraphrasing skills.
- Define and describe what is meant by summarizing.
- Demonstrate summarizing skills.

THE CHALLENGE OF LISTENING

Listening is defined in Webster's dictionary as "hearing with thoughtful attention." Wolvin and Coakley provide a more technical definition: "the process of receiving, attending to, and assigning meaning to aural and visual stimuli" (1996:69). Listening is a complex process that involves sensory, mental, and behavioural competence. Obviously, effective listeners need to hear, but simply hearing words is insufficient for listening. Skilled listeners also must be able to perceive associated relevant and often complex nonverbal information, such as voice tone and gestures, which support, enhance, or contradict verbal messages. As a mental process, listening involves separating relevant information from irrelevant information, assigning meaning to words and experiences, remembering, and linking related data. Put simply, listening is making sense of what has been heard. Behaviourally, proficient listeners are dynamic and responsive. They ask questions to get clarification, definitions, and examples to ensure that they have enough information to hear what the sender meant them to hear. They use summaries and statements to ensure the accuracy of their observations and conclusions, such as "Do you mean...?"

Listening is the cornerstone of counselling and is essential to understanding and relationship development. Often clients come to counselling with considerable experience of not being heard. They may have turned to family and friends for help but found that their concerns were discounted or were met with simplistic advice by people who were so anxious to help that they failed to listen with attention.

Effective counsellors and interviewers are distinguished by their capacity to listen. As a fundamental building block for the relationship, listening communicates to clients that their ideas and feelings are important. Skills such as probing and insightful empathy are incomplete unless they are balanced with competent listening. Indeed, listening must be an active partner in all other counselling skills. Listening educates counsellors about the uniqueness of their clients, thus minimizing any tendency to make erroneous assumptions. Listening encourages clients to tell their stories and disclose their feelings. In the process, they may gain enormous therapeutic value from releasing pent-up emotions. When counsellors listen to clients, clients become better able to listen to themselves. Systematic listening, punctuated with appropriate probes, clarification responses, and summaries, helps clients organize confusing and contradictory thoughts.

Listening is an act of acceptance and caring that says to clients, "Your feelings are precious and unique. I won't insult you by assuming that I know what you're going to say before you say it. I won't judge or ridicule what you say. I won't try to change you to fit my idea of what you should be." Listening means joining our clients in understanding their world, their perceptions, and their feelings.

Listening requires counsellors to be silent, but being silent does not necessarily mean that one is listening. A silent person may hear the words and even be able to repeat verbatim what has been said, but a tape recorder or a clever parrot can do the same thing. Egan (1977) introduced the term *hollow listening* to mean listening without responding. Hollow listeners are silent or use clichés such as "I know just what you mean." Hollow listeners may be attentive to the speaker, nod their heads to signal approval, and look as though they're involved, yet there is very little intimacy to the encounter. As Egan concludes, "The ultimate proof of good listening is good responding" (1977:137).

Listening in its purest form is a search for meaning. Kadushin says:

Listening is the dynamic process of attaching meaning to what we hear, making sense of aurally received, raw verbal-vocal symbols. It is a purposive, selective process in which sounds communicated by a speaker are screened, given attention, recognized, comprehended, and interpreted by the hearer. Listening is not the passive reception of sound, but the active processing of sounds we hear. It involves not only listening to sounds, but listening for sounds that would further our understanding. (1990:244)

Therefore, listening is not a passive act. Effective listeners are busy with the task of trying to comprehend what is happening for their clients. Sometimes, counsellors will be patiently quiet as they respectfully yield the right to speak to their clients. At other times, they will be vocal, with questions and directives for more detail, example, or clarification. At all times, they should carefully observe and try to understand nonverbal behaviour. Daly's distinction between perceived listening and actual listening underscores the importance of active involvement in listening: "No matter how effective, skilled, or competent an individual is in listening, unless he or she is perceived as listening by the other interactants, little may be accomplished" (cited in Wolvin and Coakley, 1996:31). Active listening, a collection of skills discussed in this and subsequent chapters, is the way that counsellors show their clients that they are listening. This is possible because they are, in fact, mentally and physically committed to the task of listening.

Good listening can be physically and emotionally exhausting. Nichols noted that "listening is hard work. It is characterized by faster heart action, quicker circulation of the blood, a small rise in bodily temperature" (cited in Wolvin and Coakley, 1996:29). It requires counsellors to focus all their intellectual and physical attention on clients so that they have the counsellors' unwavering commitment. Listening is the client's reward for talking.

Overcoming Listening Obstacles

Close-minded listeners respect only those who agree with them. Since they already have the "right" answers, there is no need to entertain new thoughts and ideas, nor is there any reason for them to seek additional information. Open-minded listeners, on the other hand, are willing to explore new ideas and are secure enough to hear different opinions. They endeavour to receive messages and understand meaning without distortion. Open-minded listening requires the participants to shift between speaking and listening while attempting to understand. Open-minded listeners use the following skills.

Being Patient. In order to make themselves understood, people need to be able to frame their ideas. Clients who lack the ability to express themselves, perhaps because they have a limited vocabulary or capacity to articulate in precise terms, use words that are vague, ambiguous, or contradictory. Others may not have sufficient awareness or insight to describe their feelings. In such circumstances, counsellors can become impatient, and this becomes an obstacle to listening. They may try to hurry the process by finishing sentences for clients who are struggling to express themselves. Or they could become lazy and content to assign their own meanings to words and phrases.

Encouraging Trust. Client messages could be incomplete or missing because of trust issues. In the beginning phase, the client may be reluctant to share. This is understandable, since the counselling relationship has yet to be tested. Consequently, the client could hold back information or feelings that are ultimately vital for understanding and present "safe" issues to test the relationship or only hint at more important concerns. As counselling progresses, clients learn that they can depend on their counsellors to respond with respect and understanding. Unfortunately, in some cases, they may learn that their counsellor cannot be trusted with feelings.

Controlling Noise. Once messages are sent, they must be received and interpreted accurately, hence the importance of conducting the counselling interview in an environment that is free from distraction and interruption. Counsellors should, of course, never discontinue an interview to answer the phone. In addition to the dangers of inadvertently breaching confidentiality, suspending the interview to attend to other business seriously impedes relationship rapport and the flow of information. Even a ringing phone left unanswered can destroy the ambience of the meeting. Similarly, pagers, fax machines, computer alerts (beeps and electronic voices) that signal incoming e-mail, and cell phones may interfere with listening and communication. Ideally, all such equipment should be turned off. Alternatively, counsellors might consider conducting the interview in an office that has no such distractions.

Staying Focused. Good listening is difficult work that requires effort to stay focused. Since we can think many times faster than others can talk, it's easy to allow our thoughts to wander. The trick is to keep our minds busy with listening. Active involvement in listening, through summarizing, paraphrasing, and asking questions, will help counsellors stay alert and focused. Mental involvement will also help counsellors concentrate and understand what's being said. For example, as they listen they can ask themselves, "What does the client mean by...?" "What are the key points of what is being said?" When they do this, counsellors should try to avoid becoming overly absorbed in figuring out what they are going to say next, as this will only divert their attention from listening.

Internal noise can also interfere with listening. Counsellors might be preoccupied with their own needs or ideas. They could be looking forward to their vacation and imagining their break. They may be under personal stress, suffering from fatigue, or engaged with thoughts of other clients. Such interference can cause counsellors to stop listening or to fail to engage in important aspects of the listening process. A counsellor who is tired might deliberately neglect to explore or define important ideas.

Controlling Assumptions. If counsellors believe that they already know what others are going to say and are not open to new information, then listening is not possible. Counsellors' apparent patient attention and silence could give the illusion that they are listening, but their assumptions and preconceptions quickly become obvious to astute clients. Typically, clients are guarded and defensive with people who have opinions different from their own. In the example below, a high-school student has just told her counsellor that she has been offered a scholarship at a prestigious university.

STUDENT: *It's one of the finest universities in the area. It's really quite an honour to have been chosen from all the applicants. My father, who never had a chance to go to university, is ecstatic.*

COUNSELLOR (CHOICE 1): *Wow! That's terrific. You must be so proud of yourself. This is really an outstanding opportunity.*

COUNSELLOR (CHOICE 2): *How do you feel about it?*

Choice 1 in this example assumes feelings and meaning. As a result, further exploration is discouraged or cut off. Choice 2 is a listening response that encourages more information. It allows for the possibility that the client might say, "I'm depressed about it. I've been going to school for 12 years and I really wanted to take a year off." Choice 2 illustrates a basic principle of effective listening: Good listeners are open to learning, and they "go to school" with every client. This requires counsellors' willingness to give up any notion that they know what others are about to say.

Managing Personal Reactions. Tension and anxiety may be aroused within the counsellor, either by the content of what a client is saying or by the manner of the client. Emotions in the client can trigger emotions in the counsellor, which, if unchecked, can lessen the counsellor's capacity to listen. For example, an angry client might stimulate fear in the counsellor. The counsellor may become preoccupied with his or her own fear or insecurity and begin to act defensively. As well, a depressed client can have a contagious effect and cause the counsellor to become similarly despondent. Certain words or messages might act as emotional triggers for counsellors and lead to faulty listening and understanding.

Many beginning counsellors react strongly to clients who have been abusive, and they erect listening barriers. They get so trapped in their own need to condemn the abhorrent behaviour that they have no room left to become aware of their clients' frames of reference. Consequently, they fail to establish any base for understanding and any credibility to promote change. Entering into the private world of clients whose behaviour and attitudes differ sharply from one's own requires emotional maturity, skill, and, often, abundant courage. Such capacities distinguish and define competent counsellors.

Sometimes counsellors become bored, particularly when dealing with clients who speak in a monotone. Clients who are repetitious and long winded can also stimulate boredom. More than a few anecdotes in the field relate that counsellors fell asleep during interviews. To stay alert during an interview, counsellors must arrive alert. They should get enough sleep and exercise, and avoid heavy lunches that might lead to drowsiness. Short breaks to take a walk, stretch, or clear the mind are important ways of sustaining energy.

When clients present difficult feelings and topics, some counsellors handle their own discomfort by becoming inappropriately quiet or silent, becoming excessively talkative, changing the subject, or offering premature advice or reassurance. Such responses may communicate that the counsellor does not understand or is not listening or, in the case of inappropriate silence, that the counsellor does not care. Counsellors need to become confident in their skills and abilities so that they can tolerate clients' feelings, reactions, and, at times, verbal assaults with a minimum of defensive reactions that obscure listening and understanding.

Knowing That Listening Does Not Mean Agreeing. Sometimes people confuse listening with agreeing. This misconception is common and is apparent in the way people talk. For example, a person might say, "I told him what I want. Why doesn't he change?" Failure to comply with one's wants and needs is used as evidence that the other person isn't listening. Similarly, people may not listen because they are afraid that this will be construed as consent. This belief is one of the main reasons that many people cannot communicate effectively. If each party to an argument tenaciously clings to his or her own beliefs without hearing the other side, then how is communication possible? Counsellors need to be cautious that they don't succumb to this fallacy. One new counsellor remarked, "If I listen to someone who abuses children, aren't I condoning it?" Counsellors need to remind themselves that listening does not mean agreeing. Weaver provides a useful perspective:

> We may listen carefully and at length to the presentation of our opponent. We may question; we may explore; we may do our best to hold our own biases in abeyance as we try to see the world through his eyes. And we may, after all this, decide that our own position is the better and cling to it still. This does not mean that we did not listen. (1972:22)

Exemplary counsellors become vigilant when they are dealing with clients who test their values and beliefs. They discipline themselves by taking extra precautions to ensure they are listening accurately. They try to become alert to any internal noise that might impair their capacity to hear. They know they are vulnerable, and they take preventive measures.

Being Aware of Blind Spots. Since everyone's frame of reference is more or less different, we can never perfectly understand how other people are experiencing their world. Our understanding is always clouded to some extent by the meanings we assign to events and by our own thoughts and feelings. Counsellors may have blind spots that make it difficult for them to hear or understand their clients. In this respect, counsellors are vulnerable when they have unrecognized or unresolved problems that are parallel to those of their clients. For example, one counsellor experienced unusual discomfort when trying to work with a client who was dealing with an unwanted pregnancy. Ten years ago, the counsellor had placed her own child for adoption, but she had never addressed the guilt she felt over the decision. Whenever her client focused on her options, the counsellor's own feelings made it tough for her to separate her feelings from the client's.

Table 4.1 on page 102 summarizes some strategies for overcoming common listening problems. These strategies are intended as ideas, rather than as recipes for responding. Each interview situation requires individualized and creative responses.

ACTIVE LISTENING

Understanding is always tentative, but it is even more speculative until we provide an opportunity for clients to confirm or deny its accuracy. Active listening is a term that describes a cluster of skills that are used to increase the accuracy of understanding. Attending, being silent, summarizing, paraphrasing, questioning, and empathizing are the essential skills of active listening. They breathe life into listening so that it becomes a continuous process of paying attention, hearing, exploring, and deepening. Active listening involves hearing what is said, as well as what is left unsaid. Counsellors need to use both their eyes and ears to ascertain meaning. Careful attention to such cues as word choice, voice tone, posture, and verbal hesitations is necessary to discover confirming or conflicting messages in the verbal and nonverbal messages. Subtle changes in voice tone or sudden shifts in the topic may signal important areas for the counsellor to explore. In one case, a 28-year-old woman, describing her career goals, mentioned her sister. As she did so, the counsellor noticed that she avoided

Table 4.1 Overcoming Listening Obstacles

Problem	Counsellor Choices
The client has problems with language, e.g., misleading word choice and difficulty verbalizing ideas.	Ask questions to clarify meaning. Pay careful attention to nonverbal communication for clues to meaning.
Messages are incomplete, ambiguous, or unclear.	Probe for detail and examples. Paraphrase to confirm understanding. Ask for definition.
Relationship problems/trust issues are resulting in client censorship of feelingsand ideas.	Show empathy. Provoke candid discussion of trust or relationship issues. Go at a slower pace, reduce questions. Communicate openness through nondefensive responses.
There is outside interference, e.g., noise and lack of privacy.	Hold phone calls, move interviews to a private setting.
There is internal interference, e.g., counsellor fatigue, difficulty concentrating, boredom, hearing impairment.	Start a personal wellness plan . Start time management. Defer the interview . Use discipline to increase concentration (e.g., mentally summarize key details). Summarize, paraphrase, empathize.
The counsellor has a loss of objectivity when dealing with ideas that are contrary to his or her values.	Use supervision or consultation to address personal issues that cloud objectivity. Become self-disciplined to explore ideas that are different.
There are cultural barriers between counsellor and client.	Enlist the client's help to understand cultural values and issues, then adapt the interview style to fit. Use translators or refer the client to a counsellor of the same culture.
Content is overwhelming for the counsellor, e.g., when the client rambles or is long winded.	Summarize to identify themes and priorities. Selectively interrupt to control the flow of the interview.
The client is inappropriately silent.	Attempt to understand the meaning of silence, then respond appropriately.
The client has speech problems (e.g., mumbling, stuttering, whispering).	Remember that problems may decrease as the counsellor becomes more familiar with the client's style. Ask the client to speak up.

eye contact and her voice dipped slightly. He asked how she felt about her sister. The woman began crying as she related how her sister had always been the favoured one in the family and how she had felt rejected by her mother. Subsequently, this relationship became a central issue in the counselling, and the client developed insight into how she was using her career as a desperate attempt to gain her mother's acceptance.

Active listening skills can also be used to defuse critical incidents. The FBI, for example, has trained negotiators to use active listening skills to handle situations involving hostages or barricaded subjects (Noesner and Webster, 1997). They found that active listening, particularly the skills of paraphrasing, empathizing, and open-ended questioning, helps subjects (i.e., hostage takers) release frustration, despair, anger, and other powerful feelings, with the result that they return to a more normal level of arousal and rational thinking. One of the reasons active listening is so effective is that it does not threaten people with an overt attempt to change them. Active listening builds rapport because it shows that the listener is non-judgmental and is interested in understanding. Individuals in crisis may erect heavy psychological defences, but "because active listening poses no threat to an individual's self-image, it can help a subject become less defensive. Thus, active listening creates fertile ground for negotiation and, eventually, change" (Noesner and Webster, 1997:16). In short, active listening is critical for nonviolent crisis intervention.

Attending, use of silence, summarizing, and paraphrasing will be explored in the following sections of this chapter. Subsequent chapters will address the skills of questioning and empathy.

Attending

Attending is a term used to describe the way that counsellors communicate to their clients that they are ready, willing, and able to listen. When coupled with understanding and appropriate verbal responses, attending promotes exploration. As a basic active listening skill, attending conveys physical and psychological commitment to the helping interview. Attending says to clients, "I'm here for you. You have my undivided attention. I'm not afraid of your feelings and what you have to say." It conveys an overall physical and psychological openness. Wolvin and Coakley (1996) use the term *energetic attention* to underscore the importance of bringing both effort and desire to listening.

Certain core attending skills are universally applicable, and counsellors can use them with confidence. First, counsellors need to ensure that their feelings, attitudes, and commitment to clients are genuine. Egan describes attending as a learned set of skills; however, he cautions that counsellors cannot fake it: "Your mind-set, what's in your heart, is as important as your visible presence. If you are not 'for' your client, if you resent working with a client, this will ooze out into your behavior" (1998:62). If a counsellor has negative feelings about a particular client, then referral to another counsellor may be warranted. On the other hand, if such negative feelings permeate a counsellor's attitude toward many clients, then additional remedies may be necessary, such as personal counselling, assistance to deal with burnout, consultation and supervision to manage feelings, or career change.

Second, providing space to clients so that they can speak begins the active listening process. This includes efforts by counsellors to control physical noise and self-discipline to curb internal distractions. Self-discipline to suspend hasty assumptions and judgments is essential. Counsellors must work to avoid reacting with verbal or nonverbal messages that express impatience, disagreement, or judgment. As noted earlier in this chapter, this may be difficult when clients present ideas that are offensive or conflict with one's values and beliefs.

Third, counsellors can show that they are attending by being on time for the interview, remembering important details, and following through with agreed-on plans. There is a certain physical and verbal presence that conveys commitment. Verbal and nonverbal behaviours such as head nods and encouraging probes convey interest. Counsellors need to bring a certain warmth to the interview, which is communicated through appropriate smiling, changes in voice tone, and expressions of caring and support. An unemployed client who reports with glee to his counsellor that he has found work has a right to expect more than a monotone "That's great."

There is general agreement that the following behaviours convey appropriate attending, particularly when they match the client's nonverbal behaviour: keeping an open posture, maintaining eye contact, leaning forward, using responsive facial expressions, giving brief encouraging comments, and speaking in a warm and pleasant tone (Egan, 1998; Kadushin, 1990; Wolvin and Coakley, 1996). Counsellors should avoid displaying a "poker face," which can easily be taken as a "don't care" attitude. Wolvin and Coakley reviewed the research and reached a number of conclusions that have implications for counsellors. Some of the highlights of their findings are summarized below:

- Individuals whose shoulders and legs are turned toward rather than away from the other person are perceived to be more empathic.
- Individuals with open body positions (e.g., arms and legs uncrossed) are perceived more positively than those with closed body positions.
- Individuals who lean toward others are perceived to possess more warmth and empathy.
- Listeners who engage in head nodding provide positive reinforcement for speakers.
- The smile is the best indicator of interpersonal warmth.
- People who engage in eye contact and gazing (looking at another person) project more attentiveness, interest, warmth, empathy, intimacy, truthfulness, sincerity, and credibility than those who do not engage in eye contact.
- Individuals who are embarrassed, ashamed, sad, submissive, guilty, or deceptive tend to have less gazing behaviour. (1996:176–83)

As with any counselling skill or procedure, attending must be applied intelligently, with respect to diversity. Counsellors should avoid rigid adherence to one style of attending. For example, the needs of a client who is embarrassed may be best served by averted or less intensive eye contact until more trust and comfort develops. As with any counselling skill, the general rule for attending is to seek to determine how attending can be communicated to this client in this situation.

Careful attention to words, phrases, and nonverbal communication opens counsellors to learning. Counsellors need to hear what is said, as well as what is not said. They need to reflect on how ideas are communicated, through tone of voice, posture, and other clues, and to listen carefully for confirming or conflicting messages. As well, they need to sift through what may be complex, sometimes confusing information to identify patterns, priorities, and areas of relevance. This work may involve the major senses of hearing, sight, smell, and touch. Although counselling work generally centres on hearing and sight, significant information can be gleaned from our other senses. For example, alcohol and some other drug use may be detected by smell.

When counsellors are patient, they give clients space to confront painful emotions and to gather their thoughts. When counsellors sit still, maintain culturally appropriate eye contact, and avoid needless questions, they do much to convey to their clients their unwavering attention. These actions focus the attention of the interview completely on clients. To accomplish this, counsellors must develop their ability to be comfortable with silence.

However, it is important to remember that effective listening involves more than silence. As Garrett points out, "One who frequently interrupts to say what he would have done under similar circumstances is not a good listener, but neither is he who sits quietly and says nothing" (1982:29). Knowing how and when to continue or interrupt silent moments during interviews is a core skill that will be explored in the next section of this chapter.

CONVERSATION 4.1

PROBLEMS LISTENING AND RESPONDING

STUDENT: I find that I'm so busy trying to think of what to say next that I miss what the client is saying.

TEACHER: Yes, it is tough. That's a common problem, even for experienced counsellors. It is hard to stay focused on what's being said without some thought of what to do next. But with practice it can be done. One trick is to think about what is being said before thinking about what to say. As you reflect on what is being said, try to identify major themes and feelings. Often, your response will emerge naturally out of this effort.

Remember that listening is hard work and you need to be "in shape" for the interview. One essential component of this is to address your psychological needs by dealing with your own issues that might make it difficult to hear clients. If you have unresolved difficulties, especially if they mirror those of your client, it will be particularly difficult to listen effectively. A second component is to make sure you fully disengage from your last client before engaging with the next. Finally, make sure you understand before you move on. Summarize, paraphrase, and ask defining questions to enhance and confirm your understanding. As a rule, the more you occupy yourself with the active demands of listening, the less you will be tempted to let your thoughts wander.

Silence

We should not break silence unless we can improve on it!
—Elbourne, 1997

Drawing on my fine command of language, I said nothing.
—Benchley, cited in Kadushin, 1990:254

The Personal Meaning of Silence. The second major active listening skill is silence. One distinguishing quality of effective counsellors is their mastery of language to communicate ideas and promote change. However, language fluency alone is insufficient. Counsellors also need to understand the importance of silence in communication. They need to balance their verbal agility with an equally strong capacity for silence.

Individuals and cultural groups show considerable differences in their comfort with silence. In some cultures, silence is a sign of respect. For many counsellors, silence is unnatural, and if pauses occur in the conversation, they become anxious and fear that their clients will see them as incompetent. They often burden themselves with pressure to fill the silent void with words. A silent pause even as short as a few seconds may lead to inner panic. Almost on reflex, they act to fill silent moments with questions and interpretations.

Some people judge silence harshly. Quieter people may be seen as unmotivated, uninterested, aloof, rejecting, and ignorant. In a discussion with a group of students in a counselling class, I asked members who rated themselves as "more verbal" to talk to "less verbal" members about their typical reactions to silence. The more verbal members made statements such as "I feel judged," "I don't think you are very interested," "I am boring you," and "I wonder if you care about what we are doing?" Their comments clearly indicated that they felt threatened by silence or viewed it as evidence of judgment or lack of interest.

In contrast, the members who rated themselves as quieter noted that they often did not have enough time to respond and revealed that they were fearful or felt inadequate. Sample comments from this group were: "You don't give me enough time to speak," "I'm scared to talk," "I worry about making a fool of myself," and "By the time I think of what to say, someone else has already said it."

Many philosophers, poets, spiritual leaders, and writers have reflected on the meaning of silence. Typically, they extol its virtues and its power, as the following samples illustrate:

"There was silence deep as death..." (Thomas Campbell)

"Silence is the perfect herald of joy." (William Shakespeare)

"Let thy speech be better than silence, or be silent." (Dionysius)

"I have often regretted my speech, never my silence." (Syrus)

"Silence is golden." (Caryle)

"Observe silence and refrain from idle talk." (Bahá'u'lláh)

"The cruelest lies are often told in silence." (Robert Louis Stevenson)

"I'll speak to thee in silence." (William Shakespeare)

"Silence gives consent." (Oliver Goldsmith)

"There is no reply so sharp as silent contempt." (Montaigne)

"Silence is one great art of conversation." (William Hazlitt)

"The world would be happier if men had the same capacity to be silent that they have to speak." (Spinoza)

"Silence is the most perfect expression of scorn." (George Bernard Shaw)

"There is an eloquent silence; it serves sometimes to approve, sometimes to condemn; there is a mocking silence; there is a respectful silence." (La Rochefoucauld)

Silence in Counselling. Counsellors may have the same anxieties about silence as other people have. Silence may heighten their sense of inadequacy as counsellors and lead to uncertainty in the interview. As a result, counsellors may become impulsive and try to fill silences too quickly.

However, counsellors who discipline themselves to allow silence in their interviews may find that their relationships take on an entirely different tone, with their clients answering their own questions and discovering their own solutions. A repertoire of skills positions counsellors for dealing with silence in an interview. Counsellors should develop comfort in allowing silence, as well as knowledge of when to interrupt silences appropriately. Knowing when to speak and when to allow silence requires some understanding of the various meanings of silence.

During silence, workers need to do more than just keep quiet; they need to *attend* to the silence. **Attended silence** is characterized by eye contact, physical and psychological focus on the client, and self-discipline to minimize internal and external distraction. Silence is not golden if it communicates lack of interest or preoccupation or if it says, "I'm not listening." This means refraining from fidgeting and from other digressions such as taking notes or answering the phone. At the same time, counsellors should not stare or turn the silence into a contest to see who is the first to break it. Counsellors should not automatically assume that silence is a measure of failure, nor should they think that a few moments of silence means that the work of counselling has stopped. Passive clients may be busy with thought, or they may be seeking to gain control or understanding of painful and forgotten feelings.

Every silent interlude will have a different meaning, and counsellors need to be astute to discover the significance of each quiet moment and the most appropriate response. Understanding the different types of silence positions counsellors to look for cues and makes it easier for them to consider appropriate responses. There are six common meanings to silence, which will be discussed in the following subsections.

1. The client is thinking.

Although all clients need time to process information and to frame their responses, some need more time than others. Some clients talk with only a momentary pause to catch their breath, but others punctuate their speech with periods of reflection. If counsellors do not allow this time for contemplation, their clients may feel disempowered or inadequate. Clients may be formulating their thoughts or feelings, only to be prematurely cut off by counsellors whose own anxiety with silence does not permit them to wait.

When clients need time to reflect, counsellors can simply remain attentive and nonverbally show their interest and involvement through eye contact, open posture, and so on. They can also verbally indicate their willingness to listen by using simple phrases such as "I sense you need some time to think. That's okay. I'll wait" and "It's okay with me if you just need to think without speaking."

2. The client is confused and unsure of what to say or do.

Sometimes questions are unclear, the focus of the interview is ambiguous, or clients do not know what is expected of them. Clients may sit in silence, shifting uncomfortably and attempting to sort out what to do next.

When clients become quiet because they are confused, allowing the silence to continue sustains or increases the clients' anxiety. These circumstances warrant interrupting the silence to clarify meaning, direction, or expectations. Rephrasing, summarizing, paraphrasing, and even repetition can help in such situations.

COUNSELLOR: *Perhaps you're confused.*

(client nods)

COUNSELLOR (CHOICE 1): *I think I might have confused you with my last question. It didn't make sense to me either. Let me reword it.*

COUNSELLOR (CHOICE 2): *Let's slow down a bit. Help me to understand what's unclear or confusing.*

Clients may have difficulty expressing their ideas, or language problems may be a barrier. Sometimes patience will suffice and clients just need a little more time to find the right word or phrase. At other times counsellors can tentatively suggest ideas or help clients label feelings.

Clients are more likely to be silent during the beginning phase of counselling and during first interviews. This is normal and usually indicates that clients are unsure of what to say or do. Consequently, they depend on the counsellor to take the lead to clarify role and direction.

3. The client is encountering painful feelings.

Interviewing and counselling can stimulate powerful feelings and memories. Counsellors who can tolerate silence give space to their clients so that they can experience and deal with pain or anxiety. In some cases, clients may be ambivalent about facing their feelings. They may be afraid of their intensity, or they may be unwilling to face their feelings, at least at this time. Silence is a chance for clients to examine the merits of continuing further or retreating to safety. Usually, such moments are obvious because the discussion is intense immediately before the silence.

When clients are struggling with powerful feelings, counsellors may need to use multiple responses. First, there are benefits to allowing this type of silence to continue. Responding with attentive silence can be very therapeutic and supportive. It says, "I am here. I understand. I have the courage to be with you as you deal with your pain."

Second, when dealing with powerful feelings, silence needs to be supported with empathy. Otherwise, there is a danger that clients will feel ignored or misunderstood. Empathy confirms that feelings have been heard, and then subsequent silence gives the client time to process. Empathy might be used to let clients know that they have been understood. As well, empathy tells clients that they have not been abandoned and that their counsellors are ready, willing, and able to be with them while they consider their feelings. Once the counsellor has expressed empathy, silence may be appropriate. In the following example, empathy frames two long silent moments.

COUNSELLOR: *As I listen to you, I'm beginning to sense your feeling of resentment that your mother continually tries to run your life.*

(15 seconds of silence)

CLIENT: *(tears in her eyes) Resentment. That's only part of it. I don't think I could ever live up to her expectations.*

(counsellor maintains eye contact, faces client)

(10 seconds of silence)

CLIENT: *But it's going to be okay. I realize that I have my own expectations to meet. It's me I have to face in the mirror.*

COUNSELLOR: *Sounds like you're beginning to accept that your mother is not going to change, and that only you have control over who you are and how you act.*

4. The client is dealing with issues of trust.

Before trust develops in the counselling relationship, clients may be hesitant to share personal information. They may communicate their reluctance through silence. This is a normal and self-protective way for people to avoid rejection and to maintain a sense of control over private matters. A different type of trust issue may arise with involuntary clients who use silence as a way to control the interview and to demonstrate hostility to the fact that they are there against their will. They use their silence to sabotage the interview. It says what the client may want to express, "I'm here, but you can't make me talk." Silence becomes a way of retaining dignity and control in a situation in which they feel disempowered.

Generally, counsellors will want to gently move the interview toward more openness and intimacy. One way to proceed is to acknowledge the risk in sharing and to candidly discuss issues of trust. A comment such as the following opens the door: "I know it's not easy to share your feelings with a stranger. You don't know me yet and you can't be sure how I might respond." Another strategy is to move at the client's pace and discuss less threatening content until trust in the relationship develops.

Sometimes it is preferable to put trust issues on the table, rather than trying to proceed when there is so much obvious resistance. Leads such as the following can be used:

COUNSELLOR: *I'd like to share a perception with you. I've noticed that whenever I ask a question, you answer me quickly, then you become rather silent. I'm worried that there might be some problems between you and me that we should discuss. Or perhaps you see it differently. In any case, I think it would help if we could discuss it. I'm certainly willing to listen to any of your concerns or feelings.*

(client is silent)

COUNSELLOR: *I'm not you, and without your help I can't understand how you feel. But I suspect you'd rather not be here. That's how I'd feel in the same circumstances.*

In the example above, the counsellor's invitations do not guarantee that the client will open up to discuss feelings of being forced to attend the interview. However, such openness to discuss the issue frequently motivates clients to be candid about their concerns. In any case, clients will have heard the invitation, and it may help to build trust.

5. Silence is the client's usual way.

Some clients are quiet by nature. They are unused to giving long or spontaneous responses, and they may be more comfortable keeping their ideas to themselves. It is important that counsellors do not consider clients' silence a personal failure and that they avoid the temptation to end any silence prematurely. Sometimes counsellors need to modify their own expectations and ways of relating to allow for the extended silences of some individuals.

As we will see in the next chapter, some interview techniques are effective in drawing out quieter clients. For example, open-ended questions that cannot easily be answered with a simple yes or no may help overcome patterns of continued silence that impede the counselling work. Another technique is to discuss with clients how silence is affecting the counselling work, then to explore ways for them to become more expressive. Sometimes clients don't understand the expectations of their counsellors, but once they do, they are willing to cooperate. Professionals should reflect on the fact that whereas they have had training on the skills and process of counselling, their clients have not. Clients may be inaccurately seen as resistant when they are just unsure what to say. This underscores the importance of workers keeping clients fully informed by taking advantage of opportunities to explain their intent and procedures. Simple statements such as the following help to demystify the counselling process:

> **COUNSELLOR:** *I'm sure there's more that you can tell me. It will help me to understand better if you tell me more details and perhaps give me a few examples.*

Counsellors can also adapt their methods by using strategies that require less verbal interaction. Children, for example, may respond more to play, art, music, and drama. Adolescent males may be more motivated to talk if the interview is conducted in conjunction with an activity such as a walk in the park or a game of pool. Counsellors are wise to remember that while they tend to be most comfortable with verbal interaction, their clients might favour other means. For example, some clients like to write in journals, which gives them a chance to think introspectively without time pressures. With these clients, counsellors might seek agreement to use relevant journal entries as reference for discussion. In the following case, a counsellor relates how poetry was used:

> The client was a 20-year-old woman who seemed, at first, reluctant to talk about her depression. Her usual responses were one-word or short answers. I remembered that she had mentioned that she liked poetry, so I asked her if she would be willing to bring some of it to our meeting. She was willing and, in fact, eager to share her work. She brought a short poem to the next session which she read to me. The poem revealed her deep depression and her preoccupation with death. Afterward, we talked about her torment at a level that would not have been otherwise possible. Each week she brought a new poem, and these poems became our starting point. As she began to feel better about herself, her poems became more buoyant and optimistic, and they became one measure of her progress.

6. The client has reached closure.

Silence happens when there is nothing more to say about a particular topic or idea. Silence is a way of saying, "I'm finished. Let's talk about something else."

When natural and appropriate closure is reached, there is a need to move on to a new subject. The counsellor may break such silence by seeking confirmation that an end point has indeed been reached. One strategy that helps to ensure that closure will not be premature is to acknowledge the possibility of closure, as well as the possibility that the client may need time to formulate more ideas. A comment such as the following acknowledges both alternatives:

> **COUNSELLOR:** *I'm thinking that we might have gone as far as we can with that idea. Or perhaps there's more you'd like to say.*

Subsequently, a transition to a new topic is appropriate, or it may be valuable to take a few moments to summarize before moving to a new area of discussion.

CONVERSATION 4.2

LEARNING TO DEAL WITH SILENCE

STUDENT: How long is a reasonable time to allow a silence to continue?

TEACHER: Without knowing the context, I cannot answer your question. Sometimes after a few seconds of silence, it is appropriate to break in and say something, but in other circumstances, an extended silence of several minutes is okay. Each situation must be looked at individually.

STUDENT: I agree, but my problem is that I get uncomfortable after a few seconds. I get so anxious that I usually rush to say something, even when I know I should keep quiet.

TEACHER: Try paying attention to what you are saying to yourself during silent moments. Watch for depreciating self-talk, such as "If I don't say something, the client will think I'm incompetent." Counter this by reminding yourself that silence has its place in counselling. If you interrupt too soon, you rob clients of important opportunities to reflect. Remember that comfort with silence can be learned, but like all skills, learning requires practice. It may help to have a glass of water so that you can take a long, slow sip to prevent speaking prematurely. Deep breathing may also help. Finally, don't overcompensate. Some silences should be interrupted.

Nonverbal Cues and Silence. Sometimes, nonverbal cues can reveal the meaning of silence. Presenting the open palms of one's hands may say, "Wait; I need time." Looking away and clenching a fist may signal an angry silence. At other times, the meaning of silence is unclear. In such situations, counsellors may choose to let the silence continue for a while to see if its meaning becomes apparent, or they may wish to seek help from their clients to understand it. Below are some sample responses that counsellors can use:

- You've (We've) become very quiet. I'm wondering what that means.
- Help me understand the meaning of your silence.
- Perhaps you're hesitant to tell me, or maybe you just need some time to think.

Although there is often ambiguity to silence and it is difficult to understand its meaning with certainty, some clues can be used to interpret silence. Table 4.2 on page 112 presents some of the messages of clients' silence. The table includes a range of nonverbal clues and ideas about how to respond to each. However, all nonverbal behaviour needs to be interpreted with extreme caution. The same behaviour may have multiple meanings. Crossed arms may suggest defensiveness but may also signal that the client is physically cold, or the client may be both defensive and cold. All nonverbal behaviour must be interpreted by considering the individual client and the overall context in which the behaviour occurs, and then it must be checked out with the client to confirm accuracy.

Encouraging Silence. Silence can serve a number of useful purposes in counselling. It provides time for experiencing feelings and time to contemplate. Insight may emerge from moments of uninterrupted thought. Therefore, it makes sense for counsellors to promote periodic silence in their interviews with clients. This may be particularly useful when

Table 4.2   Responding to Silence: Nonverbal Cues

Intended Message	What To Watch For	Counsellor Response Choices
"Please be patient. I need time to think."	One palm of hand raised 90 degrees, squinting, furrowed brow, eye movement, smiling (positive or pleasing thought).	Verbalize willingness to wait. Indicate attended silence with eye contact and other nonverbal expressions of support.
"Help—I'm confused and don't know what to do next."	Shoulder shrugging, raised palms, rapid eye movement.	Set the direction; clarify instructions. Rephrase the last response.
"You can't make me talk." "I don't want to be here."	Ignoring or providing inappropriately short answer, moving the chair back.	Communicate that it's okay not to talk. Empathize with resistance. Describe your feelings when forced to talk.
"I don't know whether to talk or not."	Starting to talk, abruptly stopping, shaking head, stuttering.	Empathize with ambivalence. Discuss the risks of sharing and not sharing.
"I'm scared of what you might think of me."	Physical withdrawal, averted eye contact, carefully measured words, whispering.	Reassure and convey a non-judgmental attitude.
"I'm overwhelmed with these feelings."	Tears, covering eyes, quivering lips, flushed face, looking at the floor, trembling.	Show empathy, use attended silence, then reveal further empathy.
"This is the way I am. I don't say much."	Low voice tone, a pattern of short answers.	Accept it as a cultural/individual norm. Gently encourage with open-ended questions. Explain the importance of sharing.
"I'm finished."	Leaning back, smiling, saying, "That's it."	Summarize. Change the topic; move on.

working with clients who are impulsive and with clients who seem reluctant to use silence. The following are examples of counsellor leads:

- I think it might be useful if we each took a quiet minute or two to think about this idea.
- Let's pause for a moment.
- It's okay with me if you want to think about it for a while.
- When you're ready, we can talk about it. In the meantime, I'm comfortable if we don't say anything.
- Occasional silence is something that may occur during our time together. Sometimes one or both of us will need time to think.

Paraphrasing

Paraphrasing is a way of restating the client's words and ideas in your own words. Paraphrasing is not the same as repeating what the client says. Repetition confirms memorization, but it does not mean that the words and ideas have been understood. Paraphrasing is a way of stating thoughts from a different angle. The defining feature of an accurate paraphrase is its interchangeability with the client's ideas. In the process, paraphrasing can help clients organize disjointed thoughts.

Paraphrasing is an important active listening skill that serves two purposes. First, paraphrasing confirms that counsellors have been listening and have understood clients. Second, paraphrasing gives clients an opportunity to correct any inaccuracies. In the beginning phase of counselling, paraphrasing is particularly important because the counsellor is just starting to understand how the client thinks and feels. Paraphrasing helps the counsellor "get on board." Paraphrasing, together with summarizing and empathizing, assists in developing the counselling relationship. As well, it helps clients to explore their problems in a way that is less forceful and directive than direct questioning techniques.

Paraphrasing concentrates on immediate client statements; it is presented without judgment and without an attempt to problem solve. The important point to remember about paraphrasing is that it does not add to or alter the meaning of a client's statement. In the example below, notice how the counsellor's paraphrase responses capture the essence of what the client has said.

> **CLIENT:** *Losing my job was just the start of a bad year. I've had big marriage problems too, and now my daughter is on the street.*
>
> **COUNSELLOR:** *You've had a number of serious things go wrong this year.*
>
> **CLIENT:** *Right now the most urgent thing is to find some way to get my daughter back home. I need to know she's safe.*
>
> **COUNSELLOR:** *So, the focus of your attention is seeing that your daughter is out of danger.*
>
> **CLIENT:** *I'd love to be able to leave my husband and move to a new city, but what would happen to my daughter? I can't be selfish.*
>
> **COUNSELLOR:** *If it were just you, you'd know what to do. But your daughter really is your priority.*
>
> **CLIENT:** *You're absolutely right. Once she's okay, then I'll take care of myself.*

Counsellors can add variety to their interviews by using a range of different lead-ins for paraphrasing. Some examples are listed below:

- Put a different way, you seem to be saying ...
- As I understand it ...
- Is this right? You're saying ...
- In other words ...
- It seems like ...
- It sounds a bit like ...

- As I hear it ...
- The picture I get is ...

It is preferable for counsellors to present paraphrases tentatively. This provides the opportunity for clients to correct errors, confirm accuracy, or provide more detail. A tentative paraphrase opens discussion for deeper exploration. Statements such as "Correct me if I'm wrong" and "Would it be fair to say ...?" suggest tentativeness.

Sometimes counsellors move too quickly by doing two things at once. In the example below, the counsellor offers a potentially useful paraphrase, then abruptly switches to a question that will move the interview in a different direction.

> **COUNSELLOR:** *As I see it, you've reached a point in your life where you're not going to take any more abuse. What do you see as your options?*

In this example, a vocal pause or short silence might have allowed the client the chance to confirm that the paraphrase was correct. Client confirmation may come from both verbal and nonverbal channels.

Paraphrasing and Empathy.

Paraphrasing and Empathy. Paraphrasing differs from empathy because it concentrates on the content of messages—information, facts, details, and descriptions—whereas empathy focuses on feelings. Paraphrasing may be less threatening to clients who have trouble discussing feelings. Paraphrasing can be used as a prelude to empathy, with empathy being introduced as clients become more trusting and willing to address their feelings.

Paraphrasing arises from words that the client has actually said, but empathy builds on verbal and nonverbal cues, responding to feelings that the client may never have identified. Paraphrasing is related to summarizing. Both paraphrasing and summarizing condense content, and both highlight key ideas in the client's communication.

The following example shows the difference between paraphrasing and empathy:

> **CLIENT:** *Not having a job is getting me down. I know it doesn't help to sit in front of the TV all day hoping someone will call with my dream job.*

> **COUNSELLOR PARAPHRASE:** *You're aware that you have to become more active in searching for a job in order to stop the downward slide.*

> **COUNSELLOR EMPATHY:** *You're aware that wishing for a job offer is making you depressed.*

In the paraphrase response the counsellor paid attention to the key message (content) in the client's statement, then restated it in different words. In the empathy response the counsellor picked up on the emotional component. Counsellors often find that simple paraphrases such as the one above have a powerful, positive effect. Paraphrasing helps clients realize that counsellors are listening and that they are interested. Subsequently, clients who feel heard and understood often release their defensiveness and fears about sharing. In turn, the process of sharing and exploring may generate new understanding or insight for clients regarding their feelings and problem situations.

CONVERSATION 4.3

EFFECTIVE PARAPHRASING

STUDENT: If the client has just said something, what's the point in restating it? I think that a client might find paraphrasing very irritating.

TEACHER: You're saying why anger your client by repeating what's obvious?

STUDENT: That right.

TEACHER: Notice that I just paraphrased what you said and you seemed okay with it.

(student nods in agreement)

TEACHER: An effective paraphrase is more than just mechanical restatement or parroting of the client's words. Verbatim restatements may irritate clients because they don't add anything to the interview. A useful paraphrase considers clients' ideas from a different perspective. Paraphrases are most potent when they invite or stimulate further elaboration and discussion. Nevertheless, I think it's best to avoid excessive use of paraphrasing or any other skill. Use paraphrasing when you need to check your perceptions and when it seems important to let a client know that you understand.

Summarizing

Summarizing is an active interviewing skill that can serve a number of purposes. First, summarizing is a way of confirming understanding and checking assumptions. Since client messages may be complex, vague, and ambiguous, it is crucial that counsellors validate their interpretations. When they summarize content, counsellors present a snapshot of their clients' main ideas in condensed format for verification.

> **COUNSELLOR:** *So far you seem to be saying that you don't see any point in trying the same old strategies. Talking to her didn't seem to work. Ignoring her was even worse. Now you're not sure what else you can do. Does that seem like an accurate summary?*

Second, summarizing is a way of organizing complex data and content by tying disjointed but related ideas together. This may provide clients with a different way to look at existing problems, thus promoting insight. Such summaries can significantly reduce a client's confusion by ordering ideas in a more coherent sequence. The example below is excerpted from the mid-point of an hour-long counselling session. Prior to this point the client had been talking about a variety of ways to manage his depression.

> **COUNSELLOR:** *Let me see if I can sum up what we've been talking about. Essentially, as you see it, you need to work on long-term solutions, some related to improving your fitness, others targeting your social life. As well, you want to look at things you can do immediately to reduce your depression, including getting a medical and looking for some fun things to do. Is that a fair way to outline our discussion?*

The counsellor's summary helps the client systematize his action plan. Summaries such as this help clients and counsellors identify priorities. By summarizing, counsellors configure their clients' problems and issues in a particular way that might give precedence to certain ideas.

Third, summarizing can be helpful in working with clients who are overly verbose, are prone to introduce irrelevant material, or wander from topic to topic. Summarizing separates what is important from what is irrelevant by focusing the interview on particular themes and content.

> **COUNSELLOR:** *From what you've been saying, it seems that your problems at work with your supervisor are your top priority. Do you agree?*

Summarizing may focus on a short time within an interview, or it can encompass a broader period, including the whole interview or the entire helping relationship. Two types of summaries are *content*, or simple, summaries and *theme* summaries. A content summary focuses on content and is an unedited condensing of the client's words. All ideas are included. A theme summary edits unnecessary detail and attempts to identify key patterns and areas of urgency. The following examples illustrate the two types of summaries:

The client, a 45-year-old male, has been describing how unhappy he has been as a welder.

> **CLIENT:** *From the first day on the job, I knew that welding wasn't for me. Even as a child, I always wanted to work with people. As a welder, I spend most of my time on my own. Last week was a good example. From Monday to Thursday, I was in the shop basement, and the only time I had any human interaction was when I went to lunch. It's not much better at home. My wife has gone back to school, so she's busy with homework every night. The kids are grown and we don't see them that often. All I seem to do is work and watch TV. With the junk on TV, that's not much of a life. The only thing worth watching is CNN.*

> **CONTENT OR SIMPLE SUMMARY:** *From the beginning, you were aware that your welding career didn't meet your long-standing need to work with people. It seems that your work, with last week as a typical example, leaves you on your own. With your wife studying and your children gone, TV offers little comfort.*

> **THEME SUMMARY:** *You're feeling isolated. Neither your job nor your home life gives you much opportunity to fulfill your long-standing need to work with people.*

Content summaries make little or no judgment about relevance. The major goal of the content summary is to organize ideas and to précis data. Theme summaries are more risky. They require interviewers to judge which information is relevant and which is irrelevant. In the above example, different interviewers might focus on different themes, depending on their mandate. A researcher investigating television programming would hear this client's statement differently than would a career counsellor or a marriage counsellor.

LIVE is an acronym that describes the four essential steps of summarizing: listen, identify, verbalize, evaluate.

Step One: Listen. During this step the task is to listen carefully to verbal and nonverbal messages that provide clues to content and meaning. Counsellors must exercise a great deal of self-discipline to avoid contaminating clients' ideas with personal bias and definition. Counsellors can ask questions, request examples, and probe for definition as ways to reduce any risk of imposing their own bias and assumptions. As well, they need to control distractions, including outside noise, daydreaming, attending to other activities, or becoming preoccupied with what to say next. Active involvement in what is being said diverts counsellors from any temptation to become distracted. Another technique to avoid distraction is to silently repeat or review client messages.

Listening means paying attention to the five *W*s: Who? What? Where? When? Why? and How? Sample questions to consider are, Whom are clients talking about? What are they saying? What are they feeling? What are they thinking? When does this happen? Where does it occur? Why does it happen? How are clients saying it?

Step Two: Identify. The primary goal of this step is to make sense of all that has been said and heard. This involves distinguishing important information from irrelevant information, identifying underlying themes and patterns, and setting priorities. It means hearing what has been said in context, or avoiding a common pitfall in listening: not seeing the forest for the trees. The counsellor's goal is to attach as similar meaning as possible to the meaning the client intended. At this step, counsellors need to remember that their perspectives are biased. What they deem significant and what their clients view as important may differ sharply. This reality underscores the importance of discussing these differences openly within the interview.

One tool that counsellors can use is to listen for key words that will help them understand how clients think. Use of the words *should* and *must* may signal self-imposed unrealistic or irrational expectations. Ellis (1993a) believes that individuals may develop excessive needs for certain things, such as achievement, approval, and love. Problems develop when these needs become translated into dogmatic "musts," and "shoulds." For example, a client might say, "I have to get my master's degree in order to be happy." In other circumstances, the word *can't* might suggest feelings of inadequacy or self-esteem problems.

Step Three: Verbalize. The goal of this step is to verbalize understanding of what the client has said in a summarization response, using words and phrases that the client can understand. Understanding is always tentative, at least until clients have an opportunity to confirm or challenge counsellors' perceptions, so this step is crucial to test the accuracy of comprehension. The move to a summarizing statement can be flagged by counsellor leads such as:

- To summarize what you have been saying ...
- If I may offer a summary ...
- To be sure I understand ...
- Let's summarize.
- Summing up ...
- Let's pause for a moment to recap.

Step Four: Evaluate. After summarizing for clients, the next step is to watch and listen carefully for signs that the summary is correct. Accurate summaries may be signalled nonverbally by the client's head nods, smiles, and relaxed posture, and verbally with short statements, such as "that's right" and "exactly." Disagreement may be direct ("No, that's not right"), or it may be nonverbal as clients move back, hesitate, or look away. Subtle clues that understanding is incomplete or inaccurate are lukewarm responses, such as "kind of," and paralinguistic cues, such as speech that is drawn out, even though the words may appear to confirm understanding. Counsellors can use questions and statements to invite confirmation. This reinforces the notion that the client's right to be heard accurately will be respected, and it empowers clients to take an active role in evaluation. Such leads include the following:

- Does my summary capture the important points?
- I'm wondering if you agree with my summary.
- Is that accurate?
- How does that sound to you?
- Have I missed anything important?
- What have I missed?
- How would you summarize what we have talked about?

Selective Perception. **Selective perception** is a term used to describe the natural tendency to avoid being overwhelmed by information by screening out material that is irrelevant. In counselling, the obvious problem is that what clients consider relevant may differ from what counsellors consider relevant. What a person deems important is likely to be influenced by one's frame of reference, which is uniquely defined through elements such as past experiences, personal values, current mood, interests, concerns, fears, prejudices, health, culture, and context. For example, a tow-truck driver looks very different when you're stuck on a dark and stormy night than when you're being towed for illegal parking. The word mother may call up images of love and support or memories of abuse and pain. The notion of selective perception was illustrated in a popular anecdote about a social worker who was surprised to discover how many of his clients developed sexual problems after he took a course on sexual counselling. Johnson underscores the dangers of selective perception: "There is evidence that you will be more sensitive to perceiving messages that are consistent with your opinions and attitudes. You will tend to misperceive or fail to perceive messages that are opposite to your opinions, beliefs, and attitudes" (1997:129).

Counsellors need to be alert to the dangers of selective perception in their own thinking and responses. They must be vigilant to make sure they understand how and when prior learning, values, and current expectations influence their interpretations. Counsellors need to be careful that they don't impose their own sense of what's important.

Of necessity, counsellors must ignore some parts of a client's communication and selectively attend to others. Typically, it is not possible to respond to everything. Consider how many ways a counsellor might respond to the following statement:

CLIENT: *You could say my life is complicated. Six months ago I started a new job and it's terrific. I'm making more money than ever. But I don't have much time to enjoy it, given that I'm working six days a week. Maybe I should just force myself to take a vacation. With my wife working too, I think it's been hard on the kids. My youngest daughter's not doing too well in school, and she seems very depressed. Most nights, she just goes to her room right after supper and shuts the door. Maybe it's just a stage and she's like all teenagers. Now I've just heard that my father can't live on his own anymore. I don't know whether to take him in with us, arrange home care, or place him in a senior's centre.*

In this example, there are many areas of potential importance (financial management, work pressures, stress, daughter, caring for parents). Let's look at some counsellor response choices:

COUNSELLOR (CHOICE 1): *Sounds like the most urgent need is to deal with your dad. Why don't we spend some time looking at the options?*

COUNSELLOR (CHOICE 2): *Sounds like you've got a lot on your plate. How do you manage your work stress? How do you support your daughter? What can you do with your father? Have I missed anything? (client says no) What's most important to you?*

Choice 1 illustrates the danger of selective perception. The counsellor assumes that caring for the father is the most urgent concern. In contrast, Choice 2 avoids this pitfall. The counsellor uses summarizing skills to identify major themes, then checks for accuracy, then encourages the client to set priorities.

Clients are also prone to selective perception, which may impair their ability to see all parts of a problem or available solutions that are within their grasp. Summarizing can be used to bring these overlooked aspects to the foreground.

COUNSELLOR: *You've told me many times that you don't see any way out of your situation. At the same time you've mentioned a couple of strategies that have worked for you in similar conditions.*

INTERVIEW 4.1 LISTENING, SILENCE, AND SUMMARIZING SKILLS

The following interview excerpt illustrates some of the important concepts from this chapter. This is the second interview with a client who is seeking help with anger management. The excerpt begins about five minutes into the interview.

DIALOGUE	ANALYSIS
Counsellor: Maybe we could take a minute to review the key points we discussed last week.	This opening comment sets the stage for a review of the last interview. This is important for reestablishing the contract. It confirms that issues that were important during the last session still remain priorities.
(three seconds of silence; client smiles and nods her head)	
	After offering a summary, it is important to confirm its accuracy. In this case, the counsellor uses the brief silence to confirm the client's (nonverbal) agreement.
Counsellor: I remember two points. First, you indicated that you wanted to find out what your triggers are—the things that lead you to lose control. Second, you wanted to explore some	This theme summary focuses on what the counsellor considers to have been the priority of the last session. Checking for client agreement is an important adjunct.

(continued)

ideas for staying in control. Have I missed anything?

Client: Yes, that about sums it up. But I don't want to become a pushover.

The client confirms partial accuracy, then adds a point that the interviewer's summary has missed. This should alert the interviewer to the client's priorities.

Counsellor: So, anger management, but not at the expense of giving up your rights.

A succinct paraphrase acknowledges the client's priority.

(ten seconds of silence)

Counsellor: You've become very quiet. I'm struggling to understand what that means.

(ten seconds of silence; client looks at the floor, tears in her eyes)

Counsellor: Perhaps this is painful for you to think about.

Initially, there is not enough information for the counsellor to understand the meaning of the client's silence. It might be tempting to move on with further questions, but the counsellor suspects that the silence is significant. A gentle statement invites the client to give meaning to her silence. Nonverbal clues (looking away, tears) suggest that the client is encountering strong feelings. The counsellor now focuses on feelings.

Client: In every relationship I've ever had, I end up being the underdog. I do everything to please my partner, but nothing for me. I always give in, but inside, it's a different story. I'm full of rage and resentment.

The client's comments suggest that she is willing to take a trust risk. This is a critical moment in the interview. The client will be watching carefully for signs of rejection.

Counsellor: Tell me more. (leans toward client, maintains eye contact)

This directive encourages the client to go on with her story. It confirms direction and is short enough not to interfere with the momentum that the client has established. Attending behaviour shows that the counsellor is interested and open to hearing the client's ideas and feelings.

Client: That's the essence of the problem. I let things build up inside, then I explode. Once, I was even fired when I blew up at my boss.

The client continues to risk. This signals that trust is growing, but the connection may still be very fragile. As we will see in Chapter 6, it is now important for the counsellor to make an empathic connection with the client's feelings.

Counsellor: So your anger is a bit like a time bomb, ticking away until you explode.

Here the counsellor paraphrases using a simile that is consistent with the client's phrasing.

Client: Exactly. (short silence)

This silence may be a simple pause that allows the client to decide what to talk about next.

(continued)

Client: But, as I think about it, it's not just my anger. I guess what I'm really afraid of is never having things go my way.

Counsellor: As I hear it, you seem to need to have more control over your life.

Client: No, that's not it. It's not control so much as validation.

The client does not accept the counsellor's paraphrase as accurate. Secure counsellors need not fear such mistakes or corrections. The client's willingness to correct the counsellor indicates her trust.

Summary

Listening is the basis for understanding and a prerequisite for relationship development. It requires considerable effort and patience to understand the messages of others as they were intended. Active listening involves the skills of summarizing, paraphrasing, questioning, and empathizing as tools to explore and deepen understanding. Verbal and nonverbal attending behaviours demonstrate to clients that counsellors are willing and able to listen. Communication entails shifts between speaking and listening, while attempting to understand. A wide range of problems, such as cultural and language barriers, difficulty in framing ideas, outside noise, ambiguity, loss of objectivity, and speech problems, can interfere with the listening process. Competent counsellors are sensitive to these problems and take steps to overcome them.

Active listening skills are tools for increasing understanding, communicating interest to clients, and letting clients know that they have been heard. Active listening involves counsellors in an ongoing process of paying attention, listening, exploring, and deepening.

Attending is the way that counsellors communicate that they are physically and psychologically committed to the helping relationship. Attending begins with a positive attitude and a genuine desire to get involved. This attitude is confirmed with behaviours such as making eye contact, assuming an open posture, and leaning toward others.

Effective counsellors need to develop the capacity for tolerating silence, as well as the wisdom to know when to interrupt silence during interviews. An important part of this skill is understanding the different types of silence. Nonverbal cues are important indicators of the meaning of silence. In addition, counsellors can seek help from their clients to understand silence. Since silence can serve useful purposes in counselling, counsellors may wish to encourage periodic silent moments of reflection.

Paraphrasing is a way of restating someone's words and ideas in your own words. Paraphrasing is important in counselling because it confirms to clients that counsellors have heard and understood them. Counsellors need to paraphrase without judging. Summarizing helps clients to organize complex thoughts and is used to focus on relevant themes and content. The acronym LIVE can be used to describe the process of summarizing: listen, identify, verbalize, and evaluate.

Exercises

1. List words, phrases, and situations that you think might be your emotional triggers.

2. Over the next week or so, pay attention to the vocal pauses and silences that you and others use in everyday and professional communication. What indicators suggest comfort with silence? Discomfort?

3. Deliberately alter your response time to experiment with using silence.

4. Ask a colleague to observe your use of silence during an interview. The following checklist may be used to stimulate discussion.

	Yes	No
The interviewer allowed the client time to think and respond.	__	__
The interviewer seemed comfortable with silence.	__	__
The interviewer attended to the silence.	__	__
The interviewer interrupted silences appropriately.	__	__

5. Explain how silence can be used effectively in counselling.

6. During interviews with some colleagues or clients, find opportune moments to call for brief periods of reflective silence, then continue the interview. Discuss with your colleague/client what the impact of the silence was on the interview.

7. Videotape an interview or ask a colleague to observe your work. Evaluate your attending behaviour. Use the following checklist to evaluate attending behaviour.

Checklist for Attending

	Yes	No
Did the Interviewer ...		
Use nonverbal behaviour that suggested comfort with and acceptance of the client's ideas?	__	__
Manage outside distractions and fidgeting?	__	__
Use questions and responses that showed openness to learning?	__	__
Give the client time to express ideas without inappropriate interruption?	__	__
Manage personal assumptions and attitudes that detracted from the counsellor's ability to be present for the client?	__	__

8. Work with a colleague to explore the effects of poor listening. As an exercise, deliberately (but subtly) violate the principles of effective listening and attending. For example, interrupt inappropriately, ask unrelated questions, switch topics prematurely, and avoid eye contact and other indicators of interest. When you are finished, discuss the experience. Discuss how it feels to not have others listen to you.

9. Paraphrase each of the following clients' statements.

   • At a party the other night, I finally met someone with whom I can carry on an intelligent conversation. He seemed interested too, but he didn't ask for my phone number.

- It's a dilemma! I don't know whether to finish the school year or drop out and get a handle on some of my debts.

- My supervisor wants to see me today. I know she wants to talk to me because I've been late for work over the last few weeks.

- Sure I get depressed. Who doesn't?

- First my car broke down, then the fridge. Now it's the plumbing. I should marry someone who is good at fixing things.

- I think that with AIDS and all the other diseases you can catch we should all take precautions. You never know who might be infected.

- Well, to put it bluntly, I think my partner has a lover. But I could forgive that. I just want our relationship to be the way it was when we first met.

- I've tried everything. I have a great résumé. I've called everyone I know. I look for a job five to six hours a day. Still, I can't find work.

- Lately, I've been thinking that there has to be more to life than work and play. I'm not even sure if I believe in God, but I need to find some meaning for my life.

- I just lost it. My anger built up and I hit her. She got so upset she packed up and left with the kids. I've never done anything like that in my whole life. I realize that I didn't solve anything by losing my temper. Now I may have ruined my marriage and turned my kids against me.

- I guess I'm going to have to find some way of dealing with my drinking problem. The other day I was so sick from drinking that I couldn't even get out of bed. I just can't let booze continue to jeopardize my work and my family.

10. Conduct an interview with a colleague on any topic of interest. As interviewer, your job is to practise paraphrasing. After each client statement, paraphrase what you think your colleague said, then watch for verbal and nonverbal indicators that your paraphrase was correct.

11. Practise summarizing skills:

   a. Conduct a five- or ten-minute interview with a colleague on any topic of interest. As interviewer, your job is to practise content summarizing skills. Periodically, try to summarize information in the interview. Make sure you understand accurately before moving on. At the conclusion of the interview, offer a complete summary of the whole session. Check with your partner to see if you were understood.

   b. Continue the interview, but now practise theme summarizing skills. Periodically, try to summarize important themes in the interview. Make sure you understand accurately before moving on. At the conclusion of the interview, offer a complete summary of the whole session. Use the following checklist to evaluate the work.

Checklist for Summarizing

	Yes	*No*
Did the Interviewer ...		
Listen patiently before responding?	—	—
Identify recurrent themes?	—	—

Look for issues and concerns that represent the client's most
   urgent priorities?   —   —

Respond with short summary statements?   —   —

Give verbal or nonverbal invitations to the client to confirm the
   accuracy of the summary?   —   —

Summarize without judgment, advice, or attempts to
   problem solve?   —   —

Use language that was consistent with the client's frame of
   reference and culture?   —   —

At the conclusion of both interviews switch roles; then discuss the experience.

Weblinks

"Listening" by D. Wayne Matthews (.pdf document)
www.ces.ncsu.edu/depts/fcs/humandev/docs/fcs2763.pdf

"Tips on Effective Listening" by Larry Alan Nadig
www.drnadig.com/listening.htm

"Listening—With Your Heart as Well as Your Ears" by Herbert G. Lingren
www.ianr.unl.edu/pubs/family/g1092.htm

INTERVIEWING SKILLS: THE SEARCH FOR MEANING

PREVIEW

After reading this chapter you should be able to:

- Describe the importance of asking questions.
- Identify and describe common questioning errors.
- Explain why clients might not answer questions.
- Define open, closed, and indirect questions.
- Describe the advantages and disadvantages of open, closed, and indirect questions.
- Demonstrate the capacity to formulate open, closed, and indirect questions.
- Explain the importance of concreteness in counselling.
- Demonstrate the ability to probe for appropriate concreteness.
- Identify key questions for every interview.
- Recognize the five different types of interview transitions.

QUESTIONING

Asking questions is an important part of active listening and serves multiple purposes. No single approach to questioning works best with every client. Counsellors must consider numerous factors, such as the goals for the session, the context in which questions are asked, and the individual needs of clients, and adapt their questioning techniques accordingly. Therefore, the best counsellors have a repertoire of techniques from which to select. They use questions to engage clients in higher-order thinking, kindle their curiosity, and prompt them to consider new possibilities.

Questions are important tools for gathering data. Counsellors listen in order to understand, but they cannot understand if they do not have sufficient information. Questions can be used to seek relevant details, definitions, and examples. By asking questions, counsellors lessen the probability that they will make assumptions. Questions are important adjuncts to empathy because they allow counsellors to explore, clarify, and define emotions. Asking the right question often has more impact on the client and the process of change than having the correct answer (Miller, 1992).

Questions focus the work of the interview on particular topics and themes. Every interview has a purpose, and this purpose determines the nature and type of questions that will be used, but the overall purpose of counselling is to empower clients to discover choices for solving problems that interfere with their lives. A series of questions can systematically lead clients through problem exploration, goal setting, and problem solving. Asking a thought-provoking question stimulates clients to begin a reflective process that can promote insight. Asking the right questions can promote awareness by leading clients to examine issues, ideas, and feelings that they might have otherwise overlooked. By sequencing questions, counsellors can teach clients logical ways of analyzing and responding to problems. Effective questioning can also help clients to make connections and uncover patterns in their thinking and problem solving.

Structured interviews follow a defined sequence of predetermined questions. Every person is asked the same question in exactly the same manner. Interviews that require counsellors to complete forms to establish clients' eligibility or to make assessments are examples of structured interviews. The distinguishing feature of structured interviews is their specific and standard questions. In structured interviews, there is little or no freedom of choice regarding the focus and pace of the interview.

Unstructured interviews permit interviewers and clients freedom to go in any direction without predetermined control or set questions. The distinguishing feature of unstructured interviews is their emphasis on flexible counsellor–client contracts. In these types of interviews, a more conversational tone is apparent and there is less rigidity concerning when and how questions are asked.

Errors In Asking Questions

Asking questions is a skill. Faulty questioning may bias answers, antagonize clients, or keep the interview at a superficial level. Insensitive questions can disregard client feelings or leave them feeling judged or abandoned. Poorly timed questions may rush the interview or frighten clients with demands for disclosure before trust has been established.

Jargon. Common sense tells us that in order for questions to be effective they must be presented so that they are clear and understandable—in other words, so they are consistent with the language or culture of the client. Counsellors, like other professionals, have their own words and language to describe their activities. Furthermore, each field of practice and each setting has abbreviations, distinctive words, and phrases that are commonly understood by the people who work there. This jargon allows for streamlined communication and helps to define activities and routines precisely. Unfortunately, jargon is often used inappropriately with clients who do not understand it, as in the following example:

> **COUNSELLOR:** *I'm assuming that this is the first time that you've gone through the intake process. After we complete your app., I can refer to you to an appropriate community resource.*

A new client may have no idea what is meant by the terms intake process and community resource or the abbreviation "app." Too embarrassed to ask, these clients may be left feeling demoralized, stupid, and incapable. Nonassertive clients frequently respond to jargon by acquiescing or pretending that they understand. Their answers may create the illusion that they understand, while, in fact, they have no idea what has been said. One woman phoned an immigrant services centre in a state of panic. She had been to the local welfare office and signed a form but had no idea what she had endorsed. Now she feared that she had made some mistake, since her monthly welfare cheque was $100 less than the previous month's.

Leading Questions. How you word a question may dramatically affect the answer. Asking your spiritual leader, "Is it all right to smoke while praying?" may get a very different answer than asking, "Is it all right to pray while smoking?" (Sudman and Bradburn, 1983:1).

Leading questions manipulate clients to choose what appears to be the preferred answer; for example, "Don't you believe it's time you took care of yourself instead of putting your husband first?" and "You like school, don't you?" bias the answers. Clients who have a high need to be liked by their counsellors and clients who tend to be compliant are especially vulnerable to leading questions. These clients are less likely to be assertive by disagreeing with their counsellors.

Counsellors may use leading questions to camouflage their own ideas. For example, the counsellor who asks, "Do you think you should be doing that?" is probably saying, "I don't think you should be doing that." Leading questions tend to corner clients, as in the following interview excerpt, in which a counsellor talks to a man about his mother.

> **COUNSELLOR:** *Given what you've been saying, it's time for action. Wouldn't you agree that allowing your mother to live alone at home is not in anyone's best interest?*
>
> **CLIENT:** *I suppose you're right.*
>
> **COUNSELLOR:** *Would you prefer to put her in a seniors' home?*
>
> **CLIENT:** *I really don't want to put her in a home. That wouldn't be right.*
>
> **COUNSELLOR:** *Don't you think this might be easier on your family than taking on the enormous problems involved in moving her in with you?*

CLIENT: *(hesitates) I suppose you're right. But ...*

COUNSELLOR: *(interrupts) I have a list of possible placements. Do you want to make some calls now?*

It's easy to see how the counsellor's agenda in the above encounter discounted the views and needs of the client. By selectively emphasizing one alternative, the counsellor allowed the client little freedom of choice. Consider how the outcome might have been different had the counsellor used the lead below.

COUNSELLOR: *Given what you've been saying, it's time for action. What do you see as your options?*

Such a lead would have allowed the client to identify alternatives such as arranging for in-home care for his mother or inviting her to live with him. The counsellor's favoured alternative is not out on the discussion table to contaminate the discussion.

Excessive Questioning. Although questions are an indispensable part of most interviews, excessive questioning can leave clients feeling interrogated and bombarded. As a response to intense questioning, some clients fail to return for a second interview. Others become increasingly defensive and terse with their responses, particularly if they are unsure of the purpose of the questions. Excessive questioning can overwhelm clients, leaving them frustrated, confused, and exhausted.

Benjamin offers this warning about conducting the counselling interview by relying on questions: "By initiating the question-answer pattern we are telling the interviewee as plainly as if we put it into words that we are the authority, the expert, and that only we know what is important and relevant ..." (1981:72). He suggests that the client may submit to the "humiliation" of questions "only because he expects you to come up with a solution to his problem or because he feels that this is the only way you have of helping him" (72). Martin (1983) warns that counsellors need to be careful not to behave as if they are conducting an investigation, by asking lots of questions. He suggests that this behaviour locks clients and counsellors into set roles. Relying on questions results in the interview digressing to "a question-and-answer interrogation in which the client waits for the counsellor to come up with the next topic" (George and Cristiani, 1986:147). Consequently, "it is not reasonable of the therapist to expect to ask a lot of questions and then have the client suddenly start self-exploration" (Martin, 1983:81).

Some clients simply do not respond well to questions. For example, involuntary clients may experience questions as an invasion of their privacy. As well, clients from some cultures may react unfavourably to questions. In such circumstances, reliance on questions will frustrate the goals of the interview. Counsellors may find that rather than getting more information, they are obtaining less. Counsellors should be alert to signs that their clients are reacting poorly to questions. For example, their clients' answers may become briefer, signalling their intention to be less cooperative. Clients also may communicate their displeasure nonverbally by shifting uncomfortably, grimacing, or averting eye contact. Some clients may refuse to answer by becoming silent, but others may be more outspoken with their disapproval, saying, "I don't see the point of all these questions." If counsellors continue with questions when it is clear that their clients are rejecting this approach, serious damage to the counselling relationship may result.

Questions put counsellors in control. To some extent, counsellors need to have control of the interview in order to establish its focus and structure. However, clients may be left feeling that they have lost control. As Leeds argues, "Because the other person is compelled to answer, the power goes to the person asking the question. Just watch the power shift when someone asks, 'Where are you going?' and you answer, 'Why do you ask?'" (1993:58).

Consequently, it is important that counsellors are able to modify their approaches to reduce or eliminate questions. Sometimes, for example, an empathic response can achieve the same purpose as a question:

> **CLIENT:** *I just don't know what I'm going to do. Since she left, I've felt lost and unsure of what I should do with my life.*

> **COUNSELLOR (CHOICE 1):** *What are some possibilities?*

> **COUNSELLOR (CHOICE 2):** *Sounds like you feel all alone and uncertain of what to do next.*

Choice 1 seeks more information from the client about what alternatives he sees for himself. This question helps move the interview toward problem solving and decision making. With Choice 2, the counsellor acknowledges the client's feelings, as well as his indecision. With both choices, the client is likely to respond by listing his options. However, the counsellor's empathy in Choice 2 is more likely to be experienced by the client as sensitive and supportive.

Counsellors may have to ask a lot of questions—for example, to determine eligibility for service or to complete an intake (first) interview. One way that counsellors can lessen the impact of excessive questions is to have periodic pauses to check how their clients are doing. For example, they might say, "I'm asking a lot of questions. How are you doing? I know it can be a bit overwhelming." Such comments convey respect and concern. Consequently, they tend to motivate and energize clients.

Not asking questions can be as serious a problem as asking too many questions. As a result, it is important for counsellors to remember to balance questions with responses that confirm understanding (summaries) and empathic responses that affirm sensitivity to feelings. Benjamin's terse observation is worth remembering: "We ask too many questions, often meaningless ones. We ask questions that confuse the interviewee, that interrupt him. We ask questions the interviewee cannot possibly answer. We even ask questions we don't want the answers to, and, consequently, we do not hear the answers when forthcoming" (1981:71).

Multiple Questions.

Multiple Questions. Multiple questions are two or more questions asked at the same time. If the questions are complementary, they are not problematic. A second question may be asked simultaneously that embellishes or clarifies the first. For example:

> **COUNSELLOR:** *How did you feel about it? How did you feel when he rejected you?*

In this example the second question does not detract from or contradict the first. Of course, the second question alone would have sufficed. In contrast, the example below illustrates how multiple questions can be confusing:

COUNSELLOR: *How did you feel about it? Did you see any other way of handling the situation?*

In this example, both questions are potentially useful, but not when they are asked simultaneously. The client has to decide which question to answer. Each will take the interview in a different direction. At their worst, multiple questions can bombard and assault clients with complex and conflicting demands. Imagine if you were the client in the following interview:

COUNSELLOR: *So, is there anything you can do? Do you think you might have told her how you felt? Or maybe you see it differently. How long do you think you can continue to hang on?*

The counsellor may be well meaning, but responses such as these complicate matters and may add to the client's confusion. Generally, counsellors need to curb any impulse to ask more than one question at a time. When they ask a question, they should wait for the answer before proceeding to another question or topic.

Irrelevant and Poorly Timed Questions.
One way that counselling interviews are distinguished from everyday conversations is that interviews have a definite purpose or intent. When counsellors know the purpose of the interview, they are able to frame questions that support that purpose. Conversely, counsellors who are unsure of the purpose are more likely to ask random questions.

Ideally, counsellors should have a purpose when they ask questions. Moreover, they should be prepared to share this purpose with their clients. They might offer a brief explanation, for example, "It would help me to understand your situation better if I asked you some questions. This will give me an idea of how you see things." Preambles such as this inform the client of the counsellor's motives and procedures. When clients know what is happening, they are less likely to be defensive and more likely to support the process.

Sometimes counsellors ask excellent questions but ask them at the wrong time, which leads to inappropriate topic change. A common error of this type occurs when counsellors ask content questions after clients have expressed their feelings. For example:

CLIENT: *I was furious with her. I never imagined that my best friend would be having an affair with my husband. We've been married for 10 years, and I thought I could trust him. I feel like a complete fool.*

COUNSELLOR: *How did you find out they were seeing each other?*

In the example above, the counsellor's question is valid, but it is timed insensitively. Since the client has just risked expressing strong feelings, the counsellor should consider empathy as the preferred response. The next chapter addresses this critical skill.

A second common error occurs when counsellors shift the topic without exploring beyond a superficial level. This can happen for several reasons. First, counsellors may be unskilled at using probes. Second, they may be overly cautious about probing, perhaps fearing that they will be invading their clients' privacy. Third, they may be fixated on problem solving, as in the following example:

CLIENT: *We fight all the time.*

COUNSELLOR: *How do you think you might cut down on the fighting?*

In this example, the counsellor jumps to problem solving far too quickly. Once a client introduces a topic, the counsellor's next step is to focus on the issue. The counsellor can use a series of questions to acquire and deepen understanding. For example, it is essential that the counsellor learn what the client means by "fight." Do they yell and scream? Do they refuse to talk to each other? Perhaps there is physical conflict.

"Why" Questions. "Why" questions should be used cautiously; as a rule, they are more threatening for clients. Why questions tend to ask for justification, and their tone often suggests judgment, disapproval, or embedded advice. The question "Why don't you leave him?" may put a client on the defensive with the implied message "You should leave." Why questions ask people to explain and justify their behaviour. Frequently, this requires a degree of insight that they simply do not have. In response, clients may make up answers or feel exposed and stupid for being unable to answer the question.

Benjamin echoes these sentiments, arguing that even when judgment is not intended by the interviewer "that is generally how the word will be understood" (1981:86). As a result, "whenever the interviewee hears the word 'why,' he may feel the need to defend himself, to withdraw and avoid the situation, or to attack" (86). Furthermore, clients may perceive why questions as advice, as in the following excerpt:

CLIENT: *I can't relate to my father anymore. He can't see that I need my independence.*

COUNSELLOR: *Why don't you just move out and be on your own?*

CLIENT: *Impossible. I've got two more years of college and I can't afford it.*

COUNSELLOR: *Why not just tell him how you feel?*

Kadushin (1990) suggests asking "what" instead of "why" questions. For example, "What prevents you from sharing your feelings?" is more helpful than "Why don't you share your feelings?" The first question seems to accept that there are explanations and reasons for the client's behaviour, whereas the second question seems to demand justification.

When Clients Do Not Answer Questions

Sometimes clients do not answer questions, or their answers may be superficial. To decide how to proceed in such cases, counsellors need to consider some of the reasons why clients might be reluctant to respond.

Not Understanding Questions. Clients may not understand questions because they have not heard them. Clients may be hard of hearing or deaf, or counsellors may be speaking too softly. As well, clients may not have been listening. Counsellors may be using words, phrases, metaphors, and expressions that are not part of their clients' repertoire. Effective counsellors are able to adapt their idiomatic language and voice volume to meet their clients' needs and expectations. They avoid using technical terms and jargon. Counsellors

become models for their clients, and one of the interesting and positive outcomes of counselling is that clients may learn how to listen. When counsellors demonstrate effective listening and responding skills, clients tend to imitate them. Alternatively, counsellors can
teach clients some tools for listening. For example, to encourage clients to summarize, leads
such as this can be used: "Please tell me in your own words what your understanding of
our agreement is. I want to make sure we both have the same understanding."

Not Understanding the Purpose. Clients have a right to know about the interview
process and the motivation for particular questions. Moreover, they are more apt to respond
when they feel included and informed. At any point in the interview, counsellors should
be prepared to state, "The reason I am asking this question is ..." Of course, if counsellors
don't have a valid reason for asking particular questions, they ought not to ask them.
Questions are crucial for accomplishing the goals of counselling, but they must be used
cautiously. Garrett suggests the following general rule: "Question for only two purposes—
to obtain specifically needed information and to direct the client's conversation from fruit-
less to fruitful channels" (1982:33).

Not Knowing the Answers. Some questions are difficult for clients to answer. The
questions may call for insight and explanations that are beyond the clients' current level of
understanding. Sometimes, clients are unable to articulate their ideas and inner feelings.
Learning disabilities also are a factor for some clients.

Believing That Their Answers Are Private. Clients may say, "That's not an
issue I care to explore." They may change the topic abruptly, or they may respond with
silence. Some clients resist questions, perhaps because of experiences of being embarrassed,
interrogated, or put on the spot. Moreover, cultural norms may discourage questions of any
type, or they may restrict the areas in which questioning is appropriate. In some cases,
clients withhold answers because they fear that their answers will not be understood or that
they will be judged. At other times, they are simply not ready or able to address the issues
the questions raise.

    Counsellors can use a number of strategies to overcome this problem. First, counsellors
should evaluate whether they have given their clients enough time to answer. Some clients are
slower to respond, and counsellors may misinterpret their silence as reluctance to speak.

    Second, counsellors might tactfully ask clients what prevented them from answering.
Sometimes, trust issues impede candour. Candid discussion of barriers to trust usually
increases trust, provided that counsellors are nondefensive. By remaining nondefensive,
counsellors demonstrate their capacity to be open and nonjudgmental. They show their ability to handle tough issues without retaliating. As well, when questions target sensitive or private information, counsellors can express empathy regarding how hard it might be to share
such personal material.

    Third, when clients do not answer questions, counsellors can respect their wishes not to
explore the particular area and shift the discussion to less threatening content. In addition, they
can stop asking questions. If counsellors continue to ask questions even though clients refuse
or dismiss them, unfortunate consequences will likely arise. Clients may become increasingly

frustrated, or they may feel inadequate because they have been unable to successfully meet their counsellors' directives. They may become increasingly angry and resistant.

Questions and Cross-Cultural Communication

Counsellors need to be careful that their counselling and questioning methods are not culturally biased. For example, people may have profound differences in how they react to questions. In a book on effective cross-cultural interviewing, McDonald makes this important observation:

> In mainstream society, a person being interviewed will barely wait before responding to a question. Aboriginal people, however, may pause before answering a question. Culturally, the pause may be related to thinking about the answer, considering whether the answer may affect the relationship between the interviewee and the interviewer, or wondering whether the question even requires an answer at all, especially if the answer appears obvious. The question of "small" talk which is so prevalent is also related to this point. Traditionally, native people do not engage in this kind of exchange. They may be judged as shy, reticent, or uncooperative by an interviewer when, in fact, the behaviour may actually indicate they feel that there is nothing worthwhile to say, so there is simply no reason to comment. (1993:19)

When attempting to relate effectively to members of various cultures, counsellors need to avoid stereotyping and overgeneralizing. Within a culture, an individual may subscribe to all, some, or none of the cultural norms. Table 5.1 on page 134 summarizes considerations for using questions appropriately.

Types of Questions

Interview vitality is heightened and more effective use of time is possible when counsellors use a variety of ways of asking questions. The effectiveness of any questioning technique depends on a number of factors, including timing, the nature of the relationship, the purpose of the interview, and the mood of the participants. Questions that are surprisingly useful with one client may generate hostility in another. Perhaps the most important point to keep in mind is that there is an art to asking questions that precludes any attempt to structure questioning in the same way for each client.

Closed Questions. **Closed questions** can be easily answered yes or no. Closed questions enable interviewers to confirm facts and obtain specific information. Since closed questions do not invite detailed responses, they can effectively bring closure to an interview or slow the pace of clients who are overly verbose. On the other hand, closed questions should be avoided with clients who tend to be succinct. For example, clients can easily dismiss the question "Do you have anything you want to talk about today?" with the answer "No." Typically, closed questions begin with words such as can, did, are, have, is, will, would, and do, as in the examples below:

- Can you tell me what you've done about it?
- Did you have an opportunity to call the school?
- Are you feeling depressed?

Table 5.1 Guidelines for Questioning	
Don't:	**Do:**
Bombard clients with questions.	Balance and add variety to the interview with a range of other skills.
Ask more than one question at a time.	
	Pause after each question to give clients time to answer.
Use leading questions to control clients and their answers.	
	Remember that summary and empathy responses are important to confirm understanding.
Use "why" questions, as they usually imply blame or convey judgment.	
	Ask questions one at a time.
Ask questions unless you have a reason for knowing or a right to have the answer.	
	Respect cultural norms and individual styles that may make certain questions inappropriate.
	Ask questions for a specific purpose.

- Have you thought about taking your own life?
- Is my understanding correct?
- Do you agree that the most important problem right now is ...?

Although clients may answer each of the above questions with yes or no, they may also choose to provide a more expansive answer to a closed question. When counsellors want a definite yes or no answer to an important question, then a closed question is preferable. In the example below, the client hints that suicide might be an issue. This possibility is too significant to be ignored, so the counsellor uses a closed question to see if this is a risk.

CLIENT: *Lately, I've been so down, I wonder what's the point of going on.*

COUNSELLOR: *Have you been thinking about killing yourself?*

Sometimes, organizations require an intake interview that requires a great deal of information. A series of closed questions is an efficient way to gather some data quickly. Unfortunately, too many closed questions may irritate clients and leave them feeling interrogated and restricted. To minimize these effects, counsellors should blend closed questions with various interview strategies, in particular, other active listening skills. Garrett suggests that "when considerable information is desired, it is often best obtained by encouraging the client to talk freely" (1982:22). This perspective is echoed by Kadushin (1990), who contends that clients are gratified when they are given freedom to explain themselves in their own way.

Open Questions. The distinguishing feature of **open questions** is the fact that they are difficult to answer with a simple yes or no. In general, open questions are preferable to closed questions. They provide a great deal of freedom for clients to answer the questions in the way they choose, with as much or as little depth as they wish. Open questions may be used to begin an interview, for example, "What brings you here today?" They may be used to explore thoughts, feelings, or behaviour: "What were you thinking?" "How did you feel?" "How did you respond?"

The vast majority of open questions are "five W" questions, which ask who, what, where, when, and why, and "how" questions, such as those listed below:

- Who knows about your situation besides your wife?
- What have you been able to do to cope with this problem?
- Where do you see this relationship going?
- When did this begin?
- Why do you think it has been difficult for you to cope? (As noted earlier, why questions should be used cautiously.)
- How do you see it?
- At what point do you think you might be ready to make a decision?

With some clients, both open and closed questions have the same result. With these clients the closed question "Did you have any feelings about what happened?" and the open alternative "How did you feel?" will generate the same response. Counsellors should avoid using the closed alternative with less verbal clients. If counsellors want an expansive answer, they should avoid using closed questions, particularly when dealing with clients who tend to provide single-word or short answers to questions. For example, instead of asking, "Did you come here for help with your résumé?" counsellors might ask questions that convey a greater expectation for detail, such as "What were your reasons for coming in today?"

Closed questions are leading when they suggest the right or expected answer to the client. In the example below, a single mother describes her situation:

CLIENT: *I often think that my kids don't give me enough respect. Just once, I'd like them to ask me how my day went. When I'm tired, they could help out more.*

COUNSELLOR: *Do you feel angry?*

CLIENT: *Sure I do. Who wouldn't?*

In this example, the client hints at strong but undefined feelings. Even though the client affirms anger, this may not be her main feeling. The client may indeed be angry, but other feelings may be dominant. However, for some clients it's easier to go in the direction suggested by the question by exploring anger than it is to shift the answer. A less biased question might be "How do you feel about this?"

Kadushin suggests that open-ended questions can be intimidating for inexperienced clients who are unsure of their expected role: "For such an interviewee, open-ended questions give him little structure, little guidance about what he is supposed to talk about and how he is supposed to talk about it" (1990:185). Straightforward discussion with such clients about expectations can be a useful way to reduce embarrassment.

Indirect Questions. **Indirect questions**, or embedded questions, are statements that act as questions. Indirect questions are a softer way of seeking information. Their wording tends to be less intimidating than more direct open and closed questions. Indirect questions are effective for breaking up the monotony and threat of constant questioning, particularly when they are combined with other skills, especially empathy. The following are some examples of indirect questions:

- I wonder whether you believe that it is possible.
- Perhaps you're feeling confused over her response.
- I'm curious about your opinion.
- Given what you've said, I would not be surprised if you decided to accept the offer.
- I have no idea what you might be thinking.
- I would not be surprised to find that you have strong feelings on the matter.
- You may have already reached a conclusion.
- Your views on this are very important to me.

CONVERSATION 5.1

ALTERNATIVES TO QUESTIONS

STUDENT: Sometimes, it feels like all I do in the interview is ask questions. I can't help but think that if I were the client I'd be really irritated. I don't want to leave clients feeling interrogated, but questions seem to be the only way to get the information I need. Do you agree?

TEACHER: You're right. There is a real danger that clients will become defensive if they feel cross-examined. By paying attention to the needs, feelings, and responses of individual clients you will be able to see if you are alienating them with too much questioning. Sometimes counselling works best if you avoid or minimize questions. For example, clients who have not yet developed trust in their counsellors may respond better in interviews when questions are minimized.

Another drawback to asking too many questions is that too much responsibility for the direction and content of the interview can be left on your shoulders. This can be disempowering for clients and can lead them to become overly dependent.

STUDENT: But are there ways to explore and get information without asking questions?

TEACHER: Yes, there are a number of skill alternatives to questions for gathering information and making assessments. Techniques such as showing empathy, summarizing, using silence, and self-disclosing may, in some situations, be more effective ways of getting details, facts, and examples.

Empathy, for example, is a powerful counselling tool that tells clients that we understand or are trying to appreciate their feelings and perspectives. Empathic responses and summaries create an essential base of trust by showing that counsellors are nonjudgmental and capable of listening and understanding. In response, clients often become more courageous and motivated to share and explore. Appropriate use of silence creates space for clients to speak. Questions are important for effective interviewing, but you should try to add variety to your interviews by using a range of skills.

Table 5.2	Types of Questions			
Type	**Description**	**Advantages**	**Disadvantages**	**Examples**
Closed questions	Questions that can be answered yes or no.	• Provide specific information. • Confirm facts, conclusions, or agreements. • Slow the pace of the interview by limiting focus. • Are easy for clients to answer.	• Restrict answers. • Repetitive closed questions can leave clients feeling interrogated.	• Will you be going to the parents' group tonight? • Did you say everything that you wanted to say?
Open questions	Questions that promote a more expansive answer.	• Allow for an unrestricted range of responses. • Empower clients by giving them increased control of answers.	• Client answers may be more time consuming. • Are more challenging for clients to answer.	• What are your plans for this evening? • How are you feeling?
Indirect questions	Statements that act as questions.	• Are less threatening than traditional questions.	• Client may choose not to respond.	• I am interested in knowing if you have plans for the evening.

CONCRETENESS

Concreteness concerns the extent to which messages convey clear and specific meanings. When communication is concrete, all participants share understanding of words, phrases, ideas, feelings, and behaviours. When communication lacks concreteness, understanding is incomplete and subject to error and distortion. "Concreteness is a way to ensure that general and common experiences and feelings such as depression, anxiety, anger, and so on are defined idiosyncratically for each client" (Cormier and Cormier, 1985:48).

Counsellors probe for concreteness not only to promote precision, but also to funnel the discussion and deepen the focus of inquiry. The importance of concreteness is underscored by George and Cristiani, who assert, "This dimension, perhaps more than empathy, genuineness and positive regard, moves the client through the helping process by encouraging the client to explore the problematic areas of his life and his relationship to others" (1986:128).

Table 5.3 rates concreteness on a continuum scale of one to three. Probes for increased concreteness should be considered at levels one and two.

Unclear or Ambiguous Messages. Concreteness is necessary because messages are often unclear or ambiguous. Communication involves alternating roles of sender and receiver. Senders must frame their ideas and feelings into words and gestures that can be

Table 5.3	Levels of Concreteness	
Level	**Description**	**Examples of Client Statements**
One	Minimal or no detail and examples to convey meaning. Nothing is said about a particular topic area.	There are some things I could comment on. I know exactly how you feel.
Two	Meaning is suggested, but content is vague, ambiguous, or inadequate.	I have the usual share of problems with my kids. I have strong feelings about my relationship with him. We'll have to get together soon.
Three	Language is precise and there is shared understanding of ideas.	My eldest child has been absent from school for two of the last three weeks. I feel disappointed and rejected when my husband forgets my birthday.

understood. Receivers, in turn, must accurately decode these ideas and feelings. Shared understanding between two people is possible only when each participant understands a message in the way that the sender intended. This is an exceedingly complex task, with considerable potential for distortion. Probes for concreteness can reduce or eliminate distortion.

People may lack the vocabulary and self-awareness to express their ideas precisely, and their messages may be incomplete, superficial, or ambiguous. A client might say, "I feel strongly about it." However, the same statement also provides the counsellor with an opportunity to help the client become more specific. Let's look at the choices:

CLIENT: *I feel strongly about it.*

COUNSELLOR (CHOICE 1): *I'm not surprised. From what you've been saying, who wouldn't feel that way.*

COUNSELLOR (CHOICE 2): *Perhaps you could be more specific. What exactly are your feelings?*

In Choice 1, the counsellor is supportive but does not probe to find out how the client is feeling. This client hints at feelings but conveys sparse information about their precise nature and intensity. Unless the counsellor probes further, as in Choice 2, assumptions and misunderstanding are the likely outcomes.

Information Gaps and Missing Data. Probes for concreteness should be considered when defining details are missing and when there are missing details or gaps in information that interfere with understanding. Such probes are used to obtain examples, quantify data, or check the client's frame of reference.

Although people may have links and similarities in their experiences and common human needs, everyone is unique. All people have different frames of reference based on their learning and experience. Consider the images that a word such as anger might evoke for various people. One person might vividly recall an abusive childhood, in which anger always led to someone getting hurt. Another might visualize screaming and hurtful words, while someone else thinks of withdrawing and saying nothing. What is "old?" To a 12-year-old, 30 might seem like old age, but to a man in his late 80s, 70 is young. Intended humour may be perceived as such, or different receivers of the message may see it as provocative, insulting, or sexist.

There is a natural tendency for each of us to make assumptions based on prior learning and experience. Someone tells us they are happy, and we ascribe our own meaning to the feeling. We hear about events or problems that we have faced ourselves, then we draw on our reactions and feelings as a base for empathy. Someone asks if we know how they feel, and we answer "Yes," without further inquiry or clarification. Although personal experience can be an enormous advantage for appreciating the problems and feelings of others, communication breakdowns are risked if we neglect to openly explore our assumptions for accuracy.

Using Simple Encouragers and Directives. The simplest way to probe for more information is to use short phrases and gestures that encourage clients to continue with their stories. Nonverbal gestures, such as head nodding, sustained eye contact, and attended silence, convey such support and interest. Short statements and directives, such as "Tell me more," "Yes, go on," "What else?" "Please expand on that," and "Un huh, hmm," can be used to sustain client sharing without interrupting the flow of the interview. A short example will illustrate.

CLIENT: *I guess I'm pretty angry.*

COUNSELLOR: *Meaning?*

CLIENT: *Our relationship is on the rocks.*

COUNSELLOR: *Tell me more.*

CLIENT: *My brother always puts me down. It's got to the point where I don't want to be around him.*

(counsellor nods, attended silence)

CLIENT: *We used to be so close. We were inseparable. In the last year, it's become so competitive.*

Using Questions. Questions are the primary tool for seeking information. Intelligent questioning can be used to get examples, define terms, or probe for detail. When counsellors think that information is incomplete or superficial, they can use questions to clarify and embellish understanding. The interview excerpt below demonstrates this process.

COUNSELLOR: *I want to make sure I understand. What do you mean when you say "competitive"?*

CLIENT: *It's something ugly. Not just wanting to win, but needing to win. It's as if everything rides on winning.*

COUNSELLOR: *Is that true for both of you?*

CLIENT: *At first it was just him. Now I'm just as bad.*

COUNSELLOR: *What's a typical example?*

Counsellors can use series of questions to explore beyond a superficial level. This procedure encourages clients to elaborate on vague statements and to get more details and supporting examples. The following excerpt illustrates:

CLIENT: *I know there are many times when I let my feelings get the better of me.*

COUNSELLOR: *What kinds of feelings?*

CLIENT: *Sometimes I let my anger build to the point where I'm ready to explode.*

COUNSELLOR: *"Ready to explode"—what does that mean?*

CLIENT: *I would never become physical and hurt someone. I'm just afraid of getting really mean and saying hurtful things.*

COUNSELLOR: *Has that happened?*

CLIENT: *Yes. (hesitates) A lot.*

COUNSELLOR: *Can you think of a good example?*

CLIENT: *My mother. She's always trying to control my life. Most of the time I just try to ignore her constant nagging. But lately it seems that every second day she phones with advice. I don't want it and I don't need it. Yesterday, I blew up at her.*

COUNSELLOR: *What did you do or say?*

CLIENT: *I told her in no uncertain terms to butt out of my life. She started to cry, then I felt guilty.*

Opening Up Sensitive Areas for Discussion. One characteristic that distinguishes exemplary professional interviewers and counsellors is their capacity to be comfortable with any topic. Skilled counsellors take the initiative to open sensitive areas up for discussion. Often, clients hint at a concern, which provides counsellors with a natural opportunity to probe for more detail and to open up the discussion to a greater level of intimacy.

CLIENT: *(avoiding eye contact) It's not easy to open up to a stranger.*

COUNSELLOR: *It is tough. You might wonder how I'm going to react or whether I will hold what you say against you.*

CLIENT: *It's just so embarrassing.*

COUNSELLOR: *One way to overcome that is to take a chance on me. I'm open to anything you have to say. I find that when I avoid talking about a tough area, it becomes even more difficult to deal with later.*

CLIENT: *Lately, I can't sleep at night because I'm wondering if I might be gay.*

Probes for concreteness are invitations to clients to trust their counsellors by revealing thoughts that they might prefer to keep hidden. Embarrassment, fear, uncertainty, taboos about taking help, and simple mistrust of the interview process, including suspicion about the motives of the interviewer, present natural barriers to sharing information. Shulman (1984) suggests that the same societal taboos that inhibit open discussion in sensitive areas also affect helping relationships. Among the taboos that Shulman identifies is reluctance to talk about sex, money, dependency, and authority. For some people, taking help from someone else suggests dependency, which may result in feelings of inadequacy. "To feel dependent is equated with feeling weak. The image of a 'real man' is of one who is independent, able to stand on his own feet, and competent to deal with life's problems by himself" (86).

Clients often view counsellors and interviewers as authority figures, and they tend to relate to them based on their prior experiences and images of people in power. In particular, people in authority "have power to hurt us, and therefore, we will, at best, hint at our feelings and reactions" (Shulman, 1984:86). To Shulman's list of common taboo areas could be added discussions of death, spiritual issues, and health, as well as others that vary between people and between cultures.

Probes for concreteness propel the interview from a superficial level of discussion to an intimate level that requires a deeper investment from everyone involved in the interview. In Chapter 1 the illusion of work concept was introduced as a kind of implicit partnership between workers and clients. In this arrangement, clients are permitted to avoid the pain and struggle that are often associated with growth, while workers can avoid the risk that purposeful challenge entails.

> We have all developed the capacity to engage in conversations which are empty and which have no meaning. It is easy to see how this ability to talk a great deal without saying much can be integrated into the helping interaction ... Workers have reported helping relationships with clients that have spanned months, even years, in which the worker always knew, deep down inside, that it was all illusion. (Shulman 1992:145)

Appropriate probes for concreteness are one way to avoid this illusion of work. (See Table 5.4 on page 144 for more information.) Skilled counsellors are continually working toward understanding the perspective and feelings of their clients. Effective interviewers and counsellors are learners, and they recognize that the best teachers are their clients. This means having the courage and assertiveness to ask difficult questions about private matters. At the same time, it means behaving responsibly by treating client responses with care. To be ethical, counsellors must question wisely, exploring only those matters that are relevant to the work and within their competence. Asking clients for more concreteness requires that counsellors are willing to invest time and energy to listen, probing responsibly only in those areas where there is legitimate work to be accomplished.

Some thoughts may be private. Lack of relationship trust may preclude full disclosure. For example, people fearing judgment or ridicule may tell others what they think they want to hear or what they believe will result in acceptance. Individuals also may distort or exaggerate messages because of past experiences. Counsellors need to know when to back off. As Garrett notes, "It is, of course, possible to probe too far. Some sleeping dogs should be left undisturbed, particularly when the interviewer is not equipped to deal with them should they be aroused. Even a skilled interviewer should use a great deal of discretion and wisdom in going beneath the surface" (1982:25).

In relationships, everyone must decide how much, when, and with whom they are willing to reveal personal thoughts and feelings. Restraint and self-censorship of some ideas and feelings are normal and necessary. Everyone differs in the degree to which they are comfortable with disclosing intimate thoughts and feelings. Some people prefer to remain private, sharing little or nothing. Others open up very slowly and only with people whom they deeply trust. Cultural norms may also influence what individuals are willing to share. Counsellors need to be alert to signs of client resistance, such as when they ask to change the subject or when their nonverbal cues signal reluctance to continue. Then they can work with the client to make an intelligent decision on whether to continue, as in the following example:

COUNSELLOR: *How did you feel when your father said that?*

CLIENT: *(shifts uncomfortably, averts eye contact) I don't know if I'm ready to discuss it.*

COUNSELLOR (CHOICE 1): *Okay. Let's talk about something else.*

COUNSELLOR (CHOICE 2): *This is a difficult area for you, and you have mixed feelings about continuing.*

In Choice 1, the counsellor moves quickly to change the subject. This will lessen the client's anxiety, but it also robs the client of the opportunity to deal with a difficult yet potentially important topic. Here, the counsellor decides how to proceed. In Choice 2, the counsellor is more patient and attempts to empathize with the client's ambivalence toward continuing. In response, the client may say, "You're right, it is tough. But I can handle it." Or the client might say, "I'd rather we talked about something else." With either client response, the counsellor has respected the client's right to self-determination.

Counsellors need to have the time to deal with the results of any probe for concreteness. Concreteness opens new avenues of inquiry, stimulates feelings, and invites clients to share at a deeper level. Consequently, the end of the interview is a poor time to begin probing. It may seem obvious, but an important principle is that interviewers should be purposeful and their questions and responses must be pertinent.

CONVERSATION 5.2

INCREASING YOUR ABILITY TO BE CONCRETE

STUDENT: Do you need a large vocabulary to help clients express themselves concretely?

TEACHER: It helps, but it's probably more important that you use the vocabulary you already have. Be curious. Ask questions. Express interest in hearing more. Seek definition of unfamiliar words or familiar words that are open to misinterpretation. Listen. These are the essential steps to concrete understanding.

Making Choices. A theme throughout this book is that effective counsellors have a broad range of alternatives for responding. When they have choices, counsellors are not locked into repetitive patterns, and interviews are more interesting and vibrant for both clients and counsellors. The following example demonstrates some of the many ways that a counsellor might respond to a client:

CLIENT: *I suppose I should have expected it. My girlfriend said she needed time to think, to "reevaluate our relationship," as she put it. It was tough, but I gave her some time alone.*

COUNSELLOR (CHOICE 1): *How did you feel about what was happening? [an open question that focuses the discussion on the client's feelings]*

COUNSELLOR (CHOICE 2): *What was your plan? [an open question concentrating on the client's behaviour and thoughts]*

COUNSELLOR (CHOICE 3): *Tell me what you planned to do (felt) (thought) (wanted to do). [directives]*

COUNSELLOR (CHOICE 4): *Sounds like this was a painful time for you. [empathic response directed to the client's feelings]*

COUNSELLOR (CHOICE 5): *I'd be interested in knowing how you handled it. [indirect question]*

COUNSELLOR (CHOICE 6): *(silence) [silence used to give the client an opportunity to continue sharing]*

COUNSELLOR (CHOICE 7): *It was hard, but you were able to give her time to reassess your relationship. [paraphrase]*

KEY QUESTIONS FOR EVERY INTERVIEW

Some interviews are highly structured with a series of questions to answer, such as a survey or a standardized assessment tool. Others are much less predictable, and the discussion may take unexpected detours. Whatever the nature of the interview, counsellors can use the following six key questions and their variations as reference points for most interviews:

- What brings you here today?
- What are your expectations of me?
- What do I need to know about your situation?
- What do you mean by ...?
- What did we accomplish?
- What have we missed?

It is important to remember that these questions are starting points. Additional interviewing and counselling skills are probably required before the targeted topic area can be considered complete.

1. What brings you here today?

One distinguishing feature of the counselling interview is that the relationship is purposeful. Consequently, it is essential that the goal of the interview be defined. Only then can counsellors structure the work to achieve this agreed-on purpose. The question "What brings you here today?" begins the process of establishing reason and direction for the interview. Of course, this direction may change as the interview progresses. Clients may develop more trust in their counsellors and decide to share more risky information or feelings. As well,

Table 5.4   Promoting Concreteness

Client Response	Analysis	Counsellor Choices
I have strong feelings about abortion.	The client does not provide enough information for the interviewer to understand the precise emotional reaction or point of view.	Describe those feelings. Tell me about those feelings.
I feel angry.	Further inquiry is necessary to prevent any natural tendency for the counsellor to attribute personal meaning to the word *angry*.	Angry? What does angry mean to you?
I hope you understand what it's like to be a single mother on welfare.	Personal experience or work with other clients could leave the counsellor open to making assumptions.	Everyone's experience is different. I need to hear what it's like for you.
There are several things missing in our relationship. My family is weird. I've learned a great deal.	Detail is lacking.	What's missing? In what ways are they weird? What are some things you have learned?
I'm fed up.	The target is missing (i.e., whom or what the person is angry with).	What are you fed up with? Whom are you fed up with?
She's really quite old.	The speaker's perspective is unclear.	How old is she?
I wish he'd show some respect.	The desired behavioural response is not detailed.	If he showed respect, what specifically would he be doing?
Everyone has a right to their views.	The client's views are not personalized.	What are your views?
Sometimes, I feel like giving up.	Sometimes is a vague modifier. *Giving up* is not defined.	When you say "sometimes," how often do you mean?

exploration within the interview may result in increased client insight that moves the work in different directions. Therefore, it is important that counsellors are alert to shifts in focus and are willing to negotiate changes in the contract when appropriate.

Shulman (1992) emphasizes the importance of discovering client priorities. He supports the assumption that clients will be committed only to those areas that they see as important. "The worker's task is not to decide what the client should be working on. Instead, using sessional contracting skills, the worker attempts to discover what the client is working on" (113). Although this approach is useful, it should not prevent counsellors from encouraging clients to work on other issues, such as with parents who are abusing their children but who do not see their discipline methods as problematic.

It is always preferable to have a repertoire of ideas for accomplishing the same task. This permits flexibility and contributes to keeping the interview interesting and individualized. Listed below are some alternative ways of asking the question "What brings you here today?"

- How would you like to spend our time together? (Because this type of open question gives maximum control to clients, it is useful for working with some reluctant clients.)
- Perhaps you might bring me up-to-date on what has happened since we last met.
- Do you have feelings and concerns from our last session that you want to address?
- What do you think would be a good starting point?
- There are a number of things we could do. For example ...
- What would you like to talk about?

2. What are your expectations of me?

This question is important for clarifying roles. Clients may come to counselling with clear ideas of what they want from their counsellors, or they may be aware only of their pain and be hopeful that some help will be forthcoming. In any case, it is important that both clients and counsellors understand their respective roles in the process. This agreement is, of course, always open to modification.

3. What do I need to know about your situation?

At the beginning of an interview or when a new topic is introduced, an open-ended question such as "What do I need to know about your situation?" empowers clients to identify areas of immediate concern or willingness to explore. This question communicates to clients that counsellors will respect their needs and wants. The question demonstrates to clients that counsellors will not make assumptions and that they are willing to listen and learn. It seems to say, "I will treat you as a person, not as a number or a category." Clients may not put forward (at least initially) their most urgent need. They may start with a safe topic to test the waters for understanding and acceptance. Once they feel more trust, they may present more serious matters.

Sample variations of this question are "What are the important things I need to understand about you and your problem?" and "Can you tell me the key points we need to explore?" Questions designed to learn about a client's situation generally target three important areas:

1. how the client *feels* about the problem—**affective area**
2. how the client *thinks* about the problem—**cognitive area**
3. what the client *is doing* about the problem—**behavioural area**

Affective Area. Sometimes solutions to problems are obvious to clients, and they do not need help with decision making or problem solving, but still they lack the capacity to cope with their dilemmas. Often, from this inability to cope results painful, perhaps debilitating feelings that are hindering their power to problem solve. How clients feel is, therefore, very important to the work of counselling, and emotions are frequently the centre of counselling work. In many circumstances, management of emotions is a prerequisite to problem solving. The question "How do you feel?" is one way to introduce feelings and to encourage clients to explore the emotional components of their problems.

Counsellors who are task oriented, with a focus on problem solving, may move the counselling interview prematurely to problem solving or, worse still, ignore feelings that are at the heart of their client's struggle. While questions can encourage expressions of emotions, the active listening skill of empathy is the foundation for working with feelings. (Empathy will be the central theme of Chapter 6.)

Cognitive Area. How people think about their difficulties is often more important than the problem itself. An event that may be no big deal to one client may represent a life-threatening crisis to another. **Self-talk** refers to the mental messages we give to ourselves. Golden and Lesh (1997) use the acronym **MOANS** for five words that often signal negative self-talk: *must, ought, always, never,* and *should.*

- I must succeed or I am worthless.
- I ought to be able to do it.
- I always screw up.
- I will never be able to get a job.
- I should feel differently.
- Everything must be perfect.

In contrast, positive self-talk builds confidence and is self-empowering. It moves people away from a victim mentality of feeling powerless. It enables individuals to deal with crisis realistically, without self-imposed rigid and punishing demands.

By seeking to understand how clients think about problems, counsellors can get valuable clues regarding important issues, such as self-esteem, motivation, and irrational thinking. Subsequently, counsellors can directly challenge clients' negative self-talk.

Sometimes, quick and dramatic counselling interventions can be achieved when counsellors challenge the rationality of the worrier. By offering facts, challenging assumptions, and inviting clients to consider the real probabilities of dreaded events, counsellors introduce much-needed critical thinking that may interrupt the worry cycle (Shebib, 1997:81). Questions that can prompt exploration of the cognitive area include:

- What do you say to yourself about this problem?
- What does your "inner voice" say?
- What messages do you give yourself that are self-defeating?
- What are you telling yourself?

Behavioural Area. Although it is important not to move too quickly to work on problem solving, an important part of work in the beginning phase involves interviewing clients to understand what they are doing and not doing about their problems. Such information is important for assessment. It tells counsellors whether their clients are active in seeking and working on solutions or whether they have become withdrawn and have given up. Some questions for exploring the behavioural area are the following:

- What have you been doing?
- What do you do just before the problem occurs?
- How do you respond?
- What did you do?
- What did you say?
- Has the way you have been handling your problem changed?
- What are some of the ways you have been coping with this issue?

4. What do you mean?

This is a central question during all phases of the interview. It ensures clarity of expression, encourages detail and example, and prevents counsellors from making erroneous assumptions about meaning. It moves the interview from superficial understanding to specific or concrete exploration.

5. What was accomplished?

This question makes evaluation part of the work, thus enabling counsellors and their clients to review progress and identify accomplishments. Evaluation reviews the counselling relationship and assists with making changes to the contract. Evaluative questions include:

- How has our work met your expectations?
- Looking back on our session, what were the things that you found helpful? Unhelpful?
- How would you like things to be the same or different next time we meet?
- What remains to be done?
- How would you evaluate the work?

CONVERSATION 5.3

WORKING WITH CHILDREN

STUDENT: Do you need to modify basic counselling and interviewing skills when working with children?

TEACHER: Yes, you have to modify your approach when working with children, but this is also true for every client. Having said that, there are some basic principles for working with children. First, you have to speak in words appropriate to the child's age and developmental level. A young child, for example, may not understand the concept of time. When my kids were young, a half-hour was "one Mr. Rogers show" and three days were "three sleeps." Second, play and art are often better ways to engage children than interviewing. Children often act out their problems during play. Third, children may not respond well to questioning, particularly to why questions. Listening, empathy, and gentle encouragement to talk are more effective. Fourth, you need to recognize that children have unique ways of expressing their feelings. As Erdman and Lampe observe, "Pouting, crying, remaining silent, laughing, fidgeting, and fighting are some of the natural means children use to express their needs and feelings, and counsellors need to recognize these as such" (1996:375).

6. What have we missed?

At the end of an interview (or as a significant topic draws to a close) the question "What have we missed?" often yields surprisingly rich information. This question provides an opportunity for clients to talk about issues and feelings that might have been missed. When clients are ambivalent about sharing some details, this question may tip the scales in favour of sharing. It empowers clients by giving them control of content and a final chance to make sure their needs are on the table for discussion. Some variations of this question are:

- What else do we need to talk about?
- What's left to explore?
- Have we covered all that is important?
- What questions haven't I asked?

In the following example, the counsellor prompts the client to examine the session:

COUNSELLOR: *Our time is almost up, and I want to make sure I haven't overlooked anything that is important to you. What have we missed?*

CLIENT: *Well, we haven't even begun to talk about how my divorce has changed my kids. In many ways, they have been the real victims.*

COUNSELLOR: *I agree with you. It's very important that we don't overlook them. Does it make sense to you to make that discussion part of our next meeting? I want to make sure there is enough time.*

CLIENT: *Yes, that makes sense.*

COUNSELLOR: *Then let's make that number one on our list for next time.*

There are some risks to opening up new areas at the end of an interview, particularly if the topic involves strong emotions for the client. In the above example, the counsellor suspected that this was a topic that needed a lot of time, so she suggested deferral to the next session. In such circumstances, the counsellor might have been tempted to ask further questions or to empathize, but these responses might have prolonged the interview beyond the time available. It is important to end the interview without leaving the client in a state of distress.

INTERVIEW TRANSITIONS

An **interview transition** occurs when the topic of conversation shifts from one subject to another. Such shifts may occur spontaneously in the course of the interview, or they may be orchestrated in order to further the objectives of the interview. The need for a transition arises in the following situations:

1. the discussion of a particular issue is finished and it is time to move on
2. the discussion triggers ideas in another area or links to earlier areas of discussion
3. the subject being discussed is too threatening or painful and a topic change is needed to reduce tension

4. the subject has limited relevance or has lost its relevance to the goals of the interview
5. a change from one phase of the interview to another is necessary (Shebib, 1997:156).

There are five types of transitions: natural, strategic, control, phase, and connect, or linking (Shebib, 1997:156).

Natural Transitions

Natural transitions arise as the discussion flows seamlessly from one topic to another, with clear links between the two topics. The most common natural transition occurs when clients mention new themes as part of the interview and counsellors use this information to jump to the new topic.

> **CLIENT:** *As I talk about my dissatisfaction with my job I realize that the same could also be said about my marriage.*

> **COUNSELLOR:** *Perhaps we could address that now. Tell me what's happening in your marriage.*

Clients are unlikely to resist natural transitions since the interview moves clearly in the direction they have suggested. The topic change is not abrupt, and transition responses indicate that counsellors have heard what their clients have just stated.

Strategic Transitions

Strategic transitions arise when counsellors make choices among topic alternatives. Imagine that a client makes a statement such as the following:

> **CLIENT:** *This has been the worst year on record for me. My finances were a disaster anyway, and now that I've lost my job, I think I'll go under. Needless to say, this hasn't been good for my marriage. I can see how hard it is on my kids. My eldest daughter seems to avoid me entirely, and I'm sure my son is on drugs. What's the point in living?*

How might the counsellor respond? Would he select finances as a priority for follow-up? Or, would he go with one of the other problems: marriage, relationships with children, drug abuse, or unemployment? Should he focus on problems or feelings or both? How a counsellor responds is a strategic decision that affects the direction of the interview, at least for the moment.

Control Transitions

Counsellors have a responsibility to orchestrate the flow of the interview. They use control transitions to manage the direction of the interview in a variety of circumstances.

Redirecting the flow of an interview is warranted when the discussion topic is irrelevant or when it prevents dialogue on more important issues. Preventing premature subject changes is crucial for ensuring concreteness or full exploration of content and feelings. Moving too quickly from topic to topic may render the interview superficial (Shebib, 1997).

Control transitions are used not to dominate clients, but rather to exercise professional duty to ensure that the interview time is productive. In practice, counsellors and their clients should share control, with counsellors giving clients as much power as possible to set the course of counselling based on their needs. Commenting on the role of counsellors, Kadushin notes that "skillful control of the interview involves giving direction without restriction; it implies stimulation and guidance without bias or pressure" (1990:356). He lists the following elements of the interview that are open to control:

1. topics to be discussed
2. sequence in which topics are discussed
3. focus within each topic
4. level of emotionality
5. person initiating the transition from one topic to another (356)

Counsellors are responsible for negotiating (contracting) with clients on the goals of counselling. Subsequently, they have an obligation to monitor and control the flow of work to support the achievement of these goals. In practice, this means making sure that there are not premature shifts in focus and that topics are fully explored and addressed. The example below illustrates a control transition.

> **COUNSELLOR:** *I think we might be moving too quickly here. We haven't had a chance to talk about your feelings. I wonder if you'd agree that we should do that before we move on to a different topic. It might help us both to understand why it's been so difficult for you to make a decision.*

In this example, the counsellor gives a brief reason for slowing down the interview and focusing on feelings. Clients who understand what is happening are much more likely to support the process.

Clients may suddenly change the subject of the interview. There may be a variety of reasons for this sudden topic shift. For example, it might indicate that they were revealing too much or that the material was too painful or personal to discuss. Consequently, counsellors need to use control transitions wisely and be mindful of the underlying feelings that client-initiated shifts signal. One way for counsellors to deal with a topic shift is to openly acknowledge the shift, then gently explore its meaning.

> **COUNSELLOR:** *Am I right in thinking that you seemed uncomfortable talking about your relationship with your father?*

> **CLIENT:** *It's not something I want to get into right now.*

> **COUNSELLOR:** *That's okay. I won't force you. On the other hand, you might decide later that you're ready.*

Counsellors can use summaries as a way to introduce control transitions. As the example below illustrates, summarizing makes the topic switch seem less abrupt. This is important because abrupt transitions, such as the one below, may appear harsh to clients and accentuate their feelings of being cross-examined.

COUNSELLOR: *So, as I understand it, drug abuse has had a significant impact on your work. Your boss has reached a point where he will support you, but only if you enter rehab. Let's shift our focus for a minute and talk about problems with your family.*

Using directives is another way of controlling the flow of an interview. Directives are short statements that provide direction to clients. Directives such as "Describe your feelings," "List your main reasons," "Give an example," "Tell me what you did," "Share your thoughts," "Tell me more," "Expand on that," "Don't move too quickly," "Describe your feelings," and "Put it in your own words" are used to control the pace of the interview and to get more information. Since overuse of directives may leave clients feeling controlled, they should be used sparingly.

Phase Transitions

In simplified terms, the work of counselling can be organized into clusters of activity. In the beginning phase, for example, problem exploration is paramount. However, at some point it becomes clear that sufficient time has been spent on problem exploration, and it is time to move on. Counsellors then use phase transitions to bridge the work of one phase to another, as illustrated by the following example:

COUNSELLOR: *I wonder if we've reached a point where it makes sense to begin talking about the changes you want to make. We could begin to discuss some of your goals, then think about how to achieve them.*

In the example below, the counsellor uses a phase transition to end the interview and to establish a link to the next session.

COUNSELLOR: *I'm impressed with your insights about how you tend to put yourself down. It seems to me that the next logical step might be to explore how to combat this tendency. If you agree, we can start with that next time.*

Generally, interviewers should proceed at a pace that their clients can manage. This does not mean that clients must always be 100 percent comfortable with the intensity of the interview. Indeed, the work of interviewing and counselling can be demanding, and exploring difficult topics can be exhausting. Here are some general guidelines for pacing:

- Move more slowly in new relationships and first encounters.
- Expect differences between clients.
- Don't expect to maintain the same intensity or an ever-increasing intensity throughout the interview—periodic "rest" periods with nonthreatening or less demanding topics can energize clients.
- End interviews with less demanding questions and responses.

Counsellors need to carefully manage interview transitions between one topic and another. As well, they should avoid rigid agendas, such as might be followed in a formal meeting, and, instead, allow some freedom of movement between topics. However, counsellors also need to be careful not to sprint from one topic to another without adequate exploration or completion.

Connect (Linking) Transitions

Connect transitions are used to join or blend ideas. Interviews often have recurrent themes. For example, a client may make continual subtle references to a need to have everything just right. The counsellor might use a connect transition to bring this theme to the foreground:

> **COUNSELLOR:** *In all your examples, you talk about how you make sure that you pay attention to every little detail. Then you seem to beat yourself up if everything isn't perfect.*

Connect transitions can have a powerful effect on clients by stimulating them to think about issues in new ways. Clients who have felt stuck and hopeless may find new energy. By connecting apparently discrete events, connect transitions allow problems to be understood from new perspectives, pressures to be seen to emanate from different sources, and new actions to be taken to lessen the pressures (Middleman and Wood, 1990:80).

CONVERSATION 5.4

NOTE TAKING

STUDENT: What are your thoughts on taking notes during an interview?

TEACHER: You first.

STUDENT: I have mixed feelings. On the one hand, I don't want to forget anything. But it seems so cold and clinical to be writing when clients are talking. It seems to take away from the intimacy of the relationship.

TEACHER: Suppose you were the client and I were taking notes.

STUDENT: I'd wonder about what you were writing about me. I'd be really scared that someone else might see the notes. I'd probably be really careful about what I said.

TEACHER: What if I told you that you could see the notes?

STUDENT: That would help. Then I'd be able to correct any mistakes. I'd really want to know who would have access to the file.

TEACHER: All clients have a right to that information. They may not ask, but, as a rule, you should tell them. You raised a good point earlier about how note taking can detract from rapport in the interview. I agree. I think it's particularly important to put the pen down when clients are talking about feelings or other private matters. On the other hand, most clients expect that you'll write down information such as phone numbers and addresses.

STUDENT: I'd prefer not to take notes at all.

TEACHER: That would be ideal. Of course, that's not always possible. There may be forms or computerized questionnaires to complete that can't be delayed until after the interview. Or you may have clients waiting, so there will be no time after the interview.

INTERVIEW 5.1 INTERVIEWING SKILLS

The following excerpt illustrates some of the important concepts from this chapter. This is the first interview with the client. The counsellor works in a community service centre that offers a variety of programs.

DIALOGUE	ANALYSIS
(During the first five minutes of the interview the counsellor and the client engage in small talk.)	Interview openings establish first impressions. A few minutes spent on small talk can help clients relax. Counsellors should not consider this time wasted.
Counsellor: Perhaps you can tell me what brings you here today. You did not tell me much on the phone, but I had the impression that you felt some urgency.	A simple phase transition begins the process of establishing the purpose of the interview. By making a link to the intake phone call, the counsellor demonstrates that the client's sense of emergency was heard. This lets the client know that the counsellor is sensitive to feelings.
Client: I've been on welfare for six months and I just can't make ends meet.	
Counsellor: Sounds rough. Tell me more.	A supportive and sympathetic reaction communicates warmth and concern. The counsellor uses a directive to seek more concreteness.
Client: It's not just the money—it's what it's doing to my kids.	
Counsellor: What do you mean?	It would be easy to assume what the client is talking about. Instead, the counsellor probes for definition.
Client: My oldest is 18. He doesn't seem to have any motivation. Sometimes he says he can hardly wait until he's 19 so he can go on welfare too.	
Counsellor: I wonder if it seems to you that being on welfare somehow connects with your son's attitude.	The counsellor uses an indirect question to ask for clarification.
Client: Sure it does. It's all he's known for the last five years.	
Counsellor: I need your help to understand what you were hoping would happen when you came here today.	The counsellor's statement initiates the working contract.
(The client explains that she would like some help to get into retraining.)	
(20 minutes later)	*(continued)*

Client: I'm willing to work anywhere, but eventually I want to find something that fits.

Counsellor: Fits?

The counsellor's response accents a key word. This is yet another way to seek more concrete information. Accenting encourages clients to say more.

Client: I'd really like to work with people.

Counsellor: I noticed earlier that as you described your volunteer work with kids, you seemed really happy.

A linking transition connects two parts of the interview.

Client: I'd love to do it full time, but there's no way.

Counsellor: What prevents you?

Client: I need to earn a living. Volunteers don't get paid. To get hired full time, I'd need to get a diploma.

The counsellor uses an open question to probe for concreteness. This will help the counsellor understand the real or imagined barriers that this client foresees.

Counsellor: Sounds like you've already looked into it. Have you thought about going back to school?

Client: Yes. Like I said earlier, I'm determined to get out of this rut. I suppose I should do something about it.

The counsellor uses a closed question to check if the client is prepared to go to school. Since the client has introduced the idea, the counsellor's question is not leading. In other circumstances, such questions might need to be avoided or approached cautiously.

Summary

Asking questions is an art. Faulty questioning may bias answers, antagonize clients, or keep the interview at a superficial level. Questions can systematically lead clients through problem solving, or they can help clients examine areas that they might otherwise overlook. It is important to balance questions with responses that confirm understanding (summaries) and empathic responses that confirm sensitivity to feelings. The best counsellors have a repertoire of techniques from which to select.

Structured interviews follow a defined sequence of predetermined questions. Unstructured interviews permit interviewers and clients freedom to go in any direction without any predetermined control.

Faulty, insensitive, and poorly timed questioning may bias clients' answers, antagonize them, or keep the interview at a superficial level. Common errors include using jargon, asking leading questions, excessively questioning, asking multiple questions, asking irrelevant or poorly timed questions, and asking "why" questions.

Clients may not answer questions for a variety of reasons. For example, they may not understand the questions or their purpose, they may not know the answers, or they may believe their answers are private. As well, cultural norms influence how people react to questions.

Closed questions can be easily answered yes or no. Open questions are difficult to answer with a simple yes or no. The vast majority of open questions will be "five W" and "how" questions. Indirect questions are statements that function as questions.

Concreteness concerns the extent to which words, phrases, and behaviours convey clear and specific meaning. When communication is concrete, all participants share understanding of language, ideas, and feelings. Probes for concreteness propel the interview from a superficial level of discussion to an intimate level that requires a deeper investment from everyone involved in the interview. A number of strategies are important for promoting concreteness, including recognizing the need for concreteness, demonstrating comfort and willingness to communicate at a deeper level, knowing when to pursue concreteness, using simple encouragers, and probing for detail with questions and directives.

The following key questions can be used as a rough template for interviews:

- What brings you here today?
- What are your expectations of me?
- What do I need to know about your situation?
- What do you mean by ...?
- What did we accomplish?
- What have we missed?

Interview transitions occur when the topic of the interview shifts from one subject to another. Such shifts may occur spontaneously in the course of the interview, or counsellors may orchestrate them in order to further the objectives of the interview. There are five different types of transitions: natural, strategic, control, phase, and connect, or linking.

Exercises

1. Classify each of the following questions as open, closed, or indirect.
   a. How do you feel about your brother?
   b. I'm puzzled over your reaction.
   c. Do you have time to see me next week?
   d. I'd like to know something about your strategy.
2. Reword the following closed questions as (a) open questions and (b) indirect questions.
   a. Are you enrolled in the secretarial program?
   b. Were you referred by the principal?
   c. Are you feeling sad?
   d. Do you want to talk about your feelings?
   e. Did you tell her how you felt?

3. Conduct an interview with a colleague. Use questions inappropriately (e.g., ask irrelevant questions, change the topic frequently, bombard with questions, and ask leading questions). After the interview is completed, discuss how it felt to be in both the interviewer and the client role.

4. Conduct a 10-minute focused interview with a colleague. Your task is to explore one topic in as much depth as possible. However, in this interview you are not allowed to ask questions. Try to use a range of skills. (Note to the client: Try not to be overly cooperative.) After the interview is over, discuss the experience.

5. As a conditioning exercise for interviewing quiet clients, conduct an interview with a colleague. Set up the interview so that your colleague does not respond verbally. Use a variety of techniques other than questions.

6. Imagine that you are responding in each situation below. Suggest follow-up responses that are open questions, closed questions, indirect or embedded questions, and directives.

   a. Counsellor: What are your feelings about your work?

       Client: I have mixed feelings.

   b. Counsellor: What do you see as the next step?

       Client: The next step is to solve the bloody problem.

   c. Counsellor: How long have you felt this way?

       Client: A long time.

   d. Counsellor: What is your sense of what she means?

       Client: I know exactly what she means.

   e. Client: You have no idea how I feel.

   f. Client: I'm really angry with you.

   g. Client: There are some significant things happening in my life right now.

   h. Client: I'm not sure I can handle this problem. I need help.

7. Each of the following client statements has one or more problems with concreteness. First, identify the concreteness problem. Second, suggest a possible counsellor response to promote concreteness.

   a. I still have feelings for her.

   b. I've given it a lot of thought.

   c. I hardly sleep at night.

   d. I've tried to control my kids, but nothing seems to work.

   e. She's an elderly person.

   f. I feel bad.

8. Each of the following counsellor statements contains phrases or jargon that may be unfamiliar to clients. Reword each, using everyday language.

   a. It seems as though your son has a lot of interpersonal difficulty, and it is generating acting-out behaviour.

b. Cognitively, he seems well within the mean.

c. It appears to me that you are feeling ambivalent.

d. After intake, it seems appropriate to make a referral to one of our community resources.

9. Work in a small group to brainstorm jargon that counsellors use. Next, reword these terms and phrases so that they are easily understandable.

10. Pick an issue that you have very strong feelings about (e.g., abortion, capital punishment, increases in tuition fees). Conduct a five- to ten-minute interview with a colleague to explore his or her views on the same topic. However, do not reveal any of your feelings or thoughts on the topic. After the interview is over, discuss the experience.

11. Watch a talk show. See if you can identify the interviewing skills that are used. Look for evidence of improper interviewing technique.

12. Conduct an extended interview with a colleague (in the client's role). Use the following questions to guide your interview:

- What brings you here today?

- What are your expectations of me?

- What do I need to know about your situation? (explore feelings, thoughts, and behaviour)

- What do you mean by ...?

- What did we accomplish?

- What have we missed?

13. Videotape an extended interview. Classify each response that you make (in the counsellor's role) in terms of type—open question, closed question, summary, and so on. Identify patterns. Are there skills that are overused or underused?

14. **Interview Aerobics**

Prepare flash cards with the names of various skills on each card (e.g., open question, closed question, paraphrase, summary, empathy, indirect question, directive, silence, wild card [any skill], self-disclosure, contracting).

Note: The exercises below are designed to help you develop a range of skills. The more comfortable you are with a wide array of responses, the more you will be able to respond based on the needs of the client and the situation.

Exercise 1: Shuffle the cards. The counsellor should listen carefully to what the client says, then select the first card in the stack and follow the directions on that card. For example, if the next card reads "closed question," the counsellor must ask a closed question, even if that might not be the best response.

Exercise 2: Work with a partner. One acts as interviewee and chooses an appropriate skill card for you to use.

Exercise 3: Conduct an interview using the cards in any order that you choose. Continue interviewing until all of the cards are used. Cards may be used more than one time.

Exercise 4: Conduct an interview using the cards in any order that you wish. However, you can use each card only once.

Exercise 5: Develop your own strategy for using the cards.

(Adapted from Shebib, 1997:161)

Weblinks

The Training Institute for Suicide Assessment and Clinical Interviewing provides information on interviewing skills as well as suicide and crisis intervention. A "Tip of the Month" Feature provides ideas on interviewing strategies.
www.suicideassessment.com/top-level/tiparchives.html

"What is motivational interviewing?" by Stephen Rollnick, Ph.D., & William R. Miller, Ph.D. (1995). *Behavioural and Cognitive Psychotherapy*, 23, 325-334.
www.motivationalinterview.org/clinical/whatismi.html

"Ethnographic Questioning in the Career Counseling Interview" by Elizabeth Banister.
www.ed.gov/databases/ERIC_Digests/ed404587.html

THE PURSUIT OF EMPATHIC UNDERSTANDING

PREVIEW

After reading this chapter you should be able to:

- Explain the importance of emotions.
- Name the basic families of emotions.
- Describe how clients' emotions can be recognized from nonverbal behaviour.
- Define what is meant by empathy.
- Define the three types of empathy: basic, inferred, and invitational.
- Explain when not to use empathy.
- Identify what to avoid when responding with empathy.
- Demonstrate the basic ability to formulate empathic responses.
- Explain the importance of "tough empathy."

EMOTIONS

Emotions play a central role in the significant events of our lives. Although they have many characteristics, some behavioral and others physiological, emotions are above all psychological. We feel proud when our loved ones do something worthy. When demeaned, we become angry or ashamed. We experience joy at the birth of our children, anxiety when threatened, and grief at the death of a loved one.
—Lazarus, 1991:3

Because the human experience is so closely connected with emotions (feelings), any study of counselling and interviewing must give priority to exploring and understanding client emotions. However, there is no consensus on the definition of emotion, the number of emotions that exist, whether some emotions are more basic than others, the commonality of emotions between cultures, and whether different emotions have different physiological attributes (LeDoux, 1995).

Emotions are defined by Barker as a "state of mind usually accompanied by concurrent physiological and behavioral changes and based on the perception of some internal or external object" (1995:110). Emotional responses trigger our bodies to respond in unique physiological ways. Historically, these responses helped humans respond in very different ways, including:

- Anger—the hands swell with blood, making it easier to use weapons or strike back; increased heart rate and adrenalin serve to increase energy and power.

- Fear—blood flow to the legs increases, making it easier to escape; the body may freeze for a moment, giving time to gauge whether hiding is a better response.

- Happiness—brain activity inhibits negative thoughts and fosters increased energy.

- Love—general bodily responses promote well-being and a general state of calm and contentment.

- Surprise—raising the eyebrows expands the field of vision, thus making it easier to figure out what is going on and to plan the best action.

- Sadness—a general drop in energy and enthusiasm creates an opportunity to mourn. (Goleman, 1995)

Counsellors work with clients' emotions in a number of ways. The counselling relationship provides safety for clients to explore and understand their feelings. Friends and family may be well meaning but poorly equipped to deal with complex emotions. They may be prone to simplistic advice giving, or they may try to change the subject when painful feelings are revealed. Counsellors, on the other hand, are able to deal with feelings. They don't tell clients how they should feel, nor do they insult or frustrate clients with quick-fix solutions. They allow clients to express emotions without needing to censor what they reveal.

The overall goal is to help clients gain **emotional literacy**, "the ability to experience all of one's emotions with appropriate intensity and to understand what is causing these feelings " (Parrott, 1997:260). In a similar vein, Goleman (1995) suggests that the ability to recognize feelings as they happen is the cornerstone of emotional intelligence and that people who are more in touch with their feelings are better able to navigate their lives, and they are more competent decision makers.

Weisinger (1998) argues that understanding emotions comes from appreciating the interactions of three components: thoughts, physiological changes, and behaviour. Johnson provides a perspective:

> Feelings are internal physiological reactions to your experiences. You may begin to tremble, sweat, or have a surge of energy. Your heart may beat faster. Tears may come. Although feelings are internal reactions, they do have outward signs. Sadness is inside you, but you cry or frown on the outside. Anger is inside you. But you may stare and shout at the person you are angry with. Feelings are always internal states, but you use overt behaviors to communicate your feelings to other people. (1997:134)

Black gives another perspective in attempting to capture the nature of joy:

> Joy may be looked on as anxiety's opposite. It, too, is a composite of feelings: delight, fulfilment, and refreshment, along with the warm glow that comes with an increased heart rate, deeper breathing, and a general relaxation of muscular tension. When we are in the midst of an experience as pleasantly exhilarating as joy, we are likely to identify it in an inner conversation with ourselves as a wonderful feeling. (1983:35)

Counsellors can help clients consider how their emotions might be interfering with decision making or everyday life. Decision making, for example, may be difficult when the clients' emotions pull them in different directions. Of course, feelings such as sadness, anger, grief, and disappointment are part of everyone's life. In fact, feelings such as grief are healing responses, and they are not usually pathological, or in need of treatment.

Diversity and Emotions

As one might expect, there are wide variations in the extent to which various cultures and individuals express emotions. While underscoring the importance of exceptions, Dodd offers the following generalizations:

> Asian cultures generally practice reserve and emotional restraint. The idea of extreme emotion, such as loud sobs during a funeral or boisterous laughter on festive occasions, would be considered too emotional. To a lesser extent, some Scandinavian cultures appear publicly reserved. Britons and Germans appear more reserved than Italians, Greeks and Czechs. (1995:121)

Ivey, Ivey, and Simek-Downing offer this interesting perspective: "There may be four participants in the interview: the counselor/therapist and his or her cultural/historical background and the client and his or her cultural/historical background" (1987:94). Their observation highlights the importance of exploring the four major participants in the interview, with the goal of understanding how the history and culture of both client and counsellor might influence interactions and perception.

Classifying and Understanding Emotions

Table 6.1 on page 162 categorizes emotions. Similar attempts may be found in Carkhuff (1981), Young (1998), and Cormier and Cormier (1985). Counsellors need to respond to the range of subtle feelings that clients express and in language that clients can understand. This table should be interpreted with caution, as word choice alone is an insufficient indicator of emotional intensity. A client who says, "I'd kill for a chocolate ice cream" is clearly

Table 6.1 Feeling Words

| Feelings | Intensity | | |
	Low Level	Medium Level	High Level
Anger	annoyed, irritated, miffed, offended, resentful, provoked, displeased, aggravated, put off, ticked, upset, disturbed	angry, mad, hostile, hateful, disgusted, inflamed, in a tiff, fed up, sore, agitated	outraged, furious, vengeful, repulsed, boiling, in a rage
Fear	alarmed, nervous, anxious, tense, uneasy, timid, bothered, apprehensive, intimidated, butterflies	frightened, scared, worried, distressed, fearful, jumpy	shocked, horrified, panicked, terrified, mortified, terrorized, cold sweat
Strength	adequate, up to the challenge, able to cope, stable	confident, capable, adept, healthy, qualified, whole, energized, dynamic, tough, strong, brave, determined, secure	invulnerable, in control, bold, potent, courageous, unbeatable
Weakness	delicate, insecure, timid, shy, small, fragile, tired, weary	weak, vulnerable, falling apart, burnt out, cowardly, helpless, useless, sick, incompetent, inadequate, unprotected, frail	defenceless, impotent, worthless, no good, powerless, exhausted, lifeless, useless
Joy	satisfied, glad, good, pleased, comfortable	happy, contented, joyful, loved, excited, optimistic, cheerful	euphoric, ecstatic, thrilled, delighted, passionate, elated, marvellous, full of life, terrific, overjoyed
Sadness	disappointed, hurt, troubled, downcast, upset, bothered	unhappy, glum, sad, depressed, melancholy, blue, lonely, dismal, pessimistic	agonized, dejected, despairing, despondent, hopeless, miserable
Confusion	distracted, muddled, uncertain, doubtful, hesitant, mixed up, unsure, indecisive	confused, baffled, perplexed, puzzled, ambivalent, stumped, jumbled, disjointed, frustrated	(in a state of) pandemonium or chaos, mystified, swamped
Shame	embarrassed, humbled, regretful	belittled, discredited, guilty, shamed, remorseful, ashamed	disgraced, scandalized, humiliated, mortified
Surprise	startled, puzzled	surprised, stunned, shocked	astonished, astounded, flabbergasted, amazed, overwhelmed, awed
Love	attracted, friendly	close, intimate, warm, tender, cherished, smitten with, doting on	loved, adored, raptured, crazy about, wild about, flip over, idolize, worship

exaggerating. Another might minimize a problem, saying, "It doesn't bother me," but context and other cues might reveal evidence of profound pain.

Although there are hundreds of words for emotions in the English language, most fall into one of ten categories or families of emotions, as in Table 6.1. As with any classification system, the categories are arbitrary tools designed to organize our thinking. One might argue for more or fewer categories. Closely related feelings (e.g., anger, outrage, and annoyance) can be considered as one category. Specific words for emotions within the categories are used to more precisely define emotional states and to provide some information about the intensity or strength of the emotion.

Sometimes people confuse feelings and thoughts. For example, the statement "I feel that this is the best alternative" expresses a point of view (thought), but it does not convey any information about the emotions involved. On the other hand, the statement "I feel confident that this is the best alternative" does express an emotion. One might think that this distinction is insignificant, but the importance of emotional clarity becomes evident if the example statement becomes "I feel outraged that this is the best alternative." To describe their emotions, clients may use specific feeling words, which they may further define with modifiers such as very. As well, clients may communicate their emotions through metaphors and nonverbal channels of communication.

Word Modifiers. Word modifiers (e.g., *very, extremely, somewhat, mostly, little*) may change the level of emotion expressed. We can expect some difference in emotional level between people who describe themselves as somewhat happy and others who say they are incredibly happy.

Metaphors. Metaphors are a way of describing something by using a symbol in a direct comparison. A client who says he is going around in circles is using a metaphor to describe his feelings of confusion.

Here are some metaphors with the possible feeling that each suggests:

- tied up in knots, in a pressure cooker (stressed)
- about to blow up, bent out of shape (furious, anger)
- on a sinking ship, down in the dumps (hopeless)
- tearing my hair out (swamped)
- in a sticky situation (vulnerable)
- between a rock and a hard place (helpless)
- butterflies in my stomach (fear or excitement)
- on top of the world, on cloud nine (happy/ecstatic)
- taken for granted (devalued)
- going around in circles, feeling pulled apart (confused)
- egg on face, like two cents (embarrassed)

Nonverbal Behaviour. Most people are familiar with the physiological reactions that occur in a moment of great fear. Our bodies, powered by increased adrenal secretion, respond automatically with elevated heart rate, rapid breathing, dry mouth, and other symptoms. Many of these reactions are clearly visible to any observer, even before any verbal declaration of fear. Nonverbal behaviour is usually outside our conscious control and is less likely to be censored. Consequently, counsellors can often trust nonverbal communication as a more reliable indicator of feelings than the verbal channel. With respect to nonverbal communication, the visual channel is the most significant. For example, research has shown that often more than 55 percent of the meaning of a message is conveyed nonverbally, accentuating the importance of understanding nonverbal communication (Wolvin and Coakley, 1996). A person's emotions may be conveyed much more accurately by their body posture and eyes than by their words. Furthermore, counsellors who are able to respond to nonverbal as well as verbal messages "project an unusual warmth, sensitivity, and perceptiveness that enhances the intimacy of the relationship" (George and Cristiani, 1986:145).

Counsellors can learn a great deal about their clients' feelings from carefully observing their manner and the way they present their ideas. Nonverbal cues act to confirm, contradict, or even substitute for verbal expressions of emotions. For example, a client might say, "I'm ecstatic," but saying it in a sarcastic manner conveys the opposite. Another common example occurs when people say, "I'm interested in what you have to say," but at the same time they continue with another activity. Below are additional examples:

Confirmation:

a.   client says, "I'm happy," accompanied by a smile

b.   client expresses anger by shaking a fist

Contradiction:

a.   client says "Yes," while shaking head

b.   client says, "I'm not angry," while shouting or avoiding eye contact

c.   client says, "It's not a big deal," while crying

Substitution:

a.   client cries, looks away, moves chair back, glares, frowns, shifts uncomfortably

b.   client uses gestures such as pointing

Counsellors need to interpret nonverbal behaviour cautiously. Typically, nonverbal behaviour can have many meanings that vary according to a multitude of factors, such as culture, context, and individual comfort level. People from some cultures, for example, interact at very close personal distance, but others experience the same personal distance as intrusive or even aggressive. Some people consider direct eye contact rude, while others view avoidance of eye contact as cold or as evidence that people are trying to hide something. In fact, for some cultural groups, lack of eye contact is considered a sign of respect and courtesy (Corey and Corey, 1989:84).

Body Language. *Kinesics* is the study of body language, including such variables as posture, facial expressions, gestures, and eye motion. Sometimes body language is easily interpreted, such as when people use gestures that have direct verbal equivalents. For example, people might point to indicate direction or use their fingers and hands to signify size or numbers. At other times, body language is ambiguous and more difficult to interpret, particularly when people communicate contradictory messages. For example, a person might be listening intently and making appropriate eye contact, but this is accompanied by fidgeting and rapid finger tapping, which seems to say, "I'm bored." Johnson offers a perspective on this difficulty:

> For one thing, the same feeling can be expressed nonverbally in several different ways. Anger, for example, can be expressed by jumping up and down or by a frozen stillness. Happiness can be expressed through laughter or tears. Any single nonverbal message, furthermore, can arise from a variety of feelings. A blush may show embarrassment, pleasure, nervousness, or even anger. Crying can be caused by sadness, happiness, excitement, grief, pain, or confusion. (1997:173)

Even a simple smile may have multiple meanings: (1) it may show warmth, pleasure, or amusement, (2) it may be an attempt to appease or humour someone in order to reduce threat or obtain approval, (3) it may reveal nervousness, or (4) it may simply be a habit with no particular meaning (Wolvin and Coakley, 1996:180). Consequently, counsellors should look for multiple indicators of meaning, rather than for a single signal.

Voice. Counsellors can learn a great deal from their clients from their voice tone, volume, and pitch. These variables can reveal if clients are depressed, euphoric, angry, or sad. For example, Kadushin (1990) concluded that anger tends to be expressed with speech that is more rapid and loud, whereas sadness is characterized by more pauses and slowness of speech. Silence is an important component of nonverbal communication (see Chapter 4). Counsellors need to be able to read nonverbal cues to decide how, when, and if they should interrupt a silent moment.

Spatial Distance. Proxemics is a term used to describe how people use space and distance. Hall's model (1959) is widely used to describe the four main distances:

1. Intimate distance is a zone of up to 0.5 m (2 feet) reserved for private exchanges of intimate thoughts and feelings.
2. Personal distance is a zone of about 0.5 to 1 m (2 to 4 feet) that is used for less intense exchanges with friends and family.
3. Social distance is a zone of approximately 1 to 3.5 m (4 to 12 feet) used for more impersonal meetings and social contact.
4. Public distance beyond 3.5 m (12 feet) is used for casual exchanges such as giving a speech or lecture.

How an individual uses space is influenced by many variables, including gender, age, culture, physical characteristics, status, various personality traits, and the nature of the relationship. For example, people tend to want more space as they become older (Wolvin and Coakley, 1996:186). Counsellors should adapt their seating to meet the needs of individual clients and situations and remember that angry clients may need more personal distance. In such situations, counsellors also need more space for safety reasons. Counsellors should also be mindful of spatial shifts during the interview. Often these changes are subtle, such as when a client shifts his or her chair back, as if to say, "I'm not comfortable with what we're talking about." Similarly, as clients lean in and move toward them, counsellors can conclude that intimacy and trust are increasing. If a client seems to be physically and psychologically withdrawing, this may be the wrong time to confront or to introduce more sensitive topics.

Counsellors need to be aware of their own nonverbal behaviour and how it might influence their clients in subtle ways. Counsellors easily communicate their displeasure by frowning, turning away from clients, or increasing the physical distance between them. Alternatively, they disclose that they like clients by smiling, using a pleasant voice tone, increasing eye contact, and leaning toward clients (Mehrabian, 1981:162).

Individual Definition

Each feeling can be experienced as positive or negative at varying levels of intensity, but this subjective determination is individually defined. Anxiety for some people can be debilitating, seriously affecting the quality of their lives. However, the same emotion for an athlete may arouse a competitive spirit, and the individual might thrive on its physiological consequences.

Circumstances and context may not be good predictors of feelings. One person might be anxious about public speaking but find the experience exhilarating, while another person is terrified by the prospect. One individual might enjoy parties and be stimulated by the chance to meet new people, but a second person looks for any excuse to avoid the panic brought on by crowded social events. Consequently, when not obvious, counsellors should ask clients what particular meaning they give to any emotional experience. In the following example, the counsellor makes assumptions, then, sensitive to the client's nonverbal message, works to correct the error.

CLIENT: *My mother is coming to visit me next week.*

COUNSELLOR: *Oh, that's nice. It's always great when you have a chance to see your folks.*

CLIENT: *(hesitating) I guess so.*

COUNSELLOR: *(picking up on the client's hesitation) How do you feel about her visit?*

CLIENT: *I dread it. My mother always wants to tell me how to run my life.*

In the above example, another valid choice would be for the counsellor to admit the error. This would model openness to the client and serve to reinforce the reality that the counsellor is not perfect. Subsequently, it may be easier for the client to be open about his or her mistake.

CLIENT: *(hesitating) I guess so.*

COUNSELLOR: *Perhaps I was too hasty in assuming you would be happy that she was coming. I should have waited until you told me how you felt.*

CLIENT: *I dread it. My mother always wants to tell me how to run my life.*

Individuals are often governed by cultural norms, and there are wide variances in the extent and manner to which they express emotions. Some value emotional expression, whereas others favour emotional restraint. Counsellors need to be careful to avoid using their own measuring criteria when attempting to understand the emotions of others. If they expect that people in crisis will be verbal and declare their pain, then they might miss the fact that the quiet child is much more in need than the one who is acting out.

Mixed Feelings

Problems and experiences are often defined and frequently complicated by multiple and seemingly contradictory feelings from two or more emotional families (see Table 6.2). A great deal of stress and confusion can arise from the pushes and pulls of competing feelings that, if unmanaged, can control a client's life. The terms *ambivalence* and *of two minds* are often used. Ambivalence is normal, and it can be a valuable help to decision making.

> **EXAMPLE:** *A woman describes the joy she felt when her son left home to begin training as a counsellor, but as she talks her eyes well up with tears. Clearly, she is experiencing a strong sense of loss, despite the fact that words speak to her pride and happiness. More accurately, both feelings exist simultaneously.*

People also have feelings about the emotions they experience. Sometimes they are very aware of these mixed feelings, sometimes not. Try this simple experiment. Close your eyes and recall a recent strong emotion, such as anger or joy. Take a moment to get in touch

Table 6.2 Common Mixed Feelings

happy/scared	This often arises in conjunction with a lifestyle change (e.g., getting married, returning to school, starting a new job, sending children to daycare, experiencing "empty nest" when children leave home).
happy/sad	Some transitional life events, such as leaving one job for another or seeing a child off to college (kindergarten, etc.), elicit these feelings. A sense of loss as well as gain is often present.
depressed/fed up	These feelings may suggest that the person has "bottomed out." Significantly, being fed up may be used as a strong motivator for change (e.g., deciding to change a self-destructive drug habit).
angry/afraid	Fear is often the most significant emotion, but anger is more commonly expressed (e.g., a parent facing a teenager who is two hours late for curfew).
hopeful/despairing	Many clients fluctuate between believing that change is possible and life will get better and that nothing will improve and further effort is futile. Developing and sustaining motivation is particularly crucial in such situations (e.g., a person coping with a life-threatening illness).
attracted/repulsed	Many people who are considering changes in their lives experience these feelings. Part of them wants things to be different, and part wants the security of their present situation, however distressful (e.g., a person contemplating leaving an abusive relationship).
love/hate	This usually arises in the face of contradictory evidence (e.g., a friend whose behaviour is erratic—sometimes loving, sometimes abusive).

with your feelings. Now try to complete this sentence, "I feel _____ about feeling (your recent strong emotion)." Many readers will find that this simple exercise leads to a deeper understanding of their emotions. Some may find guilt behind their joy. Others, fear behind their anger.

Mixed feelings are often associated with anxiety and stress, especially when the feelings require opposing responses. If a person is both attracted to and repelled by a particular choice, anxiety is likely to continue until he or she resolves the dilemma.

Mental Health Issues

Affect is a term counsellors use to describe how people express emotions such as sadness, excitement, and anger. Culture and context help to define what is considered within the "normal range." Affect is communicated through voice tone and quality, posture, facial expressions, and other nonverbal cues. Terms used to describe affect include:

- *Blunted:* Emotional expression is less than one might expect.

- *Flat:* There is an absence or near absence of any signs of emotional expression.

- *Inappropriate:* The person's manner and mood contradict what one might expect. For example, a client might laugh while describing the death of his mother.

- *Labile:* There is abnormal variability in affect, with repeated, rapid, and abrupt shifts in affective expression.

- *Restricted or constricted:* There is a mild reduction in the range and intensity of emotional expression (for more information see American Psychiatric Association, 1994:763).

Psychologists and other mental health professionals use the terms **affective disorder** or **mood disorder** to describe a variety of disturbances in mood. The most common mood disorders are depression and mania. Clients with depression are likely to experience many of the following symptoms: a depressed mood; inability to experience pleasure; loss of energy and interest in life and work; changes in appetite; sleep disturbances (especially insomnia); decrease in sexual energy; feelings of worthlessness, helplessness, guilt, anxiety, or pessimism; and thoughts of death or suicide. Clients with mania are likely to experience many of the following: abnormally elevated mood; irritability; hostility; grandiosity; over-activity; flight of ideas; decreased need for sleep; and involvement in buying sprees and other indicators of poor judgment (Nicholi, 1988:315; American Psychiatric Association, 1994). Referral to a physician should be considered as an adjunct to counselling (see Chapter 8 for more in-depth discussion).

EMPATHY

The Nature of Empathy

In everyday terms, empathy means seeing the world through someone else's eyes. For purposes of counselling, empathy is defined as "the process of accurately understanding the emotional perspective of another person and the communication of this understanding" (Shebib, 1997:177). This definition underscores the twin components of empathy: understanding and communication. A counsellor who is perceptive and adept at understanding the client's major feelings but cannot communicate that understanding is a limited helper

(Gladding, 1996:130). The primary target of empathy is to reply to feelings, but in the process counsellors typically capture elements of their clients' thoughts and situations. Responses that deal primarily with clients' thoughts may be more appropriately described as reflective responses (Garvin and Seabury, 1984).

Empathy is a central condition for all helping relationships, regardless of the counselling or therapeutic model adopted (Walrond-Skinner, 1986:113). Empathy is a fundamental building block for the helping relationship, and empathy is clearly connected to positive outcomes in counselling (Rogers, 1980). Appropriate empathy communicates understanding, builds trust, and assists in establishing the counsellor's credibility. It is widely ranked as among the highest qualities that a counsellor can possess (Shulman, 1992; Egan, 1998; Walrond-Skinner, 1986). Shulman's (1992) research, for example, concluded that empathy contributes substantially to overcoming the challenges of developing a counselling relationship. As well, his research confirmed that empathy is a powerful helping tool.

When counsellors are empathic, they are less likely to oversimplify complex problems. Because they understand more, they are less prone to insult their clients with well-meaning but unusable advice. Egan puts it bluntly when he says that empathy restrains the counsellor: "Empathy keeps helpers from doing useless things such as asking too many questions and giving premature and inept advice. Empathy puts the ball back into the client's court and thus in its own way encourages the client to act" (1990:135). Counsellors need to remember that clients have real and rational reasons for feeling as they do.

Counsellors who accept the feelings of their clients help clients accept themselves and their feelings. As Parrott observes, "Empathy communicates to clients that they are worth understanding, that their inner hopes and private fears have value" (1997:196). Rogers noted, "True empathy is always free of any evaluative or diagnostic quality. The recipient perceives this with some surprise: 'If I am not being judged, perhaps I am not so evil or abnormal as I have thought. Perhaps I don't have to judge myself so harshly.' Thus, the possibility of self-acceptance is gradually increased" (1980:154).

Rogers suggested that empathy is more than just a skill—it is a way of being with another person. As he succinctly put it, "The ideal therapist is, first of all, empathic" (1980:146). Empathy is essential for understanding, and some clients "cannot even begin to think about changing their painful situations until they are satisfied that the essence of their pain has been communicated" (Middleman and Wood, 1990:59).

Empathy assists clients in identifying and labelling feelings, which allows clients to then deal with the feelings. Moreover, with strong and supportive counsellors, clients can find the courage to deal with feelings that may have been too painful or overwhelming to address on their own. In this sense, empathy contributes to therapeutic change.

Empathy is not just for counsellors. Empathy is a skill that clients can use to improve their relationships with others. Often clients adopt the communication patterns of counsellors, so counsellors should be sensitive to what they model. Counsellor empathy models a healthy way of relating to others.

In order to effectively empathize, counsellors need to be able to demonstrate comfort with a wide range of feelings, without needing to flee from pain or grief. Just as doctors and nurses need to be able to deal with catastrophic injury without losing control or running away, counsellors must develop their capacity to work with intense feelings without needing to change the subject, intellectualize, or offer quick fixes. Sometimes, counsellors misinterpret this capacity as meaning that they need to be emotionally detached and coldly indifferent. In fact, empathic counsellors are deeply involved with their clients. Counsellors put aside or suspend their own reactions to their clients' feelings and adopt an accepting and nonjudgmental attitude. Hancock describes the importance of **controlled emotional involvement**, which she defines as "the empathic sensitivity of the worker to the client's feelings, disciplined by self-awareness, such that the worker's feelings do not inappropriately affect his or her understanding and purposeful response" (1997:131).

Rogers emphasizes the need to "sense the client's private world as if it were your own, but without ever losing the 'as if' quality ... To sense the client's anger, fear, or confusion as if it were your own, yet without your own anger, fear, or confusion getting bound up in it" (1961:284). Rogers also provides this important observation about empathy:

> You lay aside your own views and values in order to enter another's world without prejudice. In some sense it means that you lay aside your self; this can only be done by persons who are secure enough in themselves that they know they will not get lost in what may turn out to be the strange or bizarre world of the other, and that they can comfortably return to their own world when they wish. (1980:143)

CONVERSATION 6.1

INCREASING EMPATHIC VOCABULARY

STUDENT: I would really like to increase my empathy skills, but my vocabulary is so limited. I seem to know only a few feeling words, such as happy, sad, and angry. How can I increase my feeling word choice?

TEACHER: It's not necessary to have an encyclopedic vocabulary, but you should have enough word choice to capture a broad range of feelings. Study Table 6.1 for new feeling words, then take advantage of every opportunity to practise empathy and try these words. Remember that feelings are often mixed. Read books and watch TV with a special ear for discerning how people are feeling. One of the best ways is to ask others how they feel, then to listen carefully to their words. This will help sensitize you to the unique vocabulary that each individual has adopted.

Types of Empathy

Three types of empathy are basic, inferred, and invitational. In basic empathy, a counsellor mirrors what the client has explicitly said, whereas a counsellor uses inferred empathy to reach empathic understanding from less obvious clues. Invitational empathy involves strategies to encourage clients to talk about their feelings.

Basic Empathy. **Basic empathy** requires counsellors to accurately perceive their clients' feelings and concerns and to communicate that understanding. It may include labelling feelings or summarizing expressed feelings. Frequently, clients want to talk about feelings, particularly those closely related to their problem situations. When clients take the initiative to introduce feelings, it is relatively easy and nonthreatening for counsellors to respond with basic empathy. Basic empathy simply says, "I have heard how you feel and I accept your feelings without judgment." With basic empathy, no attempt is made to interpret, judge, or promote greater awareness or insight beyond that which the client has already articulated.

Despite its apparent simplicity, basic empathy can be a powerful helping tool. When people express feelings in everyday communication, they may be blocked or discouraged when others react by judging, ignoring, or giving advice. For example, one common but extremely unhelpful response is "You shouldn't feel that way." In contrast, basic empathy creates a climate in which clients do not have to defend or hide their feelings. Basic empathy responses are, for many people, an unusual and satisfying experience. As one client described it, "For the first time, I felt safe. Someone had finally listened and heard me." Hancock states that "empathy helps to establish an atmosphere that gives each client a secure feeling that this is a place where 'it's safe to be me, this me, here and now'" (1997:167).

Counsellors who punctuate their work with frequent empathy are more likely to build rapport and evoke further information from clients (Egan, 1998). Simple logic suggests that when people believe that they are accepted and understood, they are more likely to feel secure and less likely to raise defences. As a result, clients are more inclined to share and explore at a deeper level of intimacy than they would under more threatening conditions. The example below illustrates basic empathy:

> **CLIENT:** *I was ready to kill her. How could she embarrass me in front of all those people?*

> **COUNSELLOR:** *So you are angry that she didn't have enough sense to keep quiet.*

> **CLIENT:** *Angry, but also hurt. After all, she was supposed to be my best friend. How could she double-cross me?*

> **COUNSELLOR:** *Sounds like you felt betrayed.*

Empathic responses need to be presented with an air of tentativeness in order to give clients an opportunity to offer corrections. A simple pause or a question such as "Have I got it right?" can be used to achieve this end.

Inferred Empathy. **Inferred empathy**, sometimes called *advanced accurate empathy* (Egan, 1998), includes attempts to identify clients' feelings based on nonverbal cues, themes, and hints. Inferred empathy is a powerful counselling skill that enables clients to deal with feelings at a deeper level than they may have been able to express.

Some clients say that their trust level increased because their counsellors identified their feelings: "My worker seemed to know how I felt without me saying so. Finally, I felt understood." Inferred empathy may be particularly useful when working with clients who lack feeling vocabulary and clients who are unaccustomed to expressing feelings. Inferred empathy seems to say, "I have the courage and the ability to hear your feelings."

> **CLIENT:** *It was a tough situation. Here I was in front of all those people with my private life laid bare.*

> **COUNSELLOR:** *From the tears in your eyes, I suspect this was a painful and embarrassing moment for you.*

In the above example, the client seems willing to explore her experience, yet she stops short of verbally identifying her feelings. The counsellor takes a mild empathic risk and considers context and nonverbal cues to infer empathy. Inferred empathy should always be presented tentatively to allow room for correction and further exploration.

With inferred empathy, some speculation based on the evidence of feelings is necessary. Consequently, there is more risk involved than with basic empathy. There are two significant risks. First, because the data base for inferred empathy is more ambiguous, more errors are likely. Hence, counsellors should be especially tentative with inferred empathy. As well, counsellors should avoid becoming overly speculative to the point where they are simply guessing at their clients' feelings. Second, inferred empathy may be met with resistance from clients who are unwilling or unable to acknowledge their feelings. Inferred empathy picks up on subtle cues, and clients may be surprised to hear that their feelings have been communicated. They may react with anger and resentment that their feelings have been uncovered. Some clients are afraid of the intensity of their feelings, whereas others have strong needs for privacy. Thus, inferred empathy must be timed appropriately. The counselling relationship should have a reasonable level of trust, and there should be sufficient time left in the interview to process any reactions. Otherwise, it is best to defer inferred empathic responses.

Clients provide clues to their feelings in a number of ways. Clients might be embarrassed about sharing their feelings or reluctant to ask for help, so they talk about a "friend who has a problem." Understanding nonverbal behaviour is crucial. Astute counsellors learn a great deal about their clients' feelings by carefully observing changes in voice tone, sudden shifts in posture, nervous behaviour, tears, grimaces, clenched fists, finger tapping, and smiling. As well, certain behaviours could suggest feelings. For example, a boy who runs away from a group home just before a visit from his mother may be saying something about his fear and anger. A client who arrives late, refuses to take his coat off, and sits with arms folded across his chest might be saying, "I don't want to be here."

Another way that many clients share feelings is through analogies. For example, a client who compares his life to a speeding train may be expressing his fears of being out of control. Some clients hint at their feelings by asking questions such as "Do you worry about your kids when they are out late at night?" Clients who minimize problems, as in "I have a bit of a problem. Do you have a minute?" or "This is probably not important," may be signalling that they have significant issues and feelings that they need to discuss.

Tuning in, or **preparatory empathy** (Shulman, 1992), is a useful way to prepare for inferred empathy. Preparatory empathy is a preliminary phase skill that involves trying to anticipate the feelings and concerns that clients might bring up in the interview. Such advance tuning in is useful because clients often do not directly reveal their feelings. Tuning in helps workers anticipate feelings and consider how clients might communicate indirectly. Shulman gives an example of the potential value of tuning in by describing a common situation involving a new, 22-year-old worker meeting with a 38-year-old mother of seven children. The mother asked the worker, "Do you have any children?" The worker responded defensively by listing her training in child psychology. Shulman suggests that the worker missed the implicit feelings expressed by the mother—the fear that the worker will not understand her. Had she used the tuning-in skill, the worker might have been able to consider in advance the range of feelings that a mother of seven kids might have when meeting with a young counsellor who has no children. With such advance preparation, the worker might have been more sensitive to the mother's real question, perhaps responding, "No, I don't have any children. Are you wondering if I'm going to be able to understand what it's like for you having to raise so many? I'm concerned about that as well. If I'm going to help you, I'm going to have to understand, and you are going to have to help me to understand" (Shulman, 1992:58). This response might have set the stage for a discussion of the mother's feelings about workers and given the worker a chance to share her own feelings.

CONVERSATION 6.2

WHEN NOT TO USE EMPATHY

STUDENT: I don't think empathy is always such a good thing. I watched one taped interview of Carl Rogers and two other therapists interviewing the same client. If I had been Rogers' client, I would have been irritated. He seemed to continually regurgitate what the client had just said.

TEACHER: You've raised a good point. Too much empathy, particularly when you get stuck at a basic level, might leave you and your client going in circles. It's also true that if you move too fast with empathy, your clients can feel threatened and put up their defences. This is particularly true with clients who have strong needs for privacy. They may view your empathic statements as an unwanted intrusion into their feelings. Empathy invites greater relationship intimacy, and some clients are not ready for the risks that this entails. Having said that, I think it's important to remember that Rogers' client evaluated his method positively. This reminds us that clients respond differently to the same technique.

Other clients who may not be ready for empathy are those who are so caught up in their own talking that they do not even hear empathic statements. As Shea (1988) suggests, attempts to empathize with this group may actually be counterproductive because empathy interferes with what they want most—an audience to listen.

STUDENT: I think one way to handle that is to test your client's capacity for empathy with a few basic empathic statements. If they are not well received, you can back off by switching to less demanding content or more basic empathy.

TEACHER: I agree, back off, but not forever! As trust develops the client may welcome that same empathic response that he or she first rejected. To continue the list of times when empathy may not be a good idea, I'd add the following:

- when your clients reject empathy
- when it's clearly time to move on to problem solving or another activity
- when empathy is continuously misinterpreted by clients, for example as controlling.

We should always remember that counselling techniques will not work the same with all clients. Cultural norms and expectations, for example, may affect how empathy is received.

Invitational Empathy. **Invitational empathy** encourages clients to explore emotions. Counsellors can draw on their knowledge of human growth and development, such as how people tend to deal with particular life events and crises. Some clients are reluctant to share their feelings for fear of judgment, or they may believe that they shouldn't feel a particular way. Others may think they are the "only one" or that they are "crazy," "evil," or "abnormal." For example, it is common to feel some relief, even happiness (as well as grief) when a loved one who has been struggling with a painful illness dies, but a client may feel guilty for feeling this way. Invitational empathy normalizes the experience, making it easier for the client to talk about it and to accept it: "It's normal at a time like this to struggle with mixed feelings—grief, pain, comfort, and perhaps joy that her suffering is at an end."

Invitational empathy also says to the client that the counsellor is ready and able to talk about difficult feelings. By identifying and labelling feelings, the counsellor is saying, "It's okay to feel this way." In the following example, the counsellor uses invitational empathy to "give permission" to a client, who might otherwise suppress or ignore his pain, to experience and verbalize his emotions.

CLIENT: *I guess it's no big deal. So what if they know the scoop on my marital problems.*

COUNSELLOR: *A lot of people in the same situation might feel embarrassed and perhaps disappointed or angry that a friend could be so indiscreet about something said in confidence.*

In the example below, the counsellor uses nonverbal cues as a basis for invitational empathy to encourage the client to explore a difficult topic.

COUNSELLOR: *Would you mind if I shared an observation with you? I may be wrong, so I'd like your opinion.*

CLIENT: *Sure, go ahead. Say it.*

COUNSELLOR: *I notice that whenever mention of your father comes up, you seem keen to change the topic.*

(long silence, client stares at the floor)

COUNSELLOR: *Some memories are painful—maybe even too painful to talk about.*

CLIENT: *(softly, tears in his eyes) It's just that his death was so unexpected. We had a fight that morning, and I didn't even get a chance to say goodbye.*

Invitational empathy begins with questions and responses targeted to encourage clients to express feelings. Choosing a strategy to encourage the expression of feelings is influenced by the usual variables, including the amount of trust in the relationship, time constraints, culture, and the counsellor's role. Timing, for example, is one of the most important variables. Since the exploration of feelings can be time consuming, it is important for counsellors to make sure that they have enough time to complete the process. Intelligent use of silence is another important variable. Clients may need their counsellors to patiently listen and restrain themselves from filling every silent moment with words.

One way to bridge the interview into a discussion of feelings is to use invitational statements, such as "I do not know how you feel, but if you are feeling pain or loneliness, I am ready to listen." Comments such as "I need your help in understanding your feelings" can also move the interview into the affective, or feeling, area.

Frequently, natural opportunities are provided when clients share a bit about how they are feeling. Then the counsellor can use questions to encourage further sharing. Open questions such as the following promote clients to share feelings: "How are you feeling?" "What feelings best describe how you reacted?" Closed questions such as the following target specific information about feelings: "Did you feel angry?" "Is this something you feel strongly about?"

Helping clients understand the importance of addressing feelings is an important step that keeps clients involved in decision making (contracting). When counsellors inform clients and solicit their support for the process, clients' motivation is higher. Here are some sample leads:

- I think it might help if we shift our focus and talk a bit about how you feel. This might help us both to understand why your decision is so difficult.

- We haven't yet talked about your feelings. In my experience, feelings often present one of the biggest barriers.

- Until feelings are understood and accepted, they can distort our thinking and even reduce the amount of control we have over our behaviour. So, you might find it useful if we spend some time exploring how you feel.

Directives such as the following can be used to move the interview into the feeling area: "Tell me how you feel." "Let's switch our focus and talk about your feelings." Directives are one way to manage the flow and focus of the interview.

With some clients, counsellor self-disclosure, if used sparingly, is a powerful tool. "I don't know how it is for you, but I know that for many months after my marriage ended, I was in a state of shock."

Another interview tool is the use of sentence completion statements. Sentence completion statements give counsellors a way to focus feelings on a particular area, and they give freedom to clients to control the answer. For example, counsellors can make statements such as the following and ask clients to complete them:

- When I think about all my problems, I feel ...
- If I could use one feeling to describe my situation it would be ...
- When I first came for counselling I felt ...
- The feelings that I most need to deal with are ...

Invitational empathy should respect clients' rights to privacy. Compton and Galaway point out:

> It is questionable whether any client wants to be fully and totally known. There is something very frightening about someone's knowing everything about us as an individual for in knowledge lies control; so in the ordinary course of living people reveal their intimate selves only to those they trust. Without the pain of the problem and the hope that the worker can offer some help toward coping with it, few clients would be willing to share themselves with an unknown other person. (1984:238)

Four Generalizations about Empathy

Generalization One. When clients share feelings, empathy is often the preferred response. The **principle of positive reinforcement** states that "if in a given situation, somebody does something that is followed immediately by a positive reinforcer, then that person is more likely to do the same thing again" (Martin and Pear, 1992:26). Clients take an interpersonal risk when they share their feelings. Empathy serves to acknowledge this risk by conveying recognition and acceptance of the clients' feelings. In this way, it reinforces the wisdom of the risk and motivates clients to continue sharing feelings. On the other hand, when clients share feelings and they are not rewarded (reinforced) with empathy, they tend to keep their feelings more private. This underscores the importance of expressing empathy early in the relationship.

Generalization Two. Counsellors should risk expressing empathy early in the relationship. Early empathy establishes for the client that the counselling relationship is a safe place to express feelings. To become comfortable with empathy, counsellors need to over-

Table 6.3	Types of Empathy		
Type	**Description**	**Major Use**	**Comments**
Basic	Response to clearly articulated feelings	To encourage continued expression of feelings. To confirm capacity to hear feelings	Basic empathy contributes to the development of trust. It signals to clients that counsellors are willing and able to deal with feelings.
Inferred	Response to nonverbal cues and other indicators of feelings	To move feelings into the verbal channel of communication	Inferred empathy may generate more anxiety in some clients as feelings that they avoided, suppressed, or wanted to keep hidden are made visible. Inferred empathy may promote client insight.
Invitational	Encouragement of clients to talk about feelings	To stimulate discussion of feelings. To normalize feelings	Invitational empathy is useful for working with clients who are reluctant or unable to articulate feelings. Counsellor timing is critical, and counsellors should present invitational empathy in a gentle and tentative manner.

come their own fears about bringing emotions into the foreground. Shulman (1992) suggests that many workers fear that by encouraging clients to express emotions they might trigger extreme reactions, particularly suicide. As a counterargument he proposes that "the greater danger is not in the facing of feelings but in denying them. The only thing worse than living with strong emotions is the feeling that one is alone and that no one can understand" (1992:128). By helping clients express and get in touch with their feelings, counsellors can help them decrease the negative power that these feelings may have over them.

In the early part of a relationship or interview, counsellors may not have enough information to offer empathic understanding, but given its central importance, they should give priority to acquiring, maintaining, and deepening it throughout the helping relationship. Therefore, counsellors should be alert to empathic opportunities. One obvious opportunity arises whenever clients verbalize feelings. In such moments, counsellors can use basic empathy to confirm understanding. Sometimes clients reveal feelings nonverbally, and counsellors can use inferred empathy. When clients have not shared feelings, counsellors can adopt invitational empathy to encourage them to share their emotions.

Generalization Three. Counsellors should express empathy tentatively. Counsellors need to refrain from using empathy as a weapon by insisting that their clients must feel a particular way. Counsellors should look for indicators that clients have accepted their empathy and that it is accurate. Clients provide confirmation through head nods, smiles, reduction in anxiety, and verbal confirmation, for example, "That's right" or "You seem to know exactly how I'm feeling even before I tell you." Clients also implicitly confirm willingness to accept empathy when they continue to share feelings at a deeper level. Sometimes clients correct counsellors. This is an important and positive outcome of empathic risk. It enables counsellors to adjust and refine their understanding and helps them reach a point of shared meaning with their clients. Thus, empathy should be seen as an active process of developing understanding.

Generalization Four. Empathy requires flexibility in its use, including the ability to refrain from using it. Empathy is an important and powerful skill, but counsellors need to use it intelligently (see Table 6.4 for suggestions). When clients are willing to address feelings, empathic responses are effective. With some clients, empathic statements result in the opposite of what was intended. Instead of deepening trust and encouraging clients to open up, empathy arouses defences. This may happen when empathy suggests feelings that clients would prefer not to address, or it may arise when clients experience empathy as invading their personal space. When clients resist empathy by withdrawing or becoming defensive, it might be better to discontinue using it for a while.

Situational differences influence how the work of empathy unfolds. Some clients are very verbal and open with their feelings and respond positively to empathy. Others need gentle encouragement to talk about feelings, and they open up discussion of feelings gradually and in a very controlled manner. Counsellors will generally find that they encounter less resistance when they match their clients' pace.

Empathic Response Leads

Using a range of different responses adds interest and variety to the interview, but using the same words and phrases can irritate clients and reduce the energy and vitality of the interview. Having a range of leads for empathic response prevents the interview from sounding artificial. The following list provides some variations:

- So, you feel ...
- My sense is that you might be feeling ...
- From your point of view ...

Table 6.4   The Empathic Communication Process

- Listen for or probe for feelings.
- Observe non verbal indicators of emotion.
- Consider context—problem, phase, setting, relationship.
- Identify general category of feeling (e.g., anger, sadness, etc.) including mixed or ambivalent feelings.
- Identify level or intensity of emotion (i.e., low, medium, high).
- Choose an appropriate specific feeling word, phrase or metaphor.
- Formulate a tentative empathic response.
- Wait for or encourage the client to confirm or correct your empathic perception.
- Based on client response, correct or offer a deeper empathic response.

- As you see it ...
- I wonder if what you're saying is ...
- Perhaps you feel ...
- I gather that ...
- It seems to you that ...
- What I understand from what you have said is ...
- It sounds like ...
- You appear to be feeling ...

This list could easily be expanded, and counsellors should adapt it to fit the style and the language of their clients. (For additional ideas see Martin, 1983:42; Shebib, 1997:191.)

Why Achieving Empathic Understanding Is So Difficult

Empathic errors are less likely when counsellors are similar to their clients (in age, gender, race, etc.) and when they have had similar problems and experiences, provided they do not use their own experiences and background as a script for how the client must feel. Counsellors need to remember the importance of allowing for individual differences. It is critical that counsellors remember that they can never fully understand how other people feel. Through empathy, they can get a better sense of their clients' feelings, but this understanding will never be perfect. The challenge is to "see beyond conventional facades, refrain from imposing personal interpretations and judgments, and be willing to risk understanding another person's private logic and feelings, which in superficial daily contacts the counselor might see as weak, foolish, or undesirable" (Hammond, Hepworth, and Smith, 1977:3).

Empathy is perhaps the most difficult counselling skill to master. As Egan notes, "Although many people 'feel' empathy for others, the truth is that few know how to put it into words" (1998:83). Empathy demands a lot of counsellors. They must manage their own emotional and judgmental reactions. They have to find meaning and discover feelings from their clients' verbal and nonverbal communication. This can be exceptionally demanding, since clients may keep feelings hidden, suppress feelings, or lack understanding or awareness of their emotions. As well, relationship issues, including lack of trust, embarrassment, and fear of being judged, can inhibit clients from disclosing. For example, there may be societal, cultural, or personal norms that prohibit sharing of feelings. Or clients may not have the ability (language) to adequately communicate their emotions.

Further complicating the empathic process is the need for counsellors to respond right away. In an interview, there is no time for counsellors to use a thesaurus or dictionary to find the right words and there is no opportunity to consult others, rehearse their empathy, or ponder the feeling state of their clients. Empathic risk means daring to share perceived understanding with clients using concrete words and phrases.

Responses to Avoid

When attempting to express empathy, counsellors need to avoid certain responses. In particular, they need to be aware of the effect of cutoffs, empty responses, and sympathy.

Cutoffs. Cutoffs are phrases that inhibit the further expression of feeling. Counsellors who make statements such as "Don't feel" and "You should feel" are demonstrating a low level of understanding and acceptance of how their clients feel. Although such statements may have some limited supportive value, they generally force clients to defend their feelings. Similarly, when counsellors ask clients questions such as "Why do you feel ...?" a judgmental tone is present that can leave clients feeling defensive (see Chapter 5).

Another response that may inhibit clients is silence. When clients risk sharing feelings, some response (empathy) is appropriate. When counsellors fail to acknowledge feelings, they may be saying, "This is not important" or "I'm not capable of dealing with your emotions." In response, clients might feel abandoned, embarrassed, or judged.

Counsellors also cut clients off when they change the subject and when they offer advice. A subject change has a clear message, "Let's not talk about that," and advice trivializes feelings.

Empty Responses. Empty responses are devoid of content. Phrases such as "I hear what you are saying" and "I understand what you mean" convey no confirmation that the counsellor has understood. Another empty response is parroting, or repeating, what the client has said. Egan describes parroting as "a parody of empathy" (1998:96). In contrast, empathy communicates the counsellor's effort to go beyond merely hearing the words by understanding the client's feelings and perspectives. Using empathy, the counsellor rephrases the client's statements and assigns labels to feelings that the client expressed but did not name.

Clichés and platitudes such as "Everybody has to have a little pain in their life" patronize and reject clients' feelings. As Egan puts it, clichéd responses say, "You don't really have a problem at all, at least not a serious one" (1998:96).

Sympathy. Sympathy refers to concern for other people's problems and emotions and is related to our own emotional and behavioural reactions. Sympathy is our reaction, and though it is intimately connected to another's feelings, it is not the same as empathy. Empathy is a process whereby we come to understand another's feelings. When successful, empathy is objective, and the counsellor achieves understanding from the client's frame of reference.

Counsellors are human and it is normal for them to have emotional responses when listening to their clients. In fact, their reactions are the basis for compassion, an indispensable component of a caring counselling relationship. Clearly, there are moments when it is appropriate to express sympathy. This lets clients know that counsellors support them and are moved by their pain. At the same time, it is essential for counsellors to develop the ability to separate their emotional reactions (sympathy and compassion) from those of their clients. Counsellors also need to ensure that their sympathy does not detract from the client's feelings by interfering with their need to express feelings, tell their stories, and face the reality of their problems.

> **CLIENT:** *I'm really worried about telling my dad that I've dropped out of college. Even when I was a little girl my father kept saying, "You've got to get an education or you'll never get anywhere in life."*

COUNSELLOR (CHOICE 1—SYMPATHETIC REACTION): *I don't think it was very fair for him to have laid such a heavy burden on you. It always makes me kind of angry when I hear about parents pushing their kids.*

COUNSELLOR (CHOICE 2—EMPATHIC REACTION): *So, you fear that you've let your father down.*

In the above example, Choice 1 is a misguided attempt to offer support. Judgmental in tone, it shifts the focus from the client's feelings to those of the counsellor. Choice 2 expresses basic empathy, setting the stage for further exploration.

Empathy Reminders. When you express empathy, acknowledge the feelings that have been expressed (verbally and/or non verbally). You could include a brief "because" clause that summarizes content. In most situations, you will want to stop there. This gives your clients a chance to process what they have heard and to offer corrections. Alternatively, when clients experience empathy they may be motivated to share at a deeper level. Consequently, *avoid* combining empathy with subject changes and other cutoff responses, content questions, sympathy, or any other response that diverts attention away from empathy. Below are some examples of appropriate and inappropriate empathic responses.

CLIENT: *Sometimes when he speaks to me that way, I just want to go hide in a corner.*

COUNSELLOR 1 (APPROPRIATE EMPATHY): *It sounds like maybe you're feeling embarrassed.*

COUNSELLOR 2 (INAPPROPRIATE EMPATHY—SUBJECT SHIFT): *It sounds like maybe you're feeling embarrassed. Would you like to talk about ways of overcoming it?*

COUNSELLOR 3 (SYMPATHY CONFUSED WITH EMPATHY): *I feel sorry for you that he treats you that way.*

COUNSELLOR 4 (NON-EMPATHY): *There's no reason why you should have to put up with such treatment.*

COUNSELLOR 5 (NON-EMPATHY—FAILURE TO IDENTIFY FEELINGS): *You're feeling like he should stop doing that.*

Tough Empathy

It's not hard to feel caring and compassion for most people in pain, such as the aging client who loses his job, the young mother who has had a second miscarriage, and the single parent who is trying to raise children on a limited income. However, some clients may challenge counsellors' tolerance. Even the most accepting counsellors occasionally find it difficult to lay aside personal reaction, suspend judgment, and respond with empathy to clients such as the following:

- Bob, an angry 20-year-old who savagely attacked an elderly woman
- Pernell, a father who argues for the morality of sex with his children
- Eileen, an HIV-positive prostitute who asserts her right to have unprotected sex with her customers
- Ruby, a woman who rejects and attacks efforts to help

Counsellors working with clients such as these are likely to experience strong emotional reactions, and they may find it difficult to put aside their personal feelings in order to feel and express empathy. Often these are clients who appear to lack empathy and feelings for others in their lives. In fact, "the blotting out of empathy as these people inflict damage on victims is almost always part of an emotional cycle that precipitates their cruel acts" (Goleman, 1995:106).

Why then should counsellors respond with empathy to such people? First, empathy is a way for counsellors to understand how their clients think and feel. Second, as noted earlier, empathy is instrumental in forming the helping relationship, the prerequisite condition for the contract between client and counsellor. One outcome of empathy is that clients come to feel valued and understood. As a result of the empathic relationship, clients begin to reveal more, make discoveries about themselves, and alter their perspectives about themselves and others. With clients who lack empathy for others, empathy teaches them that they cannot block out feelings and that their victims do hurt.

In situations in which it is difficult for them to respond with empathy, counsellors may need to work on their own issues. For example, they can ask themselves, "What is it about this particular client that makes it difficult for me to be empathic?" "Does this client remind me of someone else (e.g., parent, former partner)?" "To what extent do I have unresolved feelings and issues that this client triggers?"

Another strategy for counsellors is to spend time getting to know the client. Usually, familiarity increases empathy.

Carl, an employment counsellor, carefully read Antonio's file. Antonio was a 19-year-old unemployed male. From all indications, Antonio was not very interested in finding a job. His mother complained that he usually slept until noon and that he rarely even read the newspaper want ads. Antonio arrived for his appointment 20 minutes late and gave out a clear message that he didn't want to be there. "How long will this take?" he asked sternly.

Carl's natural reaction was anger and disgust at Antonio's attitude. He wondered to himself why he should spend time with this client, who was clearly unmotivated. Putting his personal feelings aside, Carl decided to respond with empathy, and he gently replied, "My hunch is that you don't see much point in being here. Maybe you're even a little angry at being forced to come." Antonio, a bit surprised at Carl's perceptiveness, told him how much he resented everyone trying to run his life.

Gradually, Antonio began to let down his defences and a very different picture emerged. Antonio talked about the rejection he felt from countless employers who turned him away. Soon, it was clear to Carl that Antonio was deeply depressed. He slept late because he couldn't sleep at night. He had stopped looking for work because it was the only way he knew to deal with the pain.

Sometimes counsellors fear expressing empathy because they mistakenly believe that empathy will endorse their clients' beliefs or lifestyles. Counsellors need to remind themselves that being empathic does not mean that they have to agree with their clients' feelings or perspectives. Empathy simply attempts to say, "I understand how you feel and how you see things." In fact, clients must feel understood before they will respond to any efforts to promote change. Empathy is one of the ways that counsellors establish credibility and win the trust of their clients. When a trusting relationship exists, clients may be willing to consider other perspectives and look at the consequences of their choices.

INTERVIEW 6.1 POOR SUBSTITUTES FOR EMPATHY

The following excerpt illustrates some of the inappropriate responses that counsellors sometimes use instead of empathy. Ignoring feelings and offering empty responses, simplistic advice, and sympathy are some responses below that are inadequate substitutes for empathy.

DIALOGUE	ANALYSIS
Client (softly, with tears in her eyes): I just haven't been the same since he left. I still look out the door and expect him to come home. Counsellor: How old was he when he ran away?	Inappropriate topic shift: The client is clearly experiencing some pain, perhaps grief, and she trusts the counsellor enough to share these feelings. Generally, when clients share feelings, particularly feelings that are strong, empathy is the preferred response. The counsellor's response shifts the focus away from feelings to content. This may subtly signal to the client that the counsellor is uncomfortable with feelings. Continual shifts such as this will "train" the client not to share feelings.
Client: He was just 16. I still thought of him as my baby. Now I go to sleep at night wondering whether he's dead or alive. Counsellor: You thought of him as your baby. Now you go to sleep at night wondering whether he's dead or alive. (silence)	Parroting: Repetition at this point serves no purpose. Sometimes key words or phrases can be emphasized as a way to focus attention, but this type of parroting is inappropriate here.
Counsellor: I understand how you feel. Client (buries her face in her hands): Sometimes I just don't know whether I can go on living. If something doesn't happen soon, then ... (counsellor interrupts)	Superficial response: The counsellor tries to be supportive, but the response is empty. Until the counsellor risks empathy with specific feeling words and phrases, the client cannot know whether she has, in fact, been heard.
Counsellor: You have to think of your husband and your other children. Client: Yes, I know, but do you have any idea what I'm going through, how tough it is just to get out of bed in the morning?	Rescuing, ignoring feelings: It seems obvious that this counsellor is unable to deal with the powerful feelings that the client presents. After an ill-timed interruption, the counsellor offers a misguided and simplistic solution, while ignoring the emotions the client expressed.
Counsellor: My guess is that you feel very angry at the world, maybe even some guilt that you are somehow responsible for your son's running away. Client: No! I don't feel guilty. I was always a good mother. I think if my son were here, he'd	Inaccurate empathy: The counsellor attempts invitational empathy. Unfortunately, there is insufficient evidence to support the counsellor's conclusion that the client feels angry or guilty. The counsellor may be right, but as suggested, it is merely a guess, a poor substitute for empa-

(continued)

say that too. When he became addicted to drugs, it was more than either of us knew how to handle.

Counsellor: I hear what you are saying.

Client: So what am I supposed to do? I feel so empty and useless.

Counsellor: It's a very bad feeling.

(brief silence)

Counsellor: You shouldn't feel that way. One day your son might walk in the door. You have to go on living.

Client: I suppose you're right. Thanks for listening. It felt good to get it off my chest.

Counsellor: I'm glad I was able to help.

thy. Moreover, the counsellor is not attending to the feelings that the client has already expressed.

Superficial response: This counsellor's response has the same problems as her earlier one, "I understand how you feel."

Inaccurate empathy, lack of specificity: The counsellor attempts empathy but misses the intensity of the client's feelings. Then, the counsellor quickly shifts the focus without giving the client time to respond.

One important requirement is to accept clients' feelings without judgment and without trying to tell them how they should feel.

Sometimes clients benefit from the interview, even when the counsellor's responses are as poor as those depicted in this encounter. Simply telling one's story and verbalizing feelings can help people deal with pain or problems. However, it is much more likely that this client is ready to dismiss the counsellor. The counsellor may be just as relieved that the interview is over.

Counsellors may find wisdom in Nicholi's observation that "whether the patient is young or old, neatly groomed or dishevelled, outgoing or withdrawn, articulate or inarticulate, highly integrated or totally disintegrated, of high or low socioeconomic status, the skilled clinician realizes that the patient, as a fellow human being, is considerably more like himself than he is different" (1988:8).

INTERVIEW 6.2 EFFECTIVE USE OF EMPATHY

DIALOGUE	ANALYSIS
Client: For as long as I can remember, I've been drinking on a daily basis. It's no big deal. Counsellor (softly, while maintaining eye contact): Drinking has been part of your life and you don't see a problem with it.	The counsellor tries to proceed cautiously with basic paraphrasing. Mirroring the client's thoughts conveys that he has been heard. Suspending verbal and nonverbal judgment helps to develop trust.

(continued)

(client nods)

Counsellor: You mentioned that your family gives you a hard time about drinking. How do you feel about that?

Client: Yeah. I work hard all day. If I want to have a drink, no one has a right to tell me to stop. Drinking helps me to relax.

Counsellor: Sounds as though you resent it when others interfere with something that gives you pleasure.

Client (loudly): They should back off and mind their own business. I don't tell them how to live.

Counsellor: It's more than just resentment. Perhaps you're angry that they don't respect your right to live your life as you see fit.

Client: I guess I shouldn't be so ticked off. After all, my father was an alcoholic, and I know first-hand what it's like to live with a drunk.

Counsellor: To some extent your feelings are mixed—you feel anger because you think they should mind their own business, but you also see where they are coming from, and you are sympathetic to their fears.

Client: Well, to be perfectly honest, it's not just their fear. I don't want to drink myself to death like my father did.

Counsellor: You've done some thinking about how you'd like your life to be different. When your wife confronts you, it really touches a nerve, and you're reminded of fears you'd rather not have.

The counsellor uses an open question to encourage the client to talk about his feelings. Such statements also say to the client that the counsellor is willing to listen.

The counsellor uses inferred empathy. Although the client does not directly label his feelings, from the words, context, and nonverbal messages, the counsellor speculates that resentment might be the predominant feeling.

The client's response suggests that he is responsive to the counsellor's empathy. He signals this by continuing to share at a deeper level. This is a significant event in the interview, which should give the counsellor confidence to continue to risk empathy.

Here, again, the counsellor infers anger from the client's nonverbal expression. By labelling the anger, the counsellor gives the client "permission" to discuss his anger.

Since the counsellor accepts his anger, the client may feel less that he has to defend it.

The counsellor picks up and identifies the client's mixed feelings. Mixed feelings can often be a source of anxiety for clients, particularly if they pull their emotions in different directions.

This client was initially guarded and defensive, quick to defend his right to drink. As he finds acceptance from the counsellor, he begins to let his guard down. In some interviews, such as this one, trust can develop quickly, but more often, the counsellor requires extended patience.

The counsellor responds with inferred empathy.

(continued)

Client: No way I'm going to let that happen to me.

Counsellor: You're determined to control your drinking.

Client: I'm not going to be like my father.

Counsellor: Correct me if I'm off base, but as you talk, I wonder if a part of you is afraid that your drinking could get out of hand.

The counsellor uses a basic empathic response. A return to basic empathy gives the client some space. Counsellors should avoid constant pressure on clients to move to a higher level of intimacy. The counsellor needs to move deeper, but caution is critical to avoid moving too quickly.

The counsellor uses both confrontation and invitational empathy in this statement. Presenting the ideas in a tentative manner softens the confrontation.

Summary

Owing to the central role that emotions play in our lives, it is essential that counsellors give priority to exploring and understanding clients' feelings. Emotions are characterized by physiological as well as psychological and behavioural reactions. Ten families of emotions—anger, fear, strength, weakness, joy, sadness, confusion, shame, surprise, and love—provide a starting point for organizing thinking about emotions. To describe their emotions, clients may use specific feeling words, which they may further define with modifiers. As well, clients may communicate their emotions through metaphors and nonverbal channels of communication.

Body language, or kinesics, involves observing variables such as posture, facial expressions, gestures, and eye motion. Sometimes body language is easily interpreted, but at other times it is ambiguous and, thus, needs to be interpreted with caution.

Voice tone, volume, and pitch can help counsellors identify emotions. Voice variables can reveal if clients are depressed, euphoric, angry, or sad.

Proxemics is a term used to describe how people use space and distance. Counsellors should adapt their seating to meet the needs of individual clients. They should observe spatial shifts during the interview.

Feelings can be experienced as positive or negative, but this subjective determination is individually defined. An emotion may be debilitating for some but exhilarating for others. Circumstances and context may not be good predictors of feelings.

Mixed feelings, including contradictory emotions, are common. A great deal of stress and confusion can arise from the pushes and pulls of competing feelings, which, if unmanaged, can control a client's life.

Empathy is a core skill for all helping relationships. Empathy helps to build the helping relationship, assists clients in identifying and labelling feelings, models a healthy way of relating to others, and helps clients to accept their own feelings. Although counsellors can never know exactly how their clients feel, empathy enables them to move closer to understanding how they think and feel.

Three types of empathy are basic, inferred, and invitational. Basic empathy mirrors what the client has explicitly said, while inferred empathy attempts to reach empathic understanding from less obvious clues. Invitational empathy involves strategies to encourage clients to talk about their feelings.

Tuning in, or preparatory empathy, is a way for counsellors to prepare for inferred empathy. Preparatory empathy involves trying to estimate the feelings and concerns that clients may bring to the interview.

A variety of strategies can be used to encourage clients to express feelings, including invitational statements, questions targeted to feelings, explaining the importance of addressing feelings, providing directives, self-disclosing, and using sentence completion statements.

Four generalizations about empathy are (1) when clients share feelings, empathy is often the preferred response, (2) counsellors should risk expressing empathy early in the relationship, (3) counsellors should express empathy tentatively, and (4) empathy requires flexibility in its use, including the ability to refrain from using it.

Exercises

1. Begin a log to track your feelings. At periodic intervals (e.g., every hour), record words and phrases that best describe how you are feeling at that moment. Try to be as precise as possible, using terms that capture the essence and intensity of how you feel. Maintain your log for at least one week.

   a. What patterns or cycles are apparent? Are there times of the day or week when you are more likely to feel particular emotions?

   b. How were your emotions linked to events or people?

   c. How could you have altered your emotions, for example, to increase pleasurable feelings and decrease negative feelings?

   d. What have you learned about yourself from this exercise that will assist you in your work as a counsellor?

2. Recall the 10 families of emotions: anger, fear, strength, weakness, joy, sadness, confusion, shame, surprise, and love. Rate your ability to express each on a scale of 1 to 5.

   5 = strong ability to express the emotions within the category
   1 = unable to express the emotions within the category

   a. What are the emotions that you have more difficulty expressing? Are there feelings you would never express?

   b. How do your ability and willingness to share emotions vary depending on the person you are with?

3. Would you find it easier to tell your friends (your parents, family, etc.) that you love them or that you are angry with them?

4. What did you learn about expressing emotions when you were growing up? Discuss and compare your experiences with a colleague.

5. Describe in detail how you feel, think, and act when you experience specific emotions. For example, you might write, "When I feel scared I want to escape. My breathing is shallow. I tend to look away. I become quiet. I think I might vomit." To increase your aware-

ness, imagine a situation in which you are experiencing a particular emotion. Alternatively, when you experience an emotion, focus intensely on the experience and record your observations.

6. Share the details of an intense emotional experience with a partner. What was easy and difficult about sharing your feelings? What responses from your partner were helpful? Unhelpful?

7. For each of the following situations, predict and describe the emotions that the individual might experience. Remember that there may be many possibilities and that some experiences (although apparently negative) may result in positive emotions. What nonverbal cues might you observe in each case?

   a. man whose wife of 60 years has just died

   b. a young teenager on a first date

   c. a middle-aged man fired from his job

   d. a student denied admission to a training program

   e. a mother discovering her teenage daughter using drugs

   f. a student about to take an exam

   g. a teacher on the first day of class

   h. a person who witnessed the terrorist attack on New York city

   i. a prisoner about to be sentenced

   j. a 16-year-old with sexual identity problems

   k. a job applicant

   l. a job interviewer

   m. an angry client

   n. a client seeing a counsellor for the first time

   o. a client seeing a counsellor for the last time

   p. a patient in hospital waiting for major surgery

   q. a child entering a foster home

   r. a man who has just abused his wife

   s. a person dealing with depression

   t. a parent dealing with a child who has ADD (attention deficit disorder)

   u. a couple on the day of their marriage

   v. a couple on the day their divorce becomes final

   w. a serial killer

   x. a compulsive gambler

   y. a 12-year-old boy coming to a new school

   z. an 11-year-old girl who has been sexually abused by her father

8. Identify feeling words and phrases that best describe how each of the following clients may be feeling:

   a. "Everyone in my life keeps putting me down. Even my own children constantly criticize me."

b. *(shaking)* "Fifteen hard years with the same company and what do they do? They dump me with three weeks' notice."

c. *(a 6-year-old boy, crying)* "No one wants to play with me."

d. "When I saw the airplanes crash into the World Trade Center I just couldn't stop crying."

e. *(an ex-offender to parole officer)* "Have you ever been to jail?"

f. *(a 16-year-old boy)* "I'd rather live on the street than go to another foster home. Five foster homes in five years. I've had enough!"

g. "I didn't expect to live long enough to see the millennium."

9. Assume that the clients below are speaking to you and that an empathic response is appropriate.

a. *(client, looking at the floor)* "It's not just my job that I hate. I've lost a sense of purpose to my life. I live alone, and I have no special relationships. Most days I wonder why I should bother."

b. *(client, smiling)* "For the first time, things are really starting to come together for me. My kids are all doing well in school, my marital problems are on the upswing, and I finally put some money aside for a rainy day."

c. *(parent to a teacher)* "I don't know what to do. I know you said I should try to help my son with his homework and show some interest in his work. But he comes home from school and goes straight to his room. When I ask about his homework, he always says that there wasn't any. When I offer to help, he makes it clear he'd rather do it on his own."

d. *(teenager, crying)* "I'm pregnant. This will kill my dad, but first he'll kill me."

e. "Everyone always says how together I am. But I don't feel together. Sometimes I get so wound up that I think I'm going to burst."

f. *(man, 57, talking about his family problems)* "I have to make every decision. I can never count on my wife or kids for help."

g. *(parent to a teacher)* "My son does not have ADD. I don't care what you say. I'm not going to put him on drugs."

10. In each of the following client statements more than one feeling is expressed. Identify feeling words and phrases that best describe the mixed feelings. Next, formulate an empathic response.

a. "Thanks for seeing me today. It really felt good to get things off my chest. No one has ever listened to me the way you did. I hope you don't think I'm crazy or stupid."

b. *(eyes welling up with tears)* "It's over. I don't care to be with him any more."

c. *(shouting)* "I am calm."

d. "To tell you the truth, I'd like to just march right in, look him in the eye, and tell him exactly where to go. I don't know what to do."

e. "Finding out that my former girlfriend had my baby was totally shocking. After we broke up, she didn't even tell me she was pregnant. I'd love to be a father, but I don't want a relationship with her. Maybe it would be best if I just forgot the whole thing. But I want to do what's right."

    f.   "Living on your own is the pits. Now I don't even know where my next meal is coming from. I used to love being married. I felt like life really had meaning. But at least now I don't have to worry about being beat up by my husband every time he gets drunk. It's just so difficult. Maybe I should give him another chance."

11. The statements below may evoke strong personal reactions. Assume that the person is speaking to you and that you are responding with empathy, even though empathy may not be the preferred response.

    a.   "This country was much better when it was white and Christian. With such high unemployment, don't you think it's time to stop letting every damn immigrant into the country? No wonder I can't get a job."

    b.   "I'm not ashamed to admit it. Once in a while I hit my wife. It's no big deal."

    c.   "I don't care what you say. I won't give up on you until you become a Christian."

    d.   *(teacher)* "Your paper is really substandard. You haven't followed any of the directions. I'm really frustrated that you just don't seem ready to do the work that is necessary to be successful in this course. I'm so fed up. I don't see any way that you can pass this course."

    e.   *(employer)* "This is really hard for me to do. I've tried everything possible to cut costs, but unfortunately I'm going to have to make some major changes. I just don't know what else I can do. I have to lay you off."

    f.   *(applicant for welfare)* "Don't you even think about turning me down. I'm not leaving this office without a cheque."

    g.   *(student to teacher)* "I suppose this course is going to be like all the others. Lots of reading, a bunch of papers. I only hope there's some relevance to it all."

    h.   *(client, 35-year-old)* "I had no idea she was only 15. She was the one who wanted to have sex. From the look in her eyes I could tell she was begging for it. It's really unfair that I'm now charged with rape. Besides, 15 is old enough for some-one to make up their own mind."

    i.   "This counselling isn't very helpful. So why don't we just forget it and do what both of us really want? How about it, sweetheart? Let's go out for dinner."

    j.   "I really don't worry too much about AIDS. What can I do about it? If I'm meant to get it, then I'll get it. So what? We all have to die sometime."

    k.   "I'm not stupid. I know that he shouldn't hit me. But I guess I deserved it, the way I put him down. I should learn to keep my mouth shut. When I see him, I'll apologize."

    l.   *(client to physician, eyes brightening)* "So, I'm HIV positive. That's great. Now I can get a higher welfare rate and all those extra benefits."

    m.   *(client, with angry tone)* "No one is willing to talk to me about the fact that I might be dying. I can accept it, but every time I ask the big question people change the topic."

12. In question 11 above, what do you think are the advantages of responding with empathy?

13. Videotape a television program. While taping it, turn off the sound. Pay attention to the nonverbal communication of the actors. Watch the tape, this time with the sound turned on. How successful were you in correctly reading the nonverbal cues?

14. Interview people from different cultures, preferably people who have been in this country for only a short time. What are the differences between their use of nonverbal communication (e.g., eye contact, spatial distance, touching) and yours?

15. Conduct practice interviews with a colleague to experiment with spatial distance. Deliberately increase or decrease the distance between the two of you to learn about the effect of space. At what point did your space become violated? How did physical distance affect the quality of your verbal exchange?

16. The following is the typescript of a portion of a worker's interview. The setting is a social service agency and the worker is an employment counsellor.

    Consider the following questions:

    a.   How appropriate are the number, type, and timing of the worker's questions?

    b.   Was there evidence of abrupt changes of subject?

    c.   Were important clues to the client's feelings or concerns addressed?

    d.   What attitude does the worker convey to the client?

Counsellor: Hello. Are you Leah? I'm Mr. Short. Won't you come into my office? *(brief small talk in office)*

Counsellor: So, what is your problem? How can I help you?

Client: Well, I don't really know where to begin. Right now my life is a mess. I've gotten along well so far, but lately ... well, I'm just not coping very well. *(client pauses, wipes tears with a tissue)*

Counsellor: Okay, calm down. Try not to cry. Have you been to this agency before? By the way, how old are you?

Client: No, this is the first time. I wonder if anyone will ever give me a chance. Sometimes I feel, Why not give up? I feel so scared all the time. Don't get me wrong—I really want to work, to be independent, to buy my kids all the things I haven't been able to afford. I just don't know if I can do it. I haven't worked in 10 years. Plus, there's the problem of daycare ... the things you read ... it's hard to know whom to trust. Things just seemed so much easier when my husband was alive.

Counsellor: You say you haven't worked in 10 years. What was the last job you held? What did you do? What are your job skills?

Client: Mostly, I've worked as a secretary. It was okay, but I don't want to do that anymore. I really don't have a clue what I'd like.

Counsellor: So, you know you want to get out of clerical work, but you're unsure what else you might do or like.

Client: Yes, exactly.

Counsellor: Have you considered social services? There are lots of good programs that you could complete in a short time.

Client: No, I don't think I'd like that.

Counsellor: How can you be sure until you give it a try? Sometimes volunteer work is a really good way to find out if you like it.

Client (hesitates): Well ... I guess so.

Counsellor: Actually, I was in the same boat as you. Then I volunteered. Next thing I knew I was back in school. Now I'm working full time and loving it. I have a friend who works at the volunteer bureau. Why don't I give her a call and set up an appointment for you?

Client (hesitates): Okay ... thanks.

Counsellor: No problem. I was glad to be of help. I'll phone her, then I'll give you a call. It'll probably be next week or so.

17. The purpose of this exercise is develop your ability to "track" the flow of an interview including identifying the use of particular interviewing and counselling skills. Work with student colleagues. One student will be the counsellor, another the client with one or more observers. Videotape a fifteen-minute segment of a counselling interview and/or use a verbatim transcript of the session to assist your review. Classify each counsellor response (e.g., open question, closed question, silence, empathy, self-disclosure or mixed response). Use the following table to compile interview statistics. Place a check in the box each time a particular skill is used. Notice that the table is organized to divide the interview into time segments.

	0–5 minutes	6–10 minutes	11–15 minutes
Open question			
Closed question			
Indirect question			
Silence			
Empathy			
Self-disclosure			
Directive			
Summary			
Paraphrase			
Other (specify)			

Some questions to consider:

a. Did the counsellor use a variety of different responses?

b. To what extent did the counsellor vary his/her approach as the session progressed

c. What interview transitions were apparent? Were they appropriate? Consider, for example, whether the transition occurred prematurely before concrete understanding or exploration was completed.

d. What skills were overused or underused?

e. Which responses were productive? Which responses were counterproductive?

Weblinks

Listening and Empathy Responding—tips and ideas on the topic of empathy.
mhnet.org/psyhelp/chap13/chap13c.htm

Person-Centred Approach: Empathic Understanding
users.powernet.co.uk/bapca/Training/Empathy.htm

"Empathy, Emotional Expressiveness, and Prosocial Behaviour" by William Roberts and Janet Strayer (.pdf document)
www.cariboo.bc.ca/ae/psych/roberts/prosocal.pdf

EMPOWERMENT: THE PURPOSE OF COUNSELLING

PREVIEW

After reading this chapter you should be able to:

- Describe the elements of empowering clients.
- Identify the categories of motivational problems.
- Describe strategies for overcoming motivational problems.
- Explain the use of confrontation.
- Know the principles of effective confrontation.
- Detect when to avoid confrontation.
- Identify different types of thinking errors.
- Be aware of strategies for confronting thinking errors.
- Define reframing.
- Demonstrate the ability to assist clients by reframing.
- Explain the importance of goal setting.
- List criteria for effective goals.
- Demonstrate the ability to use problem statements as the basis for goal setting.
- Demonstrate the ability to help clients set goals.
- Identify the steps of action planning and implementation.

EMPOWERMENT AND CHANGE

In Chapter 3, the concept of empowerment was introduced and defined as the process of helping clients discover personal strengths and capacities so that they are able to take control of their lives. The foundation for empowerment in counselling is the belief that clients are capable and have a right to manage their own lives. An empowerment attitude focuses on the capacities and strengths of clients. Empowerment values and methods require counsellors to forego any need to control clients by taking on an "expert" role that puts clients in positions of dependency. Giving priority to empowerment constrains counsellors from hiding behind professional jargon. Counsellors who empower demystify the counselling process through open and nonjargonistic discussion with clients of their methods and assumptions.

Self-determination, an important component of client empowerment, is promoted by helping clients recognize choices and by encouraging them to make independent decisions. Counsellors should not do for clients what they can and should do for themselves. When empowerment is the priority, clients become the experts.

McWhirter asserts that the potentially empowering aspects of counselling include "an underlying belief in basic human potential and in clients' ability to cope with their life problems, a collaborative definition of the problem and therapeutic goals, skill enhancement and development, recognition and analysis of systemic power dynamics and an emphasis on group and community identity" (1991:226).

Often clients come from disadvantaged and marginalized groups, in which they have significant feelings of powerlessness. McWhirter defines the term powerless as "being unable to direct the course of one's life due to societal conditions and power dynamics, lack of skills, or lack of faith that one can change one's life" (1991:224). Sometimes powerlessness arises from negative self-evaluation and low self-esteem. Sometimes the systems that are set up to assist clients are themselves oppressive and contribute to powerlessness. Carniol, in describing the welfare system, observes, "As for the clients, evidence shows that they often find themselves blamed for the problems they face. They find they don't get the help they need or they don't get nearly enough to make a difference—or they get 'cut off'" (1995:3).

Similarly, racism and other prejudices may deny clients access to jobs and resources such as adequate housing. A full discussion of these realities is beyond the scope of this book, but they serve as a reminder to counsellors that they have some responsibility to advocate for progressive changes within the systems that serve clients. As well, counsellors' work involves them in advocating for clients by assisting them in accessing services and resources that will help them meet their needs. Shulman (1992) stresses the need for workers to have faith in the capacity of systems to change. Moreover, he argues that professionals have a responsibility not just to work with the problems of individuals, but also to promote social change. His view is echoed by Carniol, who ends his book with this challenge: "Social justice demands a transformation of power, including a basic redistribution of wealth—so that the practice of democracy comes within the reach of everyone, rather than being manipulated by those who now dominate the heights of our political and social structures" (1995:153).

This perspective draws counsellors into broader activities, including working to identify and remove gaps and barriers to service and encouraging more humane and accessible policies and services. In addition, as McWhirter argues, empowerment requires that clients "gain some degree of critical awareness of systemic power dynamics" (1991:225). One way counsellors can achieve this end is to provide clients with information on groups and organizations whose efforts are directed toward changing problematic elements of the system.

The beginning phase offers many clients a unique opportunity to explore their situation and their feelings. Active listening skills help clients bring long-forgotten or misunderstood feelings to the surface. Ventilation of feelings can energize clients, and it can lead to spontaneous insight into new ways of handling problems that seemed insurmountable. For some clients, the work of counselling is finished at this phase.

Other clients need additional assistance as they work to change established patterns. This may involve counsellors in one or more of five empowering activities:

1. *Motivating*. Clients may have made conscious decisions to change and their motivation may be high, but they often have mixed feelings about replacing established behaviour with new ways of behaving. Sometimes change involves a "selling" job. Clients need to convince themselves that the benefits of change outweigh the risks, and they need to develop attitudes and beliefs about their capacity for change. Counsellors can try to motivate clients to take the risk of developing and executing action plans based on measurable and achievable goals. Ultimately, the principle of self-determination requires that clients make the decision to change, but adherence to this principle does not preclude counsellors from involving clients in critical thinking about their behaviour and the wisdom of change.

2. *Confronting*. Confronting, one of the challenging skills introduced in Chapter 1, is a tool for providing new information to clients so that they critically evaluate their behaviour and ideas. Confrontation can be provocative because it challenges clients' perceptions and assumptions. It brings to the foreground issues that clients might ignore, deny, or rationalize. Confrontation may push clients to take responsibility for their actions, or it may cause them to face the painful reality of the effect of the behaviour on themselves and others.

3. *Helping clients think differently*. Sometimes clients remain stuck because they cling to established but ineffective ways of thinking. Counsellors can use range of techniques for helping clients think differently. Reframing, for example, helps clients become unstuck from the limits of their current thinking by providing alternative explanations for events.

4. *Goal setting*. Goals provide specific targets for clients to work toward. Having clear goals is essential for developing action plans or strategies to reach these targets. Goal setting is used as a first step in helping clients to plan a systematic change in their lives.

5. *Action planning*. Action planning involves setting up strategies for achieving goals. Typically, this involves helping clients identify, evaluate, and select alternatives, then helping them execute systematic action plans. As a result, clients expand their repertoire of coping skills. For example, they develop new or expanded capacities to manage feelings and to make intelligent decisions, or they learn to be assertive and able to utilize community and societal resources.

The balance of this chapter discusses the skills of motivating, confronting, helping clients to think differently, goal setting, and action planning.

MOTIVATING CLIENTS

Motivational Problems

Motivation in counselling refers to the extent to which clients are willing to involve themselves in the change process. Johnson identifies three factors that are important for motivation: "the push of discomfort, the pull of hope that something can be done to relieve the problem or accomplish a task, and internal pressures and drives toward reaching a goal" (1992:113). Thus, a person must not only want to change, but also must have some belief in his or her capacity to change.

The concept of secondary gain is a useful way of understanding why some people resist change despite the obvious pain or losses involved in maintaining their current situation. Secondary gain refers to the benefits that people derive from their problems. These benefits may include "increased personal attention, disability compensation, and decreased responsibility, as well as more subtle gratifications such as satisfying the need for self-punishment or the vengeful punishment of others who are forced to take responsibility" (Nicoli, 1988:13).

Change is stressful because it requires giving up established patterns of behaviour or thinking, and clients will differ in the extent to which they have the skill or energy to take the associated risks. The essential elements of high motivation are:

1. willingness to engage in the work of counselling

2. commitment to devote energy and resources to the change process

3. capacity to sustain effort over time and in the face of obstacles

4. sufficient self-esteem to sustain the courage to change (Shebib, 1997:252)

Counsellors can assess clients based on these four elements then design appropriate strategies to meet each client's particular need. These four elements suggest two major motivational tasks for counsellors: engaging clients to commit to change and supporting and energizing clients as they deal with the stresses of obstacles to change.

CONVERSATION 7.1

WORKING WITH "LAZY" CLIENTS

STUDENT: The clients I have the most trouble with are the lazy ones—like the ones who won't even get out of bed in the morning to go looking for a job or the clients who never follow through on commitments.

TEACHER: Sure, these clients can be exceptionally difficult and frustrating to work with. Sometimes it's hard to do, but we should discipline ourselves to be nonjudgmental regarding motivation. Although it might be tempting to label some clients as lazy, we should remember that they may have given up for good reason. Perhaps society has not provided the resources or support they need for change. Clients may have given up in order to protect themselves from the further damage to their self-esteem that would come from repeated failure. In this way, their behaviour may be seen as adaptive. It's normal for counsellors to lose patience with them and give up, but it's important to remember that that's precisely what they did to themselves—give up. That's one of the reasons they need counselling.

One way to further organize thinking about motivating clients is to classify motivational problems. Five categories are identified, but individual clients may have characteristics from more than one category. There are five categories: clients in denial, involuntary clients, burnt-out clients, ambivalent clients, and energized clients.

Clients in Denial.

Some clients do not perceive themselves as having a problem, despite the fact that their behaviour is problematic for themselves or others in their lives. Predictably, their motivation is low unless feedback, confrontation, or personal crisis can be used to overcome their denial and increase their awareness of the need for change. These clients are not thinking about change.

> **EXAMPLE:** *Andy's drinking is clearly a problem, but even though he lost his last job owing to chronic absenteeism caused by his drinking, he continues to assert that he is a social drinker.*

For these clients, counsellors need to direct their attention toward getting their clients to look at their situation and its consequences. Counsellors can provide information, offer feedback, or encourage reflection with questions such as "Is what you're doing now working to meet your needs?" Counsellors should proceed slowly when confronting denial, and they should remember that denial may be a defence mechanism that enables people to cope, perhaps by shielding them from feelings of hopelessness (George, in McNeece and DiNitto, 1998).

Involuntary Clients.

Some clients are involuntary and resent being forced into counselling. These clients may resist change because they are in denial and do not see the need for change or because their feelings about being forced into counselling have aroused their defences.

> **EXAMPLE 1:** *Rupert was referred by his employer because of his continual difficulty in getting along with co-workers. He claims that others in his work team have difficulty dealing with his assertive manner. He comes to see the counsellor, but it is quickly evident that his main motivation is to preserve his job.*

> **EXAMPLE 2:** *As a condition of probation, Harold was required by the judge to see a counsellor for help with his anger.*

However, not all involuntary clients are unmotivated. Some would not have entered counselling on their own, but once coerced they accept and even welcome the opportunity.

> **EXAMPLE:** *Chris begins withdrawing large amounts of cash from his life savings. An alert bank teller who has known Chris for some time is concerned about what appears to be a sudden change in his behaviour. She phones his son, who confronts Chris. When confronted, Chris says that he hears voices that are directing him. His son urges him to seek help, but he refuses. Reluctantly, his son consults with the family doctor, who*

arranges for Chris to be admitted to hospital for assessment. Almost immediately, Chris responds and thanks his son for his intervention.

Burnt-out Clients.
Another group of clients may be "burnt-out" from previous unsuccessful attempts at change. They may lack self-esteem and believe that they do not have the skill, capacity, or energy to change.

> **EXAMPLE:** *Peter (55) has been unemployed for almost two years, but he has not looked for a job for months. He says, "There's no work out there. Besides, who is going to hire a man of my age?"*

Seligman's (1975) concept of learned helplessness is a useful perspective for understanding these clients. People with learned helplessness come to believe that their actions do not matter. They believe that have no control over their lives and that what happens to them is more likely because of chance. Hence, they are unlikely to extend any effort to change. Their beliefs are reflected in statements such as the following:

- "You have to be at the right place at the right time to succeed."
- "If I'm successful, it's because the task was easy."
- "It doesn't matter if I work hard."
- "To get ahead, you have to know the right people."
- "There's nothing I can do about it."

These clients often come to counsellors or are referred after they have made many unsuccessful efforts to solve their problems or cope with their situation. They are often in a state of crisis, with considerable associated stress. Although they desire change, they doubt it will happen, and they believe that if change is to occur, it will be beyond their control.

Ambivalent Clients.
A common motivational challenge for counsellors is dealing with clients who are ambivalent about change. These clients may vacillate between wanting to alter their lives and resisting any shifts in their behaviour or lifestyle.

> **EXAMPLE:** *Agnes has been in an abusive relationship for years. She wishes that she could leave and start over. In fact, she has left her husband twice in the past, but each time she returned within a few weeks.*

Energized Clients.
For some clients, dissatisfaction with their current lifestyle or personal crisis precipitates a need for change, and they voluntarily seek counselling for assistance. These clients come to counselling energized and committed to the change process. Their motivation is high, and they readily engage as willing participants in counselling. Although these clients are highly motivated, their motivation may be fragile if they are not helped to deal with obstacles and setbacks that might arise as they develop and carry out action plans. They also may need help to sustain any changes they make.

> **EXAMPLE:** *Iris, a young single parent, is excited about the possibility of returning to school. She sees a school counsellor for assistance with enrolment in the high school's special program for teen moms. She has not yet considered issues such as daycare.*

Table 7.1 provides some strategies for dealing with a range of motivational challenges. Counsellors need to appropriately adapt these strategies to individual clients.

Table 7.1 Motivational Strategies		
Motivational Problem	**Counselling Goal**	**Strategy Choices for Counsellors**
Denial: clients who do not believe that they have a problem	Increase awareness of the need for change	Provide or encourage clients to seek information about their behaviour and its effect on others Provide feedback confrontation Use family and friends to influence clients to change Use authority Help clients become aware of "attractive" alternatives Use films, brochures, books, self-assessment questionnaires as tools to increase clients' insight
Involuntary: clients who resent being forced into counselling	Empower client, reduce hostility and resistance	Explore feelings and concerns openly Show empathy Self-disclose your own responses to being forced against your wish Empower clients (e.g., give them choices, involve them in decision making and goal setting) Encourage client-initiated goals (i.e., try to find an issue, however small, that interests the client)
Burnt-out: clients who have given up owing to failure or frustration, and clients who do not believe in their ability to change	Rekindle hope and optimism; improve self-esteem regarding capacity to change	Explore to assess why previous action plans failed (emphasize failure of plans, not failure of clients) Search for elements of success in previous actions Help clients understand and manage self-defeating inner talk Set small but achievable goals and develop detailed action plans Give positive reinforcement for any effort at change Reframe past failures as learning experiences Use support groups Convey hope
Ambivalent: clients who are ambivalent about changing	Resolve ambivalence in favour of change	Demonstrate empathy toward mixed feelings and pressures Avoid arguing in favour of change (this leaves the client free to argue against change) Assist clients to identify obstacles and barriers to change and help them develop ways to overcome these barriers
Energized: motivated clients who are actively seeking to change	Maintain the momentum of change	Provide positive reinforcement and encouragement Help with systematic planning and goal setting Help clients identify and deal with potential obstacles

CONFRONTING CLIENTS

For many people, confrontation suggests conflict and hostility, but in counselling, effective confrontation is not considered a hostile act. Confrontation is a way of directing clients' attention to aspects of their personality or behaviour that they might otherwise overlook. It is a tool to move clients to a higher level of understanding of themselves and others. Caring confrontation can deepen the level of trust in the counselling relationship. It is a major skill for helping clients develop fresh perspectives on themselves and their behaviour. Gilliland and James (1998) contend that caring confrontation is a way of valuing or respecting the client. They conclude that "confronting client excuses, explanations, or rationalizations is necessary to facilitate client movement toward responsible behavior" (283). Egan (1998) describes confrontation as a way to encourage clients toward more effective living.

In general, confrontation may be useful for addressing incongruities between what clients believe and the way they act; self-defeating ways of thinking and behaving; behaviour that is harmful to self or others; blind spots; blaming behaviour; communication problems; and strengths.

Types of Confrontation

Two types of confrontation are feedback confrontation and confrontation of incongruities. **Feedback confrontation** is used to provide new information to clients about who they are, including how they are perceived by others and the effects of their behaviour on others. Feedback confrontation can be used to help clients become aware of the consequences of their decisions and actions. Feedback confrontation is not reserved for negative or critical feedback—it can also be used to identify strengths.

In some cases, clients have blind spots regarding the harmful effect of their behaviour on themselves and others. They continue to behave in ways that are hurtful, yet they lack insight into how they are affecting others. Because they are unaware and fail to see their behaviour as problematic, they have no motivation to change. Feedback confrontation is designed to help clients examine the consequences of their actions. Some examples of clients' blind spots are:

- Jerry thinks of himself as humorous, but he is unaware that his jokes are offensive and sexist.

- Nathan has bad breath and body odour.

- Parvinder is unaware of how his aggressive behaviour pushes others away.

- Estelle has been in a series of relationships in which she has been battered. She does not understand how this has affected her children.

Despite its potential to be a powerful helping tool, feedback is often misused. Some counsellors avoid it, perhaps because they fear that they might alienate their clients or arouse their anger. At other times, counsellors feel the need to keep the helping relationship pleasant, so they distort or lie to clients to sustain their approval.

In fact, there are risks to confrontation, and some clients do react poorly. They may respond with hostility and attempt to question the integrity or credibility of the counsellor. Such a hostile reaction may be a type of denial, indicating that the client is simply not ready to acknowledge the validity of the confrontation. Hostile reactions are more likely when feedback or confrontation is unsolicited, but they may occur even when clients appear to be seeking information or feedback, usually out of a need for approval or support for the status quo. Counsellors also need to consider that harsh client reactions may arise for legitimate reasons. Sometimes feedback is confusing, or the manner and tone of the counsellor are abrupt. Secure counsellors are open to the possibility that they may have erred.

Confrontation of incongruities is directed at inconsistencies and mixed messages, for example:

- discrepancy between a client's verbal and nonverbal messages

    CLIENT: *(crying) It's really nothing. I'm not bothered.*

- discrepancy between a client's values or beliefs and behaviour

    CLIENT: *There's nothing more important to me than my kids. I know I haven't spent much time with them. It's just so hard to say no to my buddies when they ask me to help.*

- discrepancy between what a client says and what he or she does; for example, a client commits to look for work, yet consistently has an excuse for not acting on agreed-upon plans

In confronting discrepancies, it is important that counsellors remain calm and nonjudgmental while presenting clients with specific facts. Ivey offers these confrontation leads as suggestions: "The model sentence, 'On the one hand ..., and on the other hand ...,' provides a standard and useful format for actual confrontation. Variations include 'You say ... but you do ...,' 'I see ... at one time, and at another time, I see ...,' and 'Your words say ..., but your actions say ...'" (1982:196).

Principles for Effective Confrontation

Confrontation is an option, not a requirement. When deciding to confront, counsellors should consider a number of variables, including relevance, client receptivity, contracting, specificity, and the use of other skills in combination.

Relevance. Confrontation should serve the goals of counselling by leading the client to improved ways of behaving, thinking, and feeling. Relevant confrontation meets the needs of the client. It is inappropriate for a counsellor to use confrontation as a means to vent frustration or anger. When confrontation arises for this reason, the counsellor may frame it as being "in the client's best interests," but in reality, it is the need of the counsellor that is being met. For example, counsellors may rationalize that they are confronting clients in order to help them when, in fact, they are confronting in order to punish them (Egan, 1998).

When counsellors have feelings related to the relationship or the work, it is better if they deal with them directly by using I-statements rather than by trying to mask their feelings as helpful feedback (Gordon, 1971; Martin, 1983). I-statements are assertions about personal feelings or reactions that do not blame or judge others. Instead of saying "You don't care," an I-message would be "I feel hurt and angry when you don't answer my letters." I-statements are much less likely to cause resistance.

Client Receptivity. Confrontation must be timed appropriately to minimize defensive reactions. Counsellors can use confrontation when clients are ready and willing to take advantage of feedback or if there is a reasonable possibility that feedback can motivate them to change. Counsellors need to pay attention to timing and ensure that there is a well-developed counselling relationship to support confrontation. As a general rule, it is preferable to avoid strong confrontation in the beginning phase of counselling. Clients are more receptive and likely to accept feedback as credible when there is a relationship of trust. Otherwise clients may feel insulted and misunderstood. They may never return.

Confrontation should be timed closely to relevant behaviour, events, or circumstances. For example, if a counsellor uses confrontation to challenge a client's defensive behaviour, it is more appropriate immediately after a client is defensive rather than a week later. However, there should be enough time left in the interview to adequately handle the confrontation.

Contracting. Counsellors can use the contracting process to increase clients' acceptance of confrontation. The following excerpt provides an example of this technique:

> **COUNSELLOR:** *One of the ways I might be able to help is by sharing some of my impressions about what you're doing, or even about our relationship. What do you think?*

> **CLIENT:** *Sure. I'd appreciate that.*

> **COUNSELLOR:** *Well, let's look ahead. Suppose I wanted to give you some feedback about something I thought you were doing wrong that you were not aware of. What would be the best way for me to approach you?*

> **CLIENT:** *I don't like to be overwhelmed. And I like the good mixed with the bad.*

In the above example, the counsellor and the client are working toward agreement about how and when feedback might be given. Such contracting enables the counsellor to "customize" feedback to meet the needs and expectations of the client. Subsequently, when the counsellor offers feedback, it is much less likely to meet with resistance because it is given in a way that is most acceptable to the client. Contracting is a way of asking for the client's permission to confront or give feedback. As with all skills of counselling, counsellors must develop versatility so that they can confront or give feedback in a variety of ways. Some clients like blunt feedback; others prefer it "sandwiched" between positive statements.

Specificity. Effective confrontation needs to be specific without attacking the personality of the client.

> **COUNSELLOR (CHOICE 1—INEFFECTIVE CONFRONTATION):** *You don't seem at all interested in what's happening here. If you're too lazy to care about our work, why don't you just quit?*

> **COUNSELLOR (CHOICE 2—MORE EFFECTIVE CONFRONTATION):** *When you don't show up for appointments, I wonder whether you're as committed to your goals as you say you are.*

> **COUNSELLOR (CHOICE 3—MOST EFFECTIVE CONFRONTATION):** *I think your best work has happened on those days when you came on time and when you took the effort to focus. My*

sense is that if you could make every appointment you'd get a lot more out of our time together.

In Choice 1, the counsellor's words attack the client. The counsellor judges the client's behaviour but provides no concrete or useable information. In Choice 2, the counsellor is more effective because the confrontation is linked to specific client behaviour. Choice 3 focuses on strengths. The principle here is that people are motivated more by positive feedback than by negative feedback (Hamachek, 1982). Moreover, by focusing on strengths, clients can be clearer about what they can do that will be more effective.

Combining with Other Skills. As a rule, confrontation should be used in combination with other counselling skills, particularly empathy and support. Confrontation may involve feedback that is unsettling for clients, and empathy reminds counsellors to remain sensitive to the impact of confrontation. Counsellors should confront clients, but not without offering them assistance to develop new methods. Confrontation should be measured to avoid overwhelming clients with more than they can handle. Ideally, confrontation should not undermine the self-esteem of clients. Egan offers this valuable suggestion: "Confront only if you want to grow closer to the person you're confronting" (1977: 220). Corey and Corey reflect similar sentiments, and offer this advice to counsellors: "Challenge clients only if you feel an investment in them and if you have the time and effort to continue building the relationship with them" (1989:54).

Clients may respond defensively to feedback, but after reflection they may be more accepting. Alternatively, they may appear to be accepting but later become resentful. Thus, it is important to check with clients how they feel about the feedback or confrontation. Counsellors should monitor immediate reactions. As well, checking back with the client during the next session is a useful tool for identifying delayed reactions and for picking up on any feelings that might impair the relationship. The example below illustrates the process:

> **COUNSELLOR:** *I'm wondering how you felt about our last meeting. Remember, I shared with you some of my opinions about what you are doing that seems to distance you from your family.*

> **CLIENT:** *I almost didn't come today.*

> *(silence)*

> **COUNSELLOR:** *Because?*

> **CLIENT:** *I was embarrassed by what you thought of me.*

> **COUNSELLOR:** *You thought that I might think less of you?*

> **CLIENT:** *Yes.*

> **COUNSELLOR:** *Would you like to find out for sure what I think?*

> **CLIENT:** *Okay.*

This counsellor's strategy sets the stage to help the client correct any distortions, and it is crucial for dealing with the aftermath of confrontation. It also reinforces that any feelings about what happens in the counselling relationship can be dealt with openly.

Self-Awareness and Confrontation

Some counsellors are reluctant to confront. As Egan (1998) concludes, this is a potentially healthy position that can help counsellors guard against overusing this skill or using it in a way that is destructive to clients. However, effective counsellors need to have the ability and willingness to confront when necessary. Self-awareness regarding one's beliefs, fears, and expectations regarding confrontation is crucial to using this skill appropriately.

Sometimes, beginning counsellors (and some experienced ones too) are reluctant to confront. Here are some of their candid thoughts:

- "I was brought up to believe that if you don't have something good to say, then don't say anything at all."
- "If I confront, I might damage the relationship. I don't want to upset my clients."
- "I don't want to hurt my clients."
- "My clients might retaliate."

Most of the above beliefs arise from an erroneous understanding of confrontation as a "no holds barred" assault on clients. Such confrontation strategies should, of course, be avoided. On the other hand, refraining from confronting clients under any circumstance is an evasion of responsibility that cuts clients off from the potential benefits of new information and feedback. Competent counsellors do not withhold potentially useful feedback.

When to Avoid Confrontation

Confrontation should never be used as an outlet for a counsellor's anger or frustration. When counsellors are not in control of their own feelings, clients are more likely to view them as aggressive and to feel their confrontation is unsupportive. The counselling relationship is formed to meet the needs of clients, and responsible counsellors will forego their own needs to this end. Counsellors should be self-aware to know their reasons for wanting to confront.

Confrontation requires that counsellors are willing to invest time to help their clients understand any feedback. As well, counsellors must be available to help clients deal with any feelings that may result from the confrontation. Consequently, the end of a counselling interview is generally a poor time to confront.

Counsellors should consider their clients' ability to handle confrontation. When clients are already overwhelmed with feelings, confrontation may add to their stress but contribute little to their ability to cope. Some clients, such as those who are highly defensive and guarded, may respond poorly to confrontation. In such situations, counsellors may find it wise to delay or avoid confrontation entirely.

Although confrontation has potential for motivating clients to change and can assist clients in developing insight, misuse of confrontation can be destructive. As a rule, counsellors should use it sparingly and should be prepared to offer support and caring to ensure that confrontation does not overwhelm or devastate their clients.

HELPING CLIENTS THINK DIFFERENTLY

The fact that a client firmly defends a life style that he knows is unworkable is proof that he is in need of great assistance and support.
—Wicks and Parsons, 1984:171

Thinking Errors

Sometimes clients have difficulty breaking out of established patterns because of the way they think about issues or problems (De Bono, 1984). Five types of **thinking errors** are distortion, incomplete analysis, egocentricity, rigidity, and self-defeating thought. Of course, there may be overlap between the five categories. The five types of thinking errors that result in faulty logic are discussed below.

Distortion. This type of thinking error arises from misinterpretations, faulty assumptions, or cultural biases. If a client from a culture in which direct eye contact is discouraged works with a counsellor who interprets direct eye contact as a sign of warmth, there is a risk that the client will come to erroneous conclusions about the counsellor. He or she may determine that the counsellor is intrusive or disrespectful.

Incomplete Analysis. This error comes from failure to look at all aspects of a problem or situation. For example, prison inmates may overestimate their ability to cope with life outside jail. Their thinking may become clouded by unrealistic optimism that they will be able to avoid getting caught, or if they are apprehended, by rationalization that they will beat the charges. In addition, they may neglect to consider the long-term consequences of their criminal behaviour, a pattern of thinking that is characteristic of lifestyle or habitual criminals. Walters reached this conclusion: "Until high rate offenders realize the self-destructive nature of their superoptimism, they will continue to resist change because they are operating on the mistaken belief that they can get away with just about any crime" (1991:36). Walters attributes lazy thinking as the root of the offenders' problems. Even those with the best of intentions may find themselves in trouble because they failed to think about long-term outcomes.

Egocentricity or Lack of Empathy. Egocentricity thinking errors come from a failure or inability to consider other people's ideas or to look at how one's behaviour affects others. Clients may adopt an arrogant position of self-righteousness, being confident that their ideas and conclusions are sound. Egocentric thinkers are likely to be seen by others as aggressive and insensitive, interested in meeting only their own needs. Egocentric thinkers are not only poor thinkers, they are also poor listeners. Typically, they believe that the purpose of thinking, listening, and responding is to prove themselves right. De Bono contends that self-protection is a major impediment to thinking: "The main restriction on thinking is ego defence, which is responsible for most of the practical faults of thinking" (1985:29).

Rigidity. This common thinking problem is characterized by failure to be open to new ideas and by "black-and-white" thinking. De Bono made this important observation: "Unfortunately, Western thinking, with its argument habits, prefers to give a conclusion first and then to bring in the facts to support that conclusion" (1985:35). Rigid thinkers act as if to say, "We'll keep talking until you agree with me."

Self-Defeating Thought. Albert Ellis has written a great deal about irrational thinking and its impact on emotions and behaviour (1962; 1984; 1993a; 1993b). Ellis argues that people's belief systems influence how they respond to and understand problems and events.

When their beliefs are irrational and characterized by an unrealistic "should," they are likely to experience emotional anxiety or disturbance. This thinking is often accompanied by self-depreciating internal dialogue: "I'm no good," "Everyone must think I'm an idiot," and "No one likes me." Ellis concludes that irrational beliefs fall into three general categories with associated rigid demands or "shoulds":

1. "I (ego) absolutely must perform well and win significant others' approval or else I am an inadequate, worthless person."

2. "You (other people) must under all conditions and at all times be nice and fair to me or else you are a rotten, horrible person!"

3. "Conditions under which I live absolutely must be comfortable, safe, and advantageous or else the world is a rotten place, I can't stand it, and life is hardly worth living." (1993a:7)

Wicks and Parsons offer a similar perspective when they suggest that many clients are discouraged because they set unattainable goals: "These goals are often based on irrational, simplistic views: (1) if a person acts properly, everyone will like him; and (2) either a person is totally competent or he is completely inadequate" (1984:170).

To counteract **self-defeating thought**, people need to change their way of thinking and correct irrational beliefs.

An important way of accomplishing this is to help clients correct faulty reasoning by encouraging them to consider things differently. Table 7.2 on page 207 lists possible strategies for dealing with common thinking errors.

Reframing

Reframing is a counselling skill that helps clients shift or modify their thinking. Reframing attempts to help clients look at things differently by suggesting alternative interpretations or new meanings. It empowers clients by focusing on solutions and redefining negatives as opportunities or challenges. Cormier and Cormier (1985) emphasize that reframed ideas should be positive; for example, client stubbornness might be reframed as independence, or greediness as ambitiousness. Table 7.3 on page 208 lists some examples of reframing.

In each of the examples in Table 7.3, other counselling responses may need to be used before presenting reframed ideas. For example, exploration is important in order to fully understand the client's current perspective. As well, empathy is crucial; otherwise, clients may conclude that their feelings are discounted or trivialized.

Reframing should not be confused with issuing platitudes, such as "It's always darkest just before dawn" or other such statements, which are typically not very supportive or helpful. An example of a well-meaning but misguided reframe that people are apt to give in times of grief over the loss of a child is "You're young—you can have more children." "Because strong emotions of sadness and loss are present, most people cannot accept a reframing that does not take into account the most salient feature of their experience—the grief itself" (Young, 1998:282). Reframing does not trivialize complex problems with pat answers; rather, it offers a reasonable and useable alternative frame of reference.

Table 7.2 Helping Clients Change Thinking Patterns

Problem	Example	Counselling Choices
Distortion	A client assumes that quiet members in her social circle are "aloof and stuck-up."	Provide alternative explanations (e.g., cultural norms). Encourage clients to check the validity of assumptions (e.g., by talking with others about the meaning of their behaviour).
Incomplete Analysis	A man decides to quit drinking but neglects to consider the obstacles that he must overcome. A young man decides to quit school so he can get a job and buy a new car.	Ask questions targeted to the overlooked area. Provide or encourage clients to find new information. Confront gaps in reasoning. Encourage clients to consult others. Challenge clients to consider the long-term implications of their actions.
Egocentricity or lack of empathy	A juvenile offender has no remorse and does not consider how his crimes adversely affect people. A client does not realize that his humour is sexist and offensive to others.	Teach empathy skills. Role play (i.e., ask clients to assume others' roles). Self-disclose personal feelings. Offer feedback or encourage clients to seek feedback from others.
Rigidity	An aggressive male believes that the only alternative to his present style is to say nothing. A client is prejudiced.	Stimulate new ideas through education and information. Use brainstorming to generate alternative ideas. Identify a range of alternatives. Suggest another frame of reference (reframing). Confront blind spots. Ask clients to assume the role of devil's advocate in order to self-critique their ideas. Assist clients in identifying and critically evaluating assumptions.
Self-defeating thought	A client demands perfection. A client constantly tells herself that she is inadequate.	Encourage clients to become aware of self-defeating thought. Teach techniques such as "thought stopping" to over-come self-defeating inner dialogue.

Clark (1998) offers guidelines for the use of reframing in group counselling, but the principles apply equally well to individual counselling. His guidelines are summarized below:

1. Use reframing to help clients break out of thinking that is self-defeating, constricted, or at an impasse.

Table 7.3 Reframing	
Client's Perspective or Statement	**Counsellor's Reframed Idea**
This counselling is a waste of time.	Sounds like you've done some thinking about how our work could be more relevant to you.
I don't fit in. I come from a different culture and my ideas and values must seem strange.	Of course. Some people have not had experience with your culture and they may be frightened. Perhaps you could look at this in a different way. Your experiences might also be fascinating for people who have not lived outside the country. They might welcome your fresh ideas.
I'm very shy. When I first join a group, I usually don't say anything.	You like to be patient until you have a sense of what's happening. People who are impulsive are working to develop this skill. You also seem to want to develop alternatives, such as being more expressive in the beginning.
For the first time in 20 years, I'm without a job.	Obviously, this is devastating. At the same time, I wonder if this might also be an opportunity for you to try something different.
Whenever I'm late for curfew, my mother waits up for me and immediately starts screaming at me.	I'm curious about why she might do this. Perhaps she has trouble telling you how scared she is that something may have happened to you. It might seem strange, but her anger could be her way of saying how much she loves you.

2. Make sure that clients are not so emotionally distracted that they are unable to hear or process the reframed idea.

3. Offer a reframed idea in a tentative way that invites consideration.

4. Ensure that reframed ideas are plausible.

5. Allow clients sufficient time to consider a reframed idea. Clients with firmly entrenched perspectives may not immediately accept logical and sound reframes, but with gentle persuasion and patience, they may begin to accept new ideas.

Even though it may be obvious that a client's thinking is distorted, it may be wise to hold back on reframing until the client's problem is fully explored. Moreover, as suggested above, it is important that the client's feelings be acknowledged through empathy. Exploration and empathy ensure that the counsellor understands the client's feelings and situation, and they provide a basis for the client to consider reframed ideas as reasonable or worthy of consideration. If counsellors push clients too quickly, clients may feel devalued and misunderstood and, in response, they may resist new ideas. Empathy helps workers to establish and maintain credibility with their clients.

Counsellors can use directives to invite clients to use different language (Young, 1998). For example, when clients avoid responsibility for their actions with statements such as "I can't get organized," counsellors can challenge them by proposing that they rephrase with statements such as "I won't let myself get organized." A client might say, "She makes me feel hopeless." In response, the counsellor can propose that the client rephrase the statement by stating, "I have decided to feel helpless." The latter response underscores the client's control over personal feelings. As part of this work, counsellors can empower their clients by explaining that clients have ownership over their feelings and no one can make them feel a certain way. After offering a reframe, counsellors should check for the client's questions and reactions to it. Then, if the reframed idea is accepted, they can encourage further exploration and problem solving based on the new perspective.

Reframing can energize clients. When clients are locked into one way of thinking about their problems, their solutions are limited. When they consider new perspectives, problems that seemed insurmountable might now have new answers. Moreover, reframing can serve to redirect client anxiety away from self-blame to other rational explanations that are less self-punishing. In these ways, effective reframing empowers clients to action, problem resolution and management of debilitating feelings.

GOAL SETTING

Obstacles are those frightful things you see when you take your eyes off your goals.
—Anonymous

The Importance of Setting Goals

Goal setting is a counselling process that helps clients define in precise, measurable terms what they hope to achieve from the work of counselling. Two types of goals are outcome goals and process, or task, goals (Shebib, 1997; Jacobs, Masson, and Harvill, 1998). **Outcome goals** relate to what the client hopes to achieve from counselling. These goals have to do with changes in the client's life, such as getting a job, improving communication with a spouse, dealing with painful feelings, or managing self-defeating thoughts. **Process goals** concern the procedures of counselling, including such variables as the frequency of meetings and the nature of the counselling relationship. Process goals include the tasks clients and counsellors undertake in order to reach the outcome goal. Clearly, the purpose of counselling is to assist clients to reach appropriate outcome goals. Process goals are set as the means to this end. In practice, there may be some overlap between process and outcome goals. For example, a process goal might be to develop trust in the counselling relationship. Success in achieving this process goal might assist the client in achieving an outcome goal targeting improved communication with family and friends.

There is wide support in the counselling literature for the importance of setting goals (Egan, 1998; Young, 1998). Goal setting serves many important purposes, including giving direction, defining roles, motivating, and measuring progress.

Giving Direction. Goals help to give direction and purpose to the work of counselling. Clearly defined goals serve as beacons that guide and structure the client's actions. Goals help counsellors and clients make decisions regarding the topics and activities that are relevant to counselling. When clients are clear about their goals, they can begin to structure their thinking and action toward their attainment. Setting goals helps clients make reasoned choices about what they want to do with their lives. Goal setting helps clients prioritize these choices.

INTERVIEW 7.1 REFRAMING TECHNIQUES

The following interview excerpt illustrates how reframing might be used in a counselling session. The counsellor has been working with a community college student to help her deal with some of her fears about public speaking. Note: Reframing is only one of the ways that the counsellor might help the client deal with the situation. For example, relaxation techniques may help decrease the client's anxiety.

DIALOGUE	ANALYSIS
Client: Next week I have to make my class presentation. I'm so nervous and it's still a week away. What am I going to be like on the day of my talk?	In all phases of counselling, empathy is an important response. More than any other skill, it tells clients that they have been heard and that their feelings have been understood.
Counsellor: You're wondering, "What if I'm so rattled I can't handle it at all?"	
Client: Exactly.	
Counsellor: Let's try something different for a minute. What if it were possible to look at your fears differently?	The counsellor introduces the technique of reframing with a brief rationale. Later in the interview, the counsellor or the client may wish to discuss the rationale in more detail. The counsellor's short self-disclosure communicates understanding and a nonjudgmental attitude.
Client: What do you mean?	
Counsellor: I think it's natural when we have a problem to dwell on all its unpleasant aspects. I know that I tend to do that unless I discipline myself not to. For example, when you think of how nervous you are, you think of all the negatives, such as that you might make a fool of yourself or your mind might go blank while you're talking.	
Client (laughs): Or that I might throw up in front of everyone.	
Counsellor: Okay, those are real fears. But by considering only your fears, you become fixated on the negatives and you may be overlooking some important positives. If you can look at it differently, you might discover a whole new way of dealing with your class presentation.	
Counsellor: Want to try it? (the client nods) Okay, try to identify some positive aspects of your fear.	As a rule, it's more empowering for clients to generate their own suggestions before counsellors introduce their ideas and suggestions. In

(continued)

Client: Well, I guess I'm not the only one who is scared of public speaking.

Counsellor: So, you know that there will be other people in the class who understand and will be cheering for you to succeed.

this way clients become self-confronting and are more likely to come up with ideas that they will accept as credible.

Client: I never thought of that before. Here's another idea: Because I'm so nervous, I'm going to make sure that I'm super prepared.

Counsellor: Great. Do you think it might be possible to look at your fears differently? Consider that it's normal to be nervous. Or go a step further. Look at it positively. Maybe there's a part of it that's exciting—kind of like going to a scary movie.

The counsellor offers the client a reframed way of looking at nervousness. The client's response suggests that this notion is plausible.

Client: I did come back to school because I hated my boring job. One thing for sure, I'm not bored.

Counsellor: So the more you scare yourself, the more you get your money's worth. (the counsellor and client laugh)

Spontaneous humour adds colour and vitality to the counselling relationship.

Counsellor: Try this over the next few days. Every time you start to think negatively about your presentation, I want you to deliberately interrupt your thinking to focus on some of the positives.

Client: Okay. Do you think that will help?

Counsellor: Absolutely. (explains the theory behind thought stopping) But it takes practice, and you have to discipline yourself not to give up.

The counsellor introduces thought stopping—a technique to help clients control self-defeating thinking (Gilliland and James, 1998; Cormier and Cormier, 1985). The basic assumption is that if self-defeating thoughts are interrupted, they will eventually be replaced by more empowering, positive perspectives.

Defining Roles. Goals provide a basis for defining roles. When goals are clear, counsellors know which skills and techniques are appropriate, and clients know what is expected of them. Moreover, when counsellors know the goal of the work, they can make intelligent decisions regarding whether they have the skills, capacity, and time to work with the client. If not, they may make a referral.

Motivating. Goals motivate clients. Setting and reaching goals is therapeutic. Setting goals energizes clients and helps them develop optimism that change is possible. Simply having goals can build self-confidence. Goal achievement confirms personal capacity and further promotes action. Writing down goals may add an extra measure of motivation.

Measuring Progress. Goals help provide benchmarks of progress, including definition of when the counselling relationship should end—i.e., when the goals have been reached or their pursuit is no longer viable.

Developing Effective Goal Statements

Sometimes clients are able to clearly articulate what they hope to achieve as a result of counselling. Other times they have difficulty expressing their goals. Through systematic interviewing, counsellors can help these clients define and target their goals. In addition, workers can use their knowledge base to develop simple checklists of potential goals, customized to the common needs and problems of particular client groups. However, goals should be concrete, measurable, challenging but realistic, and "owned" by the client.

Effective Goals Are Concrete. One defining feature of a counselling relationship is that it is goal directed, but clients may begin counselling with vague and undefined goals, such as:

• "I want to feel better."

• "My husband and I need to get along better."

• "I need to make something of my life."

These goals are useful starting points, but they are useless until they are shaped into terms that are clear and concrete. In the beginning phase, the focus of counselling is to explore problems and feelings. Successful work at the beginning phase should lead to the development of goals that define and structure subsequent work. In the action phase, an important component of this work is helping clients to develop their goals as specific and measurable targets. This step is a prerequisite for action planning—the development of strategies and programs to achieve goals. Vague goals result in vague and ill-defined action plans, but explicit goals lead to precise action plans.

In Chapter 5 tools for increasing concreteness were introduced. Concreteness is the remedy for vagueness. Concreteness can add precision to unclear and ambiguous goals. For example, when clients are describing their goals, counsellors can use simple encouragers such as "Tell me more" and "Yes, go on" to get a general overview of what clients hope to achieve. This is the first step in shaping workable goals. The next step is to use questions to identify goals, define terms, probe for detail, and develop examples. This step helps to cast the emerging goals in precise language and to move from good intentions and broad aims to specific goals (Egan, 1998). Listed below are some examples of probes and directives that might be used to start the process:

• What is your goal?

• When you say you'd like to feel better, what exactly do you mean?

• Describe how your life would be different if you were able to reach your goal. Try to be as detailed as possible.

• If your problem were to be solved, what would need to be different in your life?

- What do you think would be the best resolution to your problem?
- What are some examples of what you would like to achieve?
- As a result of counselling, what feelings do you want to increase or decrease?
- What do you want to be able to do that you can't do now?
- If I could watch you being successful, what would I see?

Some clients are reluctant or unable to identify goals, and they may respond with a dead-end statement such as "I don't know" when they are asked for their goals. Some responses that might be used to break this impasse include the following: "Guess." "What might your best friend (mother, father, teacher, etc.) suggest as your goal?" "What would you like to achieve, but don't think is possible?" A good general technique is to encourage clients to visualize themselves reaching their goals.

When clients say, "I don't know," their responses may indicate friction in the counselling relationship, and this answer may be a way of sabotaging the work. In such cases, goal setting might be premature, and the focus of the interview may need to shift to relationship problem solving (immediacy). When clients say, "I don't know," they also might be saying, "I can't do it" or "I'm afraid." In such situations, suggesting a very small goal may be a starting point, for example, "If you could make just one tiny change in your life, what would it be?"

The **miracle question** (de Shazer, 1985) is widely used in brief or single-session counselling as a way to help clients who have difficulty coming up with defined goals. A typical miracle question might be formulated as follows: "Suppose that tonight while you're sleeping a miracle happens and your problem is solved. When you wake up, what will be different about your life?" Variations of this question may need to be developed to accommodate different clients. For example, some clients may object to the religious overtones in the question, and a more neutral term, such as *something remarkable*, could be used.

Effective Goals Can Be Measured.
Goals need to be able to be measured in some way. When goals are measurable, clients will be able to evaluate progress, and they will know precisely when they have reached their goals. Clear goals sustain clients' enthusiasm and motivation. Vague and unmeasurable goals, on the other hand, can result in apathy and vague action plans. Goals can be defined in terms of changes (increases or decreases) in behaviours, thoughts, or feelings.

EXAMPLE (SKILL): *"My goal is to express my opinion or ask a question once per class."*

EXAMPLE (THOUGHTS): *"My goal is to manage self-depreciating thought patterns by substituting positive affirmations."*

EXAMPLE (FEELINGS): *"My goal is to reduce anxiety."*

Whenever possible, goals should be framed in quantifiable language with questions such as "How often?" "How many times?" and "How much?" For example, a goal may be to target weight reduction of 9 kg. Goals should have some realistic schedule or target date. Counsellors should help clients determine when they are going to start working toward their goals and when they expect to reach them. For example, "Target weight reduction of 9 kg in 10 weeks." "Make five calls per day to potential employers."

Effective Goals Are Challenging But Realistic. Goals have to be something that clients can reasonably expect to achieve, even though it may require effort and commitment. Counsellors need to consider variables such as the client's interest in achieving the goals, the client's skills and abilities, and the resources (including the counsellor) that are available to help in reaching the goals. In addition, it is important to help clients set goals that will be significant to managing or changing their problem situation.

Some clients may be reluctant to set challenging goals or even to set goals at all. This could arise for a number of reasons, including:

- poor self-esteem
- fear of failure
- lack of awareness of capacity for change
- fear of change and reluctance to give up established patterns
- lack of resources to support pursuit of the goal (Shebib, 1997:210)

Addressing these issues is a prerequisite to goal setting. In addition, for complex problems and situations in which the client's capacity or self-esteem is low, setting short-term goals or subgoals is particularly useful. Short-term goals represent small, attainable steps toward long-term goals. Their achievement is important for building optimism and helping clients overcome a sense of inadequacy (Pincus and Minahan, 1973).

During the beginning phase of counselling, counsellors may develop ideas or views on what might be appropriate goals for their clients. Counsellors should share these ideas, not as prescriptions, but as starting points for negotiation regarding what needs to be done.

> *Evelyn was referred to the counsellor for help in coping with Trevor, her 18-year-old stepson, who was involved in petty crime. Evelyn's immediate goal was to encourage Trevor to move out of the house, and she hoped that the counsellor might help her do this. During the interview, it became apparent to the counsellor that Evelyn needed help developing parenting skills for dealing with Trevor and her two other teenage stepsons. Without dismissing Evelyn's objective, the counsellor suggested that this be part of their agenda.*

Effective Goals Are "Owned" by Clients. Clients need to see goals as relevant to their needs and consistent with their values. When clients are involved in the process of deciding what their goals are, they are more likely to be motivated to work toward achieving them. When clients are forced to come to counselling by a third party, they may not feel committed to any of the goals of counselling, and thus the chances of success are diminished greatly unless some mutually acceptable working agreement can be reached.

Understanding a client's values is an important part of goal setting. Some clients are motivated by spiritual values, some by material gain, and others by family values. Some clients focus on immediate gratification, while others have objectives that are long term.

> *Ming left his family in China to come to North America. He has seen his wife only once in the last five years when he returned to his country for a short visit. He maintains regular contact with her and their six-year-old son. He sends much of his monthly pay home to support his wife and extended family. Although he hopes that one day his fam-*

ily will be able to join him, he has accepted that his purpose is to position future generations of his family for a better life.

Clients sometimes set goals that require others to change, such as "I want my husband to stop treating me so badly." Counsellors need to encourage clients to form goals based on what is under their control, namely their own feelings, behaviour, and thoughts.

Client complaints and problem statements can usually be reframed as positively worded goal statements. Here are some examples:

EXAMPLE 1

CLIENT: *Everyone always takes advantage of me.*

COUNSELLOR: *Sound as though you'd like to learn to stand up for yourself.*

EXAMPLE 2

CLIENT: *I'm tired of not working.*

COUNSELLOR: *Put simply, your goal is to get a job.*

EXAMPLE 3

CLIENT: *My life is a mess.*

COUNSELLOR: *You would like to find a way to get your life in order.*

The above responses change the focus of the interview from problems to goals. Of course, the counsellor and client will have to work together to shape these vague goals into more explicit terms.

The overall goal of any counselling relationship is change, but depending on the needs of individual clients, the targets for change might focus on behaviour, feelings, thoughts, skills, relationship enhancement, or other areas of the client's life. Table 7.4 on page 216 provides examples of vague goals and specific goals.

ACTION PLANNING

Counselling is a developmental process. In the beginning phase, the focus is on the development of a strong working relationship based on a contract that describes the work to be done and the respective roles of both the counsellor and the client. The beginning phase is also concerned with problem identification and exploration. This work provides the foundation for clients and counsellors to define goals. Attention to detail in the beginning phase helps to prevent the problems that come from premature action. Problem exploration leads to goal setting, which, in turn, forms the foundation for action planning.

Problem Exploration   ⟶   Goals   ⟶   Action Planning

Goals represent the outcomes that clients are working toward. Having clear goals is a prerequisite to defining action programs for reaching these goals. Some clients, once they have their goals in mind, do not need further counselling assistance. The overall process

Table 7.4	Sample Goals	
Target Area	**Vague Area**	**Specific Goal Statements**
Behaviour	To do better in my courses	To improve my grade-point average from C to B- by the end of the semester
Feelings	To feel better	To overcome depression so I am able to enjoy life. That would include mixing socially with people and having a sense that life is worth living. I'll be more able to accept my problems without withdrawing or drowning in self-pity.
Thoughts	To stop putting myself down	To look at mistakes as normal and as learning opportunities. When I'm successful, I'll take credit. Overall, I'll be able to say to myself that I'm capable.
Skills	To get organized	To develop skill at organizing my time and setting priorities. I need to set up a schedule so I can plan at least a month in advance.
Relationship	To be able to communicate better with my husband	To reduce the number of fights that we have by not being so explosive. Instead of yelling, I need to remain calm. Instead of not listening, I need to check with him to make sure I understand what he wants too.
Health and fitness	To get in shape	To lose 5 kg over the next two months To increase my weekly running from 5 to 10 km
Spiritual	To be closer to God	To attend religious services regularly—at least once a week To make prayer a daily part of my life To read something spiritual at least once a day To walk in the forest three times a week

of developing goals, including the important work of exploring their problems in the beginning phase, is sufficient to meet their needs. Other clients may need additional coaching and support to develop and implement systematic action plans. Otherwise, goals can be quickly abandoned like well-intended but ill-conceived New Year's resolutions.

Action planning and implementation consists of a series of steps leading to the client's goal (or subgoal). Put simply, action planning involves developing strategies to help clients get where they want to go. This involves four steps: (1) identify alternatives for action, (2) choose an action strategy, (3) develop and implement plans, and (4) evaluate outcomes.

Step One: Identify Alternatives

The first task in selecting a plan is to list the range of alternatives for achieving goals. This step serves two purposes. First, it holds clients back from impulsive action based on the first alternative available, which may simply be a repeat of previous unsuccessful attempts at change. Second, it helps to ensure that clients have choices based on a full range of possibilities. When there is choice, clients can make more rational decisions.

INTERVIEW 7.2 GOAL SETTING

The following interview excerpt illustrates goal-setting techniques. Prior to this point, exploration and active listening have enabled the counsellor to develop a solid base of understanding. With this work apparently finished, it seems timely to move on to goal setting.

DIALOGUE	ANALYSIS
Counsellor: You've talked about how unhappy you've been and how it's, as you put it, "now or never." That suggests to me that you're ready to make some changes.	The counsellor recognizes the client's positive motivation for change and uses it to make a transition to goal setting. Problem statements can often be reframed to make goal statements.
Client: Yeah, I'd like to get out of the rut that I've been in for too long.	The client makes a general statement confirming motivation for change. This undeveloped goal is a useful starting point, but it is not yet an operational goal.
Counsellor: I think it might be helpful at this point to figure out what you want to achieve, what you'd like to change. This would give you something to work toward. What do you think?	The counsellor seeks to contract with the client to work on goal setting. The counsellor uses the criteria for effective goals as a reference point. As the interview progresses, other questions will be asked that help frame the goal. There is no secret agenda to this, and the counsellor might decide to review the process with the client. The final open question reaches for client input and agreement.
Client: Sounds good. I think it's time to do something. For one thing, I really haven't invested too much in my marriage. I have to change my priorities.	The client begins to identify an area for change.
Counsellor: What do you mean, change your priorities?	The counsellor requests more definition (goal specificity). This ensures that no assumptions are made.
Client: If possible, I've got to stop spending so much time at work. By the time I get home, I'm so tired that I have no energy or motivation to be involved with my family.	Often, as here, client goals are stated in the negative—i.e., in terms of what the client would like to stop doing.
Counsellor: Okay, I think I get a sense that what you'd like is to be more committed to your family. In order to do that, you'd have to cut back on work.	The counsellor attempts to help the client put an emerging goal statement in behavioural terms by reframing the idea.

(continued)

Client: Exactly.

Counsellor: Just so we can be clear, can you try to be more specific? Suppose you're successful. What will be different from the way things are now?

This request for more specificity encourages the client to reframe the goals in positive terms by stating what will be done differently.

Client: I don't understand. What do you mean?

The client is confused, but the relationship is strong enough that the client is able to ask for help.

Counsellor: Well, maybe you can't plan it out exactly, but what do you see happening in terms of the amount of time you'd like to spend with your family? Try to be specific so you'll have something to aim for.

The counsellor clarifies the question. This helps to educate the client regarding some of the criteria for goal setting.

Client (laughs): Oh, I see. You want to nail me down and close the deal. You should be a salesperson. Well, I think it's important that I free up the weekends and at least two nights a week. Sunday should be strictly family, a time to do something with the kids.

A clear goal statement has emerged, but the work is not yet finished.

Counsellor: From your excited tone, I get the sense that you'd feel really good if you could do that.

Empathy lets the client know that the counsellor has recognized the client's feelings and their importance.

Client: In my heart, it's what I've always wanted.

The client confirms acceptance of the counsellor's empathy.

Counsellor: A while back, you used the words "if possible" when you talked about cutting back on work. What problems do you anticipate?

An important part of goal setting is to assist the client to look at potential problems, including the relative advantages and disadvantages of goal attainment.

Client: I'd like to try for a management position at the company. But everyone's so competitive. I've got to put in the hours if I'm going to keep my sales above the others. And high sales is the first thing they look for when it's time for promotion.

Having identified this potential barrier, the client can address it, for example, by considering ways to overcome it, or make a decision about whether the costs involved are too high.

Counsellor: You're torn. To compete, you've got to put in the hours. But if you do that it takes away from your time and energy with the family. That's a lot of stress.

The counsellor recognizes the client's ambivalence.

(continued)

Client: Now that you point it out, it seems obvious. I've been under stress for so long, I don't even think about it any more. It's clear to me now that the price of success is just too much.

Solutions to problems, however obvious, are often not acted upon because of such ambivalence.

Counsellor: Meaning that if you have to sacrifice time with your family in order to get ahead, you're not interested. (client nods)

The counsellor's empathy provides a basis for insight.

Sounds like you've made a decision. But let me play devil's advocate. Suppose you cut back on your job and lost a promotion. How would you feel about that?

Such responses ensure that the client will not gloss over or minimize difficulties. The counsellor prevents the client from acting impulsively. By anticipating risks, the client is challenged to decide whether the costs are acceptable.

Client: It would be hard on me. But I think not nearly so hard as what's happening now. At heart, I'm really a family man. I'm certain of it. Family has to be number one. My career is important to me, but it's my second priority.

The client confirms a decision. If the counsellor is satisfied that the client has taken a serious look at all reasonable risks, it's time to move on.

Counsellor: Let's go back to your goal. What other problems do you anticipate?

(20 seconds of silence)

The counsellor challenges the client to look ahead to see if there are other risks. Similar responses are called for until all difficulties are explored.

Client: Here's one. My family is so used to getting along without me, they've developed lives of their own. I guess I can't expect them to drop everything for me.

The counsellor must be patient and give the client enough time to complete the thought process.

Counsellor: So, how can you deal with that reality?

Client: That's easy. I guess I'll just have to negotiate with the family on how much time we'll spend together.

This type of response ensures that the client sets goals and embarks on action plans with a clear sense of direction and planning. Problems may be prevented or anticipated, and the client is far less likely to face a crisis that leads to abandonment of otherwise healthy objectives.

Counsellor: One thought occurs to me. How will your boss react if you suddenly start spending less time on the job? Do you think that's something to consider?

It is appropriate for the counsellor to tentatively introduce some of her own ideas, leaving a lot of room for the client to respond. As a rule, counsellors should let the client have the first opportunity.

Adapted with permission from Shebib, 1997.

Both counsellors and clients may contribute ideas about possible plans. As well, consultation with others and brainstorming can generate ideas. Some basic rules for effective brainstorming are listed below (Egan, 1998; Shebib, 1997; Cragan and Wright, 1991; Young, 1998).

1. Do not evaluate or criticize ideas. Adherence to this principle ensures that self-censorship does not result. Clients might hold back potentially valuable and useable suggestions because they fear that they will be criticized or embarrassed.

2. Generate as many ideas as possible. Encourage wild and creative suggestions. At this stage any alternative, however bizarre, is acceptable. Counsellors can use leads such as these to encourage clients to generate ideas: "Let your imagination run wild and see how many different ideas you can come up with that will help you achieve your goals." "Don't worry for now about whether it's a good idea or a bad one." Sometimes counsellors can prompt clients to be creative by generating a few "wild" ideas of their own.

3. Emphasize quantity—more is better.

4. Look for ways to combine or "piggyback" ideas. Sometimes apparently ridiculous proposals can be modified to work. Or they can be combined with other ideas to come up with new alternatives. Some key questions for stimulating further alternatives include "How can we join suggestions?" "In what ways can we sort or rearrange these ideas?"

CASE STUDY (LISA)

Lisa, age 33, and her counsellor come up with a list of possibilities for Lisa to deal with her shyness and her need to meet more people. Some of the ideas they generated are listed below:

- *join a singles club*
- *take an acting class*
- *learn to sing*
- *put an ad in the personals column*
- *become a volunteer*
- *use counselling to role play problem situations in order to develop assertiveness*
- *forget the goal and become a nun*
- *use counselling to deal with self-depreciating inner talk*
- *try hypnosis*
- *join a social group at a place of worship*
- *participate in an assertiveness training group*

Step Two: Choose an Action Strategy

Once a creative list of alternative action strategies is identified, the next task is to assist clients in evaluating alternatives and making choices. At this point, the counsellor's role is to ensure that clients are able to make informed choices. This involves helping clients to intelligently consider each alternative with respect to a number of criteria. An obvious first criterion is that the alternative for meeting the client's goal is potentially effective. It must be sufficient to make a difference and relevant to the problem being addressed. A second criterion is that alternatives are within the capacity of the client. Otherwise, failure is inevitable. A third criterion is that alternatives are consistent with the values and beliefs of the client. A fourth is that alternatives are reviewed in terms of their potential cost. Cost might be measured by time, money, and energy expended in finding resources to execute the alternative. As well, alternatives might result in other losses for the client. For example, suppose a client wishes to end a pattern of alcohol abuse, but the person's friends are drinking buddies. If quitting drinking involves developing new activities, the potential loss of friends and social structure must be considered as a negative consequence that will have an impact on the client. Understanding and exploring this loss is important, for unless clients are aware of and prepared for these contingencies, they may be unable to sustain any efforts at changing.

Step Three: Develop and Implement Plans

Developing and implementing plans involves four substeps: (1) sequencing plans, (2) developing **contingency plans**, (3) putting plans into action, and (4) evaluating.

Effective plans are maps that detail the sequence of events leading to the final goal. Counsellors should avoid tailor-made plans in favour of customized strategies that are designed in collaboration with individual clients. Some of the important questions that need to be answered include the following:

- What specific strategies will be used?
- In what order will the strategies be used?
- What resources or support will be needed at each step?
- What are the risks and potenti
- What are the risks and potential obstacles?

Effective plans anticipate the potential obstacles that clients might encounter along the route. Once clients know and accept the possible barriers that could interfere with their plans, they can develop contingency plans to deal with these barriers. This preventive work helps to prevent clients from giving up when things don't go smoothly.

Case Study (Lisa, continued)

Lisa decided that joining a singles group would be a great way for her to meet people, but she admitted that she would probably back out before going to the first meeting. With her counsellor's help, she came up with two ideas for managing this problem. She recruited a friend to go with her to the group, and she phoned the group leader to volunteer to bring refreshments. Lisa knew that she wouldn't back down if it meant that others would be affected by her actions.

Lisa said that what bothered her most was first meeting someone. She told her counsellor, "I feel so awkward. I just don't know what to say." Her counsellor helped Lisa accept that feeling awkward is normal under such circumstances. The counsellor self-disclosed some of her own anxieties and suggested that they could role-play some ideas for handling these tough moments.

During the implementation phase, counsellors need to support and encourage clients as they deal with the stress of change. One way they can help is to remind clients that anxiety, awkwardness, and periodic slumps are normal when change is occurring. Counsellors can look for ways to reframe failure or setbacks as learning opportunities. Wilson's comments might be offered to clients:

> Although you may fail to reach the goal, there are benefits of having worked toward it. One benefit is the practical education of making the effort. Another is the opportunity to practice specific skills. A third is the recognition that meeting some goals and failing to meet others is part of the ebb and flow of life. Recognize that you probably will not achieve significant goals without some failures. Failing provides unique learning opportunities that ultimately contribute to your personal growth. (1994:18)

Empathy is particularly important at this time as a way of supporting clients in dealing with feelings that accompany change. During implementation, counsellors should also encourage clients to use family, friends, and support groups to assist them.

Step Four: Evaluate Outcomes

Effective plans include continual evaluation as part of the implementation phase. Evaluation recognizes and confirms success and is a powerful motivator. However, evaluation may uncover problems that need to be addressed. For example, it may become apparent that the goals are too unrealistic. If they are too challenging and unreachable, counsellors can help clients define smaller goals. When goals prove to be too easy, they can be modified to provide more challenge. Regular review of progress ensures that goals and action strategies remain relevant and realistic.

When evaluation reveals that the plan is unlikely to be successful, efforts can be redirected toward redesigning the plan or selecting a different strategy for action. In some cases, the client may need help that is beyond the capacity of the counsellor; in this case, referral to another counsellor or service is appropriate.

CONVERSATION 7.2

I'VE TRIED EVERYTHING

STUDENT: I get stuck when a client says, "I've tried everything and nothing seems to work."

TEACHER: You feel stuck, which is precisely how the client feels. Clients often bring out in counsellors the same feelings that they are experiencing. This reality can be a useful tool for empathy. When clients say they've tried everything, it's important not to get into a "yes, but" game, whereby counsellors generate ideas and clients dismiss them with a "yes, but" response.

STUDENT: So, what are my choices?

TEACHER: I'd be interested in exploring what the client did. Did he or she try long enough? At the right time? In the right way? Sometimes problems get worse before they get better, and clients may give up too soon. A mother might try ignoring her child when he has a tantrum. She tells you ignoring doesn't work, but she may have abandoned this tactic after a few minutes when it appeared that the intensity of her child's tantrum was increasing. In this situation, you could help her anticipate this obstacle so that she would not be demoralized when it occurred. Or maybe she was giving her child lots of nonverbal attention, not realizing how this was reinforcing the tantrum.

STUDENT: I can think of another example. One of the members of my work group was having trouble with her supervisor. She told us that there is no point in talking to him because he doesn't listen anyway. But from the way she described how she talked to him, I wouldn't listen either. She was vicious and cruel.

TEACHER: So, if she were your client, she would need some help developing awareness about how she affects others.

Summary

The foundation for empowerment in counselling is the belief that clients are capable and have a right to manage their own lives. In order to empower clients, counsellors need to forego controlling them, demystify the counselling process, promote client self-determination, advocate for progressive changes in the system, and assist clients to change established patterns of thinking and acting that are interfering with their lives. Counsellors can help clients change established patterns through five major activities: motivating, confronting, helping clients think differently, goal setting, and action planning.

Motivating involves engaging clients in a change process, as well as supporting and energizing them as they deal with the rigours of change. Counsellors may face a range of motivational challenges, and they can employ different strategies to address each of them. Five categories of motivational problems are clients in denial, involuntary clients, burnt-out clients, ambivalent clients, and energized clients.

Effective confrontation is not a hostile act. It is a way to move clients to a different level of understanding, behaving, or feeling. Confrontation can address incongruities between what clients believe and the way they act; self-defeating ways of thinking and behaving; behaviour that is harmful to self or others; blind spots; blaming behaviour; communication problems; and strengths. Confrontation should be relevant to the goals of counselling and timed appropriately to minimize defensive reactions.

Clients may have trouble breaking out of established patterns because of the way they think about problems. Thinking errors include distortion, incomplete analysis, egocentricity or lack of empathy, rigidity, and self-defeating thought. An important goal of counselling is to help clients discontinue faulty reasoning. Reframing is a tool for helping clients look at problems from another perspective. Reframing empowers clients by focusing on solutions and redefining negatives as opportunities or challenges.

Goal setting serves many important purposes, including giving direction, defining roles, motivating, and measuring progress. Effective goals need to be concrete, measurable, challenging but realistic, and owned by clients. Effective goals can be developed from problem statements.

Action planning consists of series of steps leading to the client's goal or subgoal. Selecting a plan involves systematic identification and evaluation of the possibilities for action, then choosing one or more alternative action plans. Developing and implementing plans involves four substeps: sequencing plans, developing contingency plans, putting plans into action, and evaluating.

Exercises

1. What style do you prefer others to use when they give you feedback? Compare your preference with those of your colleagues.

2. Consider the various ways in which your colleagues prefer to receive feedback. Which ways would you have most trouble with?

3. What are the essential differences between a counselling confrontation and an attack?

4. Identify the person(s) from whom you would be most receptive to receiving feedback and those from whom you would be least receptive. Give your reasons why.

5. Self-evaluate your personal comfort when confronting others.

    a. What people would you have difficulty confronting?

    b. Do you avoid confronting?

    c. Think of times when it was reasonable to confront, but you didn't. What prevented you from confronting?

    d. Finish the following sentence: When I confront, I feel ...

6. Write a short concept paper that describes what you believe are the elements of effective confrontation.

7. Hamachek says, "Do not confront another person if you do not wish to increase your involvement with that individual" (1982:230). Develop a rationale that supports this statement.

8. Work with a colleague to role-play an appropriate counsellor confrontation for each of the following situations.

    a. a client who has hygiene problems

    b. a colleague who has, in your opinion, behaved in an unprofessional manner

    c. a client who consistently arrives late for appointments

9. Identify an area in your own life that you are willing to accept feedback about (e.g., the first impressions you leave with others, your style of communication, the way others see you). Spend about 20 minutes with a friend or colleague exploring their opinions about the identified area.

    a. What were your feelings during the encounter? Did they change?

    b. What did your colleague say or do that made it easier to accept the feedback? What made it more difficult?

    c. What did you learn about giving or receiving feedback that will be useful to you in your work as a counsellor?

10. Evaluate the effectiveness of each of the confrontations below. Suggest improvements.

    a. Try to do better next time.

    b. You're an idiot.

    c. You're saying that you're okay, yet you're crying.

    d. Grow up and act your age.

    e. As long as you continue to act like a doormat, you're going to get abused. If you're serious about protecting yourself, leave him.

11. Suggest reframed responses for each of the following client statements.

    a. I can't do it.

    b. (a student counsellor) I feel so unnatural and phony expressing empathy all the time.

    c. I really want my kids to avoid making the same mistakes I did. I don't know why they don't listen to me.

    d. If he really loved me, he'd send me flowers.

    e. My life is a mess.

    f. I'm tired of being depressed all the time.

12. Name at least 10 different ways to motivate clients.

13. Evaluate how effectively the following statements meet the criteria for effective goals.

    a. to be a better person

    b. for my boss to stop hassling me

    c. to drink less

    d. to be able to disagree with someone without dismissing them or their ideas

    e. to improve my fitness by next year to the point where I can run 1 km in 15 minutes

14. Practise brainstorming techniques. Identify 30 different action strategies for a client who wishes to quit drinking.

15. Use the concepts from this chapter to practise goal setting and action planning. Pick one or more target areas (behaviour, feelings, thoughts, skills, or relationship).

Weblinks

"Counselling for Change: Evolutionary Trends in Counselling Services for Women Who are Abused and for Their Children in Canada" by Linda MacLeod
www.hc-sc.gc.ca/hppb/familyviolence/html/1change.htm

"From Policy to Practice: Exploring Victim Empowerment Initiatives in South Africa" by Juan Nel and Johan Kruger (.pdf document)
www.victimology.nl/onlpub/otherdocs/za-nelkruger.pdf

Integrative (or Win-Win) Reframing—includes links to other sites related to reframing.
www.colorado.edu/conflict/peace/treatment/wwrefram.htm

DIFFICULT SITUATIONS

PREVIEW

After reading this chapter you should be able to:

- Understand the different forms of client resistance.
- Explain reasons for resistance.
- Describe techniques for dealing with resistance.
- Explain the importance of counsellor self-awareness when dealing with clients who are resistant.
- Define intimidating and violent behaviour.
- Identify key variables for predicting which clients might become violent.
- Understand violence in relation to mental illness.
- List key questions for assessing the potential for violence.
- Describe techniques for preventing violence.
- Identify and describe the four phases of violence.
- Describe strategies for intervening at each phase of violence.
- Explain the importance of debriefing critical incidents.
- Identify debriefing techniques.

RESISTANCE

Resistance is a defensive reaction of clients that interferes with or delays the process of counselling. Simply put, "resistance is the client's opposition to change in the counseling process" (Otani, 1989:458). It is a term first introduced by Freud, who described its ever present influence on the therapeutic process: "Every step of the treatment is accompanied by resistance; every single thought, every mental act of the patient's, must pay toll to the resistance and represents a compromise between the forces urging towards cure and those gathered to oppose it" (cited in Rosenthal, 1987:3).

Resistance may act to protect clients from the stress of change. It serves to maintain the status quo against the threat that typically accompanies any change process.

Sometimes clients are resistant because they have been forced to come for counselling. They do not see the need for change and they resent being coerced. At other times, clients come voluntarily for counselling and they appear motivated to change, but they resist it because of prior bad experiences with counsellors or because they fear the unknown risks and pain of changing. In this sense, resistance is a way of maintaining the status quo and the relative stability (however painful) of the current situation. In fact, resistance can be viewed as a natural and protective reaction to change. As Young observed, "When the helper begins to disrupt long-held and cherished beliefs about the world, the client tries to protect his or her core beliefs from sweeping changes that may bring chaos" (1998:251).

Harris and Watkins echo Young's sentiments, arguing that resistance to change indicates a degree of stability that would be upset if people changed randomly. They conclude that "resistance has positive value and a counselor should expect to find some good reasons why clients don't change—at least from their point of view" (1987:17).

Sometimes clients become increasingly resistant as counselling progresses. This may signal that the process is moving too quickly or that there is unresolved conflict in the counsellor–client relationship. Resistance may also arise at critical moments in counselling, such as when counsellors challenge long-established behaviour or attempt to encourage discussion or goal setting in areas that clients would like to avoid.

Forms of Resistance

Resistance may show itself in a variety of ways, ranging from overt hostility to passivity that impedes the work. Among the range of client behaviours and signs that may suggest resistance are the following (Gladding, 1996; Young, 1998; Otani, 1989; Shulman, 1992; Corey and Corey, 1989):

1. failure to comply with the basic procedures of counselling, including keeping appointments, being on time, and paying fees
2. statements (direct or subtle) that indicate resistance, e.g., "This is a waste of time," "You can't make me cooperate," "That's none of your business," and "I don't want to be here."
3. passivity (e.g., silence, withholding information, persistent short responses such as "I don't know," extreme self-censorship of ideas and feelings). Such passivity may indicate that the client does not want to be there, or it may mean that the demands of the interview are excessive. For example, the feelings and content of the interview may be more than the client is willing or able to face.

4. diversion (e.g., changing subject, using excessive humour, making small talk, introducing irrelevant material, being overly talkative, intellectualizing). This type of resistance is a way of avoiding difficult, threatening, or incriminating content.

5. uncooperative behaviour (e.g., failure to follow through with plans or homework, false promises)

6. subtle undermining (e.g., acting seductively, attempting to redefine the counselling relationship as a friendship, excessive praising, being sarcastic)

7. creating the illusion of work, described by Shulman (1992) as engaging in conversations that appear important but that in reality are empty and have no real meaning. Interviews may be filled with apparent cooperation and verbosity, but the work does not empower clients or enable them to change.

8. nonverbal cues suggesting a passive/aggressive response, such as not making eye contact, folding arms, sitting on the edge of the seat, using an angry tone of voice, clenching fists, raising eyebrows, frowning, and sighing

9. limiting the setting (e.g., restricting discussion on certain topics by insisting that the topics are irrelevant)

Otani (1989) cautions against using a single incident as evidence of resistance. A client may become silent when a new topic is introduced. This silence may or may not be resistance, but if the client becomes silent again when the same topic is introduced, then resistance is likely.

Sometimes clients expect counsellors to be cold and indifferent. This expectation may be based on past experience with helping professionals or other persons in authority. If their prior encounters were unsatisfying, then it is understandable for clients to be cautious in similar situations and to believe that the same outcome is likely. Consequently, these clients will be quick to pick up on anything that might support that belief. Indeed, they view caring as manipulative and empathy as intrusive. Counsellors who understand the importance of such prior expectations are less likely to be taken aback by clients who reject or who are suspicious of their caring actions. As Irving Layton, a Canadian poet, commented, "The virtues of those we dislike irritate us more than their vices."

Dealing with Resistance

Some resistance is normal and perhaps desirable, so counsellors do not always have to treat resistance as problematic. In fact, most clients are resistant to some extent (Cormier and Cormier, 1985; Haley, 1987). Sheafor, Horejsi, and Horejsi note that it is common for clients to be somewhat defensive, particularly in the beginning phase: "The need to make even small changes generates some degree of discomfort in all people. Change can be particularly threatening to clients with well-established, or rather rigid beliefs, attitudes, and behavioral patterns. Fear is at the heart of such resistance" (1991:172). Skilled counsellors recognize resistance, but they are not threatened by it; instead, they consider it a clue that their clients' defences are engaged. By understanding the nature of the resistance, counsellors can open a pathway to greater understanding of their clients.

In the beginning phase of counselling, before trust and a working contract are negotiated, many clients tend to hold back. At this stage, their counsellors are strangers, and it would be unwise for clients to open up too quickly without knowing how precious personal information might be treated.

Clients who are open and candid about their resistance may present less of a challenge than those who mask their resistance with silence or feigned cooperation. When resistance is clearly labelled by clients, frank discussion seems to follow, but when clients mask their uncooperativeness, they deny being resistant when counsellors introduce the subject. Before counsellors assume that their clients are resistant, they should eliminate other factors. For example, clients who appear resistant may not understand the expectations or the process of counselling; thus, they remain cautious and guarded. Counsellors should remember that whereas they have considerable training in how to counsel, their clients have not had training in how to be a client. Unless the process is clarified, clients may remain frightened or confused. Counsellors need to be explicit regarding their expectations. They should not assume that what is obvious to them will also be obvious to their clients.

Resistance may arise for a number of reasons. These may be categorized in five major groups: (1) relationship, (2) motivational, (3) attitudinal, (4) fearful, and (5) involuntary. Client resistance may be unconscious and unintended, or it may be a deliberate act of sabotage or avoidance.

Relationship Resistance.

This type of resistance is linked to variables in the counselling relationship. Clients may be resistant because of transference reactions or simply because they feel they are not a good match with their counsellors. Sometimes clients are influenced by past experiences with counsellors. For example, if they perceived their former counsellors as rude or untrustworthy, clients might understandably be guarded and defensive with any new worker. This is a way to protect themselves from further rudeness, inconsistency, or breach of trust. Therefore, it is useful for counsellors to inquire about any past experiences that clients have had with other counsellors. This helps to bring feelings and issues into the open, including any preconceptions or fears about the current relationship. When counsellors do this they should provide a brief explanation to let their clients know they are not prying for gossip. The example below demonstrates.

COUNSELLOR: *Have you had any other experiences with counselling in the past?*

CLIENT: *Yes, my husband and I went for marital counselling about two years ago.*

COUNSELLOR: *What did you like and dislike about that experience? I'm asking because I think it will help me to understand a bit about your expectations. I'd like to learn what worked for you and what didn't.*

Resistance may also develop as a result of conflict in the current relationship. Counselling relationships, like all relationships, are subject to periodic stress and conflict. Counsellors can make mistakes and say the wrong thing, and they can offend their clients. Clients who are vulnerable may be overly sensitive, or they might misinterpret messages and feel angered. This is an inevitable reality of the chemistry of human encounters. What sets apart effective counsellors is their ability to be sensitive to clues that all is not well in their relationships. Counsellors are alert for verbal and nonverbal shifts in the tone of the interview that might signal that there is friction. Counsellors are further distinguished by their willingness and capacity to address these issues in a caring and nondefensive manner. By doing so, they not only prevent further resistance, they also build trust and understanding with their clients.

Motivational Resistance. This type of resistance results from some of the motivational problems discussed in Chapter 7. Clients who are in denial do not accept that they have a problem, even though there might be considerable evidence that their behaviour is problematic for them and others. If this is the source of resistance, one option is to provide accurate information to clients about the effects or consequences of their behaviour. With clients who deny they have an addiction problem, providing information (questionnaires, handouts, date and time of an open AA meeting, etc.) may persuade them to reassess their situation.

Some clients hold to their current mode of thinking, feeling, and acting because they lack the energy necessary for change or they are pessimistic that change is possible. Whatever the reason, these clients resist counselling because to do so appears easier and safer than embracing change. Counsellors might deal with this resistance by communicating optimism and by helping clients set small but achievable goals. By supporting and reinforcing small successes, counsellors contribute to the empowerment of their clients. In the process, it is important that counsellors express empathy regarding the challenges and fears associated with any change. Clients need to understand that they will not be humiliated or overwhelmed by the demands of counselling or change.

In Chapter 7, the concept of secondary gain was introduced as a way of understanding why people resist change. As Bezanson, DeCoff, and Stewart explain, "For some clients, the risks involved in bringing up reluctance and moving toward change are simply too great and the rewards of remaining with the status quo too powerful to be abandoned. The responsibility of counsellors is to attempt to find the resources to motivate the client to assume responsibility and accomplish the desired counselling targets" (1985:104).

Attitudinal Resistance. Some clients are resistant because they believe that taking help is a sign of weakness. They may believe, as well, that counselling will undermine their personal autonomy. One way for counsellors to address this resistance is to look for appropriate opportunities to reframe counselling as a sign of strength, rather than feebleness. Counsellors can deal with fears about loss of independence by making sure that clients are active and informed partners in the work of counselling.

Sometimes counsellors can modify hostile intentions through goal setting. The following interview excerpt provides a brief illustration:

COUNSELLOR: *What do you hope to achieve?*

CLIENT: *Nothing.*

COUNSELLOR: *What's behind that answer?*

CLIENT: *I just think that counselling is a waste of time. What good does it do to talk about problems anyway?*

COUNSELLOR: *You also seem to be saying that if counselling could in some way help you with your problems, you'd be more satisfied.*

CLIENT: *I guess so.*

Another technique described by Cormier and Cormier (1985) is to avoid direct challenges of resistance by matching the resistance statement. This strategy shows clients that their concerns have been heard and accepted. This approach is illustrated below.

CLIENT: *I just think that counselling is a waste of time. What good does it do to talk about problems anyway?*

COUNSELLOR: *Given your pessimism, it seems to me that you're wise to be cautious about what we might accomplish here.*

By responding in this way, the counsellor relieves the client of the burden of trying to convince the counsellor of the validity of his position. The client may begin to see the counsellor more as an ally. The wisdom of not attacking clients' beliefs and values directly is nicely illustrated by the following story.

> A holy man and an atheist met one day. The atheist challenged the holy man to debate, exclaiming, "I don't believe in God!" The holy man replied, "Tell me about the God you don't believe in." The atheist talked at length about the absurd wars that had been fought in the name of God. He attacked the "hypocrites" who espoused their religious values and beliefs but behaved quite the opposite. The holy man listened patiently until the atheist had said his piece. Only then did he respond: "You and I have a lot in common. I don't believe in that God either."

At the same time, counsellors need to accept some truth in criticisms, such as "Counselling isn't going to put food on my table." Harris and Watkins offer this perspective:

> Counseling cannot solve problems like discrimination and the economic punishment that goes with it. Counseling can help people choose how they want to respond to discrimination and how to take advantage of what economic resources may be available. But people who feel victimized by society see their problems as caused by circumstances outside themselves. Thus counseling, which seeks personal change, is viewed as valueless because it is society that needs changing. (1987:46)

Fearful Resistance. For most people, it is difficult to change from established routines and ways of coping. They communicate fears regarding the imagined consequences of change through resistance. Some clients have trouble with intimacy, and counselling may be seen as an unwanted intrusion that threatens their need to maintain personal distance and privacy. Depending on the situation, a variety of counselling initiatives might prove useful, including candid discussion with clients about their fears and the real risks of change. Here, again, working on small but achievable goals will be less threatening (see Chapter 7). As well, it is crucial that counsellors support and empathize with their clients' fears. Clients need to hear that they will not be pushed beyond their capacity. Sometimes limited counsellor self-disclosure can be a useful way of normalizing fears about change.

Johnson and Yanka suggest that "resistance is the opposite of motivation and is sometimes a sign that other influences on a person are stronger than the need for change" (2001:83). For example, cultural and familial values or responsibilities may prevent clients from seeking or taking help. It is important that workers understand how clients may perceive them. For example:

> Clients and others typically do not understand the limits of the social worker's span of control and ascribe more authority to the worker than is legally allowed. Clients may believe that the worker can withhold an income maintenance check if they do not do what they think the worker wants them to do. Such situations can become complex when the client acts

according to what she believes the worker wants rather than what the worker has said. (Johnson and Yanka, 2001:84)

When clients assume workers have more power than they actually have, they might withhold information, avoid meetings, or otherwise resist counselling. Frank discussion of roles, responsibilities, and the limits of power may assist in clients' fears. In cross-cultural situations, workers can try to modify their approach to be more congruent with their clients' culture, or they can use or partner with indigenous workers.

Involuntary Resistance.

Involuntary Resistance. This type of resistance stems clients' resentment at being forced to come for counselling and their inability to see a need for change. These clients may see themselves as fighting the "system," and they view the counsellor as a representative of the system (Harris and Watkins, 1987). Involuntary clients typically receive services from large bureaucratic organizations, but the structure and procedures of these agencies can work against clients. Johnson offers this viewpoint: "The complexity of rules and regulations and the inability of an organization to individualize for clients often gets in the way of the worker providing the service needed by the client. The worker may have feelings of powerlessness and may not feel appreciated by the agency. This can lead to frustrations that get in the way of responding to the client appropriately" (1992:137).

With involuntary clients, it is important to restore their sense of control and right to self-determination. These clients need to be able to answer the question "What can counselling do for me?" They need to see goals and outcomes that they desire as opposed to those that feel imposed. Counsellors need to be patient with unwilling clients by remaining nonjudgmental and caring. Counsellors can decrease resistance by demonstrating their ability to talk calmly with their clients about their reasons for not wanting to be there. Counsellors should be especially diligent about informing unwilling clients about their rights, including the limits of confidentiality. Clear, succinct statements about these issues will help to reduce their suspicions.

Table 8.1 on page 233 provides some strategies for dealing with each type of resistance. Two points need to be emphasized. First, clients may show more than one type of resistance, and second, techniques always have to be adapted and modified to meet the needs, culture, and language of each client and situation. Creativity and flexibility are essential for handling resistance. Sometimes this can mean dealing with resistance directly by inviting clients to talk about their feelings. At other times, counsellors may prefer to avoid direct challenges to resistance. For example, a counsellor who observes that a client becomes hostile when a certain topic comes up could shift the focus to a less threatening topic until more trust is developed.

Leads for Dealing with Resistance.

Leads for Dealing with Resistance. Immediacy was introduced in Chapter 3 as the process of exploring, deepening, and evaluating counselling relationships. When resistance blocks the work of counselling, immediacy provides a way to deal directly with clients' concerns regarding the counselling process or the relationship itself. As a general rule, if resistance is increasing, it is wise to deal directly with it; otherwise, the client may never return. The following leads illustrate the potential variety of responses that can be used to move the interview toward a discussion of resistance.

- How do you feel about being here?
- Do you resent being forced to see me?

Table 8.1 Strategies for Dealing with Resistance

Origin of Resistance	Description	Strategy Choice
Relationship	There is unresolved conflict in the helping relationship, or clients are defensive because of prior bad experiences with counselling.	Problem solve relationship difficulties. Discuss prior experiences with counselling, then use this information to work out contracts that clients can support (but do this in a way that does not undermine the integrity of other counsellors). Refer to other counsellors. Respond nondefensively and do not personalize.
Motivational	Clients lack motivation to change either because they see no problem or because they do not believe that change is possible.	Use confrontation to help clients become aware of problems. Use authority. Deal with learned helplessness (see Chapter 7). Communicate optimism about clients' skills and abilities. Acknowledge and reinforce all efforts and progress.
Attitudinal	Personal or cultural values define taking help as a sign of weakness.	Encourage clients to voice concerns regarding counselling. Adjust counselling methods to be culturally sensitive. Persuade clients that taking help is a sign of strength. Use strategies that fully empower and involve clients in making decisions.
Fearful	Clients are afraid of the risks and potential pain of changing.	Encourage clients to share fears, then use empathy to acknowledge feelings. Prompt candid discussion of the risks of change. Support and encourage the client. Gear pacing toward small, achievable goals. Help clients identify and deal with self-defeating inner dialogue. Target work in less threatening areas until confidence increases.
Involuntary	Clients do not want to be in counselling but have been forced by a third party (e.g., courts, school counsellor).	Encourage clients to share feelings, then empathize. Negotiate a contract to add voluntary objectives to those that are involuntary. In general, look for opportunities to give clients control, choices, and power. Help clients answer the question "What's in it for me?" Redirect the work to less threatening areas.

- If I felt forced to come, I think I'd feel quite angry.
- I'm wondering what's happening between us. Are you feeling angry toward me?
- Let's see if we can agree on what we want to accomplish.
- If I'm not mistaken, every time I mention your father you change the subject. Is that a topic you would rather avoid?
- How committed are you to making changes?
- Do you believe it's possible for you to change?
- What does it mean to you to be seeing a counsellor?
- Are you worried that I will try to force you to do something you don't want to do?

Counsellor Self-Awareness and Management of Self

Client resistance can be unsettling and demoralizing for counsellors. Counsellors who have a high need to be liked by their clients may interpret resistance as personal rejection. Resistant clients can test almost every counsellor's ability to be nonjudgmental. Therefore, it is important that counsellors find ways to depersonalize the situation. Otherwise, they run the risk of further worsening the situation by rejecting the client or retaliating in subtle ways. Frequently, counsellors respond with their own insecurities and defences. In turn, clients may view their counsellors' annoyance as proof that the situation is hopeless. In worst-case scenarios, counsellors turn against their clients and blame them for their problems. Ultimately, they look for ways to refer them in order to get rid of them. Such referrals are a way of "dumping" the client, rather than an attempt to help them meet their real needs through connection with alternative resources.

Counsellors need to be able to objectively evaluate their own conduct and take their fair share of responsibility for resistance. When counsellors have high self-awareness of their actions, they are able to monitor themselves and change their behaviour to be more effective. Weisinger underscores the importance of counsellor self-awareness when dealing with difficult clients: "By being aware, for example, that your voice is getting louder and you are becoming increasingly angry at a client who is making yet another unreasonable demand—and recognizing, of course, how important your client is to your ongoing employment—you might lower your voice, defuse your anger, and respond to your client respectfully" (1998:xx).

Bezanson, DeCoff, and Stewart link counselling's effectiveness to the ability of counsellors to handle reluctant or resistant clients: "Reluctant behaviours are the responsibility of the client; feelings of anger or anxiety with reluctant behaviours are the responsibility of the counsellor" (1985:78).

Colleagues and supervisors should be used for support when dealing with highly resistant clients, who can tax the patience of even the most dedicated counsellor. Collegial support can help counsellors unwind from tough sessions. Colleagues can help counsellors process their reactions and regain or test objectivity, and they can be a source of fresh ideas for reaching difficult clients.

Culture and Resistance

Sue and Sue (cited in Diller, 1999) present a case study that portrays how cross-cultural miscommunication can easily be misinterpreted as client resistance. The client was a

INTERVIEW 8.1 **DEALING WITH RESISTANCE**

The following interview excerpt shows some ways for dealing with client resistance. The client is a young male, age 19, who has been referred to an addiction counsellor as a condition of his probation. This excerpt is from the first interview, and it begins about 15 minutes into the interview. It is clear from the client's nonverbal behaviour that he doesn't want to be there (e.g., he has not removed his coat, he gives single-word or short answers to questions, and his voice tone is hostile).

DIALOGUE	ANALYSIS
Client: How long is this going to take? I'm really not in the mood to be cross-examined.	The counsellor decides to address the client's resistance directly. This is the first interview and some softening of the client's hostility might be expected over time, but the degree of resistance seems pronounced enough that it should be dealt with directly. In her response, the counsellor also attempts to remind the client that he does have a choice about whether to stay or go. However, this is a bit risky, since the client may decide to walk out.
Counsellor: Of course, you're free to leave at any point. But before you do, why don't we take a moment to talk straight. I know that you were forced to come here by your probation officer. I'm wondering how you feel about that.	
Client (sarcastically): It's no big deal. I can handle it.	Frequently, clients deny that they are resistant. This can be exceptionally hard to deal with, since such clients evade taking responsibility for their behaviour.
Counsellor: We do agree on one thing. You don't want to be cross-examined and I don't intend to try. You don't have to tell me about anything you don't want to talk about.	The counsellor tries to find a point of agreement, but her response is greeted by more anger. At this point, it is important that the counsellor not give up. Even though the client's response is less than ideal, he has heard what the counsellor said.
Client: Let's get one thing clear. I don't need your permission to do anything.	
Counsellor: Agreed. But since you've decided to stay, let's talk. If you're feeling angry because your probation officer thinks you need counselling, I can understand. I sure don't like it when I'm forced to do something against my will.	The counsellor tries to ally herself with the client by using self-disclosure to encourage him to talk about his resistance. She emphasizes that the client has made choices. Sometimes it is less threatening for clients when counsellors avoid questions (see Chapter 5). The client's earlier statement that he "doesn't want to be cross-examined" is a good indication that questions would be inappropriate in this interview.

(continued)

Client: It's not you. I just don't see the point. There's nothing wrong with me. I don't understand why I have to come here.

Counsellor: Sounds like you really want to stand up and say, "This is my life. Butt out."

Client: Yeah. What gives them the right to say I'm crazy?

Counsellor: And now that you're here, you might be worried that I'll do the same thing. That I'll try to get into your head, tell you what to do.

Client: Of course. Isn't that how it works? I've been to counselling before. (laughs) You guys aren't happy unless you're mucking someone up.

Counsellor (laughs): Well, we have to shrink our quota of heads.

Client (laughs): My head is staying just where it is.

Counsellor: I'm impressed that you're able to say what you want.

Client: I don't believe in playing games.

Counsellor: Me neither. So, let's talk about what's going to happen here. Let's try to work out something that works for both of us.

The counsellor's persistence works, as the client begins to open up. At this point, it is important for the counsellor to avoid becoming defensive. If she starts to "sell" her client on the merits of counselling, she may lose him.

Cautiously, the client begins to share his feelings, including his reservations about what will happen in the relationship.

A little humour from the counsellor helps build rapport, while showing empathy with the client's feelings. The counsellor's humour affirms her ability to talk about the issues without becoming defensive. When using humour, timing is crucial. What works very well in one situation might result in disaster in another.

The counsellor does not attempt to break down her client's defences, which are an important part of the way this client has coped.

There is much work to be done to establish a solid working relationship with this client. Resistance may be a reality throughout the life of the counselling relationship. However, an important beginning has been established.

13-year-old girl who was referred to a school counsellor for allegedly selling drugs. The school counsellor consulted for help in dealing with the parents, whom she described as "uncaring, uncooperative and attempting to avoid responsibility for their daughter's delinquency." Describing the case, the counsellor said that she called the parents, a Hispanic family living in San Jose, California, and talked with Mrs. Martinez. She said she asked Mrs. Martinez to come in as soon as possible to see what could be done to resolve the situation. The counsellor said Mrs. Martinez hesitated and excused herself from the phone when pressed. The counsellor said she overheard whispering, then Mr. Martinez came on the line. He also avoided and made excuses, saying he had to work and could not come in for the meeting. The counsellor emphasized the importance of the meeting for his daughter's welfare and suggested that missing work for a few hours was not important, given the gravity of the situation. The father proposed an evening meeting, but the counsellor rejected this because school policy prohibited evening meetings. Finally, the father agreed, and a meeting was set up for the next day. Mr. and Mrs. Martinez and a brother-in-law (the girl's godfather) showed up. The counsellor reported that she was upset that the brother-in-law was present, and she explained that this would unduly complicate the session. She stressed that she wanted to see only the family. The counsellor said the meeting went badly, and the parents were evasive and not forthcoming with their answers.

Diller, analyzing the counsellor's conclusions, describes the encounter as a clear case of misunderstanding cultural differences. He cites a number of erroneous assumptions. For example, "The counsellor appears unaware that in a traditional Mexican family, the wife would not make a decision without first consulting her husband" (57). The counsellor assumes that Mr. Martinez is unwilling to take off work because he is apathetic about his daughter. "Like any middle-class professional, she assumes he can make himself available during the day and even presumes to moralize at him, something he is probably not used to from a woman, about several hours of work being more important than his daughter" (57). As well, the counsellor hides behind school policy to excuse herself from accommodating an evening meeting. Finally, the counsellor has a narrow definition of family and has no appreciation of the appropriateness of the brother-in-law's presence. In Hispanic culture, godfathers are responsible for the spiritual welfare of their godchildren. In the eyes of this family, the girl was experiencing a serious spiritual crisis.

This case serves as a reminder to counsellors to be mindful of imposing their cultural values and expectations on clients. The Martinez family was clearly victimized by a culture-bound system that was unresponsive to their needs and wants. The very system that was designed to help them became oppressive. Its representative, the school counsellor, reached inaccurate and insulting conclusions because she was unable to view the Martinez family from their own frame of reference.

CONVERSATION 8.1

SAYING NO

STUDENT: What are some ways to say "no" to clients? I really hate it when I have to deny them what they want or need.

TEACHER: That's my reaction too. None of us in the helping professions wants to be seen as harsh or uncaring. Saying "no" may evoke feelings of guilt in us, as well as strong negative reactions from our clients. We really need to be able address our own emotions as well as the clients.

STUDENT: I suppose it's a reality of the business. Sometimes we have to make tough decisions such as, "Who gets the training money" and, "Who qualifies for assistance." In the residential part of the program where I work, we often have to say "no" when the kids want exceptions to the rules. No problem when you're able to give clients what they want. But what about when you have to turn down requests?

TEACHER: Even when you are saying "no" it's important that clients know you care. You need to listen and be available to respond with empathy and compassion. Find a way to show you understand, even if you are not able to give your clients what they want. Or, see if there is a way to compromise to help your client save face. What do you think?

STUDENT: I've learned a couple of things: Be direct, clear, and brief. Don't waffle, hint, or avoid the "bottom line." With kids, I've found that even when they test the limits, they may need limits and even welcome them when imposed. It increases their sense of safety and control when they learn the boundaries of acceptable behaviour.

TEACHER: I agree. I think it's important that you don't make a hasty retreat. Expect that anger, defensiveness, and counterattack are the ways that some clients respond to frustration. In extreme situations, you need to protect yourself. Anticipate potentially violent situations and take defensive action. Be sure to debrief with a colleague or supervisor after difficult encounters. If necessary, take a break to insure that your reactions do not contaminate your ability to deal with your next client objectively. Finally, remind yourself that no matter how your client reacts, you must stay in professional role.

STUDENT: When someone says "no" to me, I find it a lot easier to accept if I know why. So, I try to explain my rationale, or the policy. Then, I invite questions.

TEACHER: If you can, help your client identify other ways to meet their needs.

POTENTIALLY DANGEROUS CLIENTS

The deadliest form of violence is poverty.
—Gandhi

Many counsellors are employed by agencies in which their work may include some elements of social control (e.g., probation, involuntary clients, establishing eligibility). The nature of this work may leave counsellors increasingly vulnerable to violence (Newhill, 1995). For example, a counsellor's denial of a client's request for financial assistance may evoke retaliation.

Hospital emergency rooms are particularly dangerous places for social workers, counsellors, and other health-care professionals (Lanza et al., 1996). In one case, a 27-year-old social worker was shot, without provocation, while interviewing a client in a psychiatric emergency room, and in another case a social worker was stabbed to death by her client in her office (Newhill, 1995).

Although some statistical studies suggest that societal violence may be decreasing at a modest rate, anecdotal and some empirical evidence suggests that most of those who work in the counselling field admit that issues of personal safety are an increasing concern (Newhill, 1995). A study at one private psychiatric hospital found that the frequency of violence by male patients was 50 percent higher than a decade ago and that violence by female patients was 150 percent higher than a decade ago (Tardiff et al., 1997). Newhill's review of the literature supported the conclusion that violence against social workers is increasing. In part, this is because "social workers handle frontline situations that previous generations of workers did not encounter (for example, increased violence attributed to female, elderly, and deinstitutionalized clients and new intervention roles in domestic violence situations, police-social worker teams, custody and divorce mediation, and emergency room work)" (1995:632).

Sometimes counsellors fear their clients because their behaviour is threatening or they have a history of violent behaviour. At other times, counsellors' fears are based on intuition or hunches, the internal response to subtle signals that all is not well. In fact, some clients provide abundant reasons for fear, either because of intimidating behaviour or overtly violent acts.

Intimidating behaviour includes name calling; obscene or sexually harassing language and gestures; shouting; threatening displays of power such as fist shaking; invasion of personal space; stalking; and verbal threats. Clients also behave in an intimidating manner when they won't take no for an answer or when they refuse to leave the office. As well, clients may attack workers with personal insults, or they may intimidate them with threats to call the newspaper or civil rights groups. In general, intimidating behaviour should be controlled or managed in order to prevent escalation to violence. The following case examples of threatening behaviour are all based on real incidents:

- A new client to a welfare office says, "If I don't get some help, you'll be sorry."
- A man in his late 20s stares obstinately at an intake worker.
- An angry parent tells a child protection worker that if his child is not returned the worker will know what it's like to lose someone you love.
- A teenager in a group home refuses to comply with house rules. He tells his child-care counsellor, "I've had enough. Things are going to change around here."
- A parole officer meets a new parolee for the first time. He is pleasant and cooperative, but the parole officer can't ignore the fact that this man has a long history of assault charges and is known to have a short fuse.
- A mental health counsellor deals with her client, a young male with a history of self-destructive behaviour. It is obvious that he is not taking his medication, and he seems unusually agitated.
- A 10-year-old child who witnessed abuse at home grabs a pair of scissors and lunges toward the counsellor.

Violent behaviour means hitting, pushing, biting, slapping, kicking, throwing objects, and using weapons such as guns, knives, or syringes. It also refers to kidnapping and stalking.

- A social worker in a hospital emergency ward is threatened with a syringe by an angry HIV-positive patient.
- An angry client picks up a chair and hurls it at the counsellor.
- A client, disgruntled with the counsellor's refusal to provide him with money, spits in the counsellor's face.

It is important that counsellors do not become hypervigilant and conduct their work in constant fear. Such a stance makes it difficult for them to separate actual hazards from situations that present no real risk. Unwarranted fear of clients leads to uninformed responses. Though very real dangers exist in the workplace, by and large it is a place of safety. The challenge is to be able to answer some basic questions:

- Which clients are likely to become violent? What are the indicators of potential violence?
- Under what conditions should a client's anger be cause for concern?
- What are the skills and behaviours that can be used to de-escalate dangerous situations?

Predicting Violence

Violence rarely arises from a single cause (Roth, 1987). A complex array of psychological, social, biological, and physiological factors must be considered when assessing potential for violence. Although certain variables may be isolated as more likely risk factors, risk assessment is difficult. Every person has a unique history and circumstances, so it is difficult to predict who will become violent. There is no foolproof way to predict with certainty who is likely to become violent.

Violence may be perceived as a desperate act by an angry client to regain control and power. Multiple stressors such as poverty, the loss or absence of supportive relationships, and substance abuse may magnify a client's vulnerability. These clients may be under considerable stress and near the breaking point. Counsellors may be in positions of authority and may have to deny clients access to goods or services. Clients may perceive such denials as further threats to their fragile power, and the risk of violence may escalate. Kaplan and Wheeler suggest that "this denial may be seen not only as a personal rejection but also as a denial of his or her power as a person. This may trigger an uncontrollable need for self-assertion" (1983:343). Attacking others works as a psychological defence against feelings of shame and humiliation.

Key variables that have been found to have some validity for predicting violence include (1) past and current behaviour, (2) substance abuse, (3) age and gender, and (4) personality.

Past and Current Behaviour. The best predictor of future violence is a history of violence, and the more recent and severe the violent behaviour, the greater the risk. Kelleher's conclusion that a history of violent behaviour should always be given serious consideration is echoed consistently in the research on violence: "Although the argument can be made that historical evidence of violence is not a guaranty of future violent behavior, an understanding of any form of violent criminal activity clearly supports the contention that a history of violence is often a predictor of future violence" (1997:13).

Counsellors should be particularly interested in noting how a client has handled difficulties and frustrations in the past. Some clients who were victims of abuse as children grow up without a capacity for warmth and empathy for others, which can make them particularly oblivious to the suffering of others (Roth, 1987; Weaver, 1982). In extreme cases, violence may even bring these clients pleasure or sexual gratification. Counsellors should be interested in the level of remorse that clients show for past acts of violence. Clearly, counsellors should be most concerned about clients who show no regret. On the other hand, clients who have learned other ways of managing their anger now have more choices and are less likely to act out physically. In this respect, it might be revealing for counsellors to explore how their clients are managing stress outside the counselling relationship. For example, do they show evidence of a lack of concern for the safety of others? Are there indicators of inappropriate or uncontrolled anger? Are they typically extremely defensive, irritable, or self-centred? To what extent are they prone to impulsive behaviour? Impulsive clients might assure counsellors that they have no intent to harm anyone but 10 minutes later attack another client in the waiting room. As Newhill suggests, this type of client has no control over immediate urges, and if the counsellor points out that his or her behaviour may harm others, the client will not disagree, "but neither will he or she constructively integrate what is said" (1992:74).

Clients who have a specific plan of violent action and the means to carry it out represent an immediate risk of violent behaviour. Counsellors need to consider their professional obligations and legal requirements to warn any intended victim by examining their codes of ethics, as well as relevant legislation or legal precedent.

Substance Abuse. Common sense and empirical research suggest that intoxicated and agitated clients should be approached cautiously. Reviewing the role of drugs in violence, Roth (1987:13–14) concludes:

• Hallucinogens such as LSD and PCP, glue sniffing, amphetamines, and barbiturates have been associated with aggressive and homicidal behaviour.

• Narcotics tend to suppress violence, but individuals might become violent in order to get these drugs.

• Alcohol has a disinhibiting effect on behaviour and is implicated as the most frequent drug linked to violence.

Newhill reviewed the available research and recorded that certain drugs subdue aggression, whereas others escalate it. "Anticholinergics, antipsychotics, antidepressants, sedative hypnotics, and analgesics tend to suppress aggression. Amphetamines and withdrawal from drugs such as morphine or alcohol induce aggression" (1992:70).

Many studies link substance abuse to violent behaviour (Swanson et al., 1997; Tardiff et al., 1997). Moreover, people who abuse drugs are at an increased risk of victimization (Conway, 1996). The link between drug abuse and violent behaviour may arise, at least in part, from the fact that alcohol and other drugs are more likely to be abused in a dangerous place.

Age and Gender. The vast majority of people who are violent and who have been arrested for violent behaviour are male. The highest risk for violence is found in people from 15 to 39 years of age; in this age group, the rate of violent acts is three times that of the general population (Roth, 1987; Weaver, 1992).

Personality. Roth (1987) says that it is important to consider clients' self-esteem to assess their capacity for introspection and their tolerance for ambiguity. Some clients deal with their sense of personal fragility by lashing out at others, and they are hypervigilant in protecting themselves from perceived threats from others.

De Becker cautions that some people assume the worst possible motives and character and that they write their own scripts: "The Scriptwriter is the type of person who asks you a question, answers it himself, then walks away angry at what you said ... The things that go wrong are the work of others who will try to blame him. People are out to get him, period" (1997:148–49).

These clients believe that you are uncaring and out to get them. Whatever counsellors do and however caring their actions, these clients will react based on their expectations. They may try to control the relationship through manipulation and intimidation. This behaviour should be interpreted as a warning signal only. These clients may not escalate to violence.

Violence and Mental Illness

The question of whether people with mental illnesses are more dangerous than the general public continues to be the subject of research, debate, and controversy. A study conducted by Davis (1991) concludes that the answers to whether mentally ill people are more dangerous is uncertain. Although his review of the literature found a higher arrest rate for people with mental disorders, he notes that "a small criminal subset, perhaps wrongly diverted into the mental health system, may account for most of the offenses in the dangerousness studies" (177). Moreover, when "this subset is considered separately, most offenses by the rest of the mentally ill population are petty" (177) and arise from similar factors to those with the general public.

Newspaper headlines underscore the dangers that persons with mental illnesses present to their communities:

- "Paranoid Woman Involved in Standoff"
- "Policeman Killed by Ex-Mental Hospital Patient"
- "Schizophrenic Man Kills Wife, Then Turns Gun on Himself"
- "Voices Told Me to Kill My Child"

Not surprisingly, many people believe that there is a strong link between mental illness and violence, but advocate groups argue that the media, through selective and exaggerated reporting, have stimulated the development of false assumptions about the dangers of people with mental illnesses.

In recent decades, deinstitutionalization of psychiatric patients has resulted in unprecedented numbers of people with mental illnesses in the community. Clients with a history of severe mental illness and violence who stop taking their medications can be very dangerous, particularly if they have command hallucinations (voices and images directing them to be violent).

Harris and Rice reviewed risk appraisal work on the prediction of violence and conclude that "the factors most highly and consistently related to risk of violent behavior are historical and include age, sex, past antisocial and violent conduct, psychopathy, aggressive childhood behavior, and substance abuse. Major mental disorder and psychiatric disturbance are poor predictors of violence" (1997:1168).

Another study (Swanson et al., 1997) confirms the links between violent behaviour and substance abuse, particularly when there has been absence of recent contact with mental health service providers. A recent study concluded that predictions of violence based on a history of violence were more accurate than clinical predictions based on diagnosis (Gardner et al., 1996).

A comprehensive follow-up study of patients discharged from psychiatric hospitals concluded that former patients who do not abuse drugs are no more violent than a random population sample (Bower, 1998). Pastor concluded that unrealistic and delusional thinking tends to increase the likelihood that violence will result. He also noted, "Manic symptoms, such as irritability, increased energy or activity, psychomotor agitation and grandiosity, also increases the risk of violent behavior. A belief that 'others' are responsible for the person's misfortune increases the likelihood of striking out against those persons" (1995:1173).

Organic brain disease and head trauma may reduce a client's impulse control and cause him or her to act in ways that are dangerous to self and others. Organic disease or injury should be suspected when clients show disturbance in attention, orientation, and short-term memory (Dubovsky and Weissberg, 1986:258).

Assessing Potential for Violence

Although long-term prediction of violence is difficult, counsellors should be able to make reasonable short-term forecasts based on consideration and assessment of the following questions and issues:

1. Does the client have a history of violent behaviour and/or an arrest record for violent crime? The counsellor should review agency file records and other anecdotal evidence for information.

2. To what extent does the client appear dangerous, as evidenced by marked or escalating agitation or threatening behaviour? The counsellor should consider verbal threats as well as nonverbal expressions of aggression.

3. If the client is threatening violence, are the threats concrete and specific? Does the client have a plan? Does the client have the means to carry out the stated plan? Does the client have a weapon or access to one, especially a gun?

4. Is the client under duress from one or more stressors, such as poverty, unemployment, or loss of social support? Has there been a recent precipitating event that represents the last straw for the client?

5. What agency factors might be exacerbating the situation (e.g., missed or delayed appointments, denial of benefits)?

6. What counsellor variables might be heightening the client's anger? Is the counsellor acting in ways that the client might see as provocative? For example, is the counsellor defensive or judgmental toward the client?

7. What high-risk symptoms are present? For example, is the client experiencing command hallucinations? Is the client prone to impulsivity? Is the client near panic? Is the client narcissistic or self-centred and prone to blame others for his or her misfortune? Is the client hypersensitive to any criticism or hint of rejection?

8. Is there evidence of substance abuse?

9. Has the client failed to take psychiatric medication? Has the client cut off or failed to keep scheduled contact with a psychiatric caregiver?

10. Does the client believe that he or she is able to control his or her behaviour? Is the client socially isolated?

These questions are references for the purpose of assessment only. The presence of any of the factors does not mean that the client will necessarily become violent. However, when there are numerous strong clues that suggest violence, counsellors should proceed cautiously and look for ways to reduce risk factors to establish safety.

Preventing Violence

Many clients come to counselling in a state of crisis, with low tolerance for added stress. Consequently, it is important that agency policies and routines do not compound the risk. Congested and noisy waiting rooms, unexplained delays for appointments, insensitive receptionists, and indifference to the clients' right to privacy can exacerbate frustration. Nevertheless, even when these factors are controlled, counsellors may have to deny assistance, and clients may believe that they are denying them access to goods or services. These clients may perceive themselves as "losers" and look for ways to save face, including resistance, with statements such as "I don't have to put up with this treatment."

Agency Safety Precautions. In settings where there is significant risk for violence, procedures should be developed for dealing with potentially violent clients. In fact, employers usually have a legal responsibility to provide a safe working environment. Minimum safety precautions might include the following:

Policy. Agencies should develop policies and procedures for dealing with potentially violent situations. The agencies should review these policies regularly and incorporate them as part of in-service training for new staff. Policies should address issues such as the procedures for home visits, giving clients home phone numbers, using last names, and interviewing after hours. Generally, counsellors should not make home visits alone if there is a possibility for violence. Many counsellors who work with potentially dangerous clients use unlisted phone numbers as a way to ensure privacy and safety. In extreme situations, such as dangerous child abuse investigations, counsellors may need to be protected by police. Generally, counsellors should avoid making unescorted visits to high—crime areas, and only those counsellors with legal authority to do so should be investigating allegations of child abuse or neglect.

Staff Training. Training should address tactics for dealing with difficult clients, including those who are involuntary, angry, or acting out. Front office and reception staff should also be trained so that they can relate to clients in ways that do not escalate the clients' frustration or anger. Periodic team simulations will ensure that everyone is familiar with their roles and responsibilities. This prevents members of the team from becoming confused during a critical incident. Simulations also help staff to build confidence in themselves and trust that their colleagues are ready and available to assist.

Interviewing Procedures. Counsellors who are interviewing difficult or dangerous clients should work in offices where access to immediate help can be provided. A silent system for alerting others that a dangerous situation is developing should be implemented (e.g., panic button, encrypted phone message). Leaving the door open during the interview can allow other staff to monitor any increasing danger, but this practice may violate the client's confidentiality. Counsellors should make sure that clients have a clear path to the doorway so they can leave abruptly if they choose.

Files on clients with a history of violence should clearly document details of any past violent behaviour or threats. For some clients with a high propensity toward violence, a team approach may be desirable, with two or more persons being present during the interview. In such cases, it is usually preferable if only one person does the interviewing. This can lessen any feelings the client might have of being ganged up on. Too many people may heighten the client's anxiety. Backup help can be stationed out of sight but on quick standby for dangerous situations.

Office Design. Office furnishings should be carefully chosen to minimize risk. For example, shatterproof glass can be used, and items that are potential weapons, such as scissors, should be removed. Soft lighting and calming colours may have some modest effect on mood. As noted earlier, counsellors and clients should have an unobstructed path to the exit. The agency itself should have good external lighting. During high-risk hours, such as late at night or early in the morning, access doors should be locked, and workers should not have to walk alone to dark parking lots.

Crisis Intervention. A written script for staff that must call police or emergency backup intervention will ensure that relevant information is presented quickly and clearly. In a panic situation, people may forget basic information, such as emergency phone numbers. After a violent or hostile act, it is important to have a mechanism for debriefing. This enables the counsellor to restore a sense of equilibrium. It is important to remember that a critical incident may also affect staff who were not directly involved, including clerical, janitorial, and kitchen personnel. They too may suffer trauma. Therefore, they should be involved in the debriefing.

The Phases of Violence

The National Crisis Prevention Institute (1986) has identified four **phases of violence** that describe how crises escalate to violence (see Table 8.2 on page 253). Each phase is characterized by particular indicators and demands specific responses. In applying this or any other model, it is important to remember that individual incidents may not conform to the model. The four phases are (1) anxiety, (2) defensiveness, (3) acting out, and (4) tension reduction.

Anxiety Phase. In the anxiety phase there is a marked change in the client's behaviour. This phase represents an early warning that the client is becoming agitated. The individual may show increased signs of anxiety, including verbal challenges such as refusal to follow directions or questioning of authority. Statements such as "You can't tell me what to do," accompanied by finger pointing, may suggest escalating anger. Shea (1988) cautions that other signs of escalation, such as pacing, intense staring, and refusing to sit down, should be noted. At this point, the client may respond to gentle directives and invitations, such as "Let's talk and see if we can work things out" and "I'm willing to listen." This phase offers counsellors the best opportunity to intervene early to prevent anger from intensifying into acting-out behaviour.

Usually, clients enter the anxiety phase because of stress, which can come from multiple sources, including jobs, relationships, health, and finances. Clients define stressful events; thus, counsellors cannot measure stress just by knowing the facts about a situation.

What one client might see as an opportunity another might experience as a threat. Kelleher describes the triggering event as an incident that pushes the potentially violent person toward violence: "It is the proverbial 'straw that broke the camel's back' and, like the straw, may often be perceived by others with far less significance than it's perceived by the perpetrator" (1997:11). Before clients see counsellors, they may already be feeling helpless and abandoned. Any counsellor behaviour that the client views as provocative or rejecting may further propel the client toward violence.

Individuals who are predisposed to violence respond to stress with increasing anger and anxiety. A person's emotional reaction can also influence whether he or she might become violent. Labig observes:

> Emotional reactions that make it more likely that a person will become violent in reaction to a stressful situation are anger, hatred, blame, and terror. People who typically react emotionally in these ways are at higher risk of escalating into violence. Emotional reactions can also intervene to inhibit an individual's behavior. Empathy and guilt make it less likely that a person will strike out. (1995:24–25)

Dealing with Threats. Gavin de Becker, an expert on predicting violent behaviour, offers this strategy for dealing with threats:

> When any type of threat includes indirect or veiled references to things they might do, such as "You'll be sorry," or "Don't mess with me," it is best to ask directly, "What do you mean by that?" Ask exactly what the person is threatening to do. His elaboration will almost always be weaker than his implied threat. If, on the other hand, his explanation of the comment is actually an explicit threat, better to learn it now than to be uncertain later. (1997:117)

Counsellors need to take action when clients exhibit changes in their normal behaviour. This action could include referral for psychiatric assessment and reevaluation of medication. Immediate crisis intervention might result in moving the client out of the environment where others might be injured, for example, a crowded waiting room. As well, long-term counselling might focus on anger management or relaxation training. The immediate goal is crisis management, but the long-term goal is crisis prevention.

Counsellors should be attuned to their own fears and anxieties. Appropriate anxiety is a clue that the situation is escalating and that remedial action is necessary. De Becker (1997) argues that people have a basic intuition that tells them when all is not well, but that they often disregard the red flags of danger. It is only in the aftermath that they reflect and realize that they had sufficient information to make better choices but that they ignored it.

Defensiveness Phase. This is a late warning phase with clear indicators that the person is about to lose control. The client may become more challenging and belligerent by making direct threats and provocations. The client has become irrational, and clear warning indicators may be present, including clenching or raising of fists, grasping objects to use as weapons, and showing signs of movement toward attack (e.g., grasping the arms of the chair, denoting that they are about to rise and advance) (Shea, 1988:172).

At this point, it is crucial that counsellors refrain from reciprocating with the same aggressive behaviour that the client is using. This requires some discipline, as the counsellor's natural reaction might be to respond in kind, which only serves to escalate or precipitate violence. Decreased eye contact might be appropriate with some clients. As well, counsellors are wise to increase the physical distance between them and their clients, since potentially violent persons may have an increased need for space. Physical contact, however well intentioned, should be avoided. Sometimes counsellors try to calm clients by touching their shoulders, but this is ill advised, as clients may interpret it as aggression.

At this phase, counsellors need to be self-disciplined and remain calm. This calmness should be reflected in their voice and manner and in slow, nonjargonistic language. Counsellors who speak calmly and avoid any loud or authoritarian tone may have a contagious effect on their anxious clients. On the other hand, counsellors who match their clients' defensiveness and anger exacerbate the situation and increase the possibility of violent retaliation.

Defusing Explosive Situations. When dealing with clients who are hostile and on the verge of losing control, it is essential that counsellors maintain their own equilibrium and remain in control. Counsellors need to resist any tendency to be baited by clients into angry confrontation or retaliation, which only escalates the crisis. Moreover, if clients perceive that their counsellors are not in control, they may become more irrational.

Basic communication and counselling skills are excellent tools for both preventing violence and for dealing with clients who are on the verge of losing control. In particular, active listening skills communicate that counsellors are willing to listen to and learn about clients' wants and needs. Counsellors should remember the importance of modelling. When counsellors stay calm, clients are more likely to emulate their composure. Counsellors should try to speak calmly and avoid any mannerisms that clients might interpret as threatening (e.g., touching a client, making sudden movements, or invading a client's personal space). "Encourage the client to sit and to be comfortable. Listen, empathize, paraphrase, and summarize while avoiding defensiveness. With clients who are exhibiting early warning signs such as a noticeable escalation of anxiety, supportive and empathic responses are best, whereas an authoritarian (rigid) stance may leave the client feeling pressured or trapped" (Shebib, 1997:246).

However, some clients may misinterpret empathy as an unwanted intrusion on personal privacy and react defensively. Counsellors should be alert to clients' reactions to certain topics or questions. This will help counsellors make intelligent decisions about when it is appropriate to challenge or confront and when they should back off because the subject is clearly agitating their clients to a dangerous level. Counsellors should be careful that they don't overreact and should avoid interview topics that could be controversial.

Promoting Compromise. Clients often feel disempowered and disadvantaged. When counsellors promote compromise, they restore some balance of power in the relationship and show their willingness to reach a solution. When counsellors argue with, threaten, or ignore the needs of their clients, the clients may become increasingly belligerent. As Dubovsky and Weissberg conclude, the client "protects himself from feeling powerless, inadequate and frightened by attempting to demonstrate how powerful and frightening he can be" (1986:262).

Counsellors need to help clients find a way to save face and retain their dignity. While counsellors have the responsibility to set appropriate limits, they must not argue with, ridicule, challenge, threaten, or unfairly criticize clients. The language used by the counsellor can help to establish an atmosphere of compromise and mutual problem solving—for example, "Let's work together to find a solution we can both live with" and "I really do want to find a solution."

CLIENT: *(yelling loudly) I'm sick and tired of getting the runaround.*

COUNSELLOR: *(calmly) Your anger makes it clear to me how strongly you feel about this. I can see that this is an important issue for you. But we will work better if you stay calm and don't threaten. Let's see if there's another way to approach it.*

CLIENT: *(pacing and yelling) Are you going to help me or not?*

COUNSELLOR: *(calmly) I'm willing to work at this problem to solve it.*

(client sits, stares intently)

COUNSELLOR: *I understand that you think that this is the best solution. I also appreciate your reasoning. But there are two of us here. We need to find a solution that both of us can be satisfied with.*

CLIENT: *(loud, but not yelling) I'm trying to be reasonable.*

COUNSELLOR: *Okay, I'm listening. I'd like to hear your ideas on how to ...*

Hocker and Wilmot identify five principles for establishing effective collaboration: (1) join with the other, (2) control the process, not the people, (3) use productive communication, (4) be firm in your goals, flexible in your means, and (5) remain optimistic about finding solutions to your conflict (1995:212). They suggest a variety of means for operationalizing the principles, such as using "we" language that affirms common interests, actively listening even when you disagree, and persuading rather than coercing. As well, they emphasize the importance of separating the issues from the relationship and dealing with the important items one at a time. Such a collaborative approach requires that counsellors remain positive, creative, and constructive. The general goal must be "We, working together, can solve this problem that is confronting us" (Hocker and Wilmot, 1995:205). Dubovsky and Weissberg (1986) underscore the importance of promoting collaboration. They contend that the client "protects himself from feeling powerless, inadequate and frightened by attempting to demonstrate how powerful and frightening he can be. His threatening behavior increases if he feels he is not being taken seriously" (262).

Labig (1995) says that some people can react with intense emotion because of the emotional tone with which they are addressed. Similarly, intimidating body language such as crossed arms, staring, or a fighting stance can have the same effect.

> A loud, intense, and menacing voice can create an instantaneous emotional response in certain people. This is all it takes to push some people into retaliatory action ... Generally, the more emotionally calm and safe an individual feels, the less likely he is to become violent. The more frightening and threatening he finds his environment, the more likely he is to respond with violence. (Labig, 1995:25)

Setting Limits. In the defensive phase, clients may still respond to appropriate limits. Limits let clients know what will and what will not be tolerated, but counsellors need to apply certain principles in setting limits. Counsellors should be specific and tell clients which behaviour is inappropriate. Clients may not be aware of what is acceptable. Moreover, they may not know how their behaviour is affecting others. Limits should include enforceable consequences, and counsellors should state the consequences of noncompliance.

Clients, particularly those in institutional settings, may rely on staff to assist them with controls and limits. However, "if staff become overly anxious while managing a violent patient, the potentiality for that patient's violence increases" (Roth, 1987:246). Thus, it is important for counsellors to understand how their own behaviour may escalate a client's potential for violence. Furthermore, counsellors need to learn how to monitor their own feelings, when to ask for help, and when to terminate an interaction because they are not in control (Roth, 1987).

Acting-out Phase. At this stage, the client has lost control and has become assaultive. Protection of self and others is the primary goal. Ideally, agency procedures are operative, and counsellors who are dealing with such situations will receive immediate assistance from the staff team. Police intervention and restraint of the acting-out client may also be required. When dealing with acting-out clients, a team approach with a well-organized and trained staff is the preferred way to address the crisis. A team approach provides increased safety for everyone, including the client. A well-trained team may subdue violent clients before they injure themselves or others, but staff should be trained in techniques for physical restraint and control (for a brief description of physical control techniques see Roth, 1987:254). The team members provide support and can act as witnesses if litigation should arise as a result of the incident.

Police Intervention. Counsellors should not hesitate to call the police if a client becomes too threatening or aggressive. No counsellor is expected to risk his or her life or endure physical assault as part of the job. Sometimes clients are unwilling or unable to constrain their hostility, and police or psychiatric restraint is essential for managing the crisis. Police intervention is particularly crucial when dealing with clients who have weapons. Counsellors should not try to prevent a client who is determined to leave by blocking the exit. Counsellors who are assaulted by clients should consider laying criminal charges. This establishes the importance of clients' taking responsibility for their actions.

Tension Reduction Phase. The tension reduction, or recovery, phase is characterized by a gradual reduction in aggressive behaviour and a return to more rational behaviour. The client may still be driven by adrenalin for up to 90 minutes (Kaplan and Wheeler, 1983), so it is important that counsellors proceed cautiously to avoid reactivating aggressive acting out.

Follow-up Counselling Interventions. Clients can be counselled to become alert to their own warning signs, such as "tenseness, sweating palms, a tightening of the stomach, pressure in the chest and a surge to the head" (Morrissey, 1998:6). Once clients are aware of their own triggers, they can be counselled on appropriate diversionary tactics, such as employing relaxation techniques, taking time out, and using **assertiveness** and other behavioural response alternatives. Morrissey describes a technique that a counsellor used with a client who was on the verge of violence. The counsellor reassured the client "that he was there to help him and commended the client for coming to see him rather than acting on his feelings of rage. He also asked the client what was keeping him in control thus far and used that as proof to reinforce the fact that he could indeed control himself" (1998:6).

At the end of the tension reduction phase and after the client has returned to normal, the client may be mentally and physically exhausted and show signs of remorse and shame. Consequently, counselling can be directed toward helping the client use the experience as a learning opportunity, for example, to develop alternative responses for future similar stresses. Interview 8.2 provides an example.

Because of their communication skills training, counsellors are well prepared to teach their clients techniques for resolving conflict and crises nonviolently. The skills of counselling are also, to some extent, the skills of effective everyday communication. Communication skill training equips clients with more choices for asserting their rights and respecting others. Assertiveness training can help clients express feelings in a nonaggressive manner. When clients are able to respond assertively, they establish an atmosphere of cooperation and conflict can be peacefully resolved. Often conflict is difficult for clients to settle because they are unable to see the perspectives or feelings of others in the conflict. Clients who learn empathy and other active listening skills are better able to compromise because they are less likely to judge their own behaviour as absolutely right and that of others as absolutely wrong.

Sometimes, long before violence erupts, counsellors intuitively feel that the situation is worsening. This feeling may be based on unconscious reactions to subtle cues and indicators. Counsellors and clients might find it useful to try to concretely identify these clues.

Doing so will assist clients in becoming sensitive to those initial psychological responses that signal the imminent onset of the anxiety phase. Clients who become adept at recognizing early warning indicators are in a much better position to take early warning action, such as withdrawing from an explosive situation or switching to healthier problem-solving strategies.

Critical Incident Debriefing

Counsellors who have been assaulted or threatened with assault may be traumatized and experience symptoms such as recurrent images or thoughts of the event, distressing dreams, flashbacks, and intense stress when returning to the scene of the incident. There may be a marked decline in their ability to handle routine work tasks, and they may feel detached and isolated from colleagues. They may develop sleep difficulties and have difficulty concentrating. Frequently, they return to work in a state of hypervigilance, constantly expecting further trauma. Often they describe themselves as "numb" and unable to enjoy activities that usually gave them pleasure. When symptoms such as these are present, counsellors should consider obtaining medical assessment and/or professional counselling.

Even when counsellors are not injured, the threat of violence can be just as traumatic. Typical responses may include helplessness and thoughts of leaving the profession. These feelings may develop immediately or emerge after a delay of months or even years. Consequently, it is important to debrief critical incidents in order to lessen the shock, reduce isolation, and restore personal control. Team debriefing should take place as soon as possible after the incident. As well, some affected staff may require private debriefing. It is important that everyone, not just the professional staff, be included as a member of the team. Support and other front office staff, for example, are often intimately involved in a crisis.

Debriefing should be conducted by an objective third party in a safe setting. It should be held as soon as possible after the critical incident, usually within 24 to 72 hours in order to minimize the effects of any trauma that victims or witnesses may be experiencing. This is important in order to promote a return to the normal routine of the agency. A typical debriefing session is like a counselling interview. The debriefing should reinforce team

---

INTERVIEW 8.2 **FOLLOW-UP TO A VIOLENT INCIDENT**

In the following example, the counsellor, a group-home worker, is reviewing an incident with her client. The incident occurred two hours ago and was precipitated when the counsellor denied the client, a 16-year-old male, permission to meet with some of his friends later that night. The client smashed an ashtray on the floor and stormed out of the office while screaming obscenities.

DIALOGUE	ANALYSIS
Counsellor: Let's talk about what happened. Client: I guess I got a bit carried away. Counsellor: I was scared. Client: I'm sorry. I won't let it happen again.	Whenever possible, it's important that clients be invited to review prior incidents. By telling the client how she felt, the counsellor may be giving the client new information that will increase the client's capacity for empathy. Often, violent or acting-out clients are so preoccupied with their own needs and fears that they don't realize the impact they have on others.
Counsellor: I accept your apology.	This helps the client to retain some dignity. Notice that the counsellor's acceptance of her client's apology does not condone his behaviour, as would a statement such as "It's okay. Don't worry about it. No real harm was done."
Counsellor: It might be helpful for both of us to go over what happened to see how it might have been prevented. Client: I was still upset from seeing my mother. When you said no, it was just too much.	One goal of counselling is to help clients recognize their own early warning indicators that they are in danger of losing control.
Counsellor: It's never been easy for you to talk to your mom. You always seem to come back really wound up.	Empathy confirms that feelings have been heard and understood.
Client: Yeah, those are the days that people should stay out of my face.	The client rationalizes his behaviour, putting the responsibility on others.
Counsellor: Good point. Sounds like you know that you need some time alone when you're stressed. Client: You got it.	Without directly challenging the rationalization, the counsellor shifts the focus back on the client.
Counsellor: As we talk, I'm wondering what prevented you from taking that time. If you'd	Feedback confrontation challenges the client to consider some new alternatives.

(continued)

taken the time to cool off before approaching me, things would have been a lot different.

Client: Sure, I know I have to learn to control my temper, but once I get going I just can't seem to stop myself.

Counsellor: Put another way, your hope is to find a way to deal with your feelings so that you don't get angry and hurt someone.

The counsellor takes advantage of an opportunity to reframe the client's problem statement into a goal.

Client: I don't know if that's possible.

Counsellor: You've already shown me that you have some skill at doing this. You threw the ashtray and you said some awful things, but afterward you left the room without doing any more damage. This tells me that you have the ability to bring things under control. You need to find a way to do this a little earlier.

Acknowledgment of the client's restraint, however late he was in using it, provides a base for further development. By doing so, the counsellor reinforces nonaggressive behavioural alternatives.

interdependence. Sometimes counsellors are reluctant to ask colleagues for assistance, believing that asking for help is a sign of incompetence. One goal of a debriefing is to develop a staff culture in which asking for help is a sign of strength, rather than weakness. A critical incident debriefing generally has the following elements:

1. All team members are invited to share feelings and reactions about the current or prior incidents. Active listening can be used to promote this process. This will help individuals who were threatened or assaulted to "normalize" their own reactions. Counsellors should require little persuasion of the benefits of talking about one's feelings. They might be reminded that sharing feelings is something they routinely ask of their clients. Helping team members manage feelings is the major objective of the debriefing. At this time, it is important to identify the potential physical and emotional reactions that staff may experience. As well, information regarding services such as employee assistance programs (EAP's) that are available to staff who need additional help to manage their emotions should be detailed.

2. The team conducts a postmortem on the violent event. A thorough analysis of what transpired is used to review and reinforce procedures for dealing with violent clients. An important question for the team to consider is: "What, if anything, could we have done to prevent this incident?" For example, the team can explore whether any early warning indicators of pending violence were overlooked. They can investigate whether there were things that individuals or the agency did or did not do that contributed to the client's behaviour.

3. The team debriefing is an important "teachable moment," when staff are highly motivated toward skill development. It is a chance to explore alternative responses that might have been utilized at all stages of the critical incident. Role plays and simulations can be used to practise alternative responses. This step helps empower individuals and the team by moving them away from any tendency to feel helpless.

Table 8.2 The Phases of Violence

Phase	Strategy Choice
Preventive	Recognize risk factors. Structure the agency to reduce client stress and danger to personnel. Set up emergency response protocols. Practise crisis responses with simulations. Take steps to protect identified intended victims.
Anxiety phase	Promote clients' involvement in decision making to give them a sense of empowerment and control. Attend to changes in the clients' behaviour. Take gut instincts and threats seriously. Use empathy and reassurance to acknowledge and attend to the clients' needs.
Defensiveness phase	Set clear, reasonable, and enforceable limits. Respect clients' need for increased space. Remain calm and avoid sudden movement. Avoid using an authoritarian tone. Respond assertively. Use basic counselling skills. Search for compromises and "win-win" solutions.
Acting out phase	Call the police (do not try to disarm clients who have weapons and do not risk personal safety unless unavoidable). Try to ensure the safety of everyone, including bystanders, other staff, and the client. Use a team approach, including, if necessary and appropriate, physical restraint. Refer clients to hospital for assessment and/or medication. Try to reestablish verbal communication.
Tension reduction phase	Support the client's return to a state of calm. Re-establish communication. Elicit available family support.
Follow-up	Involve clients in long-term counselling. Help clients learn nonviolent solutions to problems. Implement consequences, if any. Conduct individual and team debriefing. When clients have plans to harm a specific victim, warn the victim and/or notify the police. Review procedures for handling disruptive clients.

Summary

Resistance is a defensive reaction by clients that interferes with or delays the process of counselling. Client resistance to counselling is common. It may be evident in a variety of ways, such as failure to cooperate with the basic routine of counselling, subtle or direct attacks, passivity, and nonverbal cues. Resistance arises for a number of reasons that may be categorized under five major groupings: (1) relationship, (2) motivational, (3) attitudinal, (4) fearful, and (5) involuntary. Counsellors can use a range of techniques for dealing with each of the five types. Client resistance may be unconscious, or it may be a deliberate act of sabotage or avoidance. Since client resistance can be unsettling for counsellors, it is important that they objectively evaluate their own feelings and behaviour when dealing with it. Counsellors need to be sensitive to the possibility that cross-cultural miscommunication can be mistaken for resistance.

Intimidating behaviour includes such things as name calling, using obscene language, shouting, threatening through displays of power such as fist shaking, invading personal space, stalking, and issuing verbal threats. Violent behaviour means hitting, pushing, biting, slapping, kicking, throwing objects, and using weapons such as guns, knives, or syringes.

Clients may become violent for a number of reasons. Although it is difficult to predict with certainty which clients will become violent, some risk factors may be isolated. The best predictor of violent behaviour is a history of violence. Substance abuse is also a common variable. Other factors that counsellors should consider when assessing risk are age, gender, and personality characteristics.

To prevent or minimize violent incidents, counselling agencies should develop policies and routines that address this issue. Simulations can be used to practise responses to potentially dangerous situations.

The four phases of violence are the anxiety, defensiveness, acting-out, and tension reduction stages. In the anxiety phase there is marked change in the client's usual behaviour, with signs of increasing agitation. To prevent anxiety from escalating, counsellors should attempt to establish a climate of cooperation and mutual problem solving. In the defensiveness phase, anxiety has increased to the point that the client is in danger of losing control. At this point, clients may still respond to appropriate limits. In the acting-out phase, the client becomes assaultive, and emergency intervention is crucial. Since the client has lost control and has become assaultive, protection of self and others is the primary goal. During the tension reduction phase, the client's aggressive energy gradual recedes, and the client returns to more rational behaviour.

It is important to debrief critical incidents in order to lessen shock, reduce isolation, and restore personal control. Team debriefing should take place as soon as possible after the incident. It should provide an opportunity for people to talk about their feelings. As well, the debriefing can be used to review what went wrong. Role plays and simulations can be used to practise alternative responses. Overall, the debriefing is designed to empower individuals and the team and to move them away from any tendency to feel helpless.

Exercises

1. Review your experiences dealing with persons who are angry, resistant, or potentially violent. What aspects of your experience will help you deal effectively with difficult situations? What aspects will impede your ability?

2. Interview counsellors from different settings regarding their experiences with violent or potentially violent clients. Discuss strategies that they have found effective.

3. Work in a small group. Assume that you are members of an inner-city needle exchange centre. Develop detailed policies and procedures for dealing with violent and potentially violent clients.

4. Suppose you review the file on your next client and discover that he was loud and abusive with his previous worker. What are some possible explanations for this client's behaviour? Suggest some strategies for working with this client.

5. Work in a small group to explore the potential benefits and risks of each of the following actions:

   a. having an unlisted phone number

   b. making home visits alone

   c. making home visits only when accompanied by a colleague

   d. conducting joint interviews for potentially hostile clients

   e. using only your first name with clients

   f. knowing that a client has a history of violence

   g. interviewing a client with a police officer present

   h. refusing to see a client with a history of violence

   i. striking a client in order to defend yourself

   j. calling the police

   k. warning an intended victim

   l. seeing a client who has been drinking

6. What is your natural reaction when someone's anger starts to escalate? Do you tend to fight back, or do you withdraw?

7. Research legal and ethical codes in order to explore your responsibility to notify intended victims of violence. Talk to counsellors and agencies in the field to get their opinions on this issue.

Weblinks

The Crisis Prevention Institute provides information about training programs and resources for nonviolent crisis information.
www.crisisprevention.com/default.htm

How To Manage Conflict In Groups
www.stw.ed.gov/products/handbook/pt7.htm

National Task Force on Violence Against Social Care Staff (UK)
www.doh.gov.uk/violencetaskforce/index.htm

VARIATIONS WITH SELECTED TARGET GROUPS

PREVIEW

After reading this chapter you should be able to:

- Demonstrate knowledge of the impact of job loss.
- Identify the four major activity target areas for employment counselling.
- Describe techniques for networking and accessing the hidden job market.
- Distinguish between traditional and nontraditional job search methods.
- Explain the use of electronic resources in an employment search.
- Explain the structure and use of DSM-IV-TR.
- Describe the characteristics of and treatment for major mental disorders, including schizophrenia, mood disorders, anxiety disorders, and eating disorders.
- Identify suicide warning signs.
- Identify strategies for dealing with clients who are suicidal.
- Identify issues and strategies for counselling clients who are HIV positive and clients who have AIDS.
- Explain the practice of brief counselling.
- Describe techniques of brief counselling.

EMPLOYMENT COUNSELLING

Unemployment can have a devastating impact on individuals and families. Aside from the obvious loss of income from not having a job, there may be significant consequences to job loss (see Bolles, 1997; Steinweg, 1990; Sunley and Sheek, 1986; Kirsh, 1983). For example, unemployment can lead to increased stress; health and mental health problems, including depression; increased suicide rate; premature death; and increased hospitalization (Kirsh, 1983). Holmes and Werbel (1992) reviewed the research on the physical and mental health effects of job loss. They found that job loss leads to higher incidence of coronary disease, hypertension, ulcers, headaches, depression, anxiety, and hostility, as well as increased family conflict and higher illness rates among children whose parents are unemployed.

For many people, a job or career is a pivotal part of their identity. A protracted period of unemployment can result in a loss of self-esteem and personality. Persons who are unemployed lose the routine of their daily lives, the structure of the workday, their sense of purpose, and the social contact with friends and colleagues at the workplace. As one unemployed journalist describes the experience, "I feel like I no longer have a life ... I'm a participant in a script that someone else has taken over" (Burman, 1988:5).

The financial impact of job loss can be devastating. Day-to-day survival can be tenuous at best as individuals and families struggle to survive on savings or meagre social assistance benefits. Financial problems become a crisis when unanticipated expenses such as car repairs, school fees, or medical bills appear. Job loss can easily result in the loss of savings, one's home, and the ability to maintain one's lifestyle, including social and recreational life. As Burman describes it, "It means not being able to reciprocate a dinner invitation, not seeing one's way clear to join a friend for lunch or a movie, and not being able to afford the price of a favourite recreation. As the weeks and months of unemployment pass, one's social orbit shrinks, placing a heavy emotional load on family relationships" (1988:xii).

Challenges and Goals for Counsellors

David Steinweg reviewed the research on counselling people who are unemployed and concludes that "recent research suggests that interventions focusing primarily on alleviating the negative consequences of job joss (e.g., financial pressures and subsequent job rejections) are not sufficient to help unemployed workers sustain a successful job search" (1990:40). He suggests that counsellors need to broaden their activities to include other counselling goals and activities.

Since sustained unemployment can be damaging to clients' self-worth and esteem, it is important for counsellors to encourage clients to maintain as much as possible their daily routine. In addition, whenever possible, clients should continue activities and commitments, such as parenting and volunteering, which enhance self-esteem.

Clients are often unemployed for reasons beyond their control, such as high unemployment rates, organizational downsizing, and economic downturns. Counsellors can help clients normalize the experience of job loss by helping them feel less isolated. They can help clients change their thinking about job loss by encouraging them not to blame themselves.

In general, employment counsellors are concerned with four major activity target areas: (1) job loss counselling, (2) career counselling, (3) job search skills, and (4) life skills counselling (see Table 9.1). An assessment interview will help counsellors determine if a client needs assistance with one or more of the four areas.

Job Loss Counselling

Job loss counselling aims to help clients regain equilibrium after being laid off and deal with the psychological stress that typically accompanies job loss and unemployment. As well, counsellors can help clients adjust to living on reduced or low incomes. They can help them access services that might help alleviate financial stress (e.g., welfare, employment insurance, loan negotiation, use of community resources such as subsidized daycare).

Self-esteem counselling is essential because it affects how job seekers market themselves. Sometimes clients develop learned helplessness as a result of repeated failure in their job search. Arnhold and Razak (1991) suggest a number of strategies for helping unemployed clients overcome learned helplessness.

1. Short-circuit self-depreciation by ignoring such remarks, challenging the basis for the remarks, and inviting clients to rationally consider changing the basis for their beliefs. Counsellors might use reframing and other techniques for changing thinking (see Chapter 7).

2. Reassure clients that "perfection is neither attainable nor expected" (103).

3. Reinforce current or past successes. "Positive comments on a neat desk, a new outfit, reliable punctuality, and other small past and present triumphs can be to the helplessness-oriented individual what a meal is to a starving person" (103).

4. Encourage action. In this respect, setting small but achievable goals can help clients break out of pessimism.

Table 9.1   Employment Counselling

Activity Area	Counselling Targets
Job loss counselling	Improving self-esteem Managing stress Managing physical needs
Career counselling	Researching careers Testing interests Testing aptitudes Researching employers
Job search skills	Overcoming barriers (e.g., age, a criminal record, racism, sexism) Writing résumés Identifying leads Networking Conducting informational interviews Getting interviews Preparing for interviews Using interview follow-up techniques Using electronic resources
Life skills counselling	Teaching work and life skills Helping with job survival

When dealing with clients who feel and act helpless it is important for counsellors to remember Arnhold and Razak's observation that "helplessness is a perception and not an accurate description of an individual. Many who are afflicted with crippling low self-esteem are in fact quite capable in some respects—the problem is that they think and feel otherwise about themselves" (102).

Amundson (1996) suggests a series of strategies that employment counsellors can use to help clients change their perspectives. These strategies include helping clients make positive affirmations, normalizing the experience of unemployment (i.e., assuring them that their feelings and reactions are normal), and encouraging them to avoid blaming themselves for unemployment. As well, counsellors can encourage clients to identify and use transferable skills (skills from other jobs, activities, hobbies, and experiences) in the job search. Amundson proposes challenging negative thinking patterns by having clients change "I can't" statements to "I won't" declarations. By changing the wording, clients can consider the power that they have to change any thinking or behaviour that might be acting as a barrier to action. Amundson also suggests giving clients specific activities that interrupt established but ineffective patterns of activity. For example, counsellors could ask clients to research employers, develop contact lists, and make phone calls. "By actively engaging in meaningful activity, with support, clients will gain confidence and will have a greater likelihood of persisting with career exploration and job search" (Amundson, 1996:160).

Career Counselling

Career counselling is appropriate for clients who do not have a clear perspective on either their interests or their abilities. The results of interest and aptitude testing are a starting point for consideration and further exploration. Counsellors should never use them as prescriptions for dictating what clients must or should do. With clear career possibilities identified, clients can then use a variety of resources to find out about the occupations that match their unique interests, values, and personal styles. This process should result in the establishment of a career goal.

Job Search Skills

Counselling in job search skills includes tasks such as researching employers and careers, preparing for job interviews, handling difficult interview questions, and following up phone calls or employment interviews. For example, counsellors can help clients anticipate interview questions, then role play answers. Video recordings can be used to help clients review their manner and the quality of their answers.

Job search skills training focuses on nontraditional job search methods, such as **networking** and using the **hidden job market** (see Table 9.2). Small groups for support and role playing may support this process.

Most uninformed job seekers rely on newspaper and other advertisements or employment agencies to find job vacancies. However, most jobs are never advertised. Only 15 to 20 percent of all jobs are filled through job ads (Angel and Harney, 1997; Farr, 1996). The remaining 80 to 85 percent of vacancies are part of what is known as the hidden job market.

Networking is the primary tool used to access the hidden job market. It involves using contacts such as friends, family, neighbours, and others who might provide information or access to others with information about job opportunities. Counsellors can assist clients by

Table 9.2 Traditional versus Modern Job Search Methods	
Traditional Search Method	**Modern Strategies**
Mail the same résumé widely to employers	Tailor multiple résumés to individual employers
Be ready to take any job	Link job and career objective to targeted employer or industry
Learn about the job after you are hired	Conduct prior research to learn about the organization Prepare for the job interview by anticipating and rehearsing questions
Emphasize specific skills and experiences	Emphasize transferable skills Use work skills derived from other areas (e.g., volunteer work, hobbies)
Gear job search to available vacancies	Gear job search to aptitude and interests and not to one type of job
Respond to job ads—"door to door" contact (dropping in on all employers in a defined geographic area to ask about job openings)	Use multiple approaches to job search, including: • networking • phone contact • use of Internet • direct contact with targeted employers • use of the hidden job market • follow-up of contacts • call back
Effort is part time and sporadic	Effort is full time

asking them to brainstorm the names of absolutely everyone they know or have known. Clients network by contacting these people to let them know that they are looking for a job. An important part of networking is asking contacts for the names of other people who might have jobs or information about potential openings. In this way, the network contact list grows dramatically, and clients gain access to people that they would not otherwise have known about.

Life Skills Counselling

Life skills counselling may be appropriate for clients who lack basic abilities in such areas as managing finances, maintaining proper hygiene, getting to work on time, and getting along with supervisors and co-workers. For clients in this category, this work is essential in order for them to become job ready. Some clients will need continued support and assistance in the workplace.

Job Clubs

Steinweg's (1990) work confirms the importance of group support as a way to reduce isolation and to buffer the adverse impact of unemployment. One of the most popular forms of group support is the **job club method** developed by Azrin and Besalel (1980). The job club method is based on the notion that looking for work is in itself a full-time job that is best done with a group of people. The job club leader provides support, job search skills training, and materials and supplies for completing a successful job hunt. Job clubs provide participants with access to phones, computers, photocopying, stationery, daily newspapers, and other sources of job leads. Secretarial assistance for producing effective résumés is provided, as well. In recent years, Internet access allows participants to use online resources for leads and information. An important part of the job club is the buddy system. Every job club participant has another member in the group who provides support and assistance.

The job club has a single goal: to help members obtain a job. Job club leaders remain unwavering in their optimism that everyone is employable and that there are job opportunities even during times of recession or depression. Job clubs typically have 8 to 12 members who meet for a period of two to three weeks. Job club counsellors use behavioural methods and standardized routines to teach participants job-finding methods. The "brief talk" rule requires counsellors to speak very briefly about a technique or procedure, usually for a maximum or one or two minutes. Participants then immediately practise the skill. Every session has specific learning objectives. By taking part in a job club, participants have an opportunity to acquire the skills of an effective job search, including how to network with family, friends, acquaintances, and others for job leads, how to develop an effective résumé, how to make phone calls to secure interviews, and how to handle interview questions. Azrin and Besalel offer this summary of the job club method:

> The general counseling style in the Job Club method is one of continuous encouragement and praise while still being very structured and task oriented. The counselor is constantly complimenting and encouraging the job seekers, speaking to each of them very frequently and yet briefly ... The counselor promotes mutual assistance among group members. He has a single overriding objective of helping each job seeker to obtain a good job and he devotes every moment of the meeting to instructing and encouraging the members in the specific activities that will help them obtain that objective. (1980:12)

Electronic Resources

In recent years, electronic technology has necessitated that clients become familiar with new strategies for managing their job and career searches. Fax machines, electronic databanks, software that guides users through résumé construction, and the Internet will likely continue to dramatically change the nature of the job search. The Internet, for example, offers unprecedented opportunities for clients to communicate with employers and other job seekers. As well, clients can visit company home pages for background information on the business, or they can search the Internet for detailed data on industry trends. The Internet has many resources for career information, self-assessment, job search tips, job bulletin boards, and government grants. The vast majority of colleges and universities now have Web sites where clients can get information on training programs and educational opportunities. The Internet can also help clients who may be considering moving by giving them geographic, economic, and demographic data. Chat rooms and other discussion groups can provide support, information, and sometimes network contacts. However, Bratina and Bratina caution, "Information found on the Internet is not necessarily accurate. Counselors should encourage job seekers to give Internet sources the same critical review they would give to other sources" (1998:21).

Many companies are now inviting applicants to submit electronic résumés via the Internet. Electronic résumés are somewhat different from traditional paper résumés. Action verbs such as planned, directed, and organized are best for paper résumés, but nouns such as bachelor's degree, teller, top 10 percent of class, and WordPerfect are best for electronic versions because computers sort and screen electronic résumés based on nouns such as these (Bratina and Bratina, 1998).

There is a wide range of Web sites of significance to Canadian employment counsellors. For example, Job Futures (**www.hrdc-drhc.gc.ca/JobFutures/english/index.htm**) offers general information on the National Occupations Classification occupational groups, including projections for future growth in these groups. The Canada WorkInfoNet (**www.workinfonet.ca/cwn/english/main.html**) highlights hot jobs and provides a variety of labour market information.

Employment Counselling and Immigrant Clients

Westwood and Ishiyama called attention to the unique employment counselling needs of culturally diverse clients. They noted that clients from immigrant minority groups often face unique problems related to "language, racial prejudice, lack of knowledge of the world of work, limited contacts or networks, lack of cultural knowledge of job finding and interviewing techniques, plus the additional stress due to the cultural adjustment to a new society" (1991:130). In dealing with these clients, counsellors need to be particularly sensitive to the cultural attitudes and norms. For example, Asian immigrant clients consider their career search in "light of the financial burden that may fall to them by virtue of their place in the family" (140). Thus, counsellors need to take family into account more than they might when dealing with clients from other cultures. Westwood and Ishiyama offer this caution for employment counsellors working with immigrants:

> Client resistance and distrust in the counseling process may be set in motion by cross-cultural insensitivities, such as the counselor's disregarding the client's age and social status and calling him or her by the first name, using excessive informality and friendliness, probing into private feelings, demanding high levels of self-disclosure and expressiveness, and giving advice. (137)

COUNSELLING PEOPLE WITH MENTAL DISORDERS

Historically, treatment of people with mental disorders was barbaric and included such practices as exorcizing, burning "witches," blood letting, whipping, starving, imprisoning, or housing in overcrowded "snake-pits," or insane asylums. During the 20th century, especially in the last 50 years, mental disorders have gradually been recognized as a health problem, and more humanitarian practices have been developed to replace procedures based on superstition, fear, and ignorance.

Over the past 40 years there has been a major shift in the delivery of mental health services from long-term treatment in hospitals to treatment of patients in the community. Today, the population of mental hospitals is only about one-fifth of what it was 30 years ago (Skidmore, Thackeray, and Farley, 1991). The development and refinement of a range of psychotropic drugs has been the driving force behind deinstitutionalization because these drugs enable patients to control hallucinations and behaviour that might otherwise preclude them from living in the community. However, this move toward community treatment has often been poorly funded, and new problems for those with mental disorders have resulted, particularly homelessness and its associated problems. Skidmore, Thackeray, and Farley (1991) estimate that as many as one-third of all homeless Americans are mentally ill. Cleghorn and Lee (1991) note that various studies have shown that in Canada and the United States:

- One out of every five people will develop a mental disorder during his or her lifetime.
- One in eight persons will be hospitalized.
- Psychiatric problems are the second leading cause of hospital admissions among those 20 to 44 years old.
- Suicide is the second leading cause of death of persons aged 15 to 39.

According to the National (USA) Institute of Mental Health (NIMH, 1998) the most severe mental disorders (schizophrenia, bipolar disorder, major depression, panic disorder, and obsessive-compulsive disorder) affect some five million American adults, and one in ten Americans experiences some disability from a diagnosable mental disorder in the course of any given year.

Psychiatric assessment and diagnosis typically involve an in-depth interview, including a thorough history of the person's situation. As well, physical examinations, including brain scans, electroencephalograms (EEGs), and lab tests, may be used to rule out organic illness (brain tumours, AIDS, drug reactions, etc.). Psychological tests may be used to assess thinking, personality, and other variables. The purpose of psychiatric diagnosis is not to label clients, but to match diagnosis to treatment decisions based on the best scientific evidence regarding which treatments are likely to be most effective with each disorder (Reid, 1989).

It is beyond the scope of this book to fully explore mental disorders. However, it is important to note that the concept is influenced by cultural and societal values. For example, at various times in history, homosexuality has been considered both an aberration and a gift. It is no longer considered a mental disorder.

It is important to remember that there may be vast differences between individuals with the same mental disorder. Psychological, social, and biological variables influence how illness manifests in each person. In addition, people with mental disorders may have concurrent problems, such as poverty, substance abuse, and social/relationship difficulties. Dual diagnosis is a term used to describe a person who has both a substance abuse addiction and a psychiatric disorder.

DSM-IV-TR

DSM-IV-TR is the **Diagnostic and Statistical Manual of Mental Disorders** published by the American Psychiatric Association. It is important to note that DSM-IV-TR was not developed as a way to classify people. Psychologists, psychiatrists, and other psychotherapists use it to classify and diagnose mental disorders. Consequently, counsellors should follow the lead of the DSM-IV-TR text, which "avoids the use of such expressions as 'a schizophrenic' or 'an alcoholic' and instead uses the more accurate, but admittedly more cumbersome, 'an individual with Schizophrenia' or 'an individual with Alcohol Dependence'" (American Psychiatric Association, 1994:xxii).

DSM-IV-TR organizes mental disorders into 16 major groups or classes. Each diagnostic class is further subdivided into specific disorders. A cursory overview of the 16 groups follows.

1. disorders usually first diagnosed in infancy, childhood, or adolescence (e.g., mental retardation, learning disorders, autism, conduct disorders, Tourette's syndrome). Disorders in this category have their onset during childhood or adolescence, but they may not be diagnosed until adulthood.

2. delirium, dementia, and amnestic and other cognitive disorders (e.g., dementia owing to HIV, Huntington's, Alzheimer's, or Parkinson's disease). The significant feature of disorders in this section is a disturbance in memory or thinking.

3. mental disorders resulting from a general medical condition. Here, the distinguishing feature is the judgment that the mental disorder is the direct result of a medical condition.

4. substance-related disorders (e.g., alcoholism and other addictions)

5. schizophrenia and other psychotic disorders. Disorders in this section are typically accompanied by psychotic symptoms such as hallucinations and delusions.

6. mood disorders (e.g., depression, bipolar disorder). The predominant feature is a disturbance in mood or feeling.

7. **anxiety disorders** (e.g., panic attacks, agoraphobia, post-traumatic stress disorder, phobias, obsessive-compulsive disorder). The predominant feature of anxiety disorders is much greater than usual anxiety or tension.

8. somatoform disorders (e.g., hypochondria or the fear that one has a serious disease). Here, the common feature is the presence of physical symptoms that suggest a medical problem, but there is no medical condition that is diagnosable.

9. factitious disorders (e.g., Munchausen syndrome). These disorders are characterized by the fact that the patient intentionally fakes symptoms in order to assume the role of patient.

10. dissociative disorders (e.g., amnesia, depersonalization disorder). Disorders in this category are characterized by significant changes in the consciousness, memory, or identity of the person.

11. sexual and gender identity disorders (e.g., pedophilia, sexual sadism). These disorders concern disturbances in sexual desire and functioning.

12. eating disorders (e.g., anorexia nervosa, bulimia nervosa). These disorders are noted by severe disturbance in eating behaviour.

13. sleep disorders (e.g., insomnia, narcolepsy). Sleep disorders are characterized by abnormalities in the amount, quality, or timing of sleep.

14. impulse control disorders not elsewhere classified (e.g., pathological gambling, pyromania, kleptomania). The essential feature of impulse control disorders is the inability to resist impulses or temptations.

15. adjustment disorders. These disorders arise from stressful events, such as the end of a relationship or loss of job.

16. personality disorders (e.g., paranoid personality disorder, obsessive-compulsive personality disorder). A personality disorder "is an enduring pattern of inner experience and behavior that deviates markedly from the expectations of the individual's culture, is pervasive and inflexible, has an onset in adolescence or early adulthood, is stable over time, and leads to distress or impairment" (American Psychiatric Association, 2000:685).

DSM-IV-TR strives to look at patients as more than just diagnostic labels. The manual recognizes that individuals are complex and that medical conditions, social circumstances, and other factors affect how people function. To facilitate a more comprehensive assessment, DSM-IV-TR uses a five-level multiaxial system, described below.

Axis I: Clinical Disorders. This axis is used to report the specific mental disorder that is being diagnosed. Two exceptions are personality disorders and mental retardation, which are reported on Axis II.

Axis II: Personality Disorders, Mental Retardation. Personality disorders and mental retardation are reported on this axis.

Axis III: General Medical Conditions. This axis is used for reporting relevant medical conditions that affect a current or past mental disorder (Axis I or Axis II). For example, hypothyroidism can cause depression; thus, the individual would be coded on Axis I with a mood disorder due to hypothyroidism and also on Axis III as hypothyroidism (American Psychiatric Association, (2000:29).

Axis IV: Psychosocial and Environmental Problems. This important axis is used for reporting significant stressors that might be contributing to the mental disorders. DSM-IV groups stressors into nine categories: (1) problems with primary support groups, (2) problems related to the social environment, (3) educational problems, (4) occupational problems, (5) housing problems, (6) economic problems, (7) problems with access to health-care services, (8) problems related to interaction with the legal system/crime, and (9) other psychosocial and environmental problems.

Axis V: Global Assessment of Functioning. This axis is used to report an individual's highest level of functioning. This axis may be used to track progress, and it may have some predictive value since people usually return to their previous highest level of adaptive functioning after an episode of illness (Klerman, 1988).The Global Assessment of Functioning (GAF) scale is used to judge a person's level of functioning. This scale is based on a continuum from 0 to 100, in which 100 represents a superior level of adaptation (American Psychiatric Association, 1994:32).

Appropriate Uses of DSM-IV-TR. Counsellors should use the DSM-IV-TR classification system as a diagnostic tool only if they have appropriate specialized clinical training. The overview in this chapter is a brief introduction to the basic structure of the manual.

Typically, individuals who use DSM-IV-TR in their counselling practice are licensed psychiatrists or those with graduate degrees in counselling or psychology and courses and supervised field practise in using it. Untrained practitioners should not attempt to make psychiatric diagnoses.

However, untrained counsellors may find that the manual is valuable for understanding the essential definitions and features of mental disorders that their clients may be dealing with. DSM-IV-TR contains valuable information regarding variations in culture, age, and gender with respect to particular mental disorders. The manual also provides counsellors with reference material on the prevalence of mental disorders, including lifetime risk, the typical patterns of disorders, and data on the frequency of specified disorders among biological family members.

DSM-IV-TR and Social Work. Whereas social workers should have a working knowledge of mental disorders and how they are classified, DSM-IV-TR does not typically meet the needs of most social workers. Social work is concerned primarily with individuals in a social context with an emphasis on helping them to deal with relationship problems, crisis events, difficulties related to inadequate resources, and problems dealing with organizations such as schools or government welfare offices. DSM-IV-TR, however useful as a tool for intellectually understanding mental disorders, is a model based on pathology and deficits. It does not address or prioritize human empowerment, which is a central objective of social work. Contemporary social workers adopt a strengths approach to problem solving that assumes the power of individuals to overcome adversity. Using a strengths approach social workers endeavour to find and respect the successes, assets, and resources of people including those resources available within their culture such as sweat lodges and other healing rituals. As Compton and Gallaway see it:

> The emphasis is on knowing them in a more holistic way: acknowledging their hopes and dreams, their needs, their resources and the resources around them, their capacities, and their gifts. The strengths perspective invites a more affirming interaction with individuals and families; as a profession, you engage them conversationally as collaborators and peers, recognizing that they and you are both experts and have a mutual interest in improving their quality of life. (1999:17)

Selected Major Mental Disorders

This section explores some of the most common mental disorders that counsellors are likely to encounter, including schizophrenia, mood disorders, anxiety disorders, and eating disorders. This section provides a very brief synopsis. It is expected that counsellors who work with people who have mental disorders will have had appropriate academic courses in the subject area, as well as supervised field practice.

Schizophrenia. Schizophrenia is a chronic (continuing) mental disorder affecting about 1 percent of the population (NIMH, 1998). In rare cases children can develop schizophrenia, but it usually starts in the late teens or early 20s for men, and in the 20s and early 30s for women. The children of a parent who has schizophrenia are 10 times more likely to develop it than children of a parent who does not have it (NIMH, 1998). Most people with schizophrenia suffer from it throughout their lives, and an estimated 1 of every 10 people with the illness dies by suicide (NIMH, 1998). Schizophrenia is believed to affect about 1 percent of the general population, with annual health-care costs in the United States exceeding $30 billion. In the United States, about 25 percent of all persons in hospital on any given day have schizophrenia (Cleghorn and Lee, 1991; Dubovsky and Weissberg, 1986).

Contrary to popular opinion, people with schizophrenia do not have split personalities, like Dr. Jekyll and Mr. Hyde. Furthermore, although some once accepted it as truth, parents do not cause schizophrenia. The current perspective on the disorder is that it is caused by an imbalance of the complex, interrelated chemical systems of the brain (NIMH, 1998), but there may be no single cause. The symptoms of schizophrenia vary between individuals, sometimes dramatically. The following symptoms are common: hallucinations, delusions, disordered thinking, and social isolation.

Hallucinations. There may be wide variation in the symptoms of persons with schizophrenia. Most sufferers, however, experience **hallucinations**, usually auditory but sometimes visual or olfactory (related to smell). These hallucinations may be voices that tell clients what to do (**command hallucinations**), or they may be visions of things that do not exist.

Hallucinations can affect any of a person's senses, causing them to hear, see, taste, touch, or smell what others do not. Auditory hallucinations are the most frequent type of hallucination and are most common for people with schizophrenia. Visual hallucinations are much less common, and they are more likely to occur as a result of acute infectious disease. Olfactory hallucinations may occur because of schizophrenia and organic lesions of the brain. Tactile hallucinations (touch) may occur as a reaction to drugs. Kinesthetic hallucinations may occur after the loss of a limb ("phantom limb") and owing to schizophrenia. Withdrawal from drugs may cause vivid hallucinations, such as the sensation that insects are crawling under the skin (delirium tremens common with alcohol withdrawal) (Nicoli, 1988). In fact, the symptoms of alcohol withdrawal may be clinically indistinguishable from schizophrenia (Reid, 1989). With auditory hallucinations, clients may hear voices that command or compliment them, but with disorders such as schizophrenia, the voices are usually hostile (Shea, 1988). These voices may be so real that clients believe that they have had broadcasting devices planted in their bodies. For example, one client was convinced that her dentist had secretly implanted receivers in her fillings. It is so real to the person that he or she cannot dismiss it as imagination.

It is important to know that a wide range of factors can cause hallucinations, including psychosis, high fever, mind-altering drugs (marijuana, psilocybin, LSD, and opium), medications, withdrawal from depressant drugs such as alcohol, brain disease and injury, epilepsy, sensory deprivation or sensory overload, oxygen deprivation, hyperventilation, hypoglycemia, extreme pain, extended fasting, dehydration, and social isolation (Nicoli, 1988; Beyerstein, 1998). Hallucinations can also occur in persons who have impaired vision but no mental disorder.

Delusions. Persons with schizophrenia may experience **delusions,** or distorted beliefs involving bizarre thought patterns. Delusions of persecution, typical in paranoid schizophrenia, may lead people to believe they are being cheated, controlled, or poisoned. Other common delusions include religious delusions (belief that one is a manifestation of God), delusions of grandeur (bizarre beliefs about one's abilities), delusions of being controlled (e.g., belief that one is being directed by radio messages), **thought broadcasting** (belief that one's thinking can be heard by others) and **thought insertion** (belief that thoughts are being inserted into one's brain by others) (Nicoli, 1988).

One client, a young university student, gives us a sense of what the world of a person with schizophrenia is like:

> I want to sue my dentist. Over the past year he has been installing radio transmitters in my fillings. Now he uses them to control me. At first he was nice, then he raped me while he worked on my teeth. Sometimes he makes me sleep with complete strangers. If I don't get them removed soon, I might be forced to do something awful ... There are others. I talked to a woman on the phone the other day. Her dentist did the same thing. We need to go underground where we can be safe from the enemy.

Disordered Thinking. Another common feature of schizophrenia is disordered thinking. Individuals may be unable to think logically, or they may jump from one idea to another without any apparent logical connection. Thinking may be so disorganized and fragmented that it is totally confusing to others.

Social Isolation. Persons with schizophrenia are often socially isolated and withdrawn. They may be emotionally numb, have poor communication skills, and show decreased motivation and ability to care for themselves.

Treatment of Schizophrenia. Antipsychotic medications are used to decrease the symptoms of the disorder—hallucinations, agitation, confusion, distortions, and delusions. A medical doctor, frequently a psychiatrist, must prescribe these medications. Counselling is an important adjunct to antipsychotic medication. Counsellors typically target their activities toward helping clients deal with the social aspects of the disease. As well, counsellors can be instrumental in encouraging clients to seek psychiatric attention when necessary, and they can support psychiatric initiatives by encouraging clients to continue with any prescribed medication. This is crucial, since about 50 percent of people with schizophrenia are noncompliant in taking their medication (Dubovsky and Weissberg, 1986).

CONVERSATION 9.1

WHEN CLIENTS ARE HALLUCINATING

STUDENT: What should I do when clients begin hallucinating?

TEACHER: Let's talk about what not to do. First, counsellors need to resist the temptation to argue with clients about the reality of their hallucinations. Although some clients are aware of when they are hallucinating and have learned to live with it, others are convinced of their authenticity and dismiss arguments to the contrary. Their experience is very real and has to be accepted as such.

Second, counsellors should avoid patronizing or humouring clients about their hallucinations, as this behaviour may promote further hallucinating.

STUDENT: Okay, but what can counsellors do?

TEACHER: Hallucinations are generally treated with antipsychotic medications. Consequently, referral to a physician or psychiatrist is essential to make sure that clients have been assessed for an appropriate medication to control their hallucinations. Subsequently, it is important to ensure that clients are taking their medication and that their dosage is appropriate.

One way that counsellors can respond without arguing is to simply state that they do not sense what their clients are sensing. They can combine this statement with empathic statements that acknowledge the feelings that clients may be experiencing as a result of their hallucinations.

Counsellors also can help clients deal with any stressors that may be increasing the frequency of hallucinations. For example, if being in large crowds or missing sleep brings on hallucinations, clients can take steps to minimize these precursors. It may be helpful to work with clients to help them learn skills for controlling their hallucinations. For example, they can discipline themselves to direct their thoughts and activities elsewhere. One researcher found that silence, isolation, and attention to oneself tend to promote hallucinations, but distraction, exploratory activity, movement, and external stimulation tend to impede hallucinations (Silva and Lopez de Silva, 1976). So, simply diverting clients' attention can be a useful strategy.

STUDENT: I learned something from one of my clients that I found helpful and profound. I remember him saying to me, "I have a mental disorder, but don't forget, I have the same needs and fears as everyone else." I was reminded that he and I were more alike than unlike each other.

Mood Disorders. The two most severe mood disorders (also known as affective disorders) are major **depression** and **bipolar disorder**, or manic-depressive illness.

Depression. About one in four women and one in ten men in North America will experience major depression during their lifetimes, but almost 90 percent of people who develop depression can be treated (Cleghorn and Lee, 1991:55). Although everyone has bad days, the depressed feelings that accompany them usually pass quickly. A clinical diagnosis of depression is made when a person's depressed mood becomes pervasive over time and interferes with the person's ability to cope with or enjoy life. In this way, depression is differentiated from the normal mood swings that everyone experiences. Depression is almost certainly more widespread that statistics suggest since it often goes untreated. In fact, it is sometimes referred to as the "common cold of mental illness." The signs of depression, sometimes described as clinical depression or major depression to separate it from ordinary sadness, can be organized into four major categories with specific symptoms:

1. **Mood distubances**

- constant sad, anxious, or empty mood
- feelings of hopelessness or pessimism
- feelings of guilt, worthlessness, or helplessness

2. Changes in Behaviour

- diminished interest or pleasure in daily activities, including sex
- decreased energy and fatigue
- withdrawal from others

3. Alterations in Thinking

- difficulty thinking, concentrating, remembering
- inability to make decisions
- recurrent thoughts of death or suicide

4. Physical Complaints

- restlessness or irritability
- fatigue or loss of energy
- sleep disturbances, including insomnia
- loss or gain of appetite and weight
- chronic pain or other persistent bodily symptoms that are not caused by physical disease
- suicide attempts (NIMH, 1998; American Medical Association, 1998, American Psychiatric Association, 1994; Cleghorn and Lee, 1991)

Scott Simmie, a Canadian journalist, describes how his depression included obsession with thoughts of suicide:

> I spent weeks in bed, unable to find a reason to get up. Sleep was my drug—the only, albeit temporary, way to escape what had befallen me. When awake I brooded, almost obsessively, on death. Pictured myself rigging pulleys so I could hang myself in the condo,... Most mornings, the first thought that entered my head was to put a gun to it. Bang. Problem solved. (Simmie and Nunes, 2001:27)

Intercontinental Medical Statistics Inc., (IMS HEALTH) compiles statistical information for the Canadian health care community. In a recent report (IMS, 2001) on diagnoses trends, they noted that visits to a doctor for depression have shown the largest increase among Canada's leading diagnoses. During the period 1995–2000, their statistics reveal that visits to doctors in Canada for depression have increased 36 percent with 7.8 million consultations with doctors for depressive disorders. Put another way, almost three percent of all physician visits were for depression. Women represented 66 percent of those diagnosed with depression. About 47 percent of individuals (male and female) diagnosed with depression were in the age group 40–59, and 31 percent were from the next largest group made up of 20–39 year-olds. Significantly, it now ranks second behind essential hypertension as the leading reason for visiting a physician. Moreover, the report suggested that almost three million Canadians have serious depression but less than one-third seeks help.

Depression is believed to caused by a complex combination of three primary variables—biological, genetic (inherited), and emotional and/or environmental (American Medical Association, 1998). Biological origins are associated with brain chemistry and hormonal activity. Research has demonstrated that some families are more likely to have members who suffer depression. Although no specific gene has been linked to depression, there appears to be ample evidence that heredity leads to an increased vulnerability to depression. Emotional and environmental causes might include stressors such as death of a loved one, job loss, or the break up of a relationship. As well, depression might be the result of a sleep disturbances, illness or drug reaction. Depression that originates from physical illness usually abates once the physical illness is treated. Depression is symptomatic of a medical condition in about 10 percent to 15 percent of all cases. Known physical causes of depression include thyroid disease, adrenal gland disorders, hyperparathyroidism, diabetes, infectious diseases such as viral hepatitis, cancer, autoimmune disorders, vitamin and mineral deficiencies, and cancer (American Medical Association, 1998, O'Conner, 1997). Thus, clients who are dealing with depression should be referred for a medical check up as an adjunct to counselling.

Current thinking suggests that it the combination of factors that results in depression. For example, if people with a predisposition to depression experience stressful life crises, they may develop depression. Subsequently, their first depressive episode may stimulate changes in brain chemistry leaving them more vulnerable to further episodes where even small stressful events can trigger depression. (American Medical Association, 1998)

Counsellors can assist people who are depressed in a number of ways including:

- helping them recognize and identify the symptoms of depression
- referring for appropriate medical examination and treatment which might include medication or hospitalization
- helping them to develop coping strategies for dealing with stress
- loss or grief counselling
- assessing and managing suicide risk
- helping them to develop cognitive/behavioural strategies for overcoming low self-esteem and other self-defeating thought patterns that often accompany depression
- supporting and understanding emotions.
- family counselling to interrupt communication patterns that contribute to or escalate depression

Bipolar Disorder. With bipolar illness, depression alternates with manic episodes. During manic periods people typically experience heightened energy, a euphoric mood, and a greatly increased sense of confidence, sometimes to the point of grandiosity. They may have sharpened and unusually creative thinking, along with a much decreased need for sleep. Or they may experience a flight of ideas (thoughts without logical connection). Although they may engage in increased goal-directed activities at work or school, they often engage in them without regard to the consequences, thus leading to irrational behaviour, such as uncontrolled buying sprees, sexual indiscretion, and foolish business investments (American Psychiatric Association, 1994; NIMH, 1998; Nicoli, 1988). Scott Simmie's recollection of his mind set when he was in the midst of the manic phase illustrates the irrationality of this state:

> Despite everything I'd been through, I was still convinced that I was in perfect health, that the
> real problem was the failure of others to recognize that something extraordinary and wonderful had happened to me. That I had been spiritually reborn. That my limitless potential
> had finally been free. (Simmie and Nunes, 2001:25)

Thus, it is very difficult, but not impossible, to persuade people to accept treatment, including hospitalization, during the manic phase of the illness. Supportive counsellors, family and friends may convince them to seek treatment, but in some cases, particularly where their behaviour becomes self-destructive or dangerous, involuntary hospitalization may be necessary.

Bipolar disorder usually begins in adolescence or early adulthood and continues throughout life. It is often not recognized as an illness, and people who have it may suffer needlessly for years or even decades. There is evidence that bipolar disorder is inherited (NIMH, 1998). Persons with untreated bipolar illness may experience devastating complications, including marital breakup, job loss, financial ruin, substance abuse, and suicide. However, almost everyone with bipolar illness can be helped through the use of medications such as lithium, which has demonstrated effectiveness in controlling both depression and mania. Bipolar disorder cannot be cured, but for most people treatment can keep the disease under control.

Anxiety Disorders.

Anxiety Disorders. Anxiety disorders are characterized by higher than normal levels of fear, worry, tension, or anxiety about daily events. High anxiety may be present without apparent reason. Four serious anxiety disorders are obsessive-compulsive disorder (OCD), phobias, panic disorder, and post-traumatic stress disorder (PTSD).

Obsessive-Compulsive Disorder (OCD). An **obsessive-compulsive disorder** involves recurrent, unwanted thoughts and conscious, ritualized, seemingly purposeless acts such as counting the number of tiles on the ceiling or needing to wash one's hands repetitively. Behavioural techniques and medication have proved effective in treating this disorder.

Phobia. A **phobia** is an irrational fear about particular events or objects. Phobias result in overwhelming anxiety in response to situations of little or no danger. Most people have phobias of one sort or another, such as fear of flying, heights, public speaking, or snakes. For the most part, people deal with their phobias through avoidance, which decreases the anxiety associated with the fear. Unfortunately, avoidance increases the fear of the particular object or situation. Treatment of phobias is necessary when they interfere with a person's capacity to lead a normal life. For example, agoraphobia (fear of open or public spaces) prevents people from leaving the safety of their homes. Treatment in such cases is essential to help clients overcome what would otherwise be severely restricted lives.

With systematic desensitization, persons with a phobia are first taught how to manage anxiety through relaxation. With the help of the counsellor, they construct a hierarchy of anxiety-provoking events associated with the phobia. Finally, they learn how to control their anxiety with progressively more difficult exposures to the anxiety-producing object or event. Other specialized behavioural techniques such as flooding, systematic desensitization, relaxation training, and pharmacologic (drug) treatment may be necessary to relieve anxiety disorders.

Panic Disorder. A **panic disorder** involves sudden attacks of terror and irrational fear, accompanied by an overwhelming sense of impending doom. During a panic attack a person may experience symptoms such as an accelerated heart rate, sweating, shaking, shortness of breath, chest pain, and nausea, as well as a fear of dying or losing control (American Psychiatric Association, 1994). Medication and psychotherapy have proved effective in treating this disorder.

Post-Traumatic Stress Disorder (PTSD). PTSD symptoms develop following traumatic events such as rape, assault, natural disasters (earthquakes, floods, etc.), war, torture, or automobile accident. Symptoms may occur immediately after the event, or they may be delayed by months or years (Nicoli, 1988). Recollections of the event result in disabling symptoms, such as emotional numbness; sleep disturbance (nightmares, difficulty sleeping); reliving the event; intense anxiety at exposure to cues that remind the person of the trauma; avoidance of activities, people, or conversations that arouse recall of the trauma; hypervigilance; and outbursts of anger (American Psychiatric Association, 1994; Nicoli, 1988). PTSD symptoms often dissipate within six months, but for others the symptoms may last years. Relaxation training and counselling are effective tools for treating this disorder.

Eating Disorders. The two most common eating disorders, anorexia nervosa and bulimia, are most likely to affect adolescent and young adult women, with about 90 percent of all those afflicted coming from this group (NIMH, 1998; Nicoli, 1988; Cleghorn and Lee, 1991). Approximately 1 percent of adolescent girls develop anorexia nervosa (NIMH, 1998) and as many as 10 percent develop bulimic disorder (Nicoli, 1988). Eventually, half of those with anorexia will develop bulimia (NIMH, 1998). Eating disorders are difficult to treat because many people refuse to admit that they have a problem and resist treatment. Counsellors and family need to persuade those affected to seek treatment, but this is hard because people with these disorders may argue that their only problem is the "nagging" people in their lives. Because of the life-threatening nature of eating disorders, involuntary treatment or forced hospitalization may be necessary, particularly when there has been excessive and rapid weight loss, serious metabolic disturbances, and serious depression with a risk of suicide.

Social and Cultural Variables. For most of recorded history, plumpness in women was deemed desirable and fashionable. During the last 50 years, particularly in Western cultures, women have been bombarded with media messages that promote slimness as the route to a successful and happy life. Societal emphasis on dieting, combined with the unrealistic body image of supermodels, contributes to an obsessive preoccupation with body image and dieting (Abraham and Llewellyn-Jones, 1997). One study found that the top wish of a group of girls aged 11 to 17 was "to be thinner," while another survey discovered that girls were more afraid of becoming fat than they were of cancer, nuclear war, or losing their parents (Berg, 1997:13). Mothers and fathers who are overly concerned or critical about their daughters' weight and physical attractiveness may put the girls at increased risk of developing an eating disorder. People pursuing professions or activities that emphasize thinness, such as modelling, dancing, or gymnastics, are more susceptible to the problem (Nicoli, 1988; NIMH, 1998).

Anorexia Nervosa. **Anorexia nervosa** occurs when people reject maintaining minimally healthy body weight. Driven by low self-esteem and an intense fear of gaining weight, people with anorexia use techniques such as purging (e.g., fasting, vomiting, taking laxatives) and excessive exercise to reduce body weight. Even though they may diet to the point of starvation and they look emaciated, they will still insist that they are too fat. Anorexia nervosa can be life threatening, and as many as 10 to 15 percent of sufferers die of the effects of prolonged starvation (Cleghorn and Lee, 1991; NIMH, 1998).

The symptoms of anorexia may include excessive weight loss, belief that the body is fat and continuation of dieting despite a lower than normal body weight, cessation of menstruation, obsession with food, eating in secret, obsessive exercise, and depression. People with anorexia are often perfectionists with superior athletic ability. There is some evidence to suggest that people with anorexia starve themselves in order to gain a sense of control in some area of their lives (NIMH, 1998).

The treatment of eating disorders requires a team approach consisting of physicians, counsellors, nutritionists, and family therapists. Group therapy may be a helpful adjunct to individual counselling to reduce isolation. Reframing and other methods for helping clients change the distorted and rigid thinking patterns associated with eating disorders may be extremely helpful (see Chapter 7). As well, antidepressant medications such as fluoxetine (Prozac) and imipramine may be used.

Bulimia. Bulimia occurs when people adopt a pattern of excessive overeating followed by vomiting or other purging behaviours to control their weight. Individuals with bulimia usually binge and purge in secret. Typically, persons with bulimia feel isolated, and they deal with their problems through overeating, then, feeling guilty and disgusted, they purge. Because they may have normal or even above normal body weight, they often hide their problem from others for years. By the time they finally seek treatment (sometimes not until in their 30s or 40s), their eating disorder is firmly entrenched and difficult to treat.

The symptoms of bulimia may include cessation of menstruation; obsession with food; eating in secret; obsessive exercise; serious depression; binging, vomiting, and other purging activities (often with the use of drugs); and disappearance in the bathroom for long periods to induce vomiting. From excessive vomiting, the outer layer of the teeth can be worn down, scarring may be present on the backs of hands (from pushing fingers down the throat to induce vomiting), the esophagus may become inflamed, and glands near the cheeks can become swollen (NIMH, 1998). Person with bulimia are at increased risk for substance abuse and suicidal behaviour.

Treating Mental Disorders

Ideally, persons with mental disorders should be dealt with through a team approach that includes psychiatrists, psychiatric social workers, social service workers, counsellors, occupational counsellors, nurses, and volunteers. As a team, they share common objectives:

1. motivating clients to seek and remain in treatment and, in severe cases, arranging for involuntary treatment

2. supporting clients to remain in the community (helping with housing, life skills training, employment, and career counselling)

3. helping hospitalized clients return to community living as soon as possible

4. assisting clients in dealing with the challenges of medication

5. educating clients and their families about the nature of their disorder

6. assisting clients in dealing with the consequences of mental disorders

7. helping clients and their families develop and use support systems, including self-help groups and professionals

Psychiatric Medications. The 1950s witnessed the introduction of powerful chemicals that have resulted in dramatic advances in the treatment of mental disorders. Medications have enabled the vast majority of persons with mental disorders to be treated and managed in the community as opposed to locked up in psychiatric facilities. Medications may be able to control the symptoms of mental disorders, such as hallucinations, but they do not cure the illness. They can increase the effectiveness of counselling by increasing the capacity of the clients to hear and respond. Many people need to take medication to control their illness for the rest of their lives.

There may be wide variations in people's reaction to medication (e.g., some respond better to one than another, some need bigger doses, some experience side effects and others do not). Medications may result in unwanted side effects, such as tardive dyskinesia (a serious side effect of antipsychotic medication characterized by uncontrollable movement), drowsiness, weakness, tremors, slurred speech, sleep disturbances, sexual dysfunction, and headaches. Some clients may stop taking medication in order to avoid these side effects.

Antipsychotic (or neuroleptic) medications such as loxapine, haloperidol, clozapine, and risperidone, are used to treat illnesses such as schizophrenia. Antipsychotic medications may be taken daily, but some medications are available through injection (once or twice a month). Injections are particularly useful for ensuring that clients take the medication. **Antimanic medications** such as lithium are used to control the manic symptoms of bipolar disorder. **Antidepressant medications** such as Prozac, Paxil, and Zolof are used to help people deal with serious depression. **Antianxiety medications** such as valium and librium are used to control serious and persistent anxiety, phobias, and panic attacks.

SUICIDE COUNSELLING

In Canada and the United States, the annual death rate from suicide is about 15 per 100 000 population, but because it is likely that a large number of suicides go unreported, the actual rate is almost certainly higher than that reported by official statistics (Cleghorn and Lee, 1991).

The American Association of Suicidology (1998) describes suicide as a permanent solution to a temporary problem. They emphasize that suicidal crises are almost always temporary and that often they are associated with problems that can be treated. Suicide intervention represents a unique challenge for counsellors. They must assess the immediate risk and intervene to prevent their clients from completing the suicide. This challenges counsellors to rapidly establish a supportive relationship. Active listening skills are crucial, for unless suicidal clients can be convinced that the counsellor is genuinely interested in their welfare, the client may cut off communication.

Warning Signs and Risk Assessment

There is no absolute way of predicting that a person will attempt suicide, but there are some important warning signs to consider. Suicide risk assessments should include careful observation and interviewing in the following key areas: threats of suicide, history of attempts, methodology, stressors, personality factors, alcoholism, social supports, and gender and demographic variables (American Association of Suicidology, 1998; Harvard Medical School, 1996; San Francisco Suicide Prevention Institute, 1998; Othmer and Othmer, 1989).

Threats of Suicide. Clients who talk about suicide or who appear preoccupied with death and dying are often at risk. Research has shown that 8 out of 10 suicidal persons give some sign of their intentions. Sometimes the clues are clear, such as when clients directly threaten to take their lives. At other times, their suicidal objectives are hinted at, such as when they start giving away their possessions, making final arrangements (e.g., expressing wishes for their funeral, writing a will), and involving themselves in increased risk-taking behaviour. Threats of suicide and other warning signs may represent a cry for help, an expression of frustration, a desire to induce guilt in others, or an effort to get rid of depressed feelings (Othmer and Othmer, 1989). Whatever the reason for the clients' suicide threats or attempts, counsellors should take them seriously.

History of Suicide Attempts. About 30 to 40 percent of suicides have made a previous attempt, and about 10 percent of those who attempt suicide succeed within 10 years. Eight times as many people make suicide attempts as those who complete suicide (Cleghorn and Lee, 1991). However, it is likely that the number of completed suicides is underreported, as some cases of what appear to be accidental deaths are, in fact, suicides.

Methodology. As a rule, clients who have a specific plan for taking their lives are at greater risk than those who do not have such a plan. Moreover, the more developed the plan and the greater the potential lethality of the proposed method, the greater the risk. For example, "hanging, shooting and jumping from high places are serious, mostly successful suicide methods" (Othmer and Othmer, 1989:267).

Stressors. Clients who are currently coping with significant stress are at greater risk. Such stressors can be broadly defined and may include such events as a recent loss (e.g., death, divorce, and loss of job, money, status, self-confidence, self-esteem, religious faith). As well, recent medical illness may be a factor. About two-thirds of the clients who commit suicide have seen a doctor shortly before their death (Hirschfeld & Russell, 1997).

Personality Changes. Counsellors should explore whether there have been recent and drastic changes in their clients' usual manner. Changes such as social withdrawal, sudden changes in their moods, loss of interest in activities that previously gave them pleasure (sex, work, friends, family, job, hobbies), increased substance abuse, changes in sleep patterns, and loss of interest in personal appearance ought to be closely assessed. As well, counsellors should look for signs of depression, apathy, anxiety, and general pessimism about the future. Not all suicidal people are depressed, nor are all depressed people suicidal. Some people contemplating suicide may seem at peace, even euphoric. However, depression should always signal to counsellors that they should assess suicide risk.

Suicide and Alcoholism. Research has shown that persons who are addicted to alcohol have an increased risk of suicide compared with the general population. Roy's (1993) review found that the lifetime risk of suicide among alcoholics is 2.2 to 3.4 percent in English-speaking countries and at least double the general population, but an astounding

60 to 120 times higher than that of the general population without psychiatric illness. Furthermore, he reported that about 20 percent of suicide victims are alcoholic.

Gender and Demographic Differences

Women attempt suicide three or four times as often as men, but men tend to use more lethal methods and account for 75 percent of all completed suicides. The ratio of attempts to suicides is about 10 to 1 (Harvard Medical School, 1998). One study (cited in Cleghorn and Lee, 1991:204) identified high-risk groups as those with a mental disorder, young people, seniors, Aboriginal people, and those in prison. They also reported that males aged 15 to 24 are at the highest risk among the young group and that these young men often choose violent means to end their lives.

A study by Devons (1996) revealed that the suicide rate for elderly people was the highest of all age groups, perhaps as high as double the rate in the general population. She suggests that the profound losses associated with aging leave elderly persons vulnerable, but early identification of depression can lead to appropriate treatment intervention.

Drugs such as antipsychotic medication, sleeping pills, antidepressants, and analgesics such as aspirin are all potential overdose drugs, especially when taken in combination with other drugs. Roberts reports that, as a rule, a lethal dose is 10 times the normal dose, but in combination with alcohol, as little as half the normal dose can result in death (1991:58).

Counselling Intervention

Suicide prevention and crisis intervention require that counsellors be aware of the dangerous myths about suicide, including the following (Devons, 1996):

Myth 1: Suicide occurs without warning signs.

Myth 2: People who talk about suicide aren't serious about killing themselves.

Myth 3: Bringing up the topic promotes suicide as an option.

Myth 4: People who attempt suicide are just trying to get attention.

Myth 5: The best response to a threat is to say, "Go ahead."

Assess the Risk. Although no counsellor can determine with certainty whether a client will try to commit suicide, knowledge of and exploration of risk factors is essential in order to make intelligent intervention. As described earlier in this section, some of the key risk factors that counsellors should consider include past attempts, current mental and physical status, the presence of a viable plan, the means to kill oneself, talk about suicide, personal losses, efforts to put one's affairs in order, and substance abuse. Counsellors need to explore these variables in a calm, nonjudgmental manner, without moralizing, and offer support and empathy throughout the process.

To assess the potential lethality of a plan, counsellors should investigate factors such as the following: lethal potential of the method (e.g., time between attempt and likely death), the extent to which the person has access to the means (e.g., presence of a gun or sleeping pills), and possibility of discovery and access to rescue.

Ask About Suicide Intent. Counsellors need to overcome any reluctance to ask clients if they have considered suicide as a solution to their problems. Roberts (1991) reports that there is clinical and empirical evidence to strongly support the value of direct inquiry. Asking about suicide will not plant the idea in the client's mind. In fact, bringing the issue into the open can relieve clients of the stress of trying to hide their intent, whereas avoiding the topic increases feelings of isolation and hopelessness in the suicidal person. As Roberts concludes, "Critically, direct inquiry gives the potentially suicidal individual permission to discuss feelings that may have seemed virtually undiscussable. Direct inquiry can bring great relief to the client—at last the inner battle of life or death can be openly discussed and explored in a safe, supportive, and accepting climate" (59).

A veiled or vague comment about suicide should always be taken seriously. When clients make statements such as "Sometimes life doesn't seem worth it" a follow-up question such as "Have you thought about killing yourself?" should be used to put the issue on the discussion table.

Implement Crisis Intervention. Counsellors have a responsibility to prevent suicide once the client makes this intent known. The immediate goal is crisis intervention to thwart clients from taking their lives. A number of strategies can be considered, including the following.

1. removing the means of suicide from the client (e.g., flushing pills down the toilet, confiscating guns). This prevents clients from acting impulsively.

2. negotiating a "no-suicide" contract. This involves an agreement that the client will not hurt him- or herself until the next contact with the counsellor, when a new contract may be negotiated. This plan might need to be very concrete and detailed, outlining exactly what the client will be doing, hour by hour, until the next contact with the counsellor.

3. emergency hospitalization. All jurisdictions have mental health legislation that defines when clients can be hospitalized. Typically, imminent risk for suicide is a compelling reason for involuntary hospitalization. Authorization from one or more physicians is usually required.

4. future linkage. This involves setting up short- and long-term goals that give the client something to anticipate. Through this process the client is diverted from the present crisis to thinking about an improved future.

5. decreasing isolation and withdrawal. For many clients, talking about their problems with a counsellor is sufficient to reverse the drive to suicide. In addition, counsellors should make every effort to recruit capable family members or friends to be with the client through the crisis phase. For their support to be helpful, the client must perceive these people as credible and supportive.

6. decreasing anxiety and sleep loss. Medication and/or hospitalization may be necessary if the risk of suicide is high or if supportive family and friends are not available.

7. treatment of coexisting problems, including addictions and mental disorders.

8. management of problems such as poverty, unemployment, and uncontrolled pain.

9. initiatives to increase self-esteem.

COUNSELLING HIV-POSITIVE CLIENTS AND CLIENTS WITH AIDS

All ethics worthy of that name are based on life, and seek to reinforce and strengthen it. What interests me is not whether there is life after death, but that there should be life before it. And that life should be a good life, not one of mere survival or constant fear of death.

—Ana Luisa Ligouri at the 12th World AIDS Conference in Geneva, July 1998, quoting the Spanish philosopher Fernando Sabater

HIV is an acronym for **Human Immunodeficiency Virus**. This virus attacks the immune system, weakening its ability to fight off infections. People may have the virus and not be aware of it, and they may have no symptoms for as long as 5 to 15 years. HIV is spread when HIV-infected blood, semen, or vaginal fluids get into the body of another person. Sharing dirty needles (through drug taking, tattooing, body piercing, etc.) and unprotected sex (anal, vaginal, and oral) are considered high-risk behaviours. HIV cannot be transmitted by hugging or kissing, nor can it be transmitted through the air by coughing or sneezing. It cannot be transmitted through water, food, or insect bites.

AIDS is the acronym for **Acquired Immune Deficiency Syndrome** caused by HIV infection, resulting in a number of different illnesses and opportunistic infections, such as karposi sarcoma (cancer), thrush, and many others. In the last 20 years more than 40 million people have tested HIV positive, and almost 12 million people have died. In 1997, it was estimated that 16 000 people a day acquired HIV.

AIDS has left at least 8 million orphans (Mann and Tarantola, 1998). Since the discovery of AIDS in 1981, remarkable progress in its treatment has been realized in the Western world. Aggressive treatment routines using antiretroviral therapies (HIV is a retrovirus) have resulted in a decline in the number of AIDS-related deaths in the industrialized nations, but a cure and a vaccine for the disease are not expected in the immediate future. In poorer nations, particularly those in Africa, where they are ill equipped to handle the massive costs of treatment, the ravage of AIDS continues unabated.

Prevention

Prevention of HIV infection is the best way of controlling the AIDS epidemic. Counsellors can play a significant role in educating target populations to prevent new HIV infections by encouraging safer sex practices particularly the use of condoms, and the use of clean needles for injection drug users.

Some clients are reluctant to be tested. In part, this may arise from their mistaken belief that there is nothing they can do about positive results. They may fear (often justifiably) that an HIV-positive diagnosis may lead others to devalue and oppress them. Fears about homophobia may lead individuals to isolate themselves from services that could provide information. Educating clients and the public about new treatments and the importance of early intervention may help to overcome their aversion to being tested.

In some jurisdictions HIV-positive test results must be reported. As a result, people may resist testing because they fear systematic discrimination. When anonymous testing is available, this is a way to encourage people to take the test.

Rapid testing with results available in as little as 15 minutes is useful for testing people who are highly anxious. These tests have high reliability, but they are always confirmed with other measurements such as a Western Bloc test.

The primary preventive goal for counsellors is to educate clients to abandon high-risk behaviours such as unprotected sex and needle sharing. This goal may involve initiatives to help clients deal with barriers to making changes (e.g., reluctance of partners to use condoms, fatalistic attitudes). A second counselling goal is to help clients resolve reluctance or ambivalence about taking an HIV test by exploring the advantages of testing. For example, counsellors might reframe the test as an opportunity to achieve peace of mind if it shows the client has no HIV infection. Counsellors can also inform clients that an HIV-positive diagnosis puts them in a better position to take advantage of new treatments and allows them to direct their focus to nutrition and wellness in order to try to keep their immune systems strong.

Counselling Clients Who Are HIV Positive

Awaiting test results is an anxious time for most clients. Counsellors may effectively use this period to help clients explore the meaning they attribute to the results. In the process, they need to support clients' feelings and fears.

Most clients who test negative experience relief. At this time, counsellors may take advantage of the opportunity to educate these clients about appropriate preventive routines.

Counsellors should also be prepared for the reality that some gay male clients feel ambivalent about negative results. "Some gay male clients may feel disappointed when anticipating or when informed that they are not HIV positive. Though the gay community has done much to provide a supportive environment for people living with HIV positive, many gay men who are HIV negative feel isolated, without support, and without a place to belong" (Kain, 1996:6).

Kain suggests that preresult counselling should address these feelings directly in order to reverse the possibility that HIV-negative men might practise unsafe sex in order to join the supported ranks of the infected. As well, this group may think that their concerns (e.g., guilt at having survived, dealing with the grief of losing friends who have died from AIDS) may be considered by others to be insignificant when compared with the problems of people who are infected.

Clients' reactions to testing positive may vary. Some clients are totally shocked, whereas others see the results as confirmation of what they already knew; some see the diagnosis as a death sentence, but others experience denial and act as though the results mean nothing (Kain, 1996). Clients who receive the results as death sentences need immediate help to deal with the psychological shock of receiving the diagnosis. At this point, counsellors should encourage clients to explore and cope with complex feelings, which might include guilt, anger, fear, despair, and thoughts of suicide. Subsequently, support and education about the realities of the disease can help them reach a more rational understanding about their future.

A particularly difficult situation arises when counselling HIV-positive men who have engaged in high-risk homosexual activity while remaining in heterosexual relationships. They need considerable support and counselling to deal with both the trauma of their diagnosis and the unique challenge of telling their partners.

Kain reminds counsellors that denial is a psychological defence that protects people from feelings that are too overwhelming, and he suggests that "unless the consequences of denying testing positive is harmful to clients, there is no reason for us to rush the process" (1996:15).

In the 1980s counselling focused on assisting clients in dealing with the shock of their diagnosis and their impending death. Now that an HIV-positive diagnosis no longer means imminent death (at least in the industrialized world), counselling goals have shifted to helping people live with the disease.

The principal focus of counselling people with HIV is to provide support for them to adopt healthy practices, including aggressive treatment that bolsters their immune systems. A second major goal is to promote lifestyle practices that prevent the spread of infection. More specific counselling activities and goals for working with clients who are HIV positive may include the following:

- providing empathy and support to help clients deal with their fears and anxieties while awaiting test results
- helping clients deal with the feelings associated with a positive test and living with the disease
- helping clients deal with the complex challenges of disclosure (to family, friends, sexual partners)
- assisting clients in dealing with issues of discrimination
- supporting clients to make lifestyle adjustments and to prevent spread of the infection, including adopting safe sex practices
- helping clients deal with the challenges of dating and maintaining relationships
- educating clients about preventive treatment, personal health, nutrition, and wellness issues
- working with families to help them understand how to create a safe and supportive environment for people who are HIV positive
- helping clients meet basic needs (living arrangements, finances, medical, transportation)
- helping clients with sexual identify confusion issues
- supporting couples where one partner is HIV-positive and one is negative
- linking clients to appropriate support groups and community services

Counselling Clients with AIDS

An AIDS diagnosis may bring to the foreground a range of reactions, including depression, despair, and preoccupation with end-of-life issues, such as matters of spirituality and suicide. An AIDS diagnosis means that people have to deal with dying young, as well as with partner and family issues. Many clients are members of communities that have experienced multiple losses, and this needs to be addressed in counselling. People with AIDS must deal directly with discrimination arising from such issues as physical stigma (fear of contagion) and the moralistic judgment of their behaviour and lifestyle. Anecdotal evidence from frontline workers is accumulating that some clients react positively to an AIDS diagnosis when it means that they will have access to medical and social assistance benefits that have previously been denied to them.

Counsellors working with people with AIDS need to make sure that they don't neglect their own needs for emotional support, and they need to find ways to sustain their energy and prevent burnout. Those who work in hospice settings may have to deal with multiple deaths each week. Counsellors need to be aware of their own grief at the loss of their clients, and they must find ways to process this grief. Support and consultation with colleagues is essential for dealing with the feelings and stress of counselling people with AIDS.

Spirituality. Frequently, clients living with HIV-positive diagnosis and AIDS raise spiritual questions regarding the meaning of life and life after death. Clients' spiritual values and beliefs are legitimate considerations in the counselling process (Kelly, 1995), and effective counsellors must be open and nonjudgmental when dealing with spirituality. It requires that they understand the different ways that individual clients might define and approach religion and spirituality. Kain underscores the importance of spirituality in counselling persons with HIV:

> We need to remember that many people living with HIV disease may feel alienated from all sources of spiritual guidance; the counseling session may be the only place where they feel comfortable enough to risk elaborating on issues of faith. At times we may be surprised to find that when we provide clients with the room to pursue spiritual matters accelerated psychological growth often occurs. (1996:117)

Counselling Goals. Counselling is not an opportunity for counsellors to convert clients to their religious beliefs. Instead, they must be open to the wide range of paths that individuals may choose for spirituality. This may be an appropriate time to refer them to an appropriate minister, rabbi, priest, and so on.

The most important counselling goal is to help clients sustain health. For example, counsellors can work with clients to ensure that they have access to the latest information regarding the disease and its treatment. This may mean referral to appropriate physicians who specialize in the area. Or it may mean helping clients use databases of information so that they make intelligent choices about their physical and psychological health and wellness. Other appropriate counselling activities and goals for working with clients with AIDS include the following:

- helping clients meet basic needs (living arrangements, finances, medical, transportation)
- assisting clients in dealing with the feelings associated with this disease, such as fear of death, depression, and fear of being abandoned
- grief counselling to help clients cope with the decline and loss of significant others who have AIDS
- helping clients find meaning and purpose to their lives, including how they wish to live out their remaining time
- helping clients deal with issues of discrimination
- assisting clients in connecting with appropriate supportive groups and services
- helping clients make decisions about end-of-life issues (e.g., increasing dependency on others, hospice care, wills, pain control, suicide)
- helping caregivers (i.e., partners, family, friends) deal with their emotional and physical stress

- supporting clients who are dying (e.g., helping with funeral arrangements, saying good-bye to significant others, exploring the process and meaning of death)
- referring clients to appropriate religious organizations for spiritual support

BRIEF COUNSELLING

Be kind whenever possible.
It is always possible.
—*Dalai Lama*

Brief counselling is an approach to counselling characterized by a focus on resources and solutions rather than problems. The purpose of brief counselling is "to provide people with a pleasant experience that turns problems into challenges, fosters optimism, enhances collaboration, inspires creativity, and, above all, helps them to retain their dignity" (Furman and Ahola, 1994:65).

How Brief Counselling Helps

Often counselling relationships are brief, sometimes limited to a few sessions, a single session, or even a brief encounter. Michael Hoyt (1994) reviewed the literature and found that single-session therapy is often the norm and that a significant number of clients and counsellors found it desirable and useful. In three systematic studies of the effectiveness of single-session therapy (SST), more than 50 percent of clients showed improvement (1994:41).

Many people solve psychological problems without professional consultation. For others, the "light touch" of a single visit may be enough, providing experience, skills, and encouragement to help them continue in their life journey (Hoyt, 1994:153).

An important assumption is that a change in some part of a client's life will affect other aspects of his or her life, including relationships with significant others. Brief counselling that helps a client achieve some success (e.g., insight, reduction of painful feelings, new skills), however small, can have a dramatic long-term impact if it switches the client to a position of optimism from a point of despair, and a ripple effect occurs. "When clients alter their behaviors ever so slightly, it causes a chain reaction in response to the initial change. Those affected by the change find themselves adjusting their responses, which in turn elicits further changes in clients" (Sklare, 1997:11).

When clients come voluntarily for counselling, they may have already established a certain momentum for change. In fact, some clients realize progress while waiting for their first scheduled appointment.

De Shazer (1985) argues that it is not necessary to spend time searching for the root causes of a problem, nor is it necessary to have elaborate knowledge about the problem. In brief counselling, the goal is to help clients do something different to improve their situation, rather than repeating the same ineffectual solutions.

Brief counselling may help in many ways. Because of its emphasis on action and change, brief counselling helps clients to become "unstuck" from ineffectual ways of thinking, feeling, and acting. Clients can be encouraged to reframe by focusing their attention on what's working, thus interrupting their preoccupation with problems and failure. This focus may generate or renew the clients' optimism that change is possible. Brief counselling, even a single session, can be therapeutic for clients if they are able to unload pent-up feelings. A caring and empathic counsellor can encourage such ventilation and reassure clients that their reactions and feelings are normal. This can significantly reduce any feelings of isolation by disputing the belief that many clients hold: "I'm the only one who feels this way."

Brief counselling can also provide important information to clients. For example, they can be referred to appropriate alternative services. Or they can be given information that might help them deal with their situation. Finally, brief counselling can be used to demystify the counselling process and to help clients understand what they might reasonably accomplish in counselling. In this way brief counselling may be useful for motivating reluctant clients to engage with or to continue with counselling.

Brief or single-session therapy is not appropriate for all clients. It is less likely to be effective with client groups such as the following: clients who need inpatient psychiatric care, including those who are suicidal; clients with schizophrenia, bipolar disorder, or drug addiction; clients who need help in dealing with the effects of childhood abuse; and clients with chronic eating disorders (Hoyt, 1994).

Selected Brief Counselling Techniques

Helping Clients Get on Track. Counsellors need to shift their own thinking away from believing that they have to stay with clients until the clients' problems are solved and their lives are in order. For example, counsellors might assist clients to organize their thinking about grieving, but the process of grieving is normal and might last a long time, and counsellors do not have to be present for the whole of that grieving process (Walter and Peller, 1994). Counselling ends with the client still grieving but with a much greater sense of control and of being on track. If clients have a plan in mind for dealing with their problems, they have the capacity to put that plan into action, and they are implementing that process, counsellors should consider getting out of their way.

Looking for Exceptions. Huber and Backlund (1991) propose working with the exceptions to the times when clients are having difficulty. They contend that regardless of the severity of their clients' problems, there are moments when clients are managing their troubles. Moments such as when anxious persons feel calm, acting-out children listen to their parents, and angry people are peaceful can be studied to discover potentially successful answers to chronic problems. Huber and Backlund believe that clients become fixated on their problems and on what doesn't work. By doing so, they often fail to notice those times when their problems have abated. In fact, they often continue to repeat or exaggerate "solutions" that have already proved unworkable. Using this approach, counsellors ask clients to focus on those moments, however rare, when they are coping successfully.

> So when clients are asked, "What is different about those occasions when your child obeys you or at least responds more receptively to your requests?" or "What is different about those times that you're not angry or only minimally upset?" the counselor is requesting that clients report on experiences to which they have paid almost no attention ... As a consequence, they have given little or no credence to the more successful manner in which they were resolving what at other times they experience as a persistent difficulty. (66)

Working with exceptions provides a dramatic and quick way to motivate and energize clients to think about solutions rather than problems. In the following brief excerpt, the counsellor uses the technique of working with exceptions to assist a client who is having trouble dealing with her teenage son.

COUNSELLOR: *From what you've been saying, it's a rare moment when you and your son can sit together and talk calmly.*

CLIENT: *Maybe once or twice in the last year.*

COUNSELLOR: *Let's look at those two times. I'm really curious about what was different about them that enabled you to talk without fighting. Pick one time that worked best.*

CLIENT: *That's easy. My son was excited because he was going to a rock concert and he was in a really good mood. I felt more relaxed too. He just seemed more approachable that day.*

COUNSELLOR: *Have you considered that part of your success might have to do with your mood? Perhaps your son was more approachable because you were more relaxed.*

CLIENT: *Interesting point.*

COUNSELLOR: *Let's explore that a bit further. Because you were more relaxed, what else was different about the way you handled this encounter?*

CLIENT: *I didn't feel stressed so I think I was more open to listen to him.*

COUNSELLOR: *What were you doing differently?*

CLIENT: *I let him talk without jumping in to argue.*

The counsellor's goal in the above interview is to find what works, then to encourage the client to apply successful solutions more frequently. The process is as follows:

1. Identify exceptions to those times when the client is having difficulty.
2. Explore what was different about those times, including what (specifically) the client was doing differently.
3. Identify elements (e.g., behaviour, setting, timing) that contributed to a successful solution.
4. Help the client increase the frequency of the success elements when dealing with the problem situation.

Clients are often more experienced using ineffectual strategies to deal with their problems. Despite the fact that these strategies do not work, clients may compulsively repeat them to the point where they give up and conclude that their problems are hopeless. Consequently, counsellors need to encourage clients to apply the elements of success. Techniques such as a behavioural rehearsal (role-play) that focuses on systematic exploration of the elements of success can be used. Counsellors need to encourage clients to pay attention to what they are doing when they are managing their problem, as in the following case:

Rodney came to counselling asking for help to quit what he described as "compulsive marijuana use." He was concerned that he might slip into heavy drug use. The counsellor asked him to observe what he was doing when he was not using marijuana and what he did to overcome his urge to use. This technique empowered Rodney by helping him become aware of successful strategies he was already using. Subsequently, he was encouraged to increase the frequency of these successful behaviours.

Using Solution Talk. Furman and Ahola (1994) introduced the idea of "solution talk" as a way to evoke a solution-oriented focus to the counselling interview. The goal is to create a climate of discovery and action. For example, in order to get clients to notice their skills and capacities, counsellors can use statements and questions such as the following:

- You have dealt with this problem for a long time. Many people would not have survived. How did you manage to keep going? What strengths were you able to draw on?
- When you've successfully coped, how did you do it?

In addition, counsellors need to be alert for opportunities to reinforce clients' strengths. Personal qualities, actions that underscore their determination, attitudes, positive decisions, accomplishments, effort toward change, courage in the face of adversity, and so forth, can all be used to bolster clients' sense of capacity and self-esteem.

Clients may already have a rich understanding of their problems and the ways in which they might be solved. Counsellors need to tap their clients' expertise about possible answers to their problems. The central assumption here is that clients have the capacity to resolve their distress.

- What solutions have you already tried?
- What would your best friend advise you to do?
- Suppose one day you received an invitation to give a lecture to professionals about the kind of problem you have had to live with. What would you tell them? (Furman and Ahola, 1994:51)
- In order to solve your problem, what will you have to do?

Creative solution finding can be stimulated with statements and questions such as these:

- Let's try to identify something different for you to do to solve your problem.
- Let's brainstorm ideas. Don't censor anything. The wilder the idea, the better.

Reframing was introduced in Chapter 7 as a way to help clients modify their thinking. Reframing suggests another way of looking at problems, which, in turn, generates new ways of looking at solutions. The miracle question (Sklare, 1997; Hoyt, 1994) can also be used to direct clients to thinking about solutions:

- If a miracle occurred and your problem were solved, what would be different in your life?

How could you make the miracle happen? What would you have to do differently? A variation is to use the miracle question to probe for examples of success and exceptions to clients' problems:

- Tell me about the times when part of this miracle has already happened, even just a little bit. (Sklare, 1997:68)

The Change Continuum. The basic idea behind this technique is to assist clients to become motivated in the direction of positive change. A central assumption is that it is not necessary for the counsellor to be present for the whole change process. The counsellor's role is to promote/assist with small changes in the direction of larger goals.

Step One: Draw a continuum such as the one illustrated below. The continuum will be used to assist clients to represent where they are, what direction they are heading, and where they would like to be.

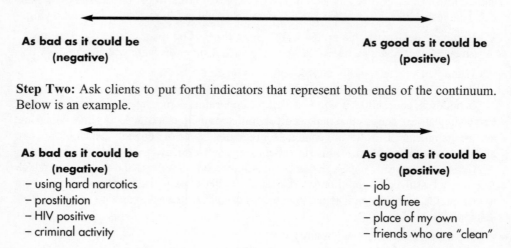

| **As bad as it could be** | **As good as it could be** |
| **(negative)** | **(positive)** |

Step Two: Ask clients to put forth indicators that represent both ends of the continuum. Below is an example.

As bad as it could be	**As good as it could be**
(negative)	**(positive)**
– using hard narcotics	– job
– prostitution	– drug free
– HIV positive	– place of my own
– criminal activity	– friends who are "clean"

Step Three: Use questions such as the following to promote discussion and exploration.

• At this time in your life, where are you on the continuum?

• Where would you like to be?

• What direction are you heading?

• What might cause or help you to change directions?

• What would be an indicator that you are moving in the right direction?

Step Four: Suggest to clients that the direction they are heading is more important that where they are on the continuum. Your role may be limited to assisting them to change direction. Help clients identify incremental steps towards their final goal. Remember: "less frequent" and "less severe" can also signal progress.

Summary

Job loss or unemployment can have a significant impact on a person's well-being. Issues of self-esteem and identity and financial consequences can lead to increased stress and mental health problems. Employment counsellors deliver service in four major areas: (1) job loss counselling, (2) career counselling, (3) job search skills, and (4) life skills counselling.

Modern job search methods differ significantly from traditional strategies. Modern strategies focus on a targeted approach to particular careers and employers with customized résumés and use of the hidden job market through networking. Electronic technology has necessitated that clients become increasingly familiar with new strategies for managing their job and career search.

The job club method is a group approach that provides support, job search skills training, and materials and supplies necessary to complete a successful job hunt. Job clubs provide participants with phones, computers, photocopying, stationery, and daily newspapers and other sources of job leads.

The last 40 years have witnessed dramatic shifts in the delivery of services to people with mental disorders. Deinstitutionalization, propelled by the introduction of new medications, has enabled the majority of people with mental disorders to live in the community.

DSM-IV is the Diagnostic and Statistical Manual of Mental Disorders published by the American Psychiatric Association. Psychologists, psychiatrists, and other psychotherapists use it to classify and diagnose mental disorders. A multiaxial system is a comprehensive evaluation that includes not only mental disorders, but also medical conditions, psychosocial and environmental problems, and an assessment of a client's overall level of functioning.

Schizophrenia is a serious mental illness that results in a range of symptoms, including hallucinations, delusions, disordered thinking, and social isolation. There may be wide variations in the symptoms people experience.

The two most severe mood, or affective, disorders are major depression and bipolar illness. Major depression affects as many as one in four women and one in ten men in North America. The defining symptoms of depression include feelings of hopelessness and difficulty sleeping, thinking, or concentrating, and they may include thoughts of suicide.

Anxiety disorders are characterized by greater than normal levels of fear, worry, tension, or anxiety about daily events, or there may be high anxiety without apparent reason. Four serious anxiety disorders are obsessive-compulsive disorder (OCD), phobias, panic disorder, and post-traumatic stress disorder (PTSD).

The two most common eating disorders, anorexia nervosa and bulimia, are most likely to affect adolescent and young adult women. Eating disorders can be life threatening, and involuntary hospitalization is necessary in some cases.

There is no certain way to predict that a person may attempt or complete suicide, but certain warning signs and risk factors can be considered. The principal risk factors include past attempts, current mental and physical status, the presence of a viable plan and the means to kill oneself, talk about suicide, personal losses, efforts to put one's affairs in order, and substance abuse.

Counsellors have important educational roles to play in preventing the spread of HIV infection. Counsellors can help by promoting practices such as safer sex, particularly the use of condoms, and the use of clean needles for injection drug users. The principal focus of counselling people with HIV is to provide support for them to adopt healthy practices, including aggressive medical treatment that bolsters their immune systems. When working with people with AIDS, counsellors may cover a wide range of areas, including helping clients deal with depression and the possibility of premature death.

Often counselling relationships are limited to a few sessions or even a single session. Nevertheless, these brief encounters have the potential to be helpful for clients. Brief counselling works on the assumption that a change in some part of a client's life will affect other aspects of his or her life, including relationships with significant others. One major technique of brief counselling is working with the exceptions to the times when clients are having difficulty. Counsellors can help clients study moments such as when anxious people feel calm to discover potentially successful answers to chronic problems. A second major technique is to focus the work of counselling on solutions to problems.

Exercises

1. If you were responsible for defining mental illness, how would you define it?
2. How do you think the following affect families and society?
   a. mental illness
   b. learning that a family or community member is HIV positive
   c. learning that a family or community member has AIDS
   d. losing a job
   e. eating disorders
3. For what reasons might a person stop taking psychiatric medication?
4. Browse through the magazine section at a local newsstand. How many publications can you identify in which a feature story related to dieting is highlighted on the cover? How many of these articles include discussion about realistic dieting, body image, and weight?
5. Examine your own attitudes and beliefs about mental illness. How have your values been shaped by personal experience? By the media?
6. Imagine that you tested positive for HIV. What feelings and challenges might you face in dealing with your situation?
7. Do you believe that it is ethically acceptable for counsellors to openly explore with their clients without judgment their clients' desire to kill themselves? Should counsellors be required to prevent clients in advanced stages of AIDS from killing themselves?
8. Review your personal experiences with death and dying. How might these experiences help or hinder your work if you were counselling clients with AIDS?
9. How might you respond to a client who says, "I'm not going to get AIDS. I'm not gay."
10. Your client is HIV positive but continues to engage in unsafe practices. Explore your ethical, moral, and legal responsibilities—for example, the dilemma of whether to reveal the client's HIV status to a known sexual partner. What if this client is a prostitute?
11. Work with a partner. Use selected brief counselling techniques from this chapter to help him or her deal with a problem area.

Weblinks

The Centre for Addiction and Mental Health, an Ontario-based centre, provides resources for professionals, clients, and their families on addiction and mental health issues (formerly the Clark Institute of Psychiatry and Addictions Research Foundation).
www.camh.net/mental_health/index.html

American Association of Suicidology
www.suicidology.org/index.html

Canada WorkInfoNet provides career, education, and labour market information.
www.workinfonet.ca/cwn/english/main.html

C h a p t e r

CULTURAL DIVERSITY: THE FUTURE OF COUNSELLING

PREVIEW

After reading this chapter you should be able to:

- Describe the diverse nature of Canadian society.
- Define the three types of immigrants.
- Describe how counsellors can avoid stereotyping.
- Define worldview and its importance to counselling.
- Explain why realities such as oppression and racism impact counselling.
- Explain the key elements of cross-cultural understanding.
- Identify the unique issues that counsellors might encounter in multicultural counselling.
- Identify strategies and guidelines for multicultural counselling.
- Describe First Nation people's worldviews.
- Demonstrate knowledge of skills and attitudes necessary for working with First Nations people.
- Explain the importance of traditional healing practices.
- Describe the importance of spirituality and multicultural counselling.

THE CANADIAN CONTEXT

No matter how similar we are, there will be differences. No matter how different we are, there will be similarities.
—Pedersen, 2001:18

Canada is a vast country with a relatively small population, most of which resides within 350 km of the southern border. Most of the country remains a virtual wilderness; population concentration is found in the relatively few number of major cities. Immigration policies in the latter part of the twentieth century increased the need for counsellors to develop skills to relate to increasingly heterogeneous caseloads. In fact, typical counselling caseloads in Canada are characterized by diversity in terms of culture, age, race, gender, and sexual orientation. It is a certainty that counsellors will work with clients who have different cultural backgrounds than their own. The 1996 Canadian Census[1] revealed the rich ethnic mix of the Canadian population. Table 10.1 on page 294 shows that among Canada's 28 million people (estimated by Statistics Canada at 31 million as of July 2000), more than 4 and 1/2 million speak a mother tongue other than English or French, Canada's two official languages. While culture is defined by many variables including religion, dress, customs, and food, language is a major defining variable. Table 10.2 on page 295 shows that about 20 percent of Canada's people were born in another country and immigrated to Canada.

The Immigration Act identifies three types of immigrants: family class, refugees, and independent immigrants (Isajiw, 1999). Family class immigrants are those sponsored by close relatives of Canadian citizens or permanent residents. A refugee claimant is one who is seeking protection as defined by the United Nations' Geneva Convention Relating to the Status of Refugees. Independent immigrants include entrepreneurs, investors, skilled workers (based on identified demographic needs), and assisted relatives (those who have a relative in Canada willing to help them become established).

Canada and the United States

Comparisons of Canadian internal approaches to ethnic relations with the United States often suggest that the American "melting pot" contrasts with the Canadian "cultural mosaic." The assumption is that the United States promotes integration of cultures whereas Canadians encourage preservation of ethnic culture. However, studies have shown that the differences between the two countries are not as distinct as the two models suggest (Isajiw, 1999). In fact, the US more closely resembles the Canadian mosaic metaphor than the melting pot. In both countries, the tendency is for ethnic groups to retain their distinct individual identity. Of course, each culture contributes to the national identity and it is, in turn, subject to its influence. One clear example is the extent to which the non-Asian population celebrates the Chinese New Year.

Nevertheless, Isajiw (1999) highlights one important difference in race relations between Canada and the US:

> In the US the largest groups setting priorities for ethnic relations are Blacks, now called Afro-Americans, and the Hispanics, mainly immigrants from Latin America, particularly Mexico.

---

1. As this book went to press results from the 2001 census were being compiled. Current statistical information is available at Statistics Canada's Web site: **www.statcan.ca/start.html**.

Table 10.1 Population by Mother Tongue, 1996 Census, Canada	
Total Population	28 528 125
English	16 890 615
French	6 636 660
Non-official languages	4 598 290
Chinese	715 640
Italian	484 500
German	450 140
Polish	213 410
Spanish	212 890
Portuguese	211 290
Punjabi	201 785
Ukrainian	162 695
Arabic	148 555
Dutch	133 805
Philipino	133 215
Greek	121 180
Vietnamese	106 515
Cree	76 840
Inuktitut (Inuit)	26 960
Other non-official languages	1 198 870

Source: Statistics Canada, 2001a. Adapted from the Statistics Canada Website
< www.statcan.ca/english/Pgdb/People/Population/demo18a.htm >.

In Canada, the two main groups that set priorities are, above all, the French of Quebec, and the Native Peoples. (58)

In Canada, First Nations claims for self-government and territorial rights have reached a much higher profile than in the US. French Canadian struggles for cultural equality and preservation of their language parallel those of Hispanics in the US. For French Canadians, language has become the principal battleground for preserving their cultural heritage; however, the issue of Quebec separation from Canada continues to remain important. Increases in Asian immigration to Canada have also greatly impacted the cultural mix of many areas, particularly large urban centres such as Vancouver, Toronto, and Montreal. Isajiw (1999) suggests that substantial increases in immigration has resulted in tension:

Yet, the mood in the country appears to be an uneasy balance between an understanding and acceptance of the immigrants and feelings of suspicion and even moderate hostility towards them and towards minority ethnic groups in general. A factor in this mood is a degree of racist feeling against the predominately non-white immigrants. (93)

Table 10.2 Immigrant Population by Place of Birth and Period of Immigration, 1996 Census, Canada	
Place of birth	**Total—Immigrant Population**
All countries	4 971 070
Southern Europe	714 380
United Kingdom	655 540
Eastern Asia	589 420
Northern and Western Europe	514 310
Eastern Europe	447 830
South-east Asia	408 985
Southern Asia	353 515
Caribbean and Bermuda	279 405
Central and South America	273 820
United States	244 695
Africa	229 300
West-central Asia and the Middle East	210 850
Oceania and Other	49 025

Source: Statistics Canada, 2001b. Adapted from the Statistics Canada Website
< www.statcan.ca/english/Pgdb/People/Population/demo35a.htm >.

As well, economic stressors, including company downsizing and consequent unemployment, can result in the scapegoating of immigrants and minorities who are unfairly blamed for societal problems.

STEREOTYPES

Counsellors are expected by their codes of ethics to appreciate and respect the uniqueness and individuality of each client and to avoid being blinded by stereotyping groups and cultures. Stereotyping may be defined as holding firm judgments about people based on preconceptions. This is illustrated by such statements as, "Jews are miserly," and "Indians can't hold their liquor." Abundant evidence of stereotypes can be found in ethnic jokes that typecast and smear various ethnic groups.

Avoid Stereotyping

It is critical that counsellors realize and accept that people from different cultures have different standards of behaviour, and that they will often respond to or interpret actions in widely divergent ways. Counsellors can study particular cultures and they may reach conclusions that support certain broad generalizations about that culture, but this is no guarantee that any one member of that culture will adhere to the defining norms of their subgroup. Consequently, counsellors should make no assumptions. In fact, clients are simultaneously under the influence of many cultural groups, each of which may exert powerful, but contradictory leverage.

> **EXAMPLE:** *Baljit, a twenty-year-old East Indian woman, is a first generation Canadian. Her parents emigrated from India shortly before her birth. They retain many of the values of their traditional culture including the expectation that Baljit will have an arranged marriage. Baljit respects her parents, but this conflicts with her growing desire to choose her own marriage partner. She also wants to honour her spiritual traditions. Baljit is active in the Indian community, but she also has many Caucasian friends.*

Thus a client like Baljit belongs "to multiple groups, all of which influence the client's perceptions, beliefs, feelings, thoughts, and behavior. The counselor must be aware of these influences and of their unique blending or fusion in the client if counseling is to be successful" (Patterson, 1996:230). In general, one's personal culture is influenced by many factors including: family of origin, social circle, community, and education. As well, it may change over time and be influenced by catastrophic events such as illness and war, or by economic realities such as poverty.

Although individuals within cultural or other groups tend to share certain values and customs, individual differences may prevail and any one person within the group may or may not conform to the cultural norms. There may also be wide diversity within the same group. In Canada, for example, there are many First Nations including (to name only a few) Algonquin, Blackfoot, Cree, Haida, and Ojibway.

Exploring and understanding the culture, language, and history of the populations counsellors work with is an important step in preventing stereotyping. To some extent, books and films can provide this knowledge base, but direct contact and experience with different cultures is a better way to learn. Counsellors can gain this experience in a number of ways, such as by visiting ethnic districts, attending cultural festivals, and cultivating friendships with a diversity of people. However, it is important to remember that a member of a particular culture does not necessarily hold the cultural values that characterize that culture. Within any culture there can be a wide range of individual differences. Even members of an individual family may exhibit wide variations in their cultural identity.

CROSS-CULTURAL UNDERSTANDING

Worldview

Worldview is the looking glass through which clients see the world. Dodd (1995) describes worldview as:

> ...a belief system about the nature of the universe, its perceived effect on human behavior, and one's place in the universe. Worldview is a fundamental core set of assumptions explaining cultural forces, the nature of humankind, the nature of good and evil, luck, fate, spirits, the power of significant others, the role of time, and the nature of our physical and natural resources. (105)

Because the worldviews of counsellors and their clients may involve different belief systems based on different assumptions and explanations, communication misunderstanding can easily occur. Counsellors may, for example, encounter clients whose essential worldview is fatalistic, i.e., they believe that they have little control over what happens to them, and that luck is the primary factor governing their fate. This has profound implications for counselling, and it may serve to explain (at least partially) why such clients may persist with passivity and pessimism.

Culture is not an adjunct to counselling; it provides the essential context for understanding and responding to clients. It is not "something to be gotten over or gotten around in order to get on with the real business" (Ruskin & Beiser, 1998:438). Counsellors need to understand how cultural origin influences their clients' behaviour and worldview. Similarly, they need to be aware of how their own cultural past influences their assumptions and responses. Moreover, counsellors need to remember that they are members of a professional community that adheres to a specific social/political ideology, and they hold to a belief system that may be at odds with that of their clients. This awareness is a prerequisite for developing consciousness to insure that they don't impose their worldview on their clients. By developing such consciousness, they can avoid some of the problems described by Evans et al. (1979) who reported that:

> Workshops on listening skills conducted in Alaska and the Canadian Northwest Territories have floundered on the critical issue of cultural differences. Eye contact among some Eskimos and Inuit is considered inappropriate and distracting. In the US, patterns of eye contact among Blacks sometimes differ from those of Whites. Individuals in the Middle East stand closer together when they talk than people in the United States and Canada; therefore, interviewing at what is considered normal distance in America would be uncomfortable for individuals from Egypt or Lebanon. The direct approach of staying on one topic and focussing on problems may be inappropriate for some Asian populations who may prefer more indirect, subtle approaches. (12)

Ross (1992) suggests we should expect differences that will lead to different interpretations of our words and actions. He proposes that,

> ... whenever we find ourselves beginning to draw negative conclusions from what the other has said or done, we must take the time to step back and ask whether those words and acts might be open to different interpretations, whether that other person's actions may have a different meaning from within his cultural conventions. (5)

Ethnic Minorities

Experience with Counselling. Capuzzi and Gross (2001) report that research has demonstrated that ethnic minority clients tend to seek help from mainstream counselling agencies only in emergency situations. As well, they noted that they are typically not satisfied with the outcomes of counselling and they "may distrust the counseling experience which may be viewed as intrusive, objectifying, and dehumanizing" (417). "Overlooking client strengths, misreading nonverbal communication, and misunderstanding family dynamics are among the most common errors made in cross-cultural helping. Behaviors motivated by religion and spirituality, family obligation, and sex roles are often misunderstood" (Sheafor, Horejsi, Horejsi, 2000:169).

Reviewing some of the literature, Ruskin & Beiser (1998) concluded that Asians were more likely to avoid seeking mental health services because of the fear of the possible stigma. They were less likely to accept referrals for assistance and they typically terminate

service more prematurely than Caucasians. This is not surprising given Ivey's (1995) observation that "traditional counseling and therapy theory are White, male, Eurocentric, and
middle-class in origin and practice"(p.55).

A Canadian study reached this conclusion:

> Ethnic groups in Canada avoid the mental health system because they feel that barriers imped-
> ing access to appropriate services are often insurmountable. They also feel that, even if they
> sometimes succeed in overcoming barriers, the treatment they receive is inappropriate or
> ineffective ... Large cultural groups who have been in Canada for generations also feel dis-
> enfranchised from care. (Canadian Task Force, 1988:37)

Various ethnic groups may differ in their expectations regarding counselling. While
Western-trained counsellors may favour more passive approaches that empower clients to
develop solutions to problems, others may expect that the helper will be more active and give
them directive answers.

Barriers. Turner and Turner (2000) identify two barriers that prevent culturally sensitive practice from being the norm:

1. Ignorance regarding the "underlying philosophy, structural, and technological alter-
   ations" that are necessary.

2. Inability or reluctance to develop agency services from a "one-size fits all" approach
   to one founded on respect for multicultural diversity.

Recent Immigrants and Refugees. There are unique challenges for counsellors
who work with recent immigrants, particularly those who do not speak English or French.
These challenges are magnified when clients are refugees, who may be poorly prepared for
life in Canada.

> Not only is their arrival usually preceded by an arduous, often dangerous journey, their flight
> was usually precipitated by social, ethno-racial, religious, or political strife—even war. Many
> refugees have been the victims of, or witnessed, torture and other atrocities. (Turner & Turner,
> 2001:171)

Counsellors who cannot draw on their own experiences for understanding need to be
willing to actively learn from these clients about the enormous trauma and suffering they have
experienced. Such empathic interest will help them to avoid duplicating the experience of
many survivors of concentration camps who were prevented from getting treatment and
assistance "because the examining psychiatrists were unable to comprehend the enormity of
their suffering" (Ruskin & Beiser, 1998:428).

EXAMPLE: *Parivash fled from her home in the Middle East after a long period of religious
prosecution. Her father and her brother were both executed for refusing to deny their faith,
although she claims the official explanation cited various fictitious crimes against the state.
As a teenager she was imprisoned and was subjected to torture, but without explanation she
was released from jail. At this time, her eldest brother remains imprisoned with his fate
unknown. Newly arrived in Canada, Parivash has only marginal English, but strong determination to make a new life. Her spiritual commitment remains central to her worldview.*

Socio-Political Realities

Typically, when dealing with ethnic minority clients, there are socio-political realities that cannot be ignored. Often, these are rooted in history and are associated with oppressive racism. In Canada, this is particularly relevant when working with First Nations clients whose cultures, including their languages, spirituality, customs, leadership, and social structure, were eroded through colonization and systematic undermining by Canadian government policies and legislation (Poonwasie & Charter, 2001; Backhouse, 1999). Thus, counsellors should not be surprised to find that their culturally different clients present with suspicion and caution expecting that counselling will be yet another experience where overt or subtle evidence of bias will come to the foreground. Sue and Sue (1999) argue that counsellors need to remember that "... many problems encountered by minority clients reside externally to them (bias, discrimination, prejudice, etc.) and they should not be faulted for the obstacles they encounter. To do so is to engage in victim blaming" (29). Summarizing their perspective on culturally different clients, they suggest that "Suspicion, apprehension, verbal constriction, unnatural reactions, open resentment and hostility, and passive or cool behaviour may all be expressed" (39). They conclude that culturally effective counselling requires professionals to have the capacity to understand these behaviours nonjudgementally, avoid personalizing them, and that they be able to resolve questions of their credibility.

Counsellors should acknowledge racial differences early in the relationship. Davis and Proctor (1989) argue that:

> Acknowledgment by the worker of a worker-client dissimilarity will convey to the client the worker's sensitivity and awareness of the potential significance of race to the helping relationship. It will also convey to the client that the worker probably has the ability to handle the client's feelings regarding race. (120)

They suggest questions such as, "How do you think my being white and you being non-white might affect our working together?" be used along with statements that voice openness to discuss issues related to culture. When counsellors and clients are from different cultures, frank discussion of their differences is an opportunity to "put on the table" variables related to dissimilar values and perspectives that might otherwise adversely impact the work. Although this is an important process with all clients, it should be a priority whenever there are sharp differences between counsellors and clients. This will assist counsellors to understand their clients' worldviews, including their priorities for decision making.

COUNSELLOR: *Clearly, you and I are very different. I wonder if it might help me to spend a bit of time talking to you about your culture and your take on things.*

CLIENT: *Lots of people here in Canada think it's rather odd that my wife's mother and father live with us. But, they just don't understand.*

COUNSELLOR: *What don't they understand?*

CLIENT: *In Canada, kids grow up and once they reach 19 or 20, they can't wait to get away from home to establish their independence. In our culture, we want to be with our families as much as possible. Living with our parents is natural and expected. We don't see it as a burden. It's a great blessing that we can be together.*

Diversity and Individual Differences

As noted earlier in this chapter, there have been dramatic shifts in the demographics of Canada with a significant increase in non-White populations. In some cities and provincial areas, non-White populations have, or soon will become, the majority. The implications of these changes have meant that counsellors are increasingly called on to serve clients from diverse cultures. Speight et al. (1991) caution counsellors against seeing multicultural counselling as something different from "regular" counselling. They warn against using a "multicultural 'cookbook' with each group receiving a 'recipe' that includes a checklist of the group's characteristics and some instructions regarding how the counselling should proceed" (30). Such an approach may result in stereotypes and in a failure to recognize individual differences. Respect for diversity challenges counsellors to modify their approaches to fit the needs and expectations of their clients. Counsellors need to become alert to any conflicts between how they see and do things and the different worldviews that drive their clients' perceptions and actions. Two key questions need to be considered:

1. To what extent does the client hold cultural values and traditions consistent with his or her own culture of origin?

2. What cultural values and traditions are unique to this individual, i.e., different from their own culture of origin?

Counsellors do not have to struggle to answer these questions on their own. As emphasized earlier, clients can be used as consultants. Given encouragement, they can be rich sources of information and understanding. Additionally, the process of inquiry serves to deepen the development of the basic foundation of counselling, namely the counsellor/client relationship. In fact, this approach empowers clients, and it should be followed with all clients, not just those who are culturally different.

KEY ELEMENTS OF CROSS-CULTURAL UNDERSTANDING

A multicultural orientation to counselling begins with a quest to understand our own worldview, then continues with curiosity and willingness to discover the unique and personal worldview of the client. Although different priorities may emerge for each client, the following broad areas should be considered:

1. Individual identity and role within family and community

2. Verbal and emotional expressiveness

3. Relationship expectations

4. Style of communication

5. Language

6. Personal priorities, values, and beliefs

7. Time orientation

Individuality and Family

When working with clients of different cultures, it is important to determine where the client's identity emphasis lies: within the individual or within the family/community (Hackney and Cormier, 2001). North Americans place high value on individuals becoming independent from their family, but in many cultures, separation from family is not sought or desired. In North America, rugged individualism tends to be prized, but among many Asian and Hispanic groups greater priority is given to family and community (Sue & Sue, 1990). In general, counsellors should remember that for many African, Asian, Middle Eastern, and First Nations clients, "individual identity is always subsumed under the mantle of family" (Ruskin & Beiser, 1998:427). Consequently, counsellors need to consider whether clients would expect that extended family or even members of their community should be included in counselling. For example, many African, Asian, Middle Eastern, and First Nations people expect that their families will be involved (Ruskin & Beiser, 1998).

Culturally sensitive counsellors need to be aware of the influence of extended family in decision making. Consider, for example, the potential dilemmas regarding confidentiality with the client who comes from a family where the family leader, not the client, is responsible for decisions regarding counselling. There may be sharply different role and relationship expectations between cultures. Culture-bound counsellors, who define a healthy male-female relationship as one based on equal division of household responsibilities, will find themselves in difficulty if they try to impose their assumptions on a family who hold a more traditional gender division of roles and power.

Although all cultures tend to have at least some respect for their elders, some cultures place very high value on the elders of the community. Many Africans, especially younger ones, defer decision making until they consult with older family members, and in Asian cultures, elders may be valued more than one's children (Dodd, 1995). The North American tendency to stress individuality and personal decision making might be regarded as disrespectful to parents in many African, Middle Eastern, and Asian cultures. In these cultures, "to honor one's parents throughout life is considered one of the highest virtues" (Dodd, 1995:117). Obligation to one's family or even to the community may take precedence over self, and failure to fulfill one's obligation may bring shame and embarrassment to the family.

Counsellors should consider family and community helping networks that exist within their clients' cultural community. Such natural helping opportunities should be utilized as adjuncts or alternatives to professional counselling. However, involving others should be with the permission of the client, except under unusual circumstances such as when the client is incapacitated or incapable of making an informed choice.

People, for example First Nations and Middle Easterners, may include the deceased as part of their natural helping network. Many Iranians believe that deceased relatives can appear in their dreams to offer guidance and support. Morrisseau (1998), from the Ontario Couchiching First Nation, eloquently describes his belief:

> Since all life is based on a circle, and a circle has no beginning and no end, life cannot end in death but rather takes on a different form and meaning. When we understand "all our relations," we will know our ancestors are just as much a part of us today as when they were physically walking Mother Earth. In this sense, we are never alone. Our relations are still present to help us. (90)

The 1978 Iranian revolution resulted in large numbers of Iranians, mostly Muslims and Baha'is, coming to Canada. Shahmirzadi (1983) noted that Iranians are highly family-oriented and counsellors can expect that elder relatives may accompany them to counselling. As well, Iranians will tend to be formal, particularly when dealing with people in authority, so last names should be used until familiarity is established.

Verbal and Emotional Expressiveness

An important consideration is the client's beliefs regarding emotional expression and disclosure of personal information. The western approach to counselling "involves heavy dependence on verbal expressiveness, emotional disclosure, and examination of behavior patterns" (Hackney and Cormier, 2001:121). This may be in stark contrast to other cultures, notably Asian and Hispanic where emotional control is favoured. Also, what is acceptable in one culture may be offensive in another. For example, what is considered assertive behaviour in North America might be seen as arrogance in other parts of the world, and what North Americans interpret as shyness might be defined as respectful behaviour elsewhere.

Many counsellors place heavy emphasis on exploration of problems and feelings as a means to assist clients to develop insight and understanding. This course of action may conflict with the approach favoured by some cultures, namely to ignore feelings by concentrating on activity. Sue and Sue (1990) highlight this issue:

> Rather than introspection and self-analysis, which many Third World people may find unappealing, the concrete tangible approach of behavioral counseling is extremely attractive. The Rogerian condition of paraphrasing, reflecting feelings, and summarizing can be incompatible with cultural patterns. Blacks, for example, may find the patient, waiting and reflective type of a nondirective technique to be antagonistic to their values. (163-164)

Similarly, Sue and Sue (1999) observe that since many Asians have difficulty expressing their feelings openly to strangers, counsellor attempts to empathize and interpret feelings may result in shaming the client. Consequently, they propose more indirect or subtle responses: "In many traditional Asian groups, subtlety is a highly prized art, and the traditional Asian client may feel much more comfortable when dealing with feelings in an indirect manner" (45). Whereas Western counselling methods tend to emphasize open expression and exploration of feelings as a method to develop insight and manage pain, many cultural groups do not favour this approach. First Nations people, for example, may feel threatened by demands for personal disclosure, particularly from non-native counsellors (Diller, 1999). Sue and Sue observe that many Asians believe that "the reason why one experiences anger or depression is precisely that one is thinking about it too much! ... 'Think about the family and not about yourself' is advice given to many Asians as a way of dealing with negative affective elements" (1999: 65). Consequently, counsellors should consider that keeping one's emotions private is for some cultures an indicator of maturity. This will assist counsellors to avoid negatively labelling such clients as resistant, uncooperative, or depressed. However, this does not rule out open discussion between counsellors and clients about the merits of dealing with repressed or painful feelings.

Versatile counsellors will be able to shift from introspective approaches that emphasize insight and exploration of feelings when this shift meets the needs of culturally different clients. For example, action based strategies that focus on developing skills or accessing resources may be more culturally appropriate. This shift has equal validity when working with clients with limited economic means whose primary need may relate to getting a job, finding housing, or feeding their families.

Alexander & Sussman (1995) suggest creative approaches to multicultural counselling that draw on the minority client's everyday life experiences. Culturally relevant music, for example, might be used in waiting rooms as a way of welcoming clients. Similarly, agency and office architecture and art should be culturally inviting.

Relationship Expectations

Clients from some cultural groups may have expectations that test the North American guidelines for counsellors. Ruskin and Beiser (1998) provide examples related to the field of psychiatry that parallel the challenges faced by counsellors.

> In many cultures, people expect to express positive feelings by giving a gift. Should a therapist accept patients' gifts? Is this an aspect of transference that must always be interpreted? Is a gift a bribe? Giving a gift to a therapist may be a culturally appropriate expression of gratitude and respect. Depriving the patient of this culturally sanctioned process may invoke feelings of hurt pride, shame, or anger that interfere with the therapy. Inviting the psychiatrist to family ceremonies and special occasions may at first seem inappropriate, but is not at all unusual. In such instances, the therapist may be well advised to consult with other therapists or culturally literate colleagues before making a decision. (437)

EXAMPLE: *Joyce, a young social worker, recalled how she became anxious when her client, a Jamaican single parent, told her that she wished to give her a gift to thank her for her help. Joyce did not want to insult the woman by refusing the gift, but she was acutely aware that her client was poor and could barely afford to feed her family. Moreover, she was concerned that she not violate professional ethics. Fortunately, her client resolved the dilemma when she presented Joyce with a grapefruit tied with a red ribbon. For Joyce's client, the grapefruit had great symbolic value.*

Another area where counsellors need to carefully navigate concerns physical contact and culture. Cultural groups differ on the extent that touch is expected or tolerated, with further issues related to gender a complicating factor. Both the Canadian Counselling Association and the Canadian Association of Social Workers codes of ethics are silent on the issue except to prohibit contact of a sexual nature. The National Association of Social Workers (1996) code outlines the responsibility of social workers to set "culturally sensitive boundaries" (Standard 1.10) regarding physical contact, but no specific guidance beyond this directive is offered.

There are cross cultural variations on how people greet each other and the spatial distance that is maintained during conversation or greeting. Whereas a handshake is common in North America, others may bow, hug, nod, or kiss on introduction, and this may vary depending on setting, degree of intimacy, or nature of the relationship. Vietnamese men do not shake hands with women or their elders, nor do two Vietnamese women shake hands (Dodd, 1995). Another variation concerns how people greet each other. Some clients are comfortable with first names only, but others are more formal and prefer to use titles. Some cultures expect one to greet the head of a family or elders first (Dodd, 1995). Iranians, who favour formality, may stand up when counsellors enter or leave the room (Shahmirzadi, 1983). Iranian same sex members stand closer than in North America, but opposite sex members are likely to be further away (Shahmirzadi, 1983).

Relationships between various cultures may have historic roots of friction and oppression. Counsellors may expect that the feelings minority group clients have towards the dominant culture will influence the counselling relationship, particularly when counsellors are perceived to be representatives of the controlling culture. In some cases feelings such as anger and suspicion will be overtly expressed, but they may also be unexpressed, and revealed only through subtle or indirect ways. Clients who are overly compliant or ingratiating may, in fact, be masking their anger or hiding the fact that they feel inadequate in a relationship of unequal power. In any case, clients will carefully observe how counsellors process and deal with their feelings, with the future of the relationship and/or whether they will return for a second session hinging on their counsellors' capacity to address such feelings non defensively.

Many clients, such as Iranians, have limited experience with counselling (Shahmirzadi, 1983). Consequently, it is important that roles and procedures be defined clearly, a step that is, of course, important for all counselling relationship regardless of experience with the process.

Style of Communication

Some clients are expressive and keen to talk about their experiences and feelings, whereas others are more reserved and carefully guard their privacy. Some clients like to get to the point and task quickly, but others prefer to informally build up to it. Clients may also differ sharply in their nonverbal communication style, including how comfortable they are with eye contact, their need for physical space and distance, their comfort with touch, their concept of time, and how they use silence. Some clients find that a conversational distance of one to one and a half metres is comfortable, whereas others find the same distance intrusive. For example, many people from the Middle East stand close enough to breathe on others. "In fact, the breath is like one's spirit and life itself, so sharing your breath in close conversation is like sharing your spirit" (Dodd, 1995:166).

Generally, First Nations people tend to speak softer, have less eye contact (indirect gaze), and their responses tend to have more delays (silence) (Sue & Sue, 1999). A similar style is evident among Asians who also maintain a low key approach and are more likely to defer to persons in authority. McDonald (1993) offers this simple, but impressive suggestion: "Interviewers must also be careful to remember that a response is not necessarily over when the speaker pauses. There may be more. Give time for full expression" (19).

In the dominant Caucasian Canadian community eye contact is experienced as a sign of listening and showing respect. Conversely, lack of eye contact may be seen as evasive and inattentive. In other cultures casting one's eyes downward is the sign of respect. For Navaho Indians and many other First Nations people, direct eye contact communicates harsh disapproval (Dodd, 1995). Ross (1992) relates some important principles he learned from a Native mentor and elder from Northern Ontario, Charlie Fisher, who commented on communication errors Ross made in speaking to an elder of the local First Nations community:

> Verbal expressions of praise and gratitude are embarrassing and impolite, especially in the presence of others. The proper course is to quietly ask the person to continue making his contribution next time around.

> Looking someone in the eye, at least among older people in the community, was a rude thing to do. It sends a signal that you consider that person in some fashion inferior. The proper

way to send a signal of respect was to look down or to the side, with only occasional glances up to indicate attention. (3)

Ross also notes that Mr. Fisher reassured him that his errors probably did not offend the elder who "knew, after all, that a great many white men simply hadn't learned how to behave in a civilized manner" (4).

Language

Counsellors need to listen carefully to the vocabulary and idioms that their clients use to express ideas and feelings. The more that counsellors can match their clients' style, the greater their rapport with them will be. When counsellors use jargon or unfamiliar words, clients may feign understanding, or the experience may leave them feeling vulnerable and disempowered. Of course, counsellors also need to avoid talking down to clients.

Words may have different meanings or connotations for different cultures. The word "school" may evoke terror from some First Nations people who associate the term with the abuses of residential schools. Counsellors should also consider the degree of formality that may be expected by clients. Addressing clients as Mr. or Mrs. may be much more appropriate than use of first names. Some clients may see indiscriminate use of first names as overly familiar and insulting.

Culturally different clients are often particularly attuned to nonverbal communication (Sue & Sue, 1999) and they will respond very quickly to subtle indicators of counsellor bias. In counselling, they may test counsellors with questions about their racial views and attitudes to measure how much they can be trusted. Counsellors' nonverbal responses to such inquires will often reveal more about their real views than their words.

Racial Labels. It is important for counsellors to use appropriate terms when referring to their clients. African Americans have historically been called Coloured, Negro, black and more recently African American. Reviewing the literature, Paniagua (1998) concluded that the term African American is more acceptable since it does not emphasize skin colour, but includes reference to cultural heritage and the African connection. Since some clients may have different preferences—preferring to be called black, for example—it is prudent for workers to ask clients what they favour. In Canada, the term First Nations is preferred, but in the US, American Indian is more commonly favoured.

Personal Priorities, Values, and Beliefs

Everyone is differently motivated. Some people are career oriented, and others are driven by spiritual beliefs. Counsellors may find themselves working with clients whose views and attitudes on such major issues as gender equality, spirituality, and sexuality differ sharply from their own. When counsellors understand their clients' priorities, they are in a much better position to support decision making and problem solving that is consistent with their clients' beliefs. Counsellors need to be self-aware and to have self-discipline in keeping their personal views and values from becoming a burden to their clients. If counsellors cannot work with reasonable objectivity, referral may be necessary.

For some clients, ideas and values that define personal and familial responsibilities and priorities are deeply rooted and defined in the traditions of their culture. There may be little room for individual initiative and independent decision making that is separate from considerations of family and one's position in the hierarchy of the family. For these clients, family and community are their sources of help and this reality has enormous implications for counsellors. To proceed without understanding, involving, or considering central family figures predestines counselling initiatives to failure.

European and North American notions of healthy adaptation include a focus on "self-reliance, autonomy, self-actualization, self-assertion, insight, and resistance to stress" (Diller, 1999:61). In contrast, Asians have different value priorities that include "interdependence, inner enlightenment, negation of self, transcendence of conflict, and passive acceptance of reality" (Diller, 1999:61). Thus, individualism and personal assertion are not as important for Asians as they tend to be for the dominant cultures of Canada. In order to process information correctly and make accurate assessments, "counsellors need to determine what is relevant behaviour within the client's current cultural context that may be quite different from that of the dominant group" (Arthur & Stewart, 2001:8). For example, they need to know when the value of family or tribal responsibility supersedes personal need. Thus, all behaviour must be interpreted based on its learned and cultural origins.

Pedersen (2001) offers an amusing, but profound, comment on the natural tendency to assume that others see the world the same as ourselves: "We have been taught to 'do unto others as you would have them do unto you' whether they want it done unto them or not!" (21)

A client's personal values can be identified through interviewing or simple tests and questionnaires. Lock (1996), for example, utilizes an inventory that assists people to rank order 21 different values (e.g., need for achievement, creativity, power, wealth, etc.) based on their relative priority.

Beliefs About How People Should Act. This includes clients' beliefs about receiving help from counsellors. Do they believe that taking help is a sign of weakness? Do they think that families should be able to solve their own problems without outside intervention? Who do they believe should initiate conversations? What are their expectations of the role of the counsellor? What expectations do they have of people in authority? How do they feel men and women should relate to each other?

Clients from some cultures will tend to defer to authority and wait for their counsellors to take the lead in the interview, rarely volunteering information or taking the initiative. They may be reluctant to challenge the authority of their counsellors or even to admit that they do not understand.

Time Orientation

There are interesting and important differences between cultures regarding how they view time. The dominant Canadian society tends toward preoccupation with time, with people's lives divided and regulated by appointments and time constraints. The common saying "Time is money," describes the drive towards getting ahead and making progress. Other societies may be less future oriented and more focused on the present or past. Consider, for example, the importance that Asians and First Nation peoples place on one's ancestors and elders in defining one's life. First Nations peoples are more grounded in the present and "artificial division of time, as in making schedules, is disruptive to the natural pattern" (Sue & Sue, 1999:110).

COUNSELLING IMMIGRANTS AND MULTICULTURAL CLIENTS

Multiculturalism has been described as a "fourth force" in counselling, supplementing psychodynamic (emphasis on thoughts and feelings), behavioural, and humanist counselling ideologies (Pedersen & Locke, 1996). Diversification of society has made it imperative that counsellors develop new attitudes and skills in order to deliver effective service to their multicultural clientele, particularly since research has shown that "many traditional counseling approaches are not effective (and in some cases are even harmful) when used among culturally and racially diverse client populations" (D'Andrea, 1996:56).

Each client has unique values and beliefs and each may belong to many different cultures at the same time. Since within-group cultural differences may actually exceed between-group differences, "all counselling, and, in fact, all communications are inherently and unavoidably multicultural" (Pedersen, 2001:18).

Immigrants to Canada face a wide range of practical problems that may result in them coming for or being referred for counselling. Examples of the issues that counsellors might expect to emerge when working with immigrants include:

1. Language. Clearly, one of the most challenging problems for any immigrant is to acquire sufficient knowledge of the country's language so that they can participate in the society.

2. Unemployment. For many immigrants, coming to Canada results in loss of status, as credentials acquired in their home country may not be accepted in Canada. For some, the problems are insurmountable and they never return to their former occupations.

3. Poverty. Immigrants who have escaped oppressive conditions may have been forced to leave their possessions and wealth behind. Others may be required to take entry level or minimum wage jobs in Canada and, as a result, subsist on marginal income.

4. Discrimination. Discrimination can frustrate an immigrant's ability to find employment and housing. Moreover, the experience of discrimination can evoke feelings of bitterness or hostility and affect their psychological well-being.

5. Culture shock. This phenomenon, which may be experienced in varying degrees, can include such feelings as bewilderment, increased self-consciousness, embarrassment, shame, and loss of self-esteem.

6. Parent-child relationship problems. As a rule, children learn the host language quicker than their parents and they make a quicker adaptation to Canada. Parents may adapt by over reliance on their children for translation or interacting with their new country. Fears for their children may lead them to become over protective, which can lead to parental child conflicts or acting out behaviour.

7. Male-female role adjustment issues. Clients may come from cultures where male dominance is accepted and embedded in the routines and beliefs of their society.

Table 10.3 on page 308 summarizes major guidelines for working with multicultural clients.

Table 10.3 Guidelines for Multicultural Work

1. Openly acknowledge and discuss differences in race, gender, sexual orientation, and so forth.

2. Avoid stereotyping by exploring individual differences. Encourage clients to teach you about their values, beliefs, and customs. Physical appearance does not necessarily mean that a person speaks the language or adheres to the values or customs of the culture they appear to represent. Relate to the client as an individual.

3. Remember that spiritual and religious values are important components of multicultural understanding.

4. Increase multicultural awareness through personal study, professional development, and personal involvement (e.g., cultivate multicultural friendships, attend multicultural events).

5. Seek to understand how historical events such as residential schools and internment of Japanese Canadians influence current beliefs and behaviour.

6. Explore how system problems such as poverty, unemployment, agency policy/procedure, and systemic prejudice affect your client. Whenever possible, advocate for appropriate systemic change. For example, examine how agency structure or policy may be skewed to serve dominant groups while excluding minorities.

7. Remain non-defensive when dealing with clients who have experienced discrimination. Expect that they may be distrustful, sometimes hostile, towards professionals who represent what they perceive as the oppressive power of the dominant group.

8. Be alert to how language, including nonverbal variables, can have different meanings for people.

9. Adapt counselling strategies and goals to meet the needs of individual clients instead of expecting clients to fit into your style and expectations. Consider cultural context when working with all clients, especially ethnic minority clients.

10. Pay particular attention to family, community, or tribal expectations and roles. (Who makes important decisions? Who should be invited to counselling meetings?)

11. Make self-awareness a priority. Understand and appreciate how your culture, attitude, beliefs, customs, experience, and religion influence what you say and do in counselling.

12. Seek and use natural helping networks including family and community resources. For example, encourage First Nations clients to access and use traditional healing practices (as appropriate).

13. Basic needs (food, shelter, employment) may need to be discussed first.

14. When dealing with clients for whom English is a second or subsequent language, speak slower (not louder). Sometimes single words or phrases are easier for them to understand than complete sentences.

15. If you are using a translator, look at your client, not the translator.

Learning From Clients

Given the range of diverse clients that counsellors work with, it is not realistic to expect that counsellors can know about the cultural values and customs of all groups. Consequently, counsellors need to use each client as a source of information by asking clients to teach them about their beliefs. Smith and Morrisette (2001) stress the importance of counsellors avoiding the "expert role" when working with First Nations people by becoming students of the client's culture. Simple questions such as, "What do you think I need to know about your culture and values in order for me to understand your situation?" can start the process. Such inquiries not only educate and empower counsellors with relevant material, but they also communicate to clients that they will not be stereotyped.

Every client represents diversity with his/her own cultural mix. In this respect, Kadushin's (1983) comments on cultural attitudes are particularly relevant:

> What may ultimately be more important than knowledge is an attitude. The interviewer needs to feel with conviction that her culture, way of life, values, etc., are only one way of doing things; that there are equally valid ways, not better or worse, but different. Cultural differences are easily transmuted into cultural deficiencies. There needs to be an openness and receptivity toward such differences and a willingness to be taught by the client about such differences . . . Because the interviewer is less likely to have had the experience which permits empathic understanding of the racially different interviewee, she needs to be more ready to listen, less ready to come to conclusions, more open to guidance and corrections of her presuppositions by the interviewee. (304)

FIRST NATIONS CLIENTS

Throughout the period of colonization and the evolution of Canada as a nation state, we maintained ourselves as a distinct social and political order. We retained our identity as a distinct society, as a nation. We continued to possess and exercise our right of self-government, a right recognized in both international and domestic law. We have never relinquished our right of self-determination.
—Chief Joe Mathias, 2001

One way for counsellors to deepen their knowledge about aboriginal issues is through film. Since 1996, the National Film Board of Canada has supported the Aboriginal Filmmaking Program. The Board has a rich variety of culturally informative and sensitive films that explore Aboriginal issues such as (to name a few) cultural heritage, healing practices, arts, family, and sweat lodges. On line resource catalogues are available at **www.nfb.ca**.

First Nations Worldviews

First Nations people view mental and physical health in a unique way. "Illnesses, both mental and physical, are thought to result from disharmony of the individual, family, or tribe from the ways of nature and the natural order. Healing can only occur when harmony is restored" (Diller, 1999:61). Traditional healing practices are directed at restoring this harmony. Jack Lawson, a Native addictions counsellor summarized his approach in an interview:

> We sit in a talking circle, but it is the issues we talk about that are important. The issues have to do with Native culture, identity, how they see themselves as Native People, the effects of stereotyping, justified anger, positive identity development, and ceremony. And we use ritual

objects, and ceremonies as part of the process: eagle feathers and pipes, smudging, sweat lodges, and so on, introducing our culture into the treatment process and acknowledging what they are going through ritually and with ceremonies. Such a process fits naturally with our cultural understanding of health and sickness. We also discuss the effects of oppression, while at the same time addressing the issues around denial, relapse prevention planning, and recovery maintenance. (Diller, 1999:171)

Poonwassie and Charter (2001) attempted to describe the clash of worldviews that occurred when European Christians encountered Aboriginal peoples:

European Christian Canadians believed that they were meant to dominate the Earth and its creatures. The Aboriginal peoples believed that they were the least important creatures of the universe and that they were dependent upon the four elements (fire, water, earth and air) and all of creation for survival. (65)

Working With First Nations People

McDonald (1993) offers a number of pointers for working with First Nations people that are summarized below:

1. In contrast to mainstream Canadian society where responses are quick, First Nations people may pause before offering a response.
2. First Nations people tend not to engage in "small talk." As a result, they may be misjudged as "shy, reticent, or uncooperative by an interviewer when, in fact, the behaviour may actually indicate they feel that there is nothing worthwhile to say, so there is no reason to comment" (19).
3. First Nations people may appear stoic or unconcerned because of a belief that it is improper to share personal feelings or information with a stranger.
4. Expect short and direct answers to questions. As well, there may be a cultural tendency not to "volunteer" information.
5. Lack of eye contact from First Nations people may mean respect for the person.

Poonwassie and Charter (2001), and others stress the importance of accepting First Nations practices as valid and preferred alternatives:

In order to facilitate community empowerment, all those who collaborate with Aboriginal communities in healing initiatives must understand and accept that Aboriginal peoples have practiced viable healing methods based on their worldview throughout their history, and these methods must be recognized and accepted as equal to Euroamerican therapeutic approaches. (70)

Smith and Morrissette (2001) conducted a study of the experiences of white counsellors who work with First Nations clients. Some of their key observations and conclusions are summarized below:

- Honouring difference, and maintaining flexibility and creative approaches, is critical to effective counselling. A central part of this is willingness of counsellors to understand First Nations experiences and culture in terms of their traumatic historical context.

- Counselling relationships may need to include extended families, elders, and traditional healers. Counsellors need to believe in the community's capacity to solve its own problems.

- Willingness to learn from clients, elders, and Native co-workers is important to relationship development and success in counselling. Counsellors must be willing to relinquish the expert role and adopt "a willingness to have one's knowledge challenge, to work with uncertainty, and seek guidance from the Native community..." (80).

- Counsellors need to respect and be open to the power of Native spirituality. They need to be willing to become involved in community events, which may test and redefine contemporary professional boundaries.

These conclusions are echoed by Choney, Berryhill-Paapke and Robbins (1995) who also remind counsellors to consider such variables as "differences in communication styles, gender role definitions, Medicine, and social support networks including family relationships" (87).

CONVERSATION 10.1

WHO ARE THE ABORIGINALS?

STUDENT: I have trouble sorting out all the terms. For instance, who are the Aboriginals?

FIRST NATIONS COUNSELLOR: Aboriginals refer to the descendants of the original inhabitants of North America. In Canada, the Constitution defines three groups of Aboriginal people—Indian, Métis, and Inuit—each of which has unique culture—language, custom, religious practices, and so forth. Métis have mixed First Nation and European ancestry. They may have cultures influenced by their ancestral roots such as French, Scottish, Ojibway, and Cree. The 1996 census reported that there are 204 000 Métis in Canada. Inuit are the descendants of the original people of the North, formerly known as Eskimos. The country's 40 000 Inuit live in northern regions of Canada, but you should know that Inuit also live in Alaska, Greenland, and Siberia. Indians are all Aboriginals who are not Inuit or Métis. You should know that many Aboriginal people prefer the term "First Nation" instead of Indian.

In Canada, there are more than 500 000 Indians and 60 percent live on more than 600 reserves, land reserved for the exclusive use of the First Nation. Each band or First Nation has its own governing system. As you might expect, the members of each First Nation are uniquely bonded by common values, traditions, and practices from their ancestral heritage.

STUDENT: What is meant by the term Status Indian?

FIRST NATIONS COUNSELLOR: In fact, there are three legal terms that apply to Indians in Canada: Status Indians, Non-Status Indians, and Treaty Indians. Status Indians are registered under the Indian Act and have access to certain rights and programs. Treaty Indians have Status and are members of a First Nations community that has signed a treaty with the government that gives them certain land, hunting, fishing, and monetary rights. Precise treaty rights will vary between various First Nations.

STUDENT: What is the Indian Act?

FIRST NATIONS COUNSELLOR: This is an 1876 Canadian law that outlines the federal government's role in regulating and managing Indian reserve lands. You should know that it is controversial. Aboriginal self-government refers to governments designed, established, and administered by Aboriginal peoples. As well, you should also know that our history includes much pain as we were robbed of our land and our children were removed to abusive residential schools where they were forbidden to practise their culture or speak their language. In the boarding schools, the goal was to make the children forget their Indian culture and adopt

White and Christian values. Government policies were based on the assumption that we were primitive and that we needed to adopt the culture of the European settlers. Canadian governments systematically attacked the tribal systems and this has resulted in marginalization and a loss of identity for First Nations peoples.

Traditional Healing Practices

For First Nations People, various practices and ceremonies are used where the "underlying goal of these ceremonies is almost always to offer thanks for, create, and maintain a strong sense of connection through harmony and balance of mind, body, and spirit with the natural environment" (Garrett, Garrett, & Brotherton, 2001:18). Examples of the various ceremonies include sweat lodge, vision quest, and powwow. They are used in a number of ways such as "honoring or healing a connection with oneself, between oneself and others (relationships; i.e., family, friends, and community), between oneself and the natural environment, or between oneself and the spirit world" (19). In the tradition of First Nations people, life is embraced through the senses which includes the awareness of medicine, which might include physical remedies (herbs and spices) but also extends beyond:

> Medicine is in every tree, plant, rock, animal, and person. It is in the light, the soil, the water, and the wind. Medicine is something that happened 10 years ago that still makes you smile when you think about it. Medicine is that old friend who calls you up out of the blue because he or she was thinking about you. There is medicine in watching a small child play. Medicine is the reassuring smile of an elder. There is medicine in every event, memory, place, person and movement. There is even medicine in empty space if you know how to use it. And there can be powerful medicine in painful or hurtful experiences as well. (Garrett et al, 2001:22)

Elders are being reaffirmed as central figures and many First Nations people are once again adopting traditional holistic healing approaches. Poonwassie and Charter (2001) include the following examples:

- Medicine wheels
- Story telling
- Teaching and sharing circles
- Various ceremonies (e.g., sundances, medicine lodges, fasts, sweats, pipe ceremonies, moon ceremonies, give-aways, and potlatches)
- Use of traditional role models such as elders, healers, medicine people, traditional teachers, or healthy community members

SPIRITUALITY AND COUNSELLING

The 1996 census did not survey religion affiliation, but some important trends are evident from a review of the 1981 and 1991 census data (Statistics Canada, 1993[a]). In 1981, about 88 percent of the people of Canada reported that they were Catholic (47.3 percent) or Protestant (41.2 percent). Only 4.1 percent of the population came from other groups (7.4 percent identified as having no religious affiliation). By 1991, the percentage that was either Catholic or Protestant had dropped to about 82 percent and there were dramatic percentage increases in the numbers that reported membership in other groups. For example, the number of Muslim, Buddhist, Hindu, and Sikh followers doubled. Clearly, the trends are evident and it is expected that similar significant increases will be apparent when the 2001 census data is released.

Counsellors may hesitate or be uncomfortable about making spirituality a component of counselling. Fear of imposing one's values and beliefs, general discomfort with discussing religious issues, and lack of knowledge or skill in addressing religious issues—all may lead counsellors to unnecessarily avoid making spiritual beliefs a target for counselling discussion. Many counselling texts fail to address or even mention this important dimension. One major counselling textbook with more than 600 pages is totally silent on the issue. When spirituality is addressed, typically the discussion is confined to ethical issues, usually confined to discussion of the professional requirement that practitioners respect and accept diversity. However, spiritual and/or religious dimensions, often intimately entwined with culture, are beginning to receive increased attention in the literature and professional organizations. For example, The Association for Spiritual, Ethical, and Religious Values in Counseling has been formed under the auspices of The American Counseling Association. The majority of people are likely to report some religious affiliation or conviction. Moreover, for some individuals and many cultural sub groups, religious organization plays a central role in their social lives and it may be seen as a major source of support. Indeed, all cultures have important religious perspectives that must be understood as part of the process of understanding clients and their worldviews. Consequently, counsellors should not refrain from work in this important area, particularly when it meets the needs and expectations of their clients.

Counsellors may work in a religious setting where their work is clearly framed within the teaching of their particular faith. Such religious counselling is guided by the values and beliefs of the sponsoring religion. Spiritual counselling, on the other hand, involves framing counselling within the client's spiritual values and beliefs. Counsellors who practise spiritual counselling understand their own religious position, but their counselling work is based on their clients' spiritual convictions. This requires that counsellors are comfortable with religious diversity, and that they have sufficient awareness and control so that their personal views are not imposed on their clients. Examples of spiritual issues that might be discussed in counselling include:

- emotional struggles to reconcile emerging personal beliefs that are in conflict with one's religious background (e.g., a client "losing his/her faith")
- feelings such as guilt that emerge from life style choices that are in conflict with one's religious values (e.g., a client contemplating an abortion, but conflicted due to spiritual teaching that forbid abortions)
- exploring client feelings such as anger towards God (e.g., client whose child has died provides an opportunity to assist the client to consider loss and grief in light of his/her own spiritual/religious beliefs)
- familial conflict (e.g., common law unions in violation of religious laws)
- family discord related to one's level of involvement (e.g., children who lose interest in attending religious services)
- meaning of life (e.g., exploring experiences that clients describe as spiritual or religious in order to discern the meaning of these experiences for them)

- death and dying (e.g., position regarding an afterlife, meaning of tests and difficulties)
- establishing life plan or problem solving that is consistent with spiritual values (e.g., dealing with a marriage breakdown when religious teachings abhor divorce)

Frequently, cultural identity is meshed with religious identity. To understand culture, counsellors must understand religion and spirituality. Religion influences the way that people think; it shapes their values and it sways their behaviour. Ethnic customs, calendar observances, music, and art may all be rooted in religious beliefs and practices. For many cultural minorities (and some from the dominant culture) their lives centre around their religious institution.

Ethnic minority clients may be more inclined to seek help from elders and religious leaders from within their own community. Clients with a strong religious connection will respond best to counselling initiatives that take into account their spiritual community, values, and practices. This might include helping them to access and consider relevant sacred writings as well as helping them to use the resources and practices of their faith, including prayer and meditation. Conversely, counsellors who are not informed, or do not consider spiritual issues when they are important for their clients, will have difficulty establishing credibility in the counselling relationship. Not surprisingly, research has demonstrated that highly religious clients do better in counselling and are less likely to drop out prematurely when they are matched with counsellors who have similar religious values (Kelly 1995). Members of the Baha'i faith, who tend to come from a variety of ethnic origins, generally strive to obtain counselling services from professionals who are versed in their faith. Cultural understanding, while important, is secondary to spiritual connection.

Counsellors who are versed in the spiritual teachings of their clients' belief system should discuss with them the extent that they wish counselling to be framed within tenets of their faith. Counsellors who are not versed in the spiritual teachings of their clients can establish credibility by demonstrating that they are open to spiritual elements as their clients experience them. Subsequently, they can best assist clients by helping them to articulate and/or sort out spiritual/religious issues. Kelly (1995) offers this perspective:

> A counselor who understands and respects the client's religious dimension is prepared to enter that part of the client's world. At this point the counselor does not need an expert knowledge of the client's particular spiritual or religious belief but rather an alert sensitivity to this dimension of the client's life. By responding with respectful understanding to the spiritual/religious aspect of the client's problem, the counselor in effect is journeying with the client, ready to learn from the client and to help the client clarify how his or her spirituality or religiousness may be understood and folded into fresh perspectives and new decisions for positive growth and change. (117)

Empathic responses are powerful ways to respect clients and to communicate understanding of clients' feelings. An illustrative counsellor response to a client struggling with spiritual issues might be "Seems like you're feeling a bit lost or disconnected. This frightens you and you're looking for a way to find spiritual peace."

In the same way that there are wide variations within cultures, it is important to remember that there may be variations within religions. For some, religion and spirituality are central to their lives and all of their decisions and choices in life are considered in the context of their spiritual commitment. Others may identify with a particular religious belief, but their involvement and the extent that religion influences their actions may be marginal.

Moreover, complexity is increased because individuals may give a different interpretation to religious teachings. Clients may self-identify as spiritually oriented, but they may not be affiliated with any organized religion, or they may be members of a particular faith but report that spirituality is not central to their lives.

Counsellors need to acquire a broad knowledge of the world's major religions. This is a formidable task considering the wide array of beliefs and traditions that exist. In Canada, counsellors will certainly encounter clients from the following groups: Christianity, Judaism, Islam, Hinduism, Buddhism, and Baha'i. Although basic knowledge can be obtained from books, this should be supplemented with appropriate field exploration. Many faiths permit visitors at religious ceremonies and sponsor public information events.

CONVERSATION 10.2

PRAYING WITH CLIENTS

STUDENT: What should you do if a client asks you to pray with him/her?

COUNSELLOR: It's unlikely that you'd ever get such a request in a secular or non-religious setting. However, in religious settings, or when clients seek help from counsellors affiliated with an organized religion, prayers might be used at the beginning and the end of a session. For clients this helps to establish the spiritual nature of this particular counselling work. Clients who come for religious counselling will not be surprised that this is part of the process; indeed, they might expect such a spiritual frame. In a secular setting, most counsellors and agencies would agree that it is usually inappropriate to pray with clients. They might witness a client who wishes to pray, but not participate actively.

STUDENT: In fact, it did happen to me. I have a field placement at a hospital where I was assisting a Catholic woman. Her husband was terminally ill and she asked if I would join the family as they celebrated last rites with their priest. I accepted, but I wonder if perhaps I've broken any ethical or professional rules.

COUNSELLOR: From the circumstances you describe I don't believe that anyone could reasonably accuse you of unprofessional conduct. In a situation such as this I think you need to ask two important questions. First, did you interfere with your client's right to self-determination? The request was initiated by your client and, given the context, your response seems supportive and appropriate. What's important is that you did not impose your religious views on her. Second, did you violate the legitimate boundaries of your role? It doesn't appear that you compromised your role with her by entering into a dual relationship. This would occur if you started to meet her outside of your professional mandate, for instance, if you agreed to accompany her to church on a regular basis. Or, if you invited her to attend one of your religious ceremonies. In fact, you may have enhanced your capacity to work with her in that you gained further insight into her spiritual values and beliefs. A colleague of mine works with persons who are terminally ill. He says that his clients who are near death will occasionally ask him to be present while they perform a spiritual ritual or prayer. He says he's willing to be present and supportive, but that he does not participate. To me that seems to be the key. Kelly (1995) argues that when a counsellor and a client have the same religious values, the counsellor may accept an invitation to participate in a prayer, but he advises extreme caution.

STUDENT: Suppose clients ask what religion you are. Or, if they asked you to teach them something about your religion. What then?

COUNSELLOR: Our role in situations such as this is to help clients make informed choices based on independent investigations. You might answer the question about your religion directly, then ask what prompted the question. If appropriate to your role and mandate you could assist them to explore spiritual questions, but this must be done from a position of neutrality without any attempt to persuade clients toward your personal belief system. This would clearly interfere with their rights to self-determination. As for teaching them your religion, I wouldn't go there. Instead, refer clients to religious specialists to help them meet their spiritual and prayer needs.

STUDENT: When prayer and spirituality are important for clients, I think it's okay to assist to set goals and action plans that will help them fulfil this need.

COUNSELLOR: Sure, and this might include encouraging them to use prayer—if they believe that this is an important part of their life.

STUDENT: I also think that it's okay to pray for your clients. A significant part of the population believes that others will benefit from our prayers. So, why should we deny our clients this benefit?

ACHIEVING CROSS-CULTURAL COMPETENCY

In recent years there has been a shift toward a broader definition of culture and multicultural competence to include factors such as sexual orientation, physical disability, and socio-economic status (Fuertes, Bartolomeo & Nichols, 2001) .

The term diversity refers to the wide range of variations in terms of lifestyle, culture, behaviour, sexual orientation, age, ability, religion, and so on. Johnson offers this perspective on diversity:

> The human diversity approach considers human behavior from the stance of cultural relativity. It sees normal behavior as an irrelevant concept and behavior as functional or dysfunctional relative to the social situation in which a person is functioning. What may be functional in one situation may be dysfunctional in another. Deviations of developmental patterns found in different cultures should not be considered as necessarily abnormal. (1992:7)

Respect and acceptance of diversity compels counsellors to be sensitive and aware of their own cultures as well as those of their clients. Competent counsellors don't just tolerate diversity; rather, they welcome and value individual and cultural differences. Cross cultural counselling competence requires counsellors to adjust their approaches to understand and respond effectively to clients with a different worldview. In order to achieve knowledge about the factors that shape their client's worldviews:

> Counsellors need to possess knowledge about the history, values, and socialization practices of cultural groups within Canadian society, and how their heritages, including the socio-political issues facing these groups may have influenced their personal and social development... Cultural knowledge includes information about the client's cultural roots, values, perceived problems and preferred interventions, as well as any significant within group diversity, including differing levels of socioeconomic status, acculturation and racial-identity commitment. (Arthur & Stewart, 2001:7)

Sue, Arredondo, and McDavis (1992) have proposed a series of multicultural counselling competencies as the basis of counsellors' education, training, and practice. These competencies and standards have gained wide acceptance in the counselling field and have been adopted within the American Counseling Association. They are organized into three clusters: counsellor awareness of own values and biases, counsellor awareness of clients' worldviews, and culturally appropriate intervention strategies which in turn are detailed in terms of the counsellor's attitudes and beliefs, knowledge, and skills. These competencies are reproduced in Table 10.4 on page 318.

AWARENESS OF SELF

Counselors who presume that they are free of racism seriously underestimate the impact of their own socialization.
—*Pedersen, 1994: 58*

Culturally competent counsellors are committed to understanding their own ethnic and value base. They consider how factors such as their own race, culture, sexual orientation, and religion shape their worldview and impact their work with clients who are different from them. They strive to develop and demonstrate understanding and comfort with diversity.

Counsellors must constantly question the relevance of their behaviour, values, and assumptions for particular clients and cultures. **Ethnocentrism** is the inclination to judge others negatively in relation to one's own cultural values and norms. Counsellors who work from an ethnocentric perspective may be predisposed to discount the importance of cultural traditions and beliefs. Worse still, they may see cultural traits as something to be treated or changed because they use their traditions, standards, and majority norms as a measure of normal behaviour. Respect for individual and cultural diversity implies more than just tolerance. It requires counsellors to accept that other cultures and lifestyles are equally valid, albeit different. This is an ethical responsibility for professional counsellors. For example, Standard A.9 of the Canadian Counselling Association's Code of Ethics directs counsellors to pursue knowledge and experiences that help them understand diversity:

> Counsellors strive to understand and respect the diversity of their clients, including differences related to age, ethnicity, culture, gender, disability, religion, sexual orientation, and social-economic status.

Typically, counsellors are well-meaning individuals who see themselves as moral and accepting. Thus, as Sue and Sue (1999) suggest, it may be very difficult for them to understand how their actions may be hurtful to their minority clients. As examples:

- Stereotyping, for example, accepting the commonly held, but erroneous belief that First Nations people can't hold their liquor.

- Adhering to counselling strategies that are culture bound, for example, by not adapting to the approach favoured by many people of colour, namely that "the helper is more active, self-disclosing and not adverse to giving advice and suggestions where appropriate" (Sue & Sue, 1999:29).

- Belief that one's own cultural heritage and way of doing things is superior. Unchecked, this can lead to oppression.

Table 10.4 Cross-cultural Competencies

I. Counsellor Awareness of Own Cultural Values and Biases

A. Beliefs and Attitudes

1. Culturally skilled counsellors have moved from being culturally unaware to being aware and sensitive to their own cultural heritage and to valuing and respecting differences.

2. Culturally skilled counsellors are aware of how their own cultural background and experiences, attitudes, and values and biases influence psychological processes.

3. Culturally skilled counsellors are able to recognize the limits of their competencies and expertise.

4. Culturally skilled counsellors are comfortable with differences that exist between themselves and clients in terms of race, ethnicity, culture, and beliefs.

B. Knowledge

1. Culturally skilled counsellors have specific knowledge about their own racial and cultural heritage and how it personally and professionally affects their definitions and biases of normality-abnormality and the process of counselling.

2. Culturally skilled counsellors possess knowledge and understanding about how oppression, racism, discrimination, and stereotyping affect them personally and in their work. This allows them to acknowledge their own racist attitudes, beliefs, and feelings. Although this standard applies to all groups, for White counsellors it may mean that they understand how they may have directly or indirectly benefited from individual, institutional, and cultural racism (White identity development models).

3. Culturally skilled counsellors possess knowledge about their social impact upon others. They are knowledgeable about communication style differences, how their style may clash or facilitate the counselling process with minority clients, and how to anticipate the impact it may have on others.

C. Skills

1. Culturally skilled counsellors seek out educational, consultative, and training experiences to enrich their understanding and effectiveness in working with culturally different populations. Being able to recognize the limits of their competencies, they (a) seek consultation, (b) seek further training or education, (c) refer out to more qualified individuals or resources, or (d) engage in a combination of these.

2. Culturally skilled counsellors are constantly seeking to understand themselves as racial and cultural beings and are actively seeking a nonracist identity.

II. Counsellor Awareness of Client's Worldview

A. Attitudes and Beliefs

1. Culturally skilled counsellors are aware of their negative emotional reactions toward other racial and ethnic groups that may prove detrimental to their clients in counselling. They are willing to contrast their own beliefs and attitudes with those of their culturally different clients in a nonjudgmental fashion.

2. Culturally skilled counsellors are aware of their stereotypes and preconceived notions that they may hold toward other racial and ethnic minority groups.

(continued)

B. Knowledge

1. Culturally skilled counsellors possess specific knowledge and information about the particular group that they are working with. They are aware of the life experiences, cultural heritage, and historical background of their culturally different clients. This particular competency is strongly linked to the "minority identity development models" available in the literature.

2. Culturally skilled counsellors understand how race, culture, ethnicity, and so forth may affect personality formation, vocational choices, manifestation of psychological disorders, help-seeking behaviour, and the appropriateness or inappropriateness of counselling approaches.

3. Culturally skilled counsellors understand and have knowledge about sociopolitical influences that impinge upon the life of racial and ethnic minorities. Immigration issues, poverty, racism, stereotyping, and powerlessness all leave major scars that may influence the counselling process.

C. Skills

1. Culturally skilled counsellors should familiarize themselves with relevant research and the latest findings regarding mental health and mental disorders of various ethnic and racial groups. They should actively seek out educational experiences that foster their knowledge, understanding, and cross-cultural skills.

2. Culturally skilled counsellors become actively involved with minority individuals outside the counselling setting (community events, social and political functions, celebrations, friendships, neighbourhood groups, and so forth) so that their perspective of minorities is more than an academic or helping exercise.

III. Culturally Appropriate Intervention Strategies

A. Attitudes and Beliefs

1. Culturally skilled counsellors respect clients' religious and/or spiritual beliefs and values, including attributions and taboos, because they affect worldview, psychosocial functioning, and expressions of distress.

2. Culturally skilled counsellors respect indigenous helping practices and respect minority community intrinsic help-giving networks.

3. Culturally skilled counsellors value bilingualism and do not view another language as an impediment to counselling (monolingualism may be the culprit).

B. Knowledge

1. Culturally skilled counsellors have a clear and explicit knowledge and understanding of the generic characteristics of counselling and therapy (culture bound, class bound, and monolingual) and how they may clash with the cultural values of various minority groups.

2. Culturally skilled counsellors are aware of institutional barriers that prevent minorities from using mental health services.

3. Culturally skilled counsellors have knowledge of the potential bias in assessment instruments, and use procedures and interpret findings keeping in mind the cultural and linguistic characteristics of the clients.

4. Culturally skilled counsellors have knowledge of minority family structures, hierarchies, values, and beliefs. They are knowledgeable about the community characteristics and the resources in the community as well as the family.

(continued)

5. Culturally skilled counsellors should be aware of relevant discriminatory practices at the social and community level that may be affecting the psychological welfare of the population being served.

C. Skills

1. Culturally skilled counsellors are able to engage in a variety of verbal and nonverbal helping responses. They are able to send and receive both verbal and nonverbal messages accurately and appropriately. They are not tied down to only one method or approach to helping but recognize that helping styles and approaches may be culture bound. When they sense that their helping style is limited and potentially inappropriate, they can anticipate and ameliorate its negative impact.

2. Culturally skilled counsellors are able to exercise institutional intervention skills on behalf of their clients. They can help clients determine whether a "problem" stems from racism or bias in others (the concept of healthy paranoia) so that clients do not inappropriately blame themselves.

3. Culturally skilled counsellors are not averse to seeking consultation with traditional healers and religious and spiritual leaders and practitioners in the treatment of culturally different clients when appropriate.

4. Culturally skilled counsellors take responsibility for interacting in the language requested by the client and, if not feasible, make appropriate referral. A serious problem arises when the linguistic skills of the counsellor do not match the language of the client. This being the case, counsellors should (a) seek a translator with cultural knowledge and appropriate professional background or (b) refer to knowledgeable and competent bilingual counsellor.

5. Culturally skilled counsellors have training and expertise in the use of traditional assessment and testing instruments. They not only understand the technical aspects of the instruments but are also aware of the cultural limitations. This allows them to use test instruments for the welfare of the diverse clients.

6. Culturally skilled counsellors should attend to as well as work to eliminate biases, prejudices, and discriminatory practices. They should be cognizant of sociopolitical contexts in conducting evaluations and providing interventions, and should develop sensitivity to issues of oppression, sexism, and racism.

7. Culturally skilled counsellors take responsibility in educating their clients to the processes of psychological intervention, such as goals, expectations, legal rights, and the counsellor's orientation.

Source: Sue, Arredondo, and McDavis, 1992:484–86. Reprinted with permission of the American Counseling Association.

The Importance of Personal Involvement

Books, films, courses, and seminars can be invaluable sources of information for counsellors in their quest for cultural deepening and understanding. These tools can greatly deepen counsellors' intellectual knowledge and awareness about cultural customs and variations. They are important for stimulating thought and broadening knowledge about diversity. However, counsellors also need to embrace experiential learning. Multicultural events, travel, visits to various churches, synagogues, and other places of worship, will expose counsellors to the subtleties of culture including the wide variations in style and practice that exist within various groups. Multi-faith calendars can be used as a starting point to learn about the religious holidays and festivals that different people celebrate. Cultivating multicultural friendships and involvement in multicultural organizations will help counsellors broaden their worldview, increase their tolerance, and help them learn about the many different ways to make sense of the world.

Cross cultural experiential learning exposes counsellors to the reality that there may be many different ways to view and solve the same problem. Achieving cross-cultural competence will be difficult, perhaps impossible, if counsellors remain personally isolated within their own cultural community of friends and family.

> Contact with different cultures provides opportunities to rehearse adaptive functioning skills that will help us survive in the diversified global village of the future. By learning to work with those different from ourselves we already know we can develop the facility for working with future cultures that we do not yet know. (Pedersen, 2001:20)

Reminder. The importance of avoiding stereotypes needs to be emphasized. Individuals of any culture may or may not hold to the values and customs of their group. Some adhere completely, while others may be assimilated into the mainstream society. As well, physical appearance does not mean that the person speaks the language or adheres to the culture that they appear to represent.

Summary

The increased diversity of the Canadian population has made it essential that counsellors develop their understanding and capacity for working with different cultures.

Stereotyping means holding firm judgments about people based on preconceptions. Individuals may adhere strongly to the values and customs of the culture to which they belong, or their worldview may differ sharply. Counsellors must avoid assumptions while accepting that people from different cultures have different standards of behaviour. However, since it is not realistic to expect to know about all cultures, counsellors need to use clients as sources of information.

Worldview is the looking glass through which clients see the world, including their core beliefs and assumptions. Counsellors need to understand how cultural origin influences their clients' worldviews. Similarly, they need to be aware of how their own cultural past influences their assumptions and responses.

Research has shown that ethnic minority clients avoid seeking counselling, and when they do, they are typically not satisfied with the outcomes. Moreover, they may have different expectations than Western clients.

Counsellors need to be sensitive to the needs and problems faced by refugees who may have faced considerable hardship in their move to Canada. Other clients need to be understood in the context of their history that might have included oppression and racism.

The elements of cross-cultural understanding include: Individual identity and role within family and community, verbal and emotional expressiveness, relationship expectations, style of communication, use of language, personal priorities, values, and beliefs, and time orientation.

Cross-cultural counselling might address such issues as: Language, unemployment, poverty, discrimination, culture shock, parent-child relationship problems, and male-female role issues.

Successful work with First Nations people is more likely when counsellors honour differences, include extended families and elders in the process, demonstrate their openness to learn from First Nations people, and respect Native spirituality. As well counsellors need to consider differences in communication styles and gender roles. Understanding and respect of the value of traditional healing practices is essential.

Frequently, cultural identity is meshed with religious identity. To understand culture, counsellors must understand religion and spirituality.

Culturally competent counsellors try to understand their own ethnic and value base, including how factors such as their own race, culture, sexual orientation, and religion shape their worldview. They need to deepen their understanding of different cultures. Although books, films, courses, and seminars can be sources of information about cultures, counsellors also need to embrace experiential learning.

Exercises

1. In what ways do diversity issues such as ethnicity, gender, and sexual orientation affect counsellors' effectiveness?

2. Develop a personal plan for increasing your multicultural sensitivity. Include strategies for experiential learning, e.g., increasing your circle of multicultural friends, involvement in multicultural events, etc.

3. What is your emotional reaction when you meet or counsel someone from a different culture?

4. Research how mental illness may be interpreted by different cultures.

5. Describe how counsellors can be sensitive to cultural norms while honouring individual differences.

6. What are some of the barriers that clients from ethnic minorities face when seeking counselling services?

7. Explore the religions of the world. Most religious groups will welcome you as a visitor to their services, so supplement what you read in books with field trips. Acquire a multi-faith calendar as a first step in learning about the religious schedules and traditions of different groups.

8. How can counsellors assist clients to explore spiritual and religious issues without imposing their own religious values?

9. Do you think it's appropriate for counsellors to privately pray for their clients?

10. Use library databases or the on-line database of Statistics Canada (**www.statcan.ca**) to research the demographic characteristics of your community. Identify the places of birth and mother tongues of the immigrant community. Explore statistics related to Aboriginal groups in your area. What are the implications of your data for counsellors who hope to practise in your locality?

11. Invite a First Nations person to share with you some of his/her experiences in a residential school. Remember that this is a very sensitive topic, so be prepared to be empathic in response to powerful feelings that might be revealed.

12. What unique problems might arise when counsellors and clients are from the same culture?

13. Think about specific customs and beliefs that you might encounter when you work with different cultures. In what areas do you have difficulty working with objectivity? Examples: arranged marriages, male family dominance, and female genital mutilation.

14. Interview several people who are culturally different to learn about their worldviews.

15. Try to analyze the worldviews of selected TV characters. For instance, what is the worldview of Tony Soprano of *The Sopranos*? Of Archie Bunker?

16. In what ways is your worldview the same as or different from that of your parents? Your colleagues? Your teacher?

17. Pedersen (1994) says "Counselors who presume that they are free of racism seriously underestimate the impact of their own socialization" (58). Do you agree or disagree with this statement?

Weblinks

The Native Trail site is a comprehensive gateway to information on First Nations in Canada.
www.nativetrail.com/nativetrail/

The official site of Indian and Northern Affairs Canada provides extensive information on federal programs and services as well as readings on the culture and history of First Nations peoples.
www.ainc-inac.gc.ca/index_e.html

Statistics Canada 2001 census data
www.statcan.ca/english/census96/list.htm#2001

CCA CODE OF ETHICS*

Contents

---

* Reprinted with the permission of the Canadian Counselling Association. The CCA Code of Ethics was approved by the CCA Board of Directors in May 1999.

Preamble

This Code of Ethics expresses the ethical principles and values of the Canadian Counselling Association and serves as a guide to the professional conduct of all its members. It also informs the public which they serve of the standards of ethical conduct for which members are to be responsible and accountable. The Code reflects such values as integrity, competence, responsibility and an understanding of and respect for the cultural diversity of society. It is part of a social contract, based on attitudes of mutual respect and trust by which society supports the autonomy of the profession in return for the commitment of its members to act ethically in the provision of professional services.

Members of CCA have a responsibility to ensure that they are familiar with this Code of Ethics, understand its application to their professional conduct, and strive to adhere to its principles and values. Counsellors should also be familiar with other sources of information which will assist them in making informed professional decisions. These include; the laws, regulations, and policies which are professionally relevant to their working environment.

Members are accountable to both the public and their peers and are therefore subject to the complaints and disciplinary procedures of the Canadian Counselling Association. Violations of this Code, however, do not automatically imply legal liability. Such a determination can only be made by legal and judicial proceedings. This peer review process is intended to enable the Association to advise and discipline its members in response to complaints originating either with peers or the public.

Although a Code of Ethics is essential to the maintenance of ethical integrity and accountability, it cannot be a substitute for the active process of ethical decision-making. Members increasingly confront challenging ethical demands and dilemmas in a complex and dynamic society to which a simple and direct application of this code may not be possible. Also, reasonable differences of opinion can and do exist among members with respect to how ethical principles and values should be rank-ordered when they are in conflict. Therefore, members must develop the ability and the courage to exercise a high level of ethical judgement. For these reasons, the code includes a section on ethical decision making.

This Code is not a static document but will need revisions over time because of the continuing development of ethical knowledge and the emergence of consensus on challenging ethical issues. Therefore, members and others, including members of the public, are invited to submit comments and suggestions at any time to CCA.

Ethical Principles

The expectations for ethical conduct as expressed in this Code are based on the following fundamental principles:

a. respect for the dignity of persons

b. not wilfully harming others

c. integrity in relationships

d. responsible caring

e. responsibility to society

f. respect for self-determination

The CCA Process of Ethical Decision-Making

This brief overview of a process of ethical decision-making is provided here so that counsellors will have a sequence of steps to follow when making ethical decisions and resolving ethical dilemmas.

Step One—What are the key ethical issues in this situation?

This first step consists of the counsellor clearly identifying the ethical issues and/or behaviours which are of concern in the particular situation.

Step Two—What ethical guidelines are relevant to this situation?

The second important step consists of referring to the CCA Code of Ethics to see if the situation is dealt with under one or more of the articles in the Code. If there are appropriate articles (for example, on confidentiality or informed consent), following it may be sufficient to address the ethical issue. If the ethical problem is more complex, however, the following further steps will be needed.

Step Three—What ethical principles are of major importance in this situation?

The third step consists of examining the ethical principles that are important in the situation including those that may be in conflict. This would include a review of the six ethical principles as stated in this Code of Ethics.

Step Four—What are the most important principles, and what are the risks and benefits if these principles are acted upon?

The fourth step consists of choosing the most important principles and relevant ethical articles and beginning to implement some possible action by:

(a) generating alternatives and examining the risks and benefits of each,

(b) securing additional information, including possible discussion with the client

(c) consulting with knowledgeable colleagues, with provincial or CCA ethics committees, or with other appropriate sources, and

(d) examining the probable outcomes of various courses of action.

Step Five—Will I feel the same about this situation if I think about it a little longer?

Until this point, this decision-making process has concentrated on fairly cognitive, rational steps, so at the fifth step counsellors should acknowledge and include in their decision making process the feelings and intuitions evoked by the ethical challenge. In so doing, they could use such techniques as:

(a) Quest - a solitary walk in the woods or park where your emotions evoked by the ethical challenge are brought into full awareness,

(b) Incubation - "sleep on it",

(c) Time projection - projecting the ethical situation into the future and thinking about the various probable scenarios.

Step Six—What plan of action will be most helpful in this situation?

The sixth step consists of taking some action. Counsellors should follow a concrete action plan, evaluate the plan, and be prepared to correct any negative consequences that might occur from the action taken.

For a more comprehensive treatment of Ethical Decision-Making, members are directed to the CCA Counselling Ethics Casebook, available from the CCA National Office

A. Professional Responsibility

A1. General Responsibility

Counsellors maintain high standards of professional competence and ethical behaviour, and recognize the need for continuing education and personal care in order to meet this responsibility.

A2. Respect for Rights

Counsellors participate in only those practices which are respectful of the legal, civic, and moral rights of others, and act to safeguard the dignity and rights of their clients, students, and research participants.

A3. Boundaries of Competence

Counsellors limit their counselling services and practices to those which are within their professional competence by virtue of their education and professional experience, and consistent with any requirements for provincial and national credentials. They refer to other professionals, when the counselling needs of clients exceed their level of competence.

A4. Supervision and Consultation

Counsellors take reasonable steps to obtain supervision and/or consultation with respect to their counselling practices and, particularly, with respect to doubts or uncertainties which may arise during their professional work.

A5. Representation of Professional Qualifications

Counsellors claim or imply only those professional qualifications which they possess, and are responsible for correcting any known misrepresentation of their qualifications by others.

A6. Responsibility to Counsellors and other Professionals

Counsellors understand that ethical behaviour among themselves and with other professionals is expected at all time.

A7. Unethical Behaviour by Other Counsellors

Counsellors have an obligation when they have serious doubts as to the ethical behaviour of another counsellor, to seek an informal resolution with the counsellor, when feasible and appropriate. When an informal resolution is not appropriate or feasible, or is unsuccessful, counsellors report their concerns to the CCA Ethics Committee.

A8. Sexual Harassment

Counsellors do not condone or engage in sexual harassment, which is defined as deliberate or repeated verbal or written comments, gestures, or physical contacts of a sexual nature.

A9. Sensitivity to Diversity

Counsellors strive to understand and respect the diversity of their clients, including differences related to age, ethnicity, culture, gender, disability, religion, sexual orientation and social-economic status.

A10. Extension of Ethical Responsibilities

Counselling services and products provided by counsellors through classroom instruction, public lectures, demonstrations, publications, radio and television programs, computer technology and other media must meet the appropriate ethical standards of this Code of Ethics.

B. Counselling Relationships

B1. Primary Responsibility

Counsellors have a primary responsibility to respect the integrity and promote the welfare of their clients. They work collaboratively with clients to devise integrated, individual counselling plans that offer reasonable promise of success and are consistent with the abilities and circumstances of clients.

B2. Confidentiality

Counselling relationships and information resulting therefrom are kept confidential. However, there are the following exceptions to confidentiality:

(i)   when disclosure is required to prevent clear and imminent danger to the client or others;

(ii) when legal requirements demand that confidential material be revealed;

(iii) when a child is in need of protection.

B3. Duty to Warn

When counsellors become aware of their clients intent or potential to place others in clear or imminent danger, they use reasonable care to give threatened persons such warnings as are essential to avert foreseeable dangers.

B4. Client's Rights and Informed Consent

When counselling is initiated, and throughout the counselling process as necessary, counsellors inform clients of the purposes, goals, techniques, procedures, limitations, potential risks and benefits of services to be performed, and other such pertinent information. Counsellors make sure that clients understand the implications of diagnosis, fees and fee collection arrangements, record keeping, and limits to confidentiality. Clients have the right to participate in the ongoing counselling plans, to refuse any recommended services, and to be advised of the consequences of such refusal.

B5. Children and Persons with Diminished Capacity

Counsellors conduct the informed consent process with those legally appropriate to give consent when counselling, assessing, and having as research subjects children and/or persons with diminished capacity. These clients also give consent to such services or involvement commensurate with their capacity to do so.

B6. Maintenance of Records

Counsellors maintain records in sufficient detail to track the sequence and nature of professional services rendered and consistent with any legal, regulatory, agency, or institutional requirement. They secure the safety of such records and, create, maintain, transfer, and dispose of them in a manner compliant with the requirements of confidentiality and the other articles of this Code of Ethics.

B7. Access to Records

Counsellors understand that clients have a right of access to their counselling records, and that disclosure to others of information from these records only occurs with the written consent of the client and/or when required by law.

B8. Dual Relationships

Counsellors make every effort to avoid dual relationships with clients that could impair professional judgment or increase the risk of harm to clients. Examples of dual relationships include, but are not limited to, familial, social, financial, business, or close personal relationships. When a dual relationship can not be avoided, counsellors take appropriate professional precautions such as informed consent, consultation, supervision, and documentation to ensure that judgment is not impaired and no exploitation occurs.

B9. Respecting Diversity

Counsellors actively work to understand the diverse cultural background of the clients with whom they work, and do not condone or engage in discrimination based on age, colour, culture, ethnicity, disability, gender, religion, sexual orientation, marital, or socioeconomic status.

B10. Consulting With Other Professionals

Counsellors may consult with other professionally competent persons about the client. However, if the identity of the client is to be revealed, it is done with the written consent of the client. Counsellors choose professional consultants in a manner which will avoid placing the consultant in a conflict of interest situation.

B11. Relationships with Former Clients

Counsellors remain accountable for any relationships established with former clients. Those relationships could include, but are not limited to those of a friendship, social, financial, and business nature. Counsellors exercise caution about entering any such relationships and take into account whether or not the issues and relational dynamics present during the counselling have been fully resolved and properly terminated. In any case, counsellors seek consultation on such decisions.

B12. Sexual Intimacies

Counsellors avoid any type of sexual intimacies with clients and they do not counsel persons with whom they have had a sexual relationship. Counsellors do not engage in sexual intimacies with former clients within a minimum of three years after terminating the counselling relationship. This prohibition is not limited to the three year period but extends indefinitely if the client is clearly vulnerable, by reason of emotional or cognitive disorder, to exploitative influence by the counsellor. Counsellors, in all such circumstances, clearly bear the burden to ensure that no such exploitative influence has occurred, and to seek consultative assistance.

B13. Multiple Clients

When counsellors agree to provide counselling to two or more persons who have a relationship (such as husband and wife, or parents and children), counsellors clarify at the outset which person or persons are clients and the nature of the relationship they will have with each person. If conflicting roles emerge for counsellors, they must clarify, adjust, or withdraw from roles appropriately.

B14. Multiple Helpers

If, after entering a counselling relationship, a counsellor discovers the client is already in a counselling relationship then, the counsellor is responsible for discussing the issues related to continuing or terminating counselling with the client. It may be necessary, with client consent, to discuss these issues with the other helper.

B15. Group Work

Counsellors have the responsibility to screen prospective group members, especially when group goals focus on self-understanding and growth through self-disclosure. They take reasonable precautions to protect group members from physical and/or psychological harm resulting from interaction within the group, both during and following the group experience.

B16. Computer Use

When computer applications are used as a component of counselling services, counsellors ensure that: (a) client and counsellor identity is verified; (b) the client is capable of using the computer application; (c) the computer application is appropriate to the needs of the client; (d) the client understands the purpose and operation of client-assisted and/or self-help computer applications; and (e) a follow-up of client use of a computer application is provided to assist subsequent needs. In any case, computer applications do not diminish the counsellor's responsibility to act in accordance with the CCA Code of Ethics, and in particular, to ensure adherence to the principles of confidentiality, informed consent, and safeguarding against harmful effects.

B17. Referral

When counsellors determine their inability to be of professional assistance to clients, they avoid initiating a counselling relationship, or immediately terminate it. In either event, members suggest appropriate alternatives, including making a referral to resources about which they are knowledgeable. Should clients decline the suggested referral, counsellors are not obligated to continue the relationship.

B18. Termination of Counselling

Counsellors terminate counselling relationships, with client agreement whenever possible, when it is reasonably clear that: the goals of counselling have been met, the client is no longer benefitting from counselling, when clients do not pay fees charged, when previously disclosed agency or institutional limits do not allow for the provision of further counselling services.

However, counsellors make reasonable efforts to facilitate the continuation of counselling services when services are interrupted by such factors as counsellor illness, client or counsellor relocation, client financial difficulties, and so forth.

C. Consulting and Private Practice

C1. General Responsibility

Counsellors provide consultative services only in those areas in which they have demonstrated competency by virtue of their education and experience.

C2. Undiminished Responsibility and Liability

Counsellors who work in private practice, whether incorporated or not, must ensure that there is no diminishing of their individual professional responsibility to act in accordance with the CCA Code of Ethics, or in their liability for any failure to do so.

C3. Accurate Advertising

Counsellors, when advertising services as private practitioners, do so in a manner that accurately and clearly informs the public of their services and areas of expertise.

C4. Consultative Relationships

Counsellors ensure that consultation occurs within a voluntary relationship between a counsellor and a help-seeking individual, group, or organization, and that the goals are understood by all parties concerned.

C5. Informed Consent

Counsellors who provide services for the use of third parties, acknowledge and clarify for the informed consent of clients, all obligations of such multiple relationships, including purpose(s), entitlement to information, and any restrictions on confidentiality. Third parties include, courts, public and private institutions, funding agencies, employees, and so forth.

C6. Respect for Privacy

Counsellors limit any discussion of client information obtained from a consulting relationship to persons clearly involved with the case. Any written and oral reports restrict data to the purposes of the consultation and, every effort is made to protect client identity and to avoid undue invasion of privacy.

C7. Conflict of Interest

Counsellors who engage in consultation avoid circumstances where the duality of relationships, or the prior possession of information could lead to a conflict of interest.

C8. Sponsorship and Recruitment

Counsellors present any of their organizational affiliations or membership in such a way as to avoid misunderstanding regarding sponsorship or certification. They also avoid the use of any institutional affiliation to recruit private practice clients.

D. Evaluation and Assessment

D1. General Orientation

Counsellors adequately orient and inform clients so that evaluation and assessment results can be placed in proper perspective along with other relevant information.

D2. Purposes and Results of Evaluation and Assessment

Counsellors take responsibility to inform clients about the purpose of any evaluation and assessment instruments and procedures and the meaning of evaluation and assessment results.

D3. Evaluation and Assessment Competence

Counsellors recognize the limits of their competence and offer only those evaluation and assessment services for which they have appropriate preparation and which meet established professional standards.

D4. Administrative and Supervisory Conditions

Counsellors ensure that evaluation and assessment instruments and procedures are administered and supervised under established conditions consistent with professional standards. They note any departures from standard conditions, and any unusual behavior or irregularities which may affect the interpretation of results.

D5. Use of Technology

Counsellors recognize that their ethical responsibilities are not altered, or in any way diminished, by the use of technology for the administration of evaluation and assessment instruments. Counsellors retain their responsibility for the maintenance of the ethical principles of privacy, confidentiality, and responsibility for decisions regardless of the technology used.

D6. Appropriateness of Evaluation and Assessment

Counsellors ensure that evaluation and assessment instruments and procedures are valid, reliable, and appropriate to both the client and the intended purposes.

D7. Reporting Evaluation and Assessment Results

Counsellors ensure that when reporting evaluation and assessment results to clients and other individuals care is taken to provide, in an appropriate manner, accurate and sufficient information for an understanding of any conclusions and recommendations made, and to identify the basis for any reservations which might exist.

D8. Release of Evaluation and Assessment Data

Counsellors ensure that evaluation and assessment data are released only to persons qualified to interpret and use them properly.

D9. Integrity of Evaluation and Assessment Instruments and Procedures

Counsellors who use psychological tests and other assessment instruments, the value of which depends on their novelty to the client, ensure that they are limited to and safeguarded by those with the professional interest and competence to do so.

D10. Sensitivity to Diversity when Assessing and Evaluating

Counsellors proceed with caution when judging and interpreting the performance of minority group members and any other persons not represented in the group on which the evaluation and assessment instruments and procedures were standardized. They recognize and take into account the potential effects of age, ethnicity, disability, culture, gender, religion, sexual orientation, and social-economic status on both the administration of, and the interpretation of date from, such instruments and procedures.

D11. Security Maintenance

Counsellors ensure the integrity and security of evaluation and assessment instruments and procedures consistent with any legal and contractual obligations. They refrain from appropriating, reproducing, or modifying established evaluation and assessment instruments without the expressed permission and adequate recognition of the original author, publisher, and copyright holder.

E. Research and Publications

E1. Researcher Responsibility

Counsellors plan, conduct, and report on research in a manner consistent with relevant ethical principles, professional standards of practice, federal and provincial laws, institutional regulations, cultural norms, and standards governing research with human subjects.

E2. Subject Welfare

Counsellors are responsible for protecting the welfare of their research subjects during research, and avoid causing injurious psychological, physical or social effects to persons who participate in their research activities.

E3. Principal Researcher Responsibility

Counsellors when in the role of principal researcher are responsible for ensuring that appropriate ethical research practices are followed and, with respect to research involving human subjects, they obtain an independent and appropriate ethical review before proceeding with the research. Research associates involved in the research activities share ethical obligations and full responsibility for their own actions.

E4. Voluntary Participation

Counsellors ensure that participation in research is voluntary. However, involuntary participation may be appropriate when it can be shown that participation will have no harmful effects on subjects, is essential to the research, and meets ethical review requirements.

E5. Informed Consent of Research Subjects

Counsellors inform all research subjects of the purpose(s) of their research. In addition, subjects are made aware of any experimental procedures, possible risks, disclosures and limitations on confidentiality. Subjects are also told they are free to ask questions and to discontinue at any time.

E6. Research Confidentiality

Counsellors ensure that research information on subjects is confidential and the identity of participants is protected unless otherwise authorized by them, consistent with all informed consent procedures.

E7. Further Research

Counsellors have an obligation to collaborate with colleagues by making available original research data to qualified researchers who may wish to replicate or verify the research.

E8. Research Sponsors

Counsellors when conducting research obtain informed consent form sponsors and institutions and ensure that sponsors and institutions are given feedback information and proper acknowledgment.

E9. Review of Manuscripts

Counsellors who review material submitted for publication, research or other scholarly purposes respect the confidentiality and proprietary rights of those who submitted the research.

E10. Reporting Results

In reporting research results, counsellors mention any variables and conditions that might affect the outcome of the investigation orth. interpretation of the results, and provide information sufficient for others who might wish to replicate the research.

E11. Research Contributions

Counsellors give due credit through joint authorship, acknowledgment, footnote statements, or other appropriate means to those who have contributed significantly to the research and/or publication, and to those who have done previous work on the topic. For an article that is based mainly on a student thesis or dissertation, the student is listed as principal author.

E12. Submission for Publication

Counsellors do not submit the same manuscript or one essentially similar in content for simultaneous publication consideration by two or more journals. In addition, manuscripts published in whole or in substantial part in another journal or published work should not be submitted for publication without acknowledgment and permission from the previous publication.

F. Counsellor Education, Training, and Supervision

F1. General Responsibility

Counsellors who are responsible for counsellor education, training, and supervision adhere to current CCA guidelines and standards with respect to such activities and conduct themselves in a manner consistent with the CCA Code of Ethics and Standards of Practice.

F2. Boundaries of Competence

Counsellors who conduct counsellor education, training, and supervision have the necessary knowledge and skills to do so, and limit their involvement to such competencies.

F3. Ethical Orientation

Counsellors who are responsible for counsellor education, training, and supervision have an obligation to make their students, trainees, and supervisees aware of their ethical responsibilities as expressed in the CCA Code of Ethics, and Standards of Practice.

F4. Clarification of Roles and Responsibilities

Counsellors who engage in counselling supervision of students or trainees take responsibility for clarifying their respective roles and obligations.

F5. Welfare of Clients

Counsellors who engage in counselling supervision of students or trainees take steps to ensure the welfare of clients during the supervised practice period, and intervene, when necessary, to ensure that this obligation is met.

F6. Program Orientation

Counsellors responsible for counsellor education programs and training activities take responsibility to orient perspective students and trainees to all core elements of such programs and activities, including to a clear policy with respect to all supervised practice components, both those simulated and real.

F7. Relational Boundaries

Counsellors who work as counsellor educators, trainers, and supervisors establish relationships with their students, trainees, and supervisees such that appropriate relational boundaries are clarified and maintained, and dual relationships avoided.

F8. Obligation to Inform

Counsellors who work as counsellor educators, trainers, and supervisors take steps to inform students, trainees, and supervisees, at the beginning of activities associated with these roles, of all reasonably foreseeable circumstances under which confidentiality maybe breached during such activities.

F9. Self-Development and Self-Awareness

Counsellors who work as counsellor educators, trainers, and supervisors, encourage and facilitate the self-development and self-awareness of students, trainees, and supervisees, so that they learn to integrate their professional practice and personal insight.

F10. Dealing with Personal Issues

Counsellors responsible for counsellor education, training, and supervision recognize when such activities evoke significant personal issues for students, trainees, and supervisees and refer to other sources when necessary to avoid counselling those for whom they hold administrative, or evaluative responsibility.

F11. Self-Growth Activities

Counsellors who work as counsellor educators, trainees, and supervisors ensure that any professional experiences which requires self-disclosure, and engagement in self-growth activities are managed in a manner consistent with the principles of informed consent, confidentiality, and safeguarding against any harmful effects.

A p p e n d i x

CANADIAN ASSOCIATION OF SOCIAL WORKERS CODE OF ETHICS (1994)*

* This Social Work Code of Ethics, adopted by the Board of Directors of the Canadian Association of Social Workers (CASW) is effective on January 1, 1994 and replaces the CASW Code of Ethics (1983). The code is reprinted here with the permission of CASW. The copyright in the document has been registered with Consumer and Corporate Affairs Canada, Registration No. 427837.

DEFINITIONS

In this Code,
Best Interest of Client

means

(a) that the wishes, desires, motivations, and plans of the client are taken by the social worker as the primary consideration in any intervention plan developed by the social worker subject to change only when the client's plans are documented to be unrealistic, unreasonable or potentially harmful to self or others or otherwise determined inappropriate when considered in relation to a mandated requirement,

(b) that all actions and interventions of the social worker are taken subject to the reasonable belief that the client will benefit from the action, and

(c) that the social worker will consider the client as an individual, a member of a family unit, a member of a community, a person with a distinct ancestry or culture and will consider those factors in any decision affecting the client.

Client[1]

means

(a) a person, family, group of persons, incorporated body, association or community on whose behalf a social worker provides or agrees to provide a service

    (i) on request or with agreement[2] of the person, family, group of persons, incorporated body, associations or community, or

    (ii) as a result of a legislated responsibility, or

(b) a judge of a court of competent jurisdiction who orders the social worker to provide to the Court an assessment.[3]

Conduct Unbecoming

means behaviour or conduct that does not meet standard of care requirements and is therefore subject to discipline.[4]

Malpractice and Negligence

means behaviour that is included as "conduct unbecoming" and relates to social work practice behaviour within the parameters of the professional relationship that falls below the standard of practice and results in or aggravates an injury to a client. Without limiting the generality of the above,[5] it includes behaviour which results in assault, deceit, fraudulent misrepresentations, defamation of character, breach of contract, violation of human rights, malicious prosecution, false imprisonment or criminal conviction.

Practice of Social Work

includes the assessment, remediation and prevention of social problems, and the enhancement of social functioning of individuals, families, groups and communities by means of

(a) the provision of direct counselling services within an established relationship between a social worker and client;

(b) the development, promotion and delivery of human service programs, including that done in collaboration with other professionals;

(c) the development and promotion of social policies aimed at improving social conditions and equality; and[6]

(d) any other activities approved by CASW.[7]

Social Worker

means a person who is duly registered to practice social work in a province or territory or where mandatory registration does not exist, a person practising social work who voluntarily agrees to be subject to this Code.

Standard of Practice

means the standard of care ordinarily expected of a competent social worker. It means that the public is assured that a social worker has the training, the skill and the diligence to provide them with professional social work services.

PREAMBLE

Philosophy

The profession of social work is founded on humanitarian and egalitarian ideals. Social workers believe in the intrinsic worth and dignity of every human being and are committed to the values of acceptance, self-determination and respect of individuality. They believe in the obligation of all people, individually and collectively, to provide resources, services and opportunities for the overall benefit of humanity. The culture of individuals, families, groups, communities and nations has to be respected without prejudice.[8]

Social workers are dedicated to the welfare and self-realization of human beings; to the development and disciplined use of scientific knowledge regarding human and societal behaviours; to the development of resources to meet individual, group, national and international needs and aspirations; and to the achievement of social justice for all.

Professional Practice Conflicts

If a conflict arises in professional practice, the standards declared in this Code take precedence. Conflicts of interest may occur because of demands from the general public, workplace, organizations or clients. In all cases, if the ethical duties and obligations or ethical responsibilities of this Code would be comprised, the social worker must act in a manner consistent with this Code.

Nature of this Code

The first seven statements in this code establish ethical duties and obligations. These statements provide the basis of a social worker's relationship with a client and are based on the values of social work. A breach of any of these statements forms the basis of a disciplinary action. The remaining three statements are characterized as ethical responsibilities and are to be seen as being different from the ethical duties and obligations. These ethical responsibilities are not likely to form the basis of any disciplinary action if breached. However these sections may form the basis of inquiry. These ethical responsibilities may be used in conjunction with breaches of other sections of this code and may form the basis of necessary background information in any action for discipline. Of equal importance, these ethical responsibilities are desirable goals to be achieved by the social work profession which by its nature is driven by an adherence to the values that form the basis of these desirable ethical behaviours.

SOCIAL WORK CODE OF ETHICS

Ethical Duties and Obligations

1. A social worker shall maintain the best interest of the client as the primary professional obligation.

2. A social worker shall carry out her or his professional duties and obligations with integrity and objectivity.

3. A social worker shall have and maintain competence in the provision of a social work service to a client.

4. A social worker shall not exploit the relationship with a client for personal benefit, gain or gratification.

5. A social worker shall protect the confidentiality of all information acquired from the client or others regarding the client and the client's family during the professional relationship unless

   (a) the client authorizes in writing the release of specified information.

   (b) the information is released under the authority of a statute or an order of a court of competent jurisdiction, or

   (c) otherwise authorized by this Code.

6. A social worker who engages in another profession, occupation, affiliation or calling shall not allow these outside interests to affect the social work relationship with the client.

7. A social worker in private practice shall not conduct the business of provision of social work services for a fee in a manner that discredits the profession or diminishes the public's trust in the profession.

Ethical Responsibilities

8. A social worker shall advocate for workplace conditions and policies that are consistent with the Code.

9. A social worker shall promote excellence in the social work profession.

10. A social worker shall advocate change

(a) in the best interest of the client, and

(b) for the overall benefit of society, the environment and the global community.

CHAPTER 1: Primary Professional Obligation

1. A social worker shall maintain the best interest of the client as the primary professional obligation.

1.1 The social worker is to be guided primarily by this obligation. Any action which is substantially inconsistent with this obligation is an unethical action.

1.2 A social worker in the practice of social work shall not discriminate against any person on the basis of race, ethnic background, language, religion, marital status, sex, sexual orientation, age, abilities, socio-economic status, political affiliation or national ancestry.[9]

1.3 A social worker shall inform a client of the client's right to consult another professional at any time during the provision of social work services.

1.4 A social worker shall immediately inform the client of any factor, condition[10] or pressure that affects the social worker's ability to perform an acceptable level of service.

1.5 A social worker shall not become involved in a client's personal affairs that are not relevant to the service being provided.

1.6 A social worker shall not state an opinion, judgment or use a clinical diagnosis unless there is a documented assessment, observation or diagnosis to support the opinion, judgment or diagnosis.

1.7 Where possible, a social worker shall provide or secure social work services in the language chosen by the client.

CHAPTER 2: Integrity and Objectivity

2. A social worker shall carry out his or her professional duties and obligations with integrity and objectivity.[11]

2.1 The social worker shall identify and describe education, training, experience, professional affiliations, competence, and nature of service in an honest and accurate manner.

2.2 The social worker shall explain to the client her or his education, experience, training, competence, nature of service and action at the request of the client.

2.3 A social worker shall cite an educational degree only after it has been received from the institution.

2.4 A social worker shall not claim formal social work education in an area of expertise or training solely by attending a lecture, demonstration, conference, panel discussion, workshop, seminar or other similar teaching presentation.[12]

2.5 The social worker shall not make a false, misleading or exaggerated claim of efficacy regarding past or anticipated achievement with respect to clients.

2.6 The social worker shall distinguish between actions and statements made as a private citizen and actions and statements made as a social worker.[13]

CHAPTER 3:   Competence in the Provision of Social Work Services

3.   A social worker shall have and maintain competence in the provision of a social work service to a client.

3.1   The social worker shall not undertake a social work service unless the social worker has the competence to provide the service or the social worker can reasonably acquire the necessary competence without undue delay, risk or expense to the client.

3.2   Where a social worker cannot reasonably acquire the necessary competence in the provision of a service to a client, the social worker shall decline to provide the service to the client, advising the client of the reason and ensuring that the client is referred to another professional person if the client agrees to the referral.

3.3   The social worker, with the agreement of the client, may obtain advice from other professionals in the provision of service to a client.

3.4   A social worker shall maintain an acceptable level of health and well-being in order to provide a competent level of service to a client.[14]

3.5   Where a social worker has a physical or mental health problem, disability or illness that affects the ability of the social worker to provide competent service or that would threaten the health or well-being of the client, the social worker shall discontinue the provision of social work to a client

(a) advising the client of the reason and,[15]

(b) ensuring that the client is referred to another professional person if the client agrees to the referral.

3.6   The social worker shall have, maintain and endeavor periodically to update an acceptable level of knowledge and skills to meet the standards of practice of the profession.

CHAPTER 4:   Limit on Professional Relationship

4.   A social worker shall not exploit the relationship with a client for personal benefit, gain or gratification.

4.1   The social worker shall respect the client and act so that the dignity, individuality and rights of the person are protected.

4.2   The social worker shall assess and consider a client's motivation and physical and mental capacity in arranging for the provision of an appropriate service.

4.3   The social worker shall not have a sexual relationship with a client.

4.4   The social worker shall not have a business relationship with a client, borrow money from a client, or loan money to a client.[16]

4.5   The social worker shall not have a sexual relationship with a social work student assigned to the social worker.

4.6   The social worker shall not sexually harass any person.

CHAPTER 5:   Confidential Information

5.   A social worker shall protect the confidentiality[17] of all information acquired from the client or others regarding the client and the client's family during the professional relationship[18] unless

(a) the client authorizes in writing the release of specified information,[19]

(b) the information is released under the authority of a statute or an order of a court of relevant jurisdiction, or

(c) otherwise authorized under this Code.

5.1 The requirement of confidentiality also applies to social workers who work as

(a) supervisors

(b) managers,

(c) educators, or

(d) administrators.

5.2 A social worker who works as a supervisor, manager or administrator shall establish policies and practices that protect the confidentiality of client information.

5.3 The social worker may disclose confidential information to other persons in the workplace who, by virtue of their responsibilities, have an identified need to know as determined by the social worker.

5.4 Clients shall be the initial or primary source of information about themselves and their problems unless the client is incapable or unwilling to give information or when corroborative reporting is required.

5.5 The social worker has the obligation to ensure that the client understands what is being asked, why and to what purpose the information will be used, and to understand the confidentiality policies and practices of the workplace setting.

5.6 Where information is required by law, the social worker shall explain to the client the consequences of refusing to provide the requested information.

5.7 Where information is required from other sources, the social worker

(a) shall explain the requirement to the client, and

(b) shall attempt to involve the client in selecting the sources to be used.

5.8 The social worker shall take reasonable care to safeguard the client's personal papers or property if the social worker agrees to keep the property at the request of the client.

Recording Information

5.9 The social worker shall maintain only one master file on each client.[20]

5.10 The social worker shall record all relevant information, and keep all relevant documents in the file.

5.11 The social worker shall not record in a client's file any characterization that is not based on clinical assessment or fact.

Accessibility of Records

5.12 The social worker who contracts for the delivery of social work services with a client is responsible to the client for maintaining the client record.

5.13 The social worker who is employed by a social agency that delivers social work services to clients is responsible

(a) to the client for the maintaining of a client record, and

(b) to the agency to maintain the records to facilitate the objectives of the agency.

5.14 A social worker is obligated to follow the provision of a statute that allows access to records by clients.

5.15 The social worker shall respect the client's right to access to a client record subject to the social worker's right to refuse access for just and reasonable cause.

5.16 Where a social worker refuses a client the right to access a file or part of a file, the social worker shall advise the client of the right to request a review of the decision in accordance with the relevant statute, workplace policy or other relevant procedure.

Disclosure

5.17 The social worker shall not disclose the identity of persons who have sought a social work service or disclose sources of information about clients unless compelled legally to do so.[21]

5.18 The obligation to maintain confidentially continues indefinitely after the social worker has ceased contact with the client.

5.19 The social worker shall avoid unnecessary conversation regarding clients.

5.20 The social worker may divulge confidential information with consent of the client, preferably expressed in writing, where this is essential to a plan of care or treatment.

5.21 The social worker shall transfer information to another agency or individual, only with the informed consent of the client or guardian of the client and then only with the reasonable assurance that the receiving agency provides the same guarantee of confidentiality and respect for the right of privileged communication as provided by the sending agency.

5.22 The social worker shall explain to the client the disclosure of information requirements of the law or of the agency before the commencement of the provision of social work services.

5.23 The social worker in practice with groups and communities shall notify the participants of the likelihood that aspects of their private lives may be revealed in the course of their work together, and therefore require a commitment from each member to respect the privileged and confidential nature of the communication between and among members of the client group.

5.24 Subject to section 5.26, the social worker shall not disclose information acquired from one client to a member of the client's family without the informed consent of the client who provided the information.

5.25 A social worker shall disclose information acquired from one client to a member of the client's family where

(a) the information involves a threat of harm to self or others,[22]

(b) the information was acquired from a child of tender years and the social worker determines that its disclosure is in the best interests of the child.[23]

5.26 A social worker shall disclose information acquired from a client to a person or a police officer where the information involves a threat of harm to that person.

5.27 A social worker may release confidential information as part of a discipline hearing of a social worker as directed by the tribunal or disciplinary body.

5.28 When disclosure is required by order of a court, the social worker shall not divulge more information than is reasonably required and shall where possible notify the client of this requirement.

5.29 The social worker shall not use confidential information for the purpose of teaching, public education or research except with the informed consent of the client.

5.30 The social worker may use non-identifying information for the purpose of teaching, public education or research.

Retention and Disposition of Information

5.31 Where the social worker's documentation is stored in a place or computer maintained and operated by an employer, the social worker shall advocate for the responsible retention and disposition of information contained in the file.

CHAPTER 6: Outside Interest

6. A social worker who engages in another profession, occupation, affiliation or calling shall not allow these outside interests to affect the social work relationship with the client.

6.1 A social worker shall declare to the client any outside interests that would affect the social work relationship with the client.

6.2 A social worker shall not allow an outside interest:

(a) to affect the social worker's ability to practise social work;

(b) to present to the client or to the community that the social worker's ability to practise social work is affected; or

(c) to bring the profession of social work into disrepute.[24]

CHAPTER 7: Limit on Private Practice

7. A social worker in private practice shall not conduct the business of provision of social work services for a fee in a manner that discredits the profession or diminishes the public's trust in the profession.

7.1 A social worker shall not use the social work relationship within an agency to obtain clients for his or her private practice.

7.2 Subject to section 7.3, a social worker who enters into a contract for service with a client

(a) shall disclose at the outset of the relationship, the fee schedule for the social work services.

(b) shall not charge a fee that is greater than that agreed to and disclosed to the client, and

(c) shall not charge for hours of service other than the reasonable hours of client services, research, consultation and administrative work directly connected to the case.

7.3 A social worker in private practice may charge differential fees for services except where an increased fee is charged based on race, ethnic background, language, religion, marital status, sex, sexual orientation, age, abilities, socio-economic status, political affiliation or national ancestry.

7.4 A social worker in private practice shall maintain adequate malpractice, defamation and liability insurance.

7.5 A social worker in private practice may charge a rate of interest on delinquent accounts as is allowed by law.[25]

7.6 Notwithstanding section 5.17 a social worker in private practice may pursue civil remedies to ensure payment for services to a client where the social worker has advised the client of this possibility at the outset of the social work service.

CHAPTER 8: Ethical Responsibilities to the Workplace

8. A social worker shall advocate for workplace conditions and policies that are consistent with the Code.

8.1 Where the responsibilities to an employer are in conflict with the social worker's obligations to the client, the social worker shall document the issue in writing and shall bring the situation to the attention of the employer.

8.2 Where a serious ethical conflict continues to exist after the issue has been brought to the attention of the employer, the social worker shall bring the issue to the attention of the Association or regulatory body.[26]

8.3 A social worker shall follow the principles in the Code when dealing with

(a) a social worker under the supervision of the social worker,

(b) an employee under the supervision of the social worker, and

(c) a social work student under the supervision of the social worker.

CHAPTER 9: Ethical Responsibilities to the Profession

9. A social worker shall promote excellence in the social work profession.

9.1 A social worker shall report to the appropriate association or regulatory body any breach of this Code by another social worker which adversely affects or harms a client or prevents the effective delivery of a social service.

9.2 A social worker shall report to the association or regulatory body any unqualified or unlicensed person who is practising social work.

9.3 A social worker shall not intervene in the professional relationship of a social worker and client unless requested to do so by the client and unless convinced that the best interests and well-being of the client require such intervention.

9.4 Where a conflict arises between a social worker and other professionals, the social worker shall attempt to resolve the professional differences in ways that uphold the principles of this Code and the honour of the social work profession.

9.5 A social worker engaged in research shall ensure that the involvement of clients in the research is a result of informed consent.

CHAPTER 10: Ethical Responsibilities for Social Change

10. A social worker shall advocate change

 (a) in the best interest of the client, and

 (b) for the overall benefit of society, the environment and the global community.

10.1 A social worker shall identify, document and advocate for the elimination of discrimination.

10.2 A social worker shall advocate for the equal distribution of resources to all persons.

10.3 A social worker shall advocate for the equal access of all persons to resources, services and opportunities.

10.4 A social worker shall advocate for a clean and healthy environment and shall advocate the development of environmental strategies consistent with social work principles.

10.5 A social worker shall provide reasonable professional services in a state of emergency.

10.6 A social worker shall promote social justice.

NOTES

1. A client ceases to be a client 2 years after the termination of a social work service. It is advisable for this termination to be clearly documented on the case file.

2. This sub-paragraph identifies two situations where a person may be considered a voluntary client. The person who requests a social work service is clearly a voluntary client. A person also may originally be receiving services as a result of the actions of a court or other legally mandated entity. This person may receive a service beyond that originally mandated and therefore be able to terminate voluntarily that aspect of the service. A situation where a person is referred by another professional or family member clearly falls into this "voluntary service" relationship when that person agrees with the service to be provided. This type of social work relationship is clearly distinguishable from the relationship in sub-paragraph (ii) where the social worker does not seek or have agreement for the service to be provided.

3. In this situation, the social worker is providing an assessment, information or a professional opinion to a judge of competent jurisdiction to assist the judge in making a ruling or determination. In this situation, the relationship is with the judge and the person on whom the information, assessment or opinion is provided is not the client. The social worker still has some professional obligations towards that person, for example: competence and dignity.

4. In reaching a decision in Re Matthews and Board of Directors of Physiotherapy (1986) 54 O.R. (2d) 375, Saunders J. makes three important statements regarding standards of practice and by implication Code of Ethics:

(i)   Standards of practice are inherent characteristics of any profession.

(ii) Standards of practice may be written or unwritten.

(iii) Some conduct is clearly regarded as misconduct and need not be written down whereas other conduct may be the subject of dispute within a profession.

5. The importance of the collective opinion of the profession in establishing and ultimately modifying the Code of Ethics was established in a 1884 case involving the medial profession. Lord Esher, M.R. stated:

> If it is shown that a medical man, in the pursuit of his profession, has done something with regard to it which would be reasonably regarded as disgraceful or dishonourable by his professional brethren of good repute and competency", then it is open to the General Medical Council to say that he has been guilty of "infamous conduct in a professional respect.

6. This definition except paragraph (d) has been taken from An Act to Incorporate the New Brunswick Association of Social Workers, chapter 78 of the Statutes of New Brunswick, 1988, section 2.

7. The procedure for adding activities under this paragraph will be established as a bylaw by the CASW Board of Directors.

8. Taken from: *Teaching and Learning about Human Rights; A Manual for Schools of Social Work and the Social Work Profession;* U.N. Centre for Human Rights, Co-operation with International Federation of Social Workers and International Association of Schools of Social Workers, United Nations, New York, 1992.

9. This obligation goes beyond grounds of discrimination stated in most Human Rights Legislation and therefore there is a greater professional obligation than that stated in provincial legislation.

10. The term condition means a physical, mental or psychological condition. There is an implied obligation that the social worker shall actively seek diagnosis and treatment for any signs or warnings of a condition. A disclosure under this section may be of a general nature. See also 3.4.

11. The term objectivity is taken from the Québec Code of Professional Conduct. See Division 2: Integrity and Objectivity (6.0 Québec) November 5, 1979 Vol. 2 No. 30. The term objectivity is stated in the following: 3.02.01 A social worker must discharge his professional duties with integrity and objectivity.

12. The provincial associations may regulate the areas of expertise to be stated or advertised by a social worker. This will vary in each province according to its enabling legislation. Where there is not sufficient legislative base for this regulation, the claim of an expertise without sufficient training may form the basis of a determination of unprofessional conduct.

13. Even with a distinction made under this section, a social worker's private actions or statements may be of such a nature that the social worker cannot avoid the responsibilities under this Code. See also 6.2(c).

14. This section should be considered in relation to section 1.4 and involves proper maintenance, prevention and treatment of any type of risk to the health or well-being of the social worker.

15. It is not necessary in all circumstances to explain specifically the nature of the problem.

16. Where a social worker does keep money or assets belonging to a client, the social worker should hold this money or asset in a trust account or hold the money or asset in conjunction with an additional professional person.

17. Confidentiality means that information received or observed about a client by a social worker will be held in confidence and disclosed only when the social worker is properly authorized or obligated legally or professionally to do so. This also means that professionally acquired information may be treated as privileged communication and ordinarily only the client has the right to waive privilege.

Privileged communication means statements made within a protected relationship (i.e., husband–wife, professional–client) which the law protects against disclosure. The extent of the privilege is governed by law and not by this Code.

Maintaining confidentiality of privileged communication means that information about clients does not have to be transmitted in any oral, written or recorded form. Such information, for example, does not have to be disclosed to a supervisor, written into a workplace record, stored in a computer or microfilm data base, held on an audio or videotape or discussed orally. The right of privileged communication is respected by the social worker in the practice of social work notwithstanding that this right is not ordinarily granted in law.

The disclosure of confidential information in social work practice involves the obligation to share information professionally with others in the workplace of the social worker as part of a reasonable service to the client. Social workers recognize the need to obtain permission from clients before releasing information about them to sources outside their workplace; and to inform clients at the outset of their relationship that some information acquired may be shared with the officers and personnel of the agency who maintain the case record and who have a reasonable need for the information in the performance of their duties.

18. The social worker's relationship with a client can be characterized as a fiduciary relationship.

    In Fiduciary Duties in Canada by Ellis, fiduciary duty is described as follows: where one party has placed its "trust and confidence" in another and the latter has accepted—expressly or by operation of law—to act in a manner consistent with the reposing of such "trust and confidence", a fiduciary relationship has been established.

19. The "obligation of secrecy" was discussed by the Supreme Court of Canada in Halls v. Mitchell, (1928) S.C.R. 125, an action brought by a disabled CNR worker against a company doctor who had disclosed the employee's medical history, to the latter's detriment. Mr. Justice Duff reviewed the duty of confidentiality:

    We are not required, for the purposes of this appeal, to attempt to state with any sort of precision the limits of the obligation of secrecy which rests upon the medical practitioner in relation to the professional secrets acquired by him in the course of his practice. Nobody would dispute that a secret so acquired is the secret of the patient, and, normally, is under his control, and not under that of the doctor. Prima facie, the patient has the right to require that the secret shall not be divulged; and that right is absolute, unless there is some paramount reason which overrides it.

    Thus the right of secrecy/confidentiality rests squarely with the patient; the Court carefully provided that there is an "ownership" extant in the confidentiality of the personal information. Duff J. continued by allowing for "paramount" criteria which vitiates from the right:

    Some reasons may arise, no doubt, from the existence of facts which bring into play overpowering considerations connected with public justice; and there may be cases in which reasons connected with the safety of individuals or of the public, physical or moral, would be sufficiently cogent to supersede or qualify the obligations prima facie imposed by the confidential relation.

    Duff J. continued:

    The general duty of medical men to observe secrecy, in relation to information acquired by them confidentially from their patients is subject, no doubt, to some exceptions, which have no operation in the case of solicitors; but the grounds of the legal, social or moral imperatives affecting physicians and surgeons, touching the inviolability of professional confidences, are not, any more than those affecting legal advisers, based exclusively upon the relations between the parties as individuals.

20. The master file refers to all relevant documents pertaining to the client consisting of such information as demographics, case recordings, court documents, assessments, correspondence, treatment plans, bills, etc. This information is often collected through various means including electronic and computer-driven sources. However the client master file exists as one unit, inclusive of all information pertaining to the client, despite the various sources of the recording process. The description and ownership of the master file is most often defined by workplace standards or policies. The client's master file should be prepared keeping in mind that it may have to be revealed to the client or disclosed in legal proceedings.

21. A social worker may be compelled to reveal information under the section when directly ordered by the court to do so. Before disclosing the information, the social worker shall advise the court of the professional obligations that exist under this section of the Code and where reasonably possible inform the client.

22. The case of Tarasoff v. The Regents of the University of California et al. (1976), 551 p.2d 334 (Cal. Supreme Court) focused on the obligation of a psychiatrist to maintain the confidentiality of his patients' statements in their discussions. In that case the patient told the psychiatrist that the patient had an intention to kill a certain woman. When the patient actually did kill this woman, her parents brought suit alleging that the psychiatrist owed a duty to tell the woman of the danger to her.

    It was held that the psychiatrist did have a duty to tell the woman of the threat. The court recognized that the psychiatrist owed a duty to the patient to keep in confidence the statements the patient made in therapy sessions, but held there was also a duty to care to anyone whom the psychiatrist knew might be endangered by the patient. At a certain point the obligation of confidentiality would be overridden by the obligation to this third person. The psychiatrist's knowledge itself gave rise to a duty of care. What conduct would be sufficient to fulfil the duty to this third person would depend on the circumstances, but it might be necessary to give a warning that would reveal what the patient had said about the third party. The court in this case held that the psychiatrist had a duty to warn the woman about the patient's stated intention to kill her, and having failed to warn her the psychiatrist was liable in negligence. Moreover, the court stated that the principle of this duty of care belonged not just to a psychiatrist but also to a psychologist performing therapy. It would follow that the principle would also apply to social workers performing therapy.

23. For the purpose of this Code, a child of tender years shall usually be determined to be a child under the age of seven years subject to a determination by a social worker considering the child's social, physical, intellectual, emotional or psychological development.

24. This section brings the social worker's outside interest and personal actions in line with the professional duties and obligations as set out in this Code.

25. This rate shall be stated on all invoices or bills sent to the client.

26. In this situation the professional obligations outweigh any obligations to a workplace.

Glossary

Absolute Confidentiality: An assurance that client disclosures are not shared with anyone.

Action Planning: Helping clients make changes in their lives; involves setting goals, identifying strategies for change, and developing plans for reaching goals.

Active Listening: A term describing a cluster of skills that are used to increase the accuracy of understanding. Attending, using silence, paraphrasing, summarizing, questioning, and showing empathy are the basic skills of active listening.

Affect: A term that counsellors use to describe how people express emotions.

Affective Area: How clients feel.

Affective Disorders: Disturbances in mood, including depression and mania.

AIDS: An acronym for **Acquired Immune Deficiency Syndrome**. Caused by HIV infection, AIDS results in a number of different illnesses and opportunistic infections, such as tuberculosis, pneumonia, persistent diarrhea, fever, and skin cancer.

Ambivalence: Multiple, often contradictory feelings about the same problem or experience. Ambivalence, though normal, can complicate clients' decision making and add stress to their lives.

Anorexia Nervosa: An eating disorder that occurs when people reject maintaining a minimally healthy body weight. Driven by low self-esteem and an intense fear of gaining weight, people with anorexia use techniques such as purging (e.g., fasting, vomiting, taking laxatives) and excessive exercise to reduce body weight.

Antianxiety Medication: Medications such as valium and librium that are used to control serious and persistent anxiety, phobia, and panic attacks.

Antidepressant Medication: Medications such as Prozac, Paxil, and Zolof that are used to help people deal with serious depression.

Antimanic Medication: Medications such as lithium that are used to control the manic symptoms of bipolar disorder.

Antipsychotic Medication: Medications such as chlorpromazine, haloperidol, clozapine, and pisperidone that are used to treat illnesses such as schizophrenia.

Anxiety Disorders: More than normal levels of fear, worry, tension, or anxiety about daily events.

Assertiveness: Behaving and expressing thoughts and feelings in an open and honest manner that respects the rights of others.

Assumptions: Distortions or false conclusions based on simplistic reasoning, incomplete information, or bias.

Attended Silence: Counsellor silence characterized by making eye contact, physically and psychologically focusing on the client, and being self-disciplined to minimize internal and external distraction.

Attending: A term used to describe the way that counsellors communicate to their clients that they are ready, willing, and able to listen. Verbal, nonverbal, and attitudinal cues are the essence of effective attending.

Basic Empathy: A counsellor's acknowledgment of a client's clearly communicated feelings.

Behavioural Area: What clients are doing.

Bipolar Disorder: A mood disorder characterized by alternating periods of depression and abnormally heightened mood, sometimes to the point of grandiosity. Persons with bipolar disorder may behave irrationally (e.g., going on uncontrolled buying sprees, committing sexual indiscretions, and taking part in foolish business investments).

Brief Counselling: An approach to counselling characterized by a focus on resources and solutions rather than problems.

Bulimia: An eating disorder that occurs when people adopt a pattern of excessive overeating followed by vomiting or other purging behaviours to control their weight.

Burnout: A state of emotional, mental, and physical exhaustion that reduces or prevents people from performing their job.

Catharsis: Verbalization of ideas, fears, past significant events, and associations, which results in a release of anxiety or tension.

Challenging Skills: Skills used to encourage clients to critically evaluate their behaviour and ideas.

Closed Question: Questions that can easily be answered with a simple *yes* or *no* (e.g., "Did you go by yourself?").

Cognitive Area: How clients think about their situations.

Command Hallucination: Distorted perception of voices and images directing one to perform some action (e.g., attack or kill someone).

Concreteness: A term used to describe the level of specificity. It is "a way to ensure that general and common experiences and feelings such as depression, anxiety, anger, and so on are defined idiosyncratically for each client" (Cormier and Cormier, 1985:48).

Confrontation: Counselling initiatives that challenge clients to critically examine their actions and/or consider other viewpoints.

Confrontation of Incongruities: Used to point out inconsistencies in a client's verbal and nonverbal messages, values or beliefs, and behaviour.

Congruence: The capacity to be real and consistent with clients; matching behaviour, feelings, and actions.

Contingency Plan: A preventive plan that anticipates possible barriers that clients might encounter as they carry out action plans.

Contract: A negotiated agreement between counsellors and clients regarding the purpose of the work, their respective roles, and the methods and routines that will be used to reach their agreed-on objectives.

Controlled Emotional Involvement: "The empathic sensitivity of the worker to the client's feelings, disciplined by self-awareness, such that the worker's feelings do not inappropriately affect his or her understanding and purposeful response" (Hancock, 1997:131).

Core Conditions: Warmth, empathy, and genuineness.

Counselling: A process of helping clients to learn skills, deal with feelings, and manage problems.

Counselling Relationship: A time-limited period of consultation between a counsellor and a client in order to achieve a defined goal.

Countertransference: Tendency of counsellors to inappropriately transfer feelings and behaviours to clients.

Critical Incident Debriefing: A team meeting held to defuse the impact of a violent or traumatic event such as an assault on a staff member. Debriefing assists workers to normalize and deal with the feelings that may be aroused as a result of the event. As well, debriefing is used to review and revise preventive and crisis intervention procedures.

Defence Mechanisms: Mental process or reaction that shields a person from undesirable or unacceptable thoughts, feelings, or conclusions that, if accepted, would create anxiety or challenges to one's sense of self. Common defence mechanisms include denial, displacement, rationalization, suppression, and regression.

Delusion: Distorted belief involving bizarre thought patterns.

Dependent Relationship: A counselling relationship in which clients become overly reliant on their counsellors for decision making. Symptoms include excessive permission seeking, frequent phone calls or office visits for information, and inability to make simple decisions or take action without consulting.

Depression: Pervasive deflation in mood characterized by symptoms such as sadness, hopelessness, decreased energy, and difficulty concentrating, remembering, and making decisions.

Directives: Short statements that provide direction to clients on topics, information, and pace (e.g., "Tell me more.")

Diversity: Variations in terms of lifestyle, culture, behaviour, sexual orientation, age, ability, religion, and other factors.

Doorknob Communication: A phenomenon described by Shulman (1992) whereby clients bring up important issues at the end of the interview/relationship when there is little or no time to address them.

DSM-IV-TR: The **Diagnostic and Statistical Manual of Mental Disorders** published by the American Psychiatric Association. It is used by psychologists, psychiatrists, and other psychotherapists to classify and diagnose mental disorders.

Dual Diagnosis: A person who has both a substance abuse addiction and a psychiatric disorder.

Dual Relationship: A relationship in which there is both a counselling relationship and another type of relationship, such as friendship or sexual intimacy.

Duty to Warn: Professional responsibility that counsellors have to inform people whom they believe a client may harm.

Emotion: A state of mind usually accompanied by concurrent physiological and behavioural changes and based on the perception of some internal or external object.

Emotional Literacy: The ability to experience all of one's emotions with appropriate intensity and to understand what is causing these feelings (Parrott, 1997:260).

Empathy: The process of accurately understanding the emotional perspective of another person and the communication of this understanding without imposing one's own feelings or reactions.

Empowering Skills: Skills used to help clients develop confidence, self-esteem, and control over their lives.

Empowerment: The process of helping clients to discover personal strengths and capacities so that they are able to take control over their lives.

Ethical Dilemma: Situation involving competing or conflicting values or principles.

Ethics: Guidelines that define the limits of permissible behaviour.

Ethnocentrism: The inclination to judge others negatively in relation to one's own cultural values and norms.

Exploring/Probing Skills: Skills counsellors use to gather information, clarify definition, seek example, and obtain necessary detail.

Feedback Confrontation: Used to provide new information to clients about who they are, including how they are perceived by others and the effects of their behaviour on others.

Genuineness: A measure of how authentic or real one is in a relationship.

Goal Setting: A counselling process that helps clients define in precise, measurable terms what they hope to achieve from the work of counselling.

Hallucination: Hearing, seeing, tasting, touching, or smelling what others do not.

Hidden Job Market: Jobs that are not advertised or made public; 80 percent or more of all jobs are filled through the hidden job market.

HIV: An acronym for **Human Immunodeficiency Virus**. This virus attacks the immune system, weakening its ability to fight off infections. People may be unaware that they have the virus, as they may have no symptoms for as long as 5 to 15 years.

Illusion of Work: As defined by Shulman (1992:171), a process in which the worker and the client engage in a conversation that is empty and that has no real meaning.

Immediacy: A tool for exploring, evaluating, and deepening counselling relationships.

Indirect Question: Statements that imply questions (e.g., "I'm curious how you responded.").

Inferred Empathy: A counsellor's identification of a client's feelings based on nonverbal cues and indirect communication.

Interviewing: Acquiring and organizing relevant information using active listening skills, including attending, silence, paraphrasing, summarizing, questioning, and empathy.

Interview Transition: A shift in the topic of the interview.

Intimidating Behaviour: Behaviours such as name calling; using obscene or sexually harassing language and gestures; shouting; and threatening through displays of power such as fist shaking, invading personal space, stalking, and issuing verbal threats. These behaviours should be restrained in order to prevent escalation to violence.

Invitational Empathy: A tool a counsellor uses to encourage clients to explore emotions.

I-Statement: Clear assertions about personal feelings or reactions that do not blame or judge others.

Job Club Method: An intensive and structured approach to job finding based on group support and structured learning activities. The sole purpose of a job club is to help participants find work.

Leading Question: A question that suggests a preferred answer (e.g., "Don't you think our session went really well today?").

Learned Helplessness: A state of mind that occurs when individuals have learned through failure that their efforts will not result in change.

Listening: A process aimed at receiving and understanding messages without distortion.

LIVE: An acronym that describes the four essential steps in summarizing: listen, identify, verbalize, evaluate.

Miracle Question: Used in brief or single-session counselling as a way to help clients who have difficulty coming up with defined goals. The miracle question challenges clients to imagine how their lives would be different if a miracle solved their problems.

MOANS: An acronym for five words—must, ought, always, never, and should—that signals irrational or self-defeating thought.

Mood Disorders: See affective disorders.

Motivation: The extent to which clients are willing to involve themselves in the change process.

Networking: An integral part of job searching used to access the hidden job market. It involves using contacts, such as friends, family, and neighbours, who might provide information or access to others with information about possible job opportunities.

Nonhelping Behaviours: Variables that can lead to poor outcomes in counselling.

Objectivity: Ability to understand feelings, thoughts, and behaviour without allowing personal values, beliefs, and biases to interfere.

Obsessive-Compulsive Disorder (OCD): Recurrent, unwanted thoughts and conscious, ritualized, seemingly purposeless acts, such as counting the number of tiles on the ceiling or needing to wash one's hands repetitively.

Open Questions: Questions that promote expansive answers. These types of questions cannot be answered with a simple yes or no (e.g., "How do you feel about her?").

Outcome Goal: A goal related to what the client hopes to achieve from counselling.

Panic Disorder: Sudden attacks of terror and irrational fear, accompanied by an overwhelming sense of impending doom. During a panic attack a person may experience symptoms such as an accelerated heart rate, sweating, shaking, shortness of breath, chest pain, nausea, and fear of dying or losing control.

Paraphrase: A nonjudgmental restatement of the client's words and ideas in the counsellor's own words.

Phases of Counselling: Sequential steps through which counselling tends to evolve. Four phases are preliminary, beginning, action, ending.

Phases of Violence: Four-phase model (anxiety, defensiveness, acting out, and tension reduction) that describes how crises escalate to violence.

Phobia: An irrational fear about particular events or objects that results in overwhelming anxiety in response to situations where there is little or no danger.

Positive Regard: The ability of counsellors to recognize the inherent worth of people.

Post-Traumatic Stress Disorder (PTSD): Disabling symptoms such as emotional numbness, sleep disturbance (nightmares, difficulty sleeping), or reliving the event following a traumatic event such as rape, assault, natural disaster (earthquakes, floods, etc.), war, torture, or automobile accident.

Preparatory Empathy: A counsellor's attempt to consider (in advance of the interview) the feelings and concerns that the client may communicate indirectly.

Principle of Positive Reinforcement: The idea that behaviour tends to increase or continue when it is rewarded.

Process Goal: The methods and procedures that will be used in counselling to assist clients to reach their goals.

Proxemics: A term used to describe how people use space and distance in social behaviour.

Pseudo-counselling: Counselling that lacks real meaning, evidenced by irrelevant exploration of issues, use of clichés and patronizing platitudes, intellectual exploration of issues, and avoidance of subjects or feelings that involve pain in favour of "safe" topics.

Psychotherapy: Advanced counselling targeting severe emotional or behavioural difficulties or disorders.

Questioning: An active listening skill that involves probing for information to confirm understanding and seek clarification.

Reframing: Technique for helping clients to look at things differently by suggesting alternative interpretations or new meanings.

Relationship-Building Skills: Tools for engaging clients and developing trust.

Relative Confidentiality: The assumption that client disclosures may be shared within the agency with supervisors or colleagues, outside the agency with client permission, or with others because of legal requirements, such as those contained within child-abuse legislation.

Rescuing: Also called band-aiding, this involves a counsellor's actions that prevent or protect clients from dealing with issues or feelings. Rescuing arises from the counsellor's need to avoid tension and keep the session cheerful.

Resistance: Defensive reaction by clients that interferes with or delays the process of counselling.

Schizophrenia: A chronic mental disorder involving symptoms such as hallucinations, delusions, disordered thinking, and social isolation.

Selective Perception: A term used to describe the natural tendency to avoid being overwhelmed by information by screening out material that is irrelevant.

Self-Awareness: Process of becoming alert and knowledgeable about one's own way of thinking, acting, and feeling.

Self-Defeating Thought: Inner dialogue of critical messages.

Self-Determination: The principle that promotes the rights of clients to have autonomy and freedom of choice.

Self-Talk: Mental messages people give to themselves (e.g., "I'm no good.").

Silence: A tool used in counselling when the client is thinking, the client is confused and unsure of what to say or do, or the client has encountered painful feelings. Silence signals trust issues, is culturally defined, and indicates closure.

Simple Encouragers: Short phrases and gestures, such as "Tell me more," "Go on," "Uh huh," and head nods that encourage clients to continue with their stories.

Skill Clusters: Categories of skills based on their intended purpose or helping activity.

Strengths Approach: A counselling perspective that assumes the inherent capacity of people. Individuals and communities are seen to have assets and resources that can be mobilized for problem solving.

Structured Interview: An interview that follows a predetermined sequence of questions.

Summary: A way of condensing content. A simple summary focuses on content and is an unedited condensing of the client's words. Theme summaries edit out unnecessary detail and attempt to identify key patterns and areas of urgency.

Thinking Errors: Faulty reasoning caused by distortion, incomplete analysis, egocentricity, rigidity, and self-defeating thought.

Thought Broadcasting: The delusional belief that one's thinking can be heard by others.

Thought Insertion: The delusional belief that thoughts are being inserted into one's brain by others.

Transference: The tendency of clients to communicate with their counsellors in the same way that they communicated to significant people in the past.

Unstructured Interview: An interview that does not have a preset plan that restricts direction, pace, or content.

Values: What individuals and groups consider to be important or worthwhile.

Ventilation: See catharsis.

Versatility: The need for counsellors to develop a broad range of skills in order to adapt their approach to fit the distinctive complexities of each individual and context.

Violent Behaviour: Hitting, pushing, biting, slapping, kicking, throwing objects, and using weapons such as guns, knives, or syringes.

Worldview: Belief system about the nature of the universe, its perceived effect on human behaviour, and one's place in the universe. Worldview is a fundamental core set of assumptions explaining cultural forces, the nature of humankind, the nature of good and evil, luck, fate, spirits, the power of significant others, the role of time, and the nature of our physical and natural resources (Dodd: 1995:105).

An excellent general resource is http://socialpolicy.ca, which provides an online glossary of hundreds of social work terms.

References

Abraham, S., and D. Llewellyn-Jones. *Eating Disorders: The Facts*. 4th ed. New York: Oxford University Press, 1997.

Alexander, C.M., and L. Sussman. "Creative Approaches to Multicultural Counseling." In Ponterotto, J.G., J.M. Casas, L.A. Suzuki, and C.M. Alexander, *Handbook of Multicultural Counseling*. Thousand Oaks, CA: Sage Publications, 1995: 375–384.

American Association of Suicidology. [Online, cited 10 August 1998]. Available: http://www. cyberpsych.org/aas/

American Counseling Association (ACA). *Code of Ethics and Standards of Practice*. Alexandria, VA: American Counseling Association, 1995.

American Medical Association. *Essential Guide to Depression*. New York, NY: Pocket Books, 1998.

American Psychiatric Association. *Diagnostic and Statistical Manual of Mental Disorders*. 4th ed. Text Revision. Washington, DC: American Psychiatric Association, 2000.

Amundson, N.E. "Supporting Clients Through a Change in Perspective." *Journal of Employment Counseling* 33, no. 4 (1996): 155–62.

Angel, D.L, and E.E. Harney. *No One Is Unemployable: Creative Solutions for Overcoming Barriers to Employment*. Hacienda Heights, CA: WorkNet Training Services, 1997.

Armitage, A., *Social Welfare in Canada Revisited: Facing Up to the Future*. 3rd ed. Don Mills, ON: Oxford University Press, 1996.

Arnhold, R.M., and W.N. Razak. "Overcoming Learned Helplessness: Managerial Strategies for the 1990s." In *Journal of Employment Counseling* 28 (September 1991): 99–106.

Arthur, N., and J. Stewart. "Multicultural Counselling in the New Millennium: Introduction to the Special Theme Issue." In *Canadian Journal of Counselling* 35, no. 1 (2001): 3–14.

Azrin, N.H., and V.A. Besalel. *Job Club Counselor's Manual: A Behavioral Approach to Vocational Counseling*. Austin, TX: Pro-Ed., 1980.

Backhouse, C. *Colour-Coded: A Legal History of Racism in Canada, 1900–1950*. Toronto, ON: University of Toronto Press, 1999.

Barker, R.L. *The Social Work Dictionary*. 3rd ed. Washington, DC: NASW Press, 1995.

Beckman, C.S., S.G. Turner, M. Cooper, D. Polnerow, and M. Swartz. "Sexual Contact With Clients: Assessment of Social Workers' Attitudes and Educational Preparation." In *Social Work* 45, no. 3 (2000): 224.

Benjamin, A. *The Helping Interview*. 3rd ed. Boston, MA: Houghton Mifflin, 1981.

Berg, F.M. *Afraid to Eat: Children and Teens in Weight Crisis*. Hettinger, ND: Healthy Weight Journal, 1997.

Beyerstein, B.L. "Believing Is Seeing: Organic and Psychological Reasons for Hallucinations and Other Anomalous Psychiatric Symptoms." *Medscape*. [Online, cited 7 August 1998]. Available: http://www.medscape.com/Medscape/MentalHealth

Bezanson, M.L., C.A. DeCoff, and N.R. Stewart. *Individual Employment Counselling: An Action Based Approach*. Toronto, ON: University of Toronto Guidance Centre, 1985.

Black, K. Short-Term Counseling: *A Humanistic Approach for the Helping Professions*. Menlo Park, CA: Addison-Wesley, 1983.

Bolles, R.N. *The 1997 What Color Is Your Parachute: A Practical Manual for Job-Hunters and Career Changers*. Berkeley, CA: Ten Speed Press, 1997.

Bower, B. "Study Tracks Violence Among Mentally Ill." In *Science News* (May 1998): 309.

Brammer, L.M. *The Helping Relationship: Process and Skills*. 3rd ed. Englewood Cliffs, NJ: Prentice-Hall, 1985.

Brammer, L.M., and G. MacDonald. *The Helping Relationship: Process and Skills*. 7th ed. Needham Heights, MA: Allyn & Bacon, 1999.

Brammer, L.M., and E.L. Shostrom. *Therapeutic Psychology: Fundamentals of Counseling and Psychotherapy*. 4th ed. Englewood Cliffs, NJ: Prentice-Hall, 1982.

Bratina, T.G., and T.A. Bratina. "Electronic Career Search." In *Journal of Employment Counseling* 35 (March 1998): 17–25.

Brill, N.I. *Working with People: The Helping Process*. 6th ed. New York, NY: Addison-Wesley, 1998.

Burman, P. *Killing Time, Losing Ground: Experiences of Unemployment*. Toronto, ON: Thompson Educational Publishing Inc., 1988.

Canadian Task Force on Mental Health Issues Affecting Immigrants and Refugees. *After The Door Has Been Opened: Mental Health Issues Affecting Refugees and Immigrants in Canada: Report of the Canadian Task Force on Mental Health Issues Affecting Immigrants and Refugees*. Ottawa, ON: Multiculturalism and Citizenship Canada, 1988.

Capuzzi, D., and D.R. Gross. *Introduction to the Counseling Profession*. 3rd ed. Needham Heights, MA: Allyn & Bacon, 2001.

Carkhuff, R.R. *The Art of Helping*. Amherst, MA: Human Resource Development Press, 1981.

Carniol, B. *Case Critical: The Dilemma of Social Work in Canada*. 3rd ed. Toronto, ON: Between the Lines, 1995.

Chappell, R. *Social Welfare in Canadian Society*. 2nd ed. Scarborough, ON: Nelson Thomson Learning, 2001.

Choney, S.K., E. Berryhill-Paapke, and R. Robbins. "The Acculturation of American Indians: Developing Frameworks for Research and Practice." In Pedersen, P.B., and D.C. Locke, *Cultural and Diversity Issues in Counseling*. Greensboro, NC: ERIC Counseling and Student Services Clearinghouse, 1996: 73–92.

Clark, A.J. "Reframing: A Therapeutic Technique in Group Counseling." In *Journal for Specialists in Group Work* 23, no. 1 (1998): 66–73.

Cleghorn, J.M., and B.L. Lee. *Understanding and Treating Mental Illness: The Strengths and Limits of Modern Psychiatry*. Toronto, ON: Hogrefe & Huber, 1991.

Compton, B., and B. Galaway. *Social Work Processes*. 3rd ed. Homewood, IL: Dorsey Press, 1984.

———. *Social Work Processes*. 6th ed. Pacific Grove, CA: Brooks/Cole, 1999.

Corey, M., and G. Corey. *Becoming a Helper*. Pacific Grove, CA: Brooks/Cole, 1989.

Cormier, W.H., and L.S. Cormier. *Interviewing Strategies for Helpers*. Monterey, CA: Brooks/Cole, 1985.

Corsini, R.J. *Encyclopedia of Psychology*. New York, NY: John Wiley & Sons, 1984.

Cottone, R.R., and V.M. Tarvydas. *Ethical and Professional Issues in Counseling*. Englewood Cliffs, NJ: Prentice-Hall, 1998.

Cowger, C. "Assessing Client Strengths." In *Social Work* 39, no. 3 (1994): 262–268.

Cragan, J.F., and D.W. Wright. *Communication in Small Group Discussions: An Integrated Approach*. 3rd ed. St. Paul, MN: West Publishing Company, 1991.

D'Andrea, M.J. "White Racism." In Pedersen, P.B., and D.C. Locke, *Cultural and Diversity Issues in Counseling*. Greensboro, NC: ERIC Counseling and Student Services Clearinghouse, 1996.

Daniluk, J.C., and B.E. Haverkamp. "Ethical Issues in Counseling Adult Survivors of Incest." In *Journal of Counseling and Development* 72, no. 1 (1993): 16–22.

D'Augelli, A.R., J.F. D'Augelli, and S.J. Danish. *Helping Others*. Monterey, CA: Brooks/Cole, 1981.

Davis, S. "An Overview: Are Mentally Ill People Really More Dangerous?" In *Social Work* 36, no. 2 (1991): 174–80.

Davis, L.E., and E.K. Proctor. *Race, Gender, and Class: Guidelines for Practice with Individuals, Families, and Groups*. Englewood Cliffs, NJ: Prentice-Hall, 1989.

De Becker, G. *The Gift of Fear: Survival Signals That Protect Us from Violence*. Boston, MA: Little, Brown, 1997.

De Bono, E. *Six Thinking Hats*. Toronto, ON: Key Porter, 1985.

de Shazer, S. *Keys to Solution in Brief Therapy*. New York, NY: Norton, 1985.

Devons, C. "Suicide in the Elderly: How to Identify and Treat Patients at Risk." In *Geriatrics* 51, no. 3 (1996): 67–72.

Diller, J.V. *Cultural Diversity: A Primer for the Human Services*. Scarborough, ON: Brooks/Cole, 1999.

Dodd, C.H. *Dynamics of Intercultural Communication*. 4th ed. Duguque, IA: Brown & Benchmark, 1995.

DuBois, B., and K. Miley. *Social Work: An Empowering Profession*. 2nd ed. Needham Heights, MA: Allyn & Bacon, 1996.

Dubovsky, S.L., and M.P. Weissberg. *Clinical Psychiatry in Primary Care*. 3rd ed. Baltimore, MD: Williams & Wilkins, 1986.

Dumont, M. *The Absurd Healer*. New York, NY: Viking Press, 1968.

Egan, G. *You and Me: The Skills of Communicating and Relating to Others*. Belmont, CA: Brooks/Cole, 1977.

———. *The Skilled Helper*. 4th ed. Monterey, CA: Brooks/Cole, 1990.

———. *The Skilled Helper*. 6th ed. Monterey, CA: Brooks/Cole, 1998.

Elbourne, R. "Is Silence Suspicious?" [Online, cited 30 September 1997]. Available: http://home.vicnet. net.au/~gnaust/vic2/25-10.html

Ellis, A. *Reason and Emotion in Psychotherapy*. New York, NY: Stuart, 1962.

———. "Fundamentals of Rational-Emotive Therapy for the 1990s," in *Innovations in Rational-Emotive Therapy*, ed. W. Dryden and I. Hill. Newbury Park, CA: Sage, 1993: 1–32.

———. "Reflections on Rational-Emotive Therapy." In *Journal of Counseling and Clinical Psychology* 62, no. 2 (1993b): 199–201.

———. *Rational-Emotive Therapy and Cognitive Behavior Therapy*. New York, NY: Springer, 1984.

Erdman, P., and P. Lampe. "Adapting Basic Skills to Counsel Children." In *Journal of Counseling and Development* 74, no. 4 (1996): 374–77.

Evans, D.R., M.T. Hearn, M.R. Uhlemann, and A.E. Ivey. *Essential Interviewing: A Programmed Approach to Effective Communication*. Monterey, CA: Brooks/Cole, 1979.

Farr, J.M. *The Very Quick Job Search: Get a Better Job in Half the Time*. 2nd ed. Indianapolis, IN: JIST Works, 1996.

Fuertes, J.N., C. Nichols, and Bartolomeo. "Future Research Directions in the Study of Counselor Multicultural Competency." In *Journal of Multicultural Counseling and Development*, vol. 29 (Jan. 2001): 3–13.

Furman, B., and T. Ahola. "Solution Talk: The Solution-Oriented Way of Talking about Problems." In *Constructive Therapies*, ed. M.F. Hoyt. New York, NY: The Guilford Press, 1994: 41–66.

Gardner, W., C. Lidz, E. Mulvey, and E. Shaw. "Clinical versus Actuarial Predictions of Violence in Patients with Mental Illness." In *Journal of Consulting and Clinical Psychology* 64, no. 3 (1996): 602–10.

Garrett, A. *Interviewing: Its Principles and Methods*. 3rd ed. Revised and enlarged by Margaret M. Mangold and Elinor P. Zaki. New York, NY: Family Service Association of America, 1982.

Garrett, M.T., J.T. Garrett, and D. Brotherton. "Inner Circle/Outer Circle: A Group Technique Based on Native American Healing Circles." In *Journal for Specialists in Group Work,* 26, no. 1, March 2001.

Garvin, C.D., and B.A. Seabury. *Interpersonal Practice in Social Work: Processes and Procedures*. Englewood Cliffs, NJ: Prentice-Hall, 1984.

George, R.L., and T.S. Cristiani. *Counseling Theory and Practice*. 2nd ed. Englewood Cliffs, NJ: Prentice-Hall, 1986.

Gilliland, B.E., and R.K. James. *Theories and Strategies in Counseling and Psychotherapy*. 4th ed. Needham Heights, MA: Allyn & Bacon, 1998.

Gladding, S.T. *Counseling: A Comprehensive Profession*. 3rd ed. Englewood Cliffs, NJ: Prentice-Hall, 1996.

Glosoff, H.L., B. Herlihy, and E.B. Spence. "Privileged Communication in the Counselor-Client Relationship." In *Journal of Counseling and Development* 78, no. 4 (2000): 454–462.

Golden, B.J., and K. Lesh. *Building Self-Esteem: Strategies for Success in School and Beyond*. 2nd ed. Scottsdale, AZ: Gorsuch Scarisbick, 1997.

Goleman, D. *Emotional Intelligence*. New York, NY: Bantam Books, 1995.

Gordon, T. *Parent Effectiveness Training: The "No-Lose" Program for Raising Responsible Children*. New York, NY: Peter Wyden, Inc., 1971.

Grinder, J., and R. Bandler. *The Structure of Magic II*. Palo Alto, CA: Science and Behavior Books, 1976.

Hackney, H.L., and L.S. Cormier. *The Professional Counselor: A Process Guide to Helping*. 4th ed. Needham Heights, MA: Pearson Education, 2001.

Haley J. *Problem-Solving Therapy*. 2nd ed. San Francisco, CA: Jossey-Bass, 1987.

Hall, E.T. *The Silent Language*. Greenwich, CT: Fawcett Publications, 1959.

Hamachek, D.E. *Encounters with Others: Interpersonal Relationships and You*. New York, NY: Holt, Rinehart and Winston, 1982.

Hammond, C., D. Hepworth, and V. Smith. *Improving Therapeutic Communication*. San Francisco, CA: Jossey-Bass, 1977.

Hancock, M.R. *Principles of Social Work Practice: A Generic Approach*. Binghamton, NY: The Haworth Press, 1997.

Harris, G.A., and D. Watkins. *Counseling the Involuntary and Resistant Client*. College Park, MD: American Correctional Association, 1987.

Harris, G.T., and M.E. Rice. "Risk Appraisal and Management of Violent Behavior." In *Psychiatric Services* 48, no. 9 (1997): 1168–76.

Harris, H.S., and D.C. Maloney. *Human Services: Contemporary Issues and Trends*. Needham Heights, MA: Allyn & Bacon, 1996.

Hepworth, D.H., R.H. Rooney, and J. Larsen. *Direct Social Work Practice, Theory and Skills*. 5th ed. Pacific Grove, CA: Brooks/Cole, 1997.

Harvard Medical School. *Harvard Mental Health Letter* 13, no. 6 (December 1996).

Hess, H., and P. McCartt Hess. "Termination in Context." In *Social Work Processes*, 3rd ed., by B. Compton and B. Galaway. Homewood, IL: Dorsey Press, 1984, 559–70.

Hirschfeld, R.M., and J.M. Russell. "Assessment and Treatment of Suicidal Patients." In *The New England Journal of Medicine* 337, no. 13 (1997): 910–16.

Hocker, J.L., and W.W. Wilmot. *Interpersonal Conflict*. 4th ed. Dubuque, IA: Wm. C. Brown Communication, 1995.

Holmes, B.H., and J.D. Werbel. "Finding Work Following Job Loss: The Role of Coping Resources." In *Journal of Employment Counseling* 29, no. 1 (1992): 22–29.

Hoyt, M.F. (ed). *Constructive Therapies*. New York, NY: The Guilford Press, 1994.

Huber, C.H., and B.A. Backlund. *The Twenty Minute Counselor: Transforming Brief Conversations into Effective Helping Experiences*. New York, NY: The Continuum Publishing Company, 1991.

Intercontinental Medical Statistics Inc. [Online, cited March 31, 2001] Available: http://www. imshealthcanada.com/htmen/4_2_1_35.htm

Isajiw, W.W. *Understanding Diversity, Ethnicity and Race in the Canadian Context*. Toronto, ON: Thompson Educational Publishing, 1999.

Ismael., J.S. (ed). *The Canadian Welfare State: Evolution and Transition*, Edmonton, AB: The University of Alberta Press, 1987.

Ivey, A.E. *Intentional Interviewing and Counseling*. Monterey, CA: Brooks/Cole, 1982.

Ivey, A.E., M.B. Ivey, and L. Simek-Downing. *Counseling and Psychotherapy: Integrating Skills, Theory, and Practice*. 2nd ed. Englewood Cliffs, NJ: Prentice-Hall, 1987.

Ivey, A.E. "Psychotherapy as Liberation: Toward Specific Skills and Strategies in Multicultural Counseling and Therapy." In Ponterotto, J.G., J.M. Casas, L.A. Suzuki, and C.M. Alexander, *Handbook of Multicultural Counseling*. Thousand Oaks, CA: Sage, 1995: 53–72.

Jacobs, E., R. Masson, and R. Harvill. *Group Counseling Strategies and Skills*. Pacific Grove, CA: Brooks/Cole, 1998.

Jobes, D.A., and A.L Berman. "Crisis Intervention and Brief Treatment for Suicidal Youth." In *Contemporary Perspectives on Crisis Intervention and Prevention*, by A.R. Roberts. Englewood Cliffs, NJ: Prentice-Hall, 1991, 53–69.

Johnson, L.C., Yanca, S. J., *Social Work Practice: A Generalist Approach*. 7th ed. Needham Heights, MA: Allyn & Bacon, 2001.

Johnson, D.W. *Reaching Out: Interpersonal Effectiveness and Self-Actualization*. 6th ed. Boston: Allyn & Bacon, 1997.

Johnson, L.C. *Social Work Practice: A Generalist Approach*. 4th ed. Needham Heights, MA: Allyn & Bacon, 1992.

Johnson, L.C., R.W. McClelland, and C.D. Austin. *Social Work Practice: A Generalist Approach*. Canadian Edition. Scarborough, ON: Prentice Hall Allyn & Bacon Canada, 2000.

Kadushin, A. *The Social Work Interview*. 2nd ed. New York: Columbia University Press, 1983.

———. *The Social Work Interview: A Guide for Human Service Professionals*. 3rd ed. New York, NY: Columbia University Press, 1990.

Kain, C.D. *Positive HIV Affirmative Counseling*. Alexandria, VA: American Counseling Association, 1996.

Kaplan, S.G., and E.G. Wheeler. "Survival Skills for Working with Potentially Violent Clients." In *Social Casework* (June 1983): 339–46.

Keith-Lucas, A. *The Giving and Taking of Help*. Chapel Hill, NC: University of North Carolina Press, 1972.

Kell, B.L., and W.L. Mueller. *Impact and Change*. New York, NY: Appleton Century-Crofts, 1966.

Kelleher, M.D. *Profiling the Lethal Employee: Case Studies of Violence in the Workplace*. Westport, CT: Praeger, 1997.

Kelly, E.W. *Spirituality and Religion in Counseling and Psychotherapy: Diversity in Theory and Practice*. Alexandria, VA: American Counseling Association, 1995.

Kirsh, S. *Unemployment: Its Impact on Body and Soul*. Canadian Mental Health Association, 1983.

Klerman, G.L. "Classification and DSM-III-R." In *The New Harvard Guide to Psychiatry*, ed. A.M. Nicoli. Cambridge, MA: Belknap Press, 1988: 70–87.

Kottler, J.A. "When Clients Don't Get Better: Facing Failure as a Counselor." In *American Counselor* 2, no. 4 (1993): 14–19.

Labig, C.E. *Preventing Violence in the Workplace*. New York, NY: AMACOM, 1995.

Lanza, M., H. Kayne, I. Pattison, C. Hicks, S. Islam, J. Bradshaw, and P. Robins. "The Relationship of Behavioral Cues to Assaultive Behavior." In *Clinical Nursing Research* 5, no. 1 (1996): 6–28.

Lazarus, A.A., and L.E. Beutler. "On Technical Eclecticism." In *Journal of Counseling & Development* 71, no. 4 (1993): 381–85.

Lazarus, R., *Emotion and Adaptation*. New York, NY: Oxford University Press, 1991.

LeDoux, J.E. "Annual 1995." In *Annual Review of Psychology* 46 (1995): 209–35.

Leeds, D. "The Art of Asking Questions." In *Training and Development* 47, no. 1 (1993): 57–62.

Liguori, A.L. Closing comments at the 12th World AIDS Conference, Geneva, Switzerland, July 1998. [Online, cited 25 July 1998]. Available: http://www.aids98.ch/archive/ special/final_ summarysession_trackd.html

Lock, R.D. *Taking Charge of Your Career Direction*. 3rd ed. Pacific Grove, CA: Brooks/Cole, 1996.

Mann, J.M., and D.J. Tarantola. "HIV 1998: The Global Picture." In *Scientific American*, July 1998, 82–83.

Martin, D.G. *Counseling and Therapy Skills*. Belmont, CA: Brooks/Cole, 1983.

Martin, G., and J. Pear. *Behavior Modification: What It Is and How to Do It*. 4th ed. Englewood Cliffs, NJ: Prentice-Hall, 1992.

Maslow, A.H. *Motivation and Personality*. New York, NY: Harper & Row, 1954.

Mathias, Chief Joe. Quotation taken from a permanent public display. Stanley Park, Vancouver, BC, 2001.

McDonald, N. *Interviewing Aboriginal Peoples: A Guide to Effective Cross-Cultural Interviews*. Winnipeg, MB: Cross-Cultural Communications International, 1993.

McNeece, C.A., and D.M. DiNitto. *Chemical Dependency: A Systems Approach*. 2nd ed. Needham Heights, MA: Allyn & Bacon, 1998.

McWhirter, E.H. "Empowerment in Counseling." In *Journal of Counseling and Development* 69, no. 3 (1991): 222–27.

Meharabian, A. *Silent Messages: Implicit Communication of Emotions and Attitudes*. 2nd ed. Belmont, CA: Wadsworth, 1981.

Mehr, J.J. *Human Services: Concepts and Intervention Strategies*. 7th ed. Boston, MA: Allyn & Bacon, 1998.

Middleman, R.R., and G.G. Wood. *Skills for Direct Practice in Social Work*. New York, NY: Columbia University Press, 1990.

Miller, S.D. "The Symptoms of Solutions." In *Journal of Strategic and Systemic Therapies* 11, no. 1 (1992): 2–11.

Minuchin, S., and H. Fishman. *Family Therapy Techniques*. Cambridge, MA: Harvard University Press, 1981.

Morrisseau, C. *Into the Daylight: A Wholistic Approach to Healing*. Toronto, ON: University of Toronto Press, 1998.

Morrissey, M. "Safety Issues for Counselors Who Work with Violent Clients." In *Counseling Today* (February 1998): 6.

National Association of Social Workers. *Revised Code of Ethics*. Washington, D.C.: NASW Press, 1996.

National Crisis Prevention Institute. *Nonviolent Crisis Intervention: The Preventative Techniques*. Vol. 1. National Crisis Prevention Institute, 1986.

———. *Nonviolent Crisis Intervention: Therapeutic Physical Intervention*. Vol. 11. National Crisis Prevention Institute, 1987.

National Institute of Mental Health (NIMH). [Online, 5 August 1998]. Available: http://www. nimh.nih.gov/home.htm

Newhill, C.E. "Assessing Danger to Others in Clinical Social Work Practice." In *Social Service Review* (March 1992): 65–79.

———. "Client Violence Toward Social Workers: A Practice and Policy Concern for the 1990s." In *Social Work* 40, no. 5 (September 1995): 631–39.

Nicholi, A.M. (ed). *The New Harvard Guide to Psychiatry*. Cambridge, MA: Belknap Press, 1988.

Noesner, G.W., and M. Webster. "Crisis Intervention: Using Active Listening Skills in Negotiations." In *The FBI Law Enforcement Bulletin* 66, no. 8 (1997): 13–20.

O'Connor, R. *Undoing Depression: What Therapy Doesn't Teach You and Medication Can't Give You*. Toronto, ON: Little, Brown and Company, 1997.

Otani, A. "Client Resistance in Counseling: Its Theoretical Rationale and Taxonomic Classification." In *Journal of Counseling and Development* (1989): 458–61.

Othmer, E., and S.C. Othmer. *The Clinical Interview Using DSM-III-R*. Washington, DC: American Psychiatric Press, 1989.

Paniagua, F.A. *Assessing and Treating Culturally Diverse Clients: A Practical Guide*. 2nd ed. Thousand Oaks, CA: Sage, 1998

Parrott, L. *Counseling and Psychotherapy*. New York, NY: McGraw-Hill, 1997.

Pastor, L.H. "Initial Assessment and Intervention Strategies to Reduce Workplace Violence." In *American Family Physician* 52, no. 4 (1995): 1169–75.

Patterson, C.H. "Multicultural Counseling: From Diversity to Universality." In *Journal of Counseling and Development* 74, no. 3 (1996): 227–31.

Pedersen, P.B. "Multiculturalism and the Paradigm Shift in Counselling: Controversies and Alternative Futures." In *Canadian Journal of Counselling* 35, no. 1 (2001): 15–25.

Pedersen, P.B., D.C. Locke, eds. *Cultural and Diversity Issues in Counseling*. Greensboro, NC: ERIC Counseling and Student Services Clearinghouse, 1996.

Pedersen, P. *A Handbook for Developing Multicultural Awareness*. 2nd Ed. Alexandria, VA: American Counseling Association, 1994.

Pincus, A., and A. Minahan. *Social Work Practice: Model and Method*. Itasca, IL: F.E. Peacock, 1973.

Poonwassie, A., and A. Charter. "An Aboriginal Worldview of Helping: Empowering Approaches." In *Canadian Journal of Counselling* 35, no. 1 (2001): 63–73.

Reamer, F.G. *Ethical Standards in Social Work: A Critical Review of the NASW Code of Ethics*. Washington, DC: NASW Press, 1998.

Reid, W.H. *The Treatment of Psychiatric Disorders: Revised for the DSM-IIIR*. New York, NY: Brunner/Mazel, 1989.

Remley Jr., T.P., B. Herlihy, and S.B. Herlihy. "The U.S. Supreme Court Decision in Jafee v Redmond: Implications for Counselors." In *Journal of Counseling and Development* 75, no. 3 (1997): 213–18.

Roberts, A.R. *Contemporary Perspectives on Crisis Intervention and Prevention*. Englewood Cliffs, NJ: Prentice-Hall, 1991.

Rogers, C.R. *Client-Centered Therapy: Its Current Practice, Implications, and Theory*. Boston, MA: Houghton Mifflin, 1951.

———. *On Becoming a Person*. Boston, MA: Houghton Mifflin, 1961.

———. *A Way of Being*. Boston, MA: Houghton Mifflin, 1980.

Rosenthal, L. *Resolving Resistance in Group Psychotherapy*. Northvale, NJ: Jason Aronson, Inc., 1987.

Roth, L.H. *Clinical Treatment of the Violent Person*. New York, NY: Guilford Press, 1987.

Roy, A. "Risk Factors for Suicide Among Adult Alcoholics." In *Alcohol Health and Research World* 17, no. 2 (1993): 133–36.

Ruskin, R., and M. Beiser. "Cultural Issues in Psychotherapy." In Cameron, P., J. Ennis, J. Deadman, eds., *Standards and Guidelines for the Psychotherapies*. Toronto, ON: University of Toronto Press, 1998: 422–445.

Saleeby, D. *The Strengths Perspective in Social Work Practice*. 2nd ed. New York, NY: Longman, 1997.

San Francisco Suicide Prevention Institute. [Online, 10 August 1998]. Available: http://www.sfsuicide.org/facts.html

Schram, B., and B.R. Mandell. *An Introduction to Human Services Policy and Procedure*. 3rd ed. Needham Heights, MA: Allyn & Bacon, 1997.

Seligman, M.E. Helplessness: *On Depression, Development and Death*. San Francisco, CA: W.H. Freeman, 1975.

Shahmirzadi, A. "Counseling Iranians." In *The Personnel and Guidance Journal* (April 1983): 487–489.

Shea, S.C. *Psychiatric Interviewing: The Art of Understanding*. Philadelphia, PA: W.B. Sanders, 1988.

Sheafor, B.W., C.R. Horejsi, and G.A Horejsi. *Techniques and Guidelines for Social Work Practice*. 5th ed. Boston, MA: Allyn & Bacon, 2000.

———. *Techniques and Guidelines for Social Work Practice*. 5th ed. Boston, MA: Allyn & Bacon, 2000.

Shebib, B. *Counseling Skills*. Victoria, BC: Province of British Columbia, Ministry of Education, Skills and Training, 1997.

Shilling, L.E. *Perspectives on Counseling Theories*. Englewood Cliffs, NJ: Prentice-Hall, 1984.

Shulman, L. *Skills of Helping Individuals and Groups*. 2nd ed. Itasca, IL: F.E. Peacock, 1984.

———. *Skills of Helping Individuals and Groups*. 3rd ed. Itasca, IL: F.E. Peacock, 1992.

Shulz, W.E. *Counselling Ethics Casebook 2000*. Ottawa, ON: Canadian Counselling Association, 2000.

Silva, F., and M. Lopez de Silva. "Hallucinations and Behavior Modification." In *Analisis y Modificacion de Conducta* 2, no. 2 (1976).

Simmie, S., and J. Nunes. *The Last Taboo: A Survival Guide to Mental Health Care in Canada*. Toronto, ON: McClelland & Stewart, 2001.

Skidmore, R.A., M.G. Thackeray, and O.W. Farley. *Introduction to Social Work*. 5th ed. Englewood Cliffs, NJ: Prentice-Hall, 1991.

Sklare, G.B. *Brief Counseling That Works: A Solution-Focused Approach for School Counselors.* Thousand Oaks, CA: Corwin Press, 1997.

Smith, D.B., and P.J. Morrissette. "The Experiences of White Male Counsellors Who Work with First Nations Clients." In *Canadian Journal of Counselling* 35, no. 1 (2001): 74–88.

Specht, H. "Social Work and the Popular Psychotherapies." In *Social Service Review* 64, no. 3 (1990): 345–357.

Speight, S.L., L.J. Myers, C.I. Cox, and P.S. Highlen. "A Redefinition of Multicultural Counseling," *Journal of Counseling and Development* 70, no. 1 (1991): 29–36.

Statistics Canada. Catalogue no. 93-319-XPB, 1993(a).

Statistics Canada. [online]: http://www.statcan.ca/english/Pgdb/People/Population/demo18a.htm April, 2001a.

Statistics Canada. [online] http://www.statcan.ca/english/Pgdb/People/Population/demo35a.htm April, 2001b.

Steinweg, D.A. "Implications of Current Research for Counseling the Unemployed." In *Journal of Employment Counseling* 27, no. 1 (March 1990): 37–41.

Sudman, S. and N.M. Bradburn. *Asking Questions: A Practical Guide to Questionnaire Design.* San Francisco, CA: Jossey-Bass, 1983.

Sue, D.W., P. Arredondo, and R. McDavis. "Multicultural Counseling Competencies and Standards: A Call to the Profession." In *Journal of Counseling and Development* 70, no. 4 (1992): 477–86.

Sue, D.W., and D. Sue. *Counseling the Culturally Different: Theory and Practice.* 3rd ed. New York, NY: John Wiley and Sons, 1999.

Sunley, R., and G.W. Sheek. *Serving the Unemployed and Their Families.* Milwaukee, WI: Family Service America, 1986.

Swanson, J., S. Estroff, M. Swartz, R. Borum, W. Lachicotte, C. Zimmer, and R. Wagner. "Violence and Severe Mental Disorder in Clinical and Community Populations: The Effects of Psychotic Symptoms, Comorbidity, and Lack of Treatment." In *Psychiatry: Interpersonal and Biological Processes* 60, no. 1 (1997): 1–22.

Tardiff, K., P. Marzuk, A. Leon, L. Portera, and C. Weiner. "Violence by Patients Admitted to a Private Psychiatric Hospital." In *American Journal of Psychiatry* 154, no. 1 (1997): 88–94.

Thoreson, R.W., P. Shaughnessy, P.P. Heppner, and S.W. Cook. "Sexual Contact During and After the Professional Relationship: Attitudes and Practices of Male Counselors." In *Journal of Counseling and Development* 71, no. 4 (1993): 429–34.

Truax, C., and R. Carkhuff. *Toward Effective Counseling and Psychotherapy: Training and Practice.* Chicago, IL: Aldine, 1967.

Turner, J.C., and F.J. Turner (general eds.). *Canadian Social Welfare.* 2nd ed. Don Mills, ON: Collier Macmillan Canada, 1986.

———. *Canadian Social Welfare.* 4th ed. Toronto, ON: Pearson Education Canada, 2001.

Vaillant, G.E. "Defense Mechanisms." In *The New Harvard Guide to Psychiatry*, ed. A.M. Nicholi. Cambridge, MA: Belknap Press, 1988: 200–7.

Walrond-Skinner, A. *Dictionary of Psychotherapy.* London: Routledge & Kegan Paul, 1986.

Walter, J.L., and J.E. Peller. "'On Track' in Solution-Focused Brief Therapy." In *Constructive Therapies*, ed. M.F. Hoyt. New York, NY: The Guilford Press, 1994: 111–25.

Walters, G.D. "Identifying and Confronting Resistance in Lifestyle Criminal Offenders." In *Tough Customers: Counseling Unwilling Clients*, ed. G.A. Harris. Laurel, MD: American Correctional Association, 1991: 25–42.

Weaver, A.J. "Working with Potentially Dangerous Persons: What Clergy Need to Know." In *Pastoral Psychology* 40, no. 5 (1982): 313–23.

Weaver, C.H. *Human Listening: Processes and Behavior*. Indianapolis, IN: Bobbs-Merrill Company, 1972.

Weisinger, H. *Emotional Intelligence at Work*. San Francisco, CA: Jossey-Bass, 1998.

Wells, C.S., and M.K. Masch. *Social Work Ethics Day to Day: Guidelines for Professional Practice*. Prospect Heights, IL: Waveland, 1991.

Westwood, M.J., and F.I. Ishiyama. "Challenges in Counseling Immigrant Clients: Understanding Intercultural Barriers to Career Adjustment." In *Journal of Employment Counseling* 28, no. 4 (1991):130–43.

Wicks, R.J., and R.D. Parsons. *Counseling Strategies and Intervention Techniques for the Human Services*. New York, NY: Longman, 1984.

Wilson, S.B. *Goal Setting*. New York, NY: AMACOM, 1994.

Wolvin, A., and C. Coakley. *Listening*. 5th ed. Dubuque, IA: Brown & Benchmark, 1996.

Woodside, M., and T. McClam. *An Introduction to Human Services*. Belmont, CA: Brooks/Cole, 1990.

Young, M.E. *Learning the Art of Helping*. Upper Saddle River, NJ: Merrill, 1998.

Zastrow, C. *Introduction to Social Welfare: Social Problems, Services, and Current Issues*. 4th ed. Belmont, CA: Wadsworth, 1990.

Index

*Tables are indicated with a t, in **boldface**.*